Urban Life
in Contemporary
China

Martin King
Whyte

William L.
Parish

Urban Life
in Contemporary
China

The University
of Chicago Press

Chicago
and London

Martin King Whyte is professor of
sociology and associate of the Center for Chinese Studies at the University of Michigan.

William L. Parish is professor of sociology and director of the Center
for Far Eastern Studies at the University of Chicago. They are joint
authors of *Village and Family in
Contemporary China*.

THE UNIVERSITY OF CHICAGO PRESS, CHICAGO 60637
THE UNIVERSITY OF CHICAGO PRESS, LTD., LONDON

© 1984 by The University of Chicago
All rights reserved. Published 1984
Printed in the United States of America
90 89 88 87 86 85 84   1 2 3 4 5

LIBRARY OF CONGRESS CATALOGING IN PUBLICATION DATA

Whyte, Martin King.
   Urban life in contemporary China.

   Includes index.
   1. Cities and towns—China.   2. Urban economics.
3. Family—China.   4. Quality of life—China.
I. Parish, William L.   II. Title.
HT147.C48W59 1983   307.7′6′0951   83-7779
ISBN 0-226-89546-7
ISBN 0-226-89547-5 (pbk.)

Contents

Acknowledgments

This study is the product of the equal contributions of its two authors, who worked in collaboration but at separate institutions. Many individuals and institutions provided assistance and encouragement that made this final product possible.

Funding for this research came primarily from a grant from the National Science Foundation (NSF-SOC-08942), which supported both our data collection phase in Hong Kong and most of the subsequent data analysis back at our home institutions. Supplementary funds came from the Department of Sociology at the University of Michigan and from the Social Science Division and the Center for Far Eastern Studies at the University of Chicago as well as a National Endowment for the Humanities grant (RC-25746-76-1200) to the University of Chicago project on modern China.

The facilities of the Universities Service Centre and the Union Research Institute were indispensable to our work in Hong Kong. We would particularly like to thank the staff of the former institution and its director, John Dolfin, for the extraordinary amount of advice and assistance provided to us there. We were ably assisted in Hong Kong by Chen Huamei, Chen Yutong, Robert Lee, Liu Xianping, and Song Wing. Their assistance to us in interviewing, finding sources, translating, and in interpreting the Chinese urban context in general was essential to the success of this study. Back at Michigan, Andrew Walder, Michael Kozura, Linda Kaboolian, Jessica Musoke, and Pamela Meil all provided research assistance at various points, while John Sell and Michael Canjar provided invaluable advice on how to handle the mysteries of the computer. At Chicago, Grant Blank, Cheng-hung Chiang, and Doo-seung Hong provided able research assistance.

The staffs of the University of Michigan Asia Library and the University of Chicago Far Eastern Library were very helpful in helping us locate needed sources. We are grateful to the secretarial staff at the sociology department and the Center for Far Eastern Studies at Chicago in helping put together the final manuscript on computer. In making the final revisions of the manuscript Whyte benefitted from a faculty fellowship at the Center for Asian and Pacific Studies of the University of Hawaii, and the assistance of that organization and its director, Stephen Uhalley, is gratefully acknowledged.

Many friends and colleagues provided comments on our work in its earlier stages and it is impossible to thank them all here adequately. Several of the chapters here (3, 4, 7, and 8) had earlier incarnations as conference papers and the comments received on these earlier versions were of great assistance. We received assistance on sources and relevant data from Richard Barrett, Susan DeVos, Philip Emerson, David Goodman, Clifton Pannell, Sophie Sa, James Tong, and Tang Tsou. The following people read parts or all of the manuscript and offered helpful suggestions: Marc Blecher, David Buck, Andrew Cherlin, Lois DeFleur, Ray Fogelson, Tom Gold, Gail Henderson, Chu Huaizhi, Morris Janowitz, Gail Kligman, Pamela Meil, G. William Skinner, Theda Skocpol, Irving Spergel, Gerald Suttles, Tang Tsou, Andrew Walder, Yang Weiming, William Whyte, Brantley Womack, Wei Zhangling. Naturally none of our advisors and critics are responsible for the remaining defects in this volume. Francis Hsieh helped provide woodcuts used as illustrations in the book. Typing and word processing assistance was provided by Debbie Polzin, Billie Crawford, Susan Sherry, Glenn Sharrock, Angela Perez, and Kathleen Nerat.

Finally, we are grateful to our families for tolerating the disruptions in their lives that our trek off to Hong Kong occasioned, and also bearing with us while we remained absorbed in Chinese urban problems in the subsequent years. Their helpful comments, emotional support, and good humor made the long research process satisfying and productive for us.

Authors' Notes

Interviews are referenced as follows: The first two letters give the city or county that is being reported on—for example, KS = Canton, SS = Shanghai, PK or PE = Peking. The significance of the third letter varies by size of the city. In large cities such as Canton or Peking, P = neighborhoods with predominantly private housing, S or D = neighborhoods with predominantly work unit compounds, and M = mixed neighborhood or one with mostly city-owned housing. In small towns, the third letter can be H = county seat, or C = commune seat. In the fourth position there is typically a digit, indicating whether this is the first, second, third, or later person interviewed in this city from this type of neighborhood. The digits after the colon simply give the page number in the interview transcript. Thus KSM17:1 indicates a quote from the first page of an interview with the seventeenth person we encountered from a mixed neighborhood in Canton.

In the footnotes, *FBIS* refers to Foreign Broadcast Information Service, *Daily Report: People's Republic of China* (Washington, D.C.: U.S. Department of Commerce, National Technical Information Service), a translation service including both broadcast and newspaper reports.

All transliteration of Chinese terms is via the official pinyin system now used in the People's Republic of China. Terms are rendered from their Mandarin (*putong hua*) versions even if another dialect was actually used in the interview. If a personal or place name is very well known under another spelling, however (such as Peking, Canton, or Sun Yat-sen), we maintain that spelling in our text.

One yuan = approximately US $0.67 in the late 1970s at the official exchange rate.

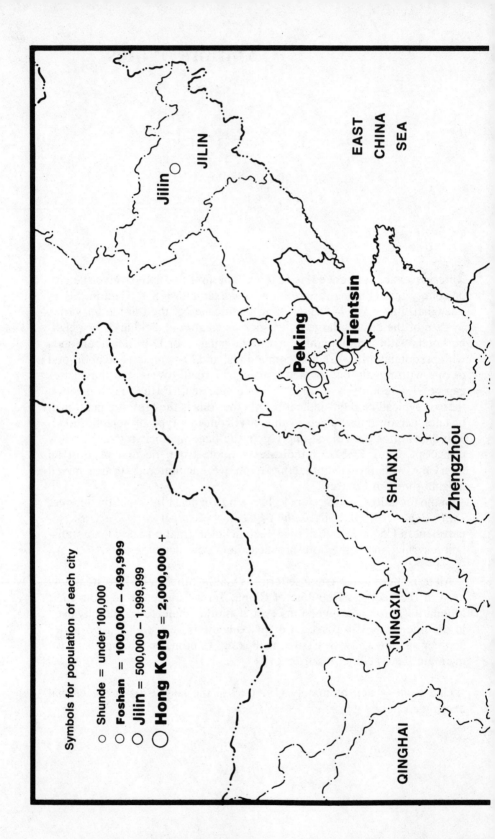

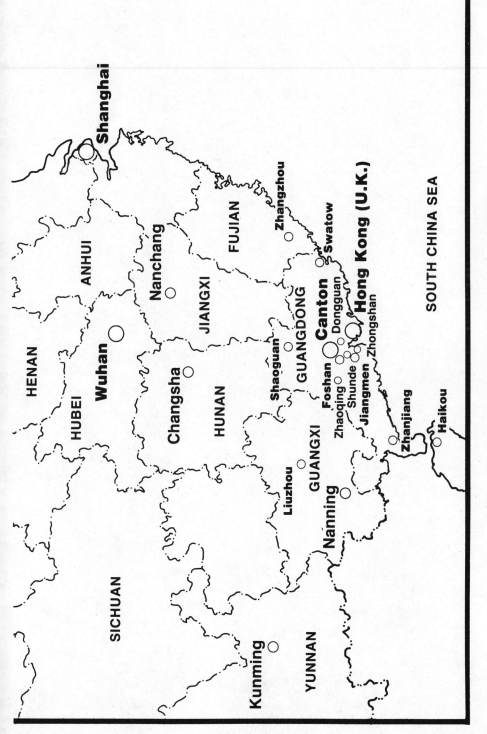

Map 1. Cities and Provinces of China (sample sites and Hong Kong)

1   Introduction

Since the start of industrialization and with increasing rapidity in recent decades, a modern city with new social forms and behavior has been spreading around the world. In Western social thought this modern city has been viewed with profound ambivalence. On the one hand it is generally assumed that modern economic development has an immutable logic that requires cities to grow and proliferate. Cities also are seen as supporting "high culture," providing a variety of resources and facilities unknown in rural villages, and, partly as a consequence, making it possible for migrants to escape from the rigid conventionalism and traditional superstitions of the countryside. The resulting opportunities for innovation and rational calculation in turn help to fuel further economic changes. There is much about modern cities, then, that is admirable and even liberating.

On the other hand, however, are the darker sides of the modern city. It seems fair to say that the predominant tone of most Western social commentary on modern cities has been negative. Cities are seen on balance as not very nice places, in spite of the virtues we have just noted. The catalogue of urban problems varies somewhat depending upon which commentator one reads, but familiar traits appear in most lists: modern cities tend to be characterized by increased bureaucratization and unresponsiveness of the authorities; stark inequalities, class and ethnic group conflicts, and the existence of an unemployed underclass; slums, neighborhood decay, and other symptoms of the inability to provide needed services for all; impersonality, anonymity, and alienation; the primacy of cash transactions and segmental role relationships over relationships between individuals as whole human beings; the fragmenting of kinship, family, and other primary ties and with them a shared sense of moral values; and rising rates of crime and other forms of deviant behavior.[1] In describing cities in developing societies the list gets even longer and includes such features as the emergence of sprawling squatter settlements fueled by rural migration, overproduction of educated youths for whom there are no jobs, and dominance of a conspicuously consuming urban elite whose life styles and concerns mirror those of elites in developed countries and have little connection with the tastes and needs of their countrymen.[2]

In most Western writing about modern cities it is assumed that such urban ills are unavoidable. They are the price paid for progress or, in the words of Sigmund Freud, they are the discontents that inevitably accompany civilization. Recently, however, this verdict has been called into question. Critics now charge that particular urban ills are not inevitable products of city life itself but are caused by the particular kind of economic or urban development that has predominated in both the developed and the Third World—capitalist development. If this view is correct, then perhaps a different form of development would produce urbanism without all of the problems heretofore associated with it.[3]

To some critics of the prevailing wisdom about urbanism the case of China seemed to provide supportive evidence. In the wave of travel reports were observations that seemed to suggest a very different form of urbanism was being created under the leadership of Mao Zedong. Cities had apparently not grown much in relative terms in spite of considerable economic development, slums and squatter settlements seemed absent, conspicuous consumption and foreign-oriented life styles were not visible, a high degree of economic equality and security seemed to prevail, unemployment seemed absent, close-knit neighborhoods and families seemed to persist, and crime, drug addiction, prostitution, and other forms of

1. Louis Wirth and many other early theorists on city life stress the negative consequences of modern urban development. A thorough discussion of a range of such views is presented in Michael P. Smith, *The City and Social Theory* (New York: St. Martin's Press, 1979). See also Morton and Lucia White, *The Intellectuals versus the City* (Cambridge: Harvard University Press, 1962).

2. The literature on these points is voluminous. See, for example, T. G. McGee, *The Urbanization Process in the Third World* (London: G. Bell, 1971); Bruce London, "Is the Primate City Parasitic? The Regional Implications of National Decision Making in Thailand," *Journal of Developing Areas* 12 (1977) 49–67; Oscar Lewis, *La Vida* (New York: Random House, 1965).

3. See the arguments presented in Smith, *The City and Social Theory,* Manuel Castells, *The Urban Question: A Marxist Approach* (Cambridge: MIT Press, 1977), and Mike Davidow, *Cities without Crises* (New York: International Publishers, 1976).

deviance seemed minor or nonexistent.[4] Did China perhaps hold a lesson of how the benefits of urbanism could be enjoyed without the ills? Might there be features of the "Chinese model" of urbanism that could be borrowed by the West or by the Third World to help them cope with their urban problems? These are the major questions that motivated the research we report in these pages.

To be more specific, we hope in this study to do several things. First and most basic, we want to give the reader a fairly comprehensive description of the way in which contemporary Chinese cities are organized, and of the nature of the social relationships that have emerged within this form of organization. In providing this descriptive overview, we will be attempting to assess just how distinctive the contemporary patterns of urban life in China really are. Does the reality of Chinese city life fit the features claimed to be part of the "Chinese model"? Have the Chinese really been able to avoid common urban ills, or are there after all "imperatives of urbanism" that even the most determined revolutionary assault cannot alter?

In attempting to deal with these questions we will also be grappling with more complex questions: What are the origins or explanations for particular features of contemporary urban organization in China? Do they reflect the influence of Chinese traditional culture? Are they the product of China's low level of economic development? Can they be explained by the set of Leninist-socialist institutions that China adopted from the Soviet Union? Do they represent innovations that the Chinese Communists introduced? Or are they after all simply the inevitable concomitants of urbanism? To deal with such questions we will in the course of this study make use of multiple kinds of comparisons—with pre-1949 Chinese cities, with contemporary non-Communist Chinese cities such as Hong Kong and Taipei, and with cities in the Third World, socialist Eastern Europe, and the capitalist West. Hopefully the use of this wide range of comparisons will help us come to a fuller understanding of why Chinese cities are organized the way they are.

A third set of issues that we address concerns whether there are distinctive problems that are produced by the "Chinese model" of urban

4. See, on a number of these points, Lawrence J. C. Ma and Edward W. Hanten, eds., *Urban Development in Modern China* (Boulder: Westview Press, 1981); Ruth Sidel, *Families of Fengsheng* (Baltimore: Penguin, 1974); C. L. Salter, "Chinese Experiments in Urban Space: The Quest for an Agrapolitan China," in *New Concepts and Technologies in Third World Urbanization,* J. Friedman, ed. (Los Angeles: UCLA School of Architecture and Urban Planning, 1974); and Charles Cell, "Deurbanization in China: The Urban-Rural Contradiction," *Bulletin of Concerned Asian Scholars* 11 (1979): 62–72.

organization, even if these are not the same as the urban ills most often noted in other societies. Here the time frame that is the primary focus in our study is important. Most of our data refer primarily to the early and mid-1970s. Some features of urban organization in China have remained relatively constant since at least the mid-1950s; others have been modified repeatedly in accord with the tides of Chinese politics. Insofar as there is a distinctive Chinese (or some would prefer "Maoist") model of urban organization, it reached its purest (or some would say most extreme) form in the period immediately following the Cultural Revolution (1966–69), and has been modified in important ways in the period since Mao's death and the purge of his radical supporters in 1976.

Our richest data in most chapters concentrate on the period immediately following the Cultural Revolution. During these years, the early and mid-1970s, when China's radical alternative was most thoroughly realized, we get the clearest demonstration of how cities might be reorganized. The analysis of problems that this alternative organization created tells us much about what makes cities tick. And in these years of the radical alternative, when equality and creating the new socialist man were stressed, we get an extreme test of the viability of many socialist ideals. During these years, the Chinese leadership self-consciously turned against many of the social forms they had learned from the Soviet Union and tried to create urban forms of their own. In so doing they provided a new test of whether alternate ways of building socialism could avoid some of the pitfalls of the Soviet model. Concentrating on this radical period also provides a better sense of the negative features to which the present Chinese leadership is reacting and the possible directions that Chinese urban policy may take in the future. Accordingly, many of our chapters conclude with a discussion of current urban policy trends and how these are linked to negative reactions against radical policies of the 1970s. In the concluding chapter we attempt an overall assessment of both the lessons of the extreme radical alternative and the direction of future urban policy.

The methods we use to answer these questions are complex and not always ideal. Although both of us have travelled to China and made first-hand observations of urban life on several occasions, neither has had the opportunity to conduct extended field research in China. When we began our research in 1977 such opportunities were not available, and although a few scholars have been able to conduct field research within China since 1979, it presently seems highly unlikely that the sort of extensive research reported here could be conducted there in the foreseeable future. In our research we relied on several sources. First and most important, we base many of our conclusions on analysis of a series of intensive, semistructured interviews we conducted in Hong Kong in 1977–78 with 133 individuals who had formerly been residents of fifty different cities, large and small, scattered around China (see map 1). The reader who wishes a detailed description of how we conducted these interviews and analyzed the results, and how we deal with problems of bias and selectivity in our data, should consult appendix 1.

Here we note simply that we used a detailed question outline to elicit details on many different aspects of the microenvironments—neighborhoods, work organizations, schools, and so forth—to enable us to reconstruct as complete as possible a picture of the corners of Chinese urban life with which each informant was familiar, including everything from political organization through patterns of family life to the quality of interpersonal relationships. In effect, then, we were collecting urban ethnographies, but at a distance. In total, those interviews consumed 1,382 hours and produced 2,369 single-spaced legal-size pages of interview transcripts plus a large number of completed standardized forms on specialized topics. To maximize objectivity we generally did not ask about the informants and their families, but about neighboring families and people they knew in their immediate environment. By this indirect method, we managed to construct a number of kinds of samples that we could subject to quantitative analysis—133 urban neighborhoods, 91 urban work organizations, 581 neighboring families, 831 marriage cases, 66 divorce cases, as well as our 50 cities.

Because informants from the areas near Hong Kong were overrepresented in our interviews, and it was only in those areas that we had something close to a full range of city sizes and urban neighborhood types described, in some places in our quantitative analysis we restrict our attention to a weighted set of data provided by informants from cities in what is called the Lingnan Region—roughly the provinces of Guangdong and Guangxi in Southeastern China. So for some topics we attempt to give an idea of the range of variation in urban social forms across the entire Chinese landscape, but when we wish to derive more precise estimates of the experience of the average urbanite we restrict our attention to this one macroregion.

In this study we also rely on a variety of supplementary sources of information—the Chinese mass media, China trip reports, and the secondary literature on Chinese society. Through cross-checking and combining sources we hope to arrive at the fullest picture of contemporary urban social organization that is possible under the circumstances. (In appendix 1 we present some figures to show how statistics calculated from our interview samples correspond with those published in the official media in China.)

This study is divided into three main parts. The first, on the political economy of Chinese cities, describes the principal economic and political structures that shape urban life in China. These include both the bureaucratic penetration of well-organized neighborhoods and work units and the emphasis on equality that reached its greatest intensity in the early and mid-1970s. This extreme bureaucratization and equality, and their consequences, are themes that we examine throughout the book. Other themes introduced in this first part include the residential stability of Chinese neighborhoods and the emerging problems with employment, housing, and consumer services. These sorts of issues have not only had a direct effect on the perceived quality of life in Chinese cities but also indirect effects on many other aspects of urban life described in other parts of the book.

The second part, on family behavior, describes how marriage, family form, birth control, and the position of women have changed since 1949. It compares this behavior to that found in other ethnically Chinese cities such as Hong Kong and Singapore, non-Chinese developing Asian cities, and to other socialist cities in Eastern Europe and the Soviet Union. With these comparisons, and additional comparisons among different families and neighborhoods in China, part 2 draws conclusions about whether China's unique political economy produces special family behavior versus behavior that only mimics that found in other, not so special settings. The focus here is on the extent to which alternatives in urban behavior can be realized and on the economic and cultural sources of these alternatives.

The third, and final, part of this book examines the quality of life in Chinese cities. Or, otherwise stated, this final section examines how far the socialist promise of eliminating "capitalist" social problems such as crime, alienation, and social isolation has been realized. Throughout this section, the promise of greater economic security is contrasted with the increased threat of political pressure. The question is whether promise or threat has had the greater influence on the quality of urban life as Chinese residents have experienced it and what the likely directions for the future are. This section permits the reexamination of many old issues about how residential mobility, occupational heterogeneity, and status striving shape the character of urban life. The very special character of Chinese cities permits an untangling of many issues in this area.

In sum, all three parts help us to better understand the links between political structures, economic institutions, family behavior, and other aspects of modern urban life. Studying the Chinese experience, particularly during the more extreme moment of the mid-1970s, offers not only a better understanding of China and its present course but also a better understanding of one's own society wherever it is.

One   Urban Political Economy

2 Chinese Urban Structure

The differences between China's urban structure and that of the West and other developing societies are many. These differences began not in the modern age but more than two thousand years ago. As Marco Polo discovered, China has had a long and elaborate urban history.

Ruled by a complex bureaucracy, the Chinese state established administrative posts throughout the empire. Symbolizing the sanctity and grandeur of the empire, each outpost came to have an elaborate structure of city walls and gates with an administrative hall at the center and officially esteemed temples scattered about.[1] Artisans, performers, soldiers, traders, servants, and a host of others joined officials in these cities. Eventually there were over two thousand county, prefectural, and provincial capitals scattered throughout the empire, and a national capital having as many as a million residents. By late imperial times, including the last three centuries before our own, perhaps six to ten percent of the Chinese population lived in cities. In absolute numbers, this meant that before the middle of the last century there were more city dwellers in China than anywhere else in the world.

These cities were distinctive not only in their size and number but also in their distribution, social function, and internal social organization. In most developing societies that had few cities prior to Western contact, there is today a very uneven distribution of cities. One or two primate cities, often port cities created by a colonial power, dominate the society, receiving disproportionate shares of modern investment, government expenditures, and rural migrants. Once one drops below this level, there is

1. See G. William Skinner, *The City in Late Imperial China* (Stanford: Stanford University Press, 1977); Chang Sen-dou, "The Historical Trend of Chinese Urbanization," *Annals of the Association of American Geographers* 53 (1963): 109–43; Paul Wheatley, "City as Symbol," (Inaugural lecture, University College, London, 1969); Gilbert Rozman, *Urban Networks in Ch'ing China and Tokugawa Japan* (Princeton: Princeton University Press, 1973).

little else until one reaches small market towns and villages. This uneven pattern of development, critics argue, helps create a dual economy, retarding the spread of development and exacerbating regional inequalities.[2]

China was in a good position to avoid some of these difficulties because of the even distribution of cities developed in the imperial period.[3] The early distribution of cities was related to domestic trade as well as administrative patterns. With the dominance of the bureaucracy, merchants never became an independent force in Chinese cities. They existed at the sufferance of the bureaucracy, often intermarrying with them and sending some of their sons into bureaucratic service to build the personal contacts needed for official protection. Despite the subordination of merchant to bureaucratic activities, domestic trade was well developed, especially along the major river routes which provided the cheapest form of transport. In each of eight major river basins—one of which is heavily represented in our sample—there developed a full range of cities, arrayed in regular order by size, in a pattern found typically only in internally well-developed economic systems that have had time to reach equilibrium. This regular distribution of cities was not limited to drainage basins. Cutting across the basins on a national scale, the joint effect of the national administrative hierarchy and regional trade networks was to produce a national distribution of cities of different sizes that was remarkably evenly spread across the landscape. Few people were very far removed from the influence of some kind of urban center.

Chinese cities were also special in their orthodoxy and their lack of separation from the surrounding countryside. From the vantage point of Western history and from the history of new cities in the Third World today, we tend to think of urban and rural life as being very distinct. In Europe, the urban populace under the leadership of the rising merchant class fought for independence from the rural aristocracy and the surrounding countryside. Cities became centers of change, and the countryside a center of orthodoxy. In traditional China the opposite situation held. Dominated by the imperial bureaucracy, cities became centers of orthodoxy, and there were few clear divisions between rural and urban. Official administrative lines tended to cut across the rural-urban divide.

2. Brian J. L. Berry and Frank E. Horton, *Geographic Perspectives on Urban Systems* (Englewood Cliffs, N.J.: Prentice-Hall, 1970), chap. 3; Bruce London, "Is the Primate City Parasitic?" *The Journal of Developing Areas* 12 (1977): 49–67.

3. For much of the discussion below, see Skinner's articles in *The City in Late Imperial China;* Rhoads Murphey, *The Fading of the Maoist Vision: City and Country in China's Development* (New York: Methuen, 1980); G. William Skinner, "Mobility Strategies in Late Imperial China," in *Regional Analysis,* vol. 1, Carol Smith, ed. (New York: Academic Press, 1976).

Cities had little in the way of an independent urban administration and could, as in the case of Canton, be split between several counties. Merchants remained subordinated to the bureaucracy and fragmented into a variety of guilds and developed no citywide organizations or class consciousness until practically the end of the imperial period. Change often came from rebellions and sectarian movements originating in the countryside.

In the official ideology, the simplicity of rural life was esteemed over the sinful pleasures of urbanism. Though officials ruled from cities, many of them had their origins in the countryside and would return to buy land and reside there once they retired from office. With a rigorous examination system for picking officials, as many as two-fifths of the new degree holders in each generation came from new stock, and often from rural areas.[4] Even those degree holders who failed to receive an official post typically spent part of their lives competing and studying in the cities and then later resided and taught in the countryside, thereby serving as a cultural bridge between the two realms. Circular mobility of this type was not restricted to the scholar-gentry. Many males, finding insufficient opportunity in family farming, left for the city in their teens to seek employment, returned periodically to the village to get married and take part in family celebrations, and then returned permanently in their forties or later to resume farming after the death of a father or brother or after they had accumulated enough savings to buy land. The prevalence of this sort of urban sojourning not only created a very unbalanced sex ratio in cities but also helped shape the cellular and somewhat rural nature of the traditional cities.[5]

The bureaucratic structures of modern cities—utility companies, police departments, welfare offices, and so forth—were absent in late imperial China, and urbanites new and old depended heavily on traditional forms of association for providing them with security and access to resources. New migrants generally sought the aid of previous migrants from their rural locality in their efforts to get established, and with sufficient numbers from one place a native place association (*tongxiang hui*) would arise to defend the interests of its members. In cities common rural origin often formed the basis for common occupations and residential location. Craft and merchant guilds of various types—of stone cutters, hat makers, cloth

---

4. Ping-ti Ho, *The Ladder of Success in Imperial China* (New York: Columbia University Press, 1962); Fei Hsiao-tung, *China's Gentry* (Chicago: University of Chicago Press, 1953); Johanna Menzel, ed., *The Chinese Civil Service* (Boston: Heath, 1963).

5. For much of the discussion below, see the articles in Skinner, *The City in Late Imperial China*, part 3; J. Stewart Burgess, *The Guilds of Peking* (New York: Columbia University Press, 1928).

sellers, pot makers, tailors, or bankers—were often based upon common rural origins (and thus a guild might coincide with a native place association and their firms often tended to be concentrated in a particular street or neighborhood). The traditional Chinese city, then, had a geography made up in large part of a jigsaw puzzle of separate craft/rural origin groups. These groups, rather than the urban bureaucracy, provided many of the services needed by residents.

While these groups were dedicated to advancing and protecting the interests of their members, they also helped to sustain ties with the rural places of origin of their members. They commonly helped organize lending associations and charitable funds to make it possible for members who died to be placed in suitable coffins and transported back to the village for burial, and if news of a flood or drought back in the village reached them, the group leadership would organize a relief drive to help alleviate the resulting famine. All of these features of traditional Chinese urbanism lead Frederick Mote to conclude that there was an "organic unity" of rural and urban in late imperial China that had no counterpart in the West.[6]

This particularistic mode of organizing social life in late imperial cities had other consequences besides lending a rural character to cities. The cellular or encapsulated form of social life hindered both class and urban consciousness. The guilds and native place associations included rich and poor, owners and employees, all locked in paternalistic association. One generally needed the introduction of family members or friends to join in the first place, and then a lengthy apprenticeship period was often involved, which established lifelong obligations. Guilds regulated not only apprenticeships, but prices, quality, competition, and member behavior, using regular worship to the patron god of the guild to sanctify the fines, boycotts, and other measures used in these efforts. Typically work was also joined with residence. Owners and their wives and children lived at the rear or above the shop or workshop, while unattached workers often slept on counters or workbenches in the shop and ate their meals with the owner's family. Even without guild organizations, neighborhoods and lanes often had a separate associational life. Neighborhood associations organized residents to provide basic urban amenities, such as street sweeping and fire protection, and might close off gates at the end of the lane to protect residents at night. Typically a neighborhood shrine to the local earth god (*tudi gong*) brought neighbors together for ritual occasions and reinforced local solidarity.[7]

6. Frederick W. Mote, "The Transformation of Nanking 1350–1400," in Skinner, *The City in Late Imperial China,* pp. 101–54.

7. In addition to the references in note 5, see Morton H. Fried, *Fabric of Society: A Study of the Social Life of a Chinese County Seat* (New York: Praeger, 1953); Lynn White, "Non-

Above the level of neighborhoods, major temples, a few large clan halls, and some of the larger guilds of merchants provided only a few extra tendons for tying the city together. Some popular temples typically drew a large following, but worship tended to be ad hoc and eclectic, depending on special need or on the birthday of the god. One went to the god of fertility, scholarship, or drought, depending on special need, or to some god who was thought locally to be particularly powerful and efficacious. There was no organized religion which might have brought a larger unity to the city.[8] Major merchant guilds were not able to bring that unity either, for ones that grew too large and powerful risked expropriation by the government. Thus, Chinese cities tended to be organized with a very strong bureaucracy above and tight communal groups below with only informal and irregular ties bringing the different levels and segments together.

Western Contact

This pattern of cellularly organized, bureaucratically dominated, and evenly spread cities began to change in the middle of the last century. Opened up to foreign trade by Britain's 1842 defeat of China in the Opium War and by a series of concessions afterwards, China's treaty ports such as Shanghai, Nanking, Tientsin, and Wuhan began to grow out of all proportion to their former importance. Scattered along the coast and up the major rivers, these cities began to shift China's balance of resources to central and coastal China. Even today, many of China's major cities owe their major period of growth to this time of foreign influence.[9]

Governmentalism in the Historical Development of Shanghai,'' in *Urban Development in Modern China,* Laurence Ma and Edward Hanten, eds. (Boulder: Westview Press, 1981). Preindustrial European cities shared in some of the same guild and household workshop structure as China, yet Max Weber still claimed that Chinese cities were significantly more cellular and that this cellular structure inhibited rational trade among the different parts of the city—hence, Europe's more rapid economic development. Max Weber, *General Economic History* (New York: Collier, 1961), chap. 28. For an approach critical of Weber's view, see William T. Rowe, ''Urban Society in Late Imperial China: Hankow, 1796–1889'' (Ph.D. dissertation, Columbia University, 1980).

8. Again Max Weber makes much of this point, arguing that the absence of a sense of brotherhood under a single god inhibited the growth of citizenship and rational trade in China (*General Economic History,* chap. 28). We will return to a more detailed discussion of religion in chap. 10.

9. For a summary of this period, see Murphey, *The Fading of Maoist Vision;* Franz Schurmann, *Ideology and Organization in Communist China* (Berkeley: University of California Press, 1968), chap. 6; David Buck, *Urban Change in China* (Madison: University of Wisconsin Press, 1978).

In these cities much of the old structure of urban life was replaced by what was new and foreign. The treaties conceded special areas in the cities to foreigners, and in these areas foreign law provided a haven for Chinese merchants and others seeking freedom from the constraints of Chinese rule. Foreigners (missionaries and others) established and ran new schools, churches, hospitals, YMCAs, and other organizations. New forms of urban administration began to be built under foreign pressure and inspiration, with professional police and fire departments, municipal councils and courts, and other modern trappings. Large industrial enterprises and chambers of commerce (formed in many cases by an alliance among merchant guilds) provided a new framework for employment in the closing days of the Manchu dynasty, and trade unions, political parties, and other unconventional associational forms began to flower after the end of imperial rule in 1911.

Yet the new order was slow in building, and neither the modern institutions nor the undermined particularistic associations were able to cope with the rapid growth of Chinese cities in the twentieth century. Economic conditions were often chaotic, inflation was a regular threat, and crime was rampant. Secret societies and gangs increasingly replaced guilds in providing what social order there was. Many people arrived in the major cities in pursuit of work that was not there, and on mornings in Shanghai in the 1940s beggars and others who had starved to death during the night had to be picked up by roving trucks. Prostitution was widespread, as was opium addiction. These ills and the control over parts of urban life by foreigners contributed to the torment in Chinese thinking about their cities.

The treaty ports symbolized both the hope of a strong, industrial modern China and her shame at foreign domination and control. Foreign domination was apparent not only in the profit which flowed abroad, but also in public symbols of Western superiority, such as the signs in the Western-style park along the waterfront in Shanghai stating that no Chinese and no dogs were allowed entry. These new urban trends undermined the distinctive characteristics of traditional Chinese cities, such as cellular associational life and close ties with the countryside, and spawned many of the urban problems that have since come to plague other societies in the Third World. It is little wonder, then, that social critics in the Republican period often railed against these new urban trends. In the words of sociologist Fei Xiaotong, in the late 1940s, "At present the growth of great urban centers is like a tumor from which China is suffering."[10]

10. Fei, *China's Gentry*, p. 138.

The leaders of the Communist movement shared these negative views and had their own reasons for hostility to Chinese urban life. Although immediately after its founding in 1921 the Chinese Communist Party was active in the cities, after 1927 it was driven into the countryside by Chiang Kai-shek and had to devise means for mounting a rural revolution while watching Chiang's Nationalist Party, and later Japanese invading armies, rule the cities. The Chinese Communists eventually developed organizational forms and policies that had roots more in the simpler ways of rural life in their refuge in Yanan than in the cosmopolitanism of the cities. They were eventually joined in the hinterland by many students and intellectuals from the coastal cities who despaired of the Nationalists ever ridding themselves of corruption and healing China's ills. Together, the Communist organizers and urban intellectuals joined in shaping a new grassroots peasant mobilization strategy which involved mobilizers living and working with those they were mobilizing, minimal economic differences between leaders and led, extreme political commitment reinforced by small group criticism sessions, and individual interests subordinated to the larger goals of the revolution. It was an extremely spartan lifestyle designed to foster high levels of commitment and solidarity.[11]

When the Chinese Communists began to sweep toward victory in their civil war with the Nationalists in 1948 they came into control of large cities for the first time—first in Manchuria, and subsequently across all of mainland China. The jaundiced way in which China's new rulers regarded the evil and corrupting cities that fell to their sieges is portrayed in vivid but perhaps extreme form in a press depiction of Shanghai soon after its capture in 1949. "Shanghai is a non-productive city. It is a parasitic city. It is a refugee city. It is a paradise of adventurers. In a word, Shanghai is a city where consumption is greater than production; indeed one may even say a city where waste is greater than consumption."[12] Although some radical elements among the new rulers advocated dispersing up to half of the population of cities such as Shanghai to the countryside, more moderate voices prevailed, and the Chinese Communists did not adopt the radical measures against urbanism that their Cambodian pupils later did. The leadership of the CCP recognized that much of the strength and vitality of Chinese society depended upon her cities, and that ways had

11. For a general discussion of the Yanan policies and ethos, see Mark Selden, *The Yenan Way in Revolutionary China* (Cambridge: Harvard University Press, 1971). For some caveats on how spartan and egalitarian the Yanan base area society really was, see Simon Leys, *Chinese Shadows* (New York: Viking, 1977).

12. Quoted in Richard Gaulton, "Political Mobilization in Shanghai," in *Shanghai: Revolution and Development in an Asian Metropolis,* Christopher Howe, ed. (Cambridge: Cambridge University Press, 1981), p. 46.

to be found to purge them of their evils and utilize their strengths. They set about this task immediately, utilizing the experiences they had gained in their rural base areas, advice and models borrowed from their Soviet allies, and ad hoc experiments and improvisations designed to cope with unfamiliar problems.[13]

Some of the fundamental goals of the Chinese Communists in this urban reform effort can be stated fairly simply. Foreign control and influence should be eliminated.[14] (Extraterritoriality had been renounced by China's wartime allies in 1943, but substantial foreign ownership and control as well as cultural influence remained.) Cities should become spartan and productive places with full employment, secure jobs with a range of fringe benefits, minimal income and life style differences, an end to conspicuous consumption and lavish spending, and with decent consumption standards for all. Crime, prostitution, drug addiction, begging, and other social evils should be eliminated. Private enterprise should give way after a period to socialist property relations, and eventually to the classless Communist society of the future. Along the way superstitions, religious worship, gambling, acquisitiveness, arranged marriages, female subordination, and all the other holdovers from feudal and bourgeois society should be eliminated, and a "new socialist man" should become dominant. To pave the way for these changes, each urban family and individual should become part of a tight-knit organizational structure subordinated to the Communist Party and designed to facilitate mobilization of maximum human energies to achieve these lofty goals. The specifics of these various goals and how the CCP has tried to achieve them should become clear as we discuss a range of aspects of contemporary Chinese urban organizations in the remainder of this and in succeeding chapters.

City Size and Stability

Some of the urban reform efforts designed to meet these goals were adopted immediately, while others were held in abeyance until further economic development, socialist transformation, or other preconditions had prepared the way. As noted in chapter 1, in some ways the effort to

13. On this early era, see Schurmann, *Ideology and Organization;* Derk Bodde, *Peking Diary, 1948–1949* (1950; reprinted, New York: Fawcett, 1967); Noel Barber, *The Fall of Shanghai* (New York: Coward, McCann and Geoghegan, 1979); Gaulton, "Political Mobilization"; Kenneth Lieberthal, *Revolution and Tradition in Tientsin* (Stanford: Stanford University Press, 1980); Ezra Vogel, *Canton under Communism* (Cambridge: Harvard University Press, 1969).

14. Soviet influence was extremely important during the 1950s, of course, but it was seen in a different light, as influence invited in by the government and capable of being eliminated—as in fact happened after 1960.

develop a distinctive form of urban life in China did not reach its peak until the Cultural Revolution decade. But many basic policies and structures used to organize China's cities were adopted during the 1950s and continue to shape the nature of urban life today. One of these policies involved the attempt to control the growth of large cities and to redistribute resources to the interior.

In the early 1950s, frightened by the possibility of Korean War attacks on industrial resources concentrated in coastal cities and eager to have the whole country share in the benefits of development, the government began to shift resources to old as well as newly created cities in the interior. The profits from former treaty ports such as Shanghai began to subsidize investment in interior cities such as Lanzhou, Zhengzhou, and Xian.[15] Some labor-intensive factories and much of their skilled labor force were moved from Shanghai to the interior. Some cotton mills, for example, were moved to central Henan to be nearer to where cotton was grown. Even parts of some universities were relocated to interior provinces. Shanghai, concentrating on more technologically sophisticated industries, continued to grow in output, but with some labor intensive industries dispersed to the interior, there was less need to bring new labor into the city. The government also invested heavily in an interior railroad network, thereby linking its interior cities together and further spurring their growth.[16]

Besides positive investment in smaller cities in the interior, the government eventually moved to dampen migration into all cities and especially the very largest cities. This was not accomplished easily. In the 1950s rural land reform, collectivization, and then communization, plus a continuing gap between rural and urban living standards, drove successive waves of migrants into the cities.[17] These waves threatened to undermine the government's program of full urban employment and to drive up the state's expenditures on housing, schools, parks, and other social needs just when it was trying to increase investment in industry. When various other control efforts failed, these problems culminated in 1958 in tough new laws to limit urban migration.[18]

Henceforth, individuals were forbidden to migrate to a city unless they had been specifically recruited to do so—for example, to fill an urban job

15. Nicholas Lardy, *Economic Growth and Distribution in China* (Cambridge: Cambridge University Press, 1978).

16. C. K. Leung, *China: Railway Patterns and National Goals,* Research Paper no. 195 (Chicago: University of Chicago, Department of Geography, 1980).

17. For details for one city, see Lynn White, *Careers in Shanghai* (Berkeley: University of California Press, 1978).

18. These regulations are translated in H. Y. Tien, *China's Population Struggle* (Columbus: Ohio State University Press, 1973), appendix L.

or to enroll in an urban university. Urban economic enterprises had strict limits placed on their wage fund, and were forbidden to hire extra regular staff members without special permission. Even marriage to an urbanite did not entitle one to move into a city in order to live with one's spouse. The result of such measures was to create a rigid urban hierarchy of limited access that still persists. At the bottom are peasants, classified as members of "agricultural households," who are generally unable to move into urban places to establish residence—even into nearby commune towns.[19] Next come those in nonagricultural households living in rural towns, then those in county towns, district cities, provincial capitals, and finally in the three national level cities—Peking, Tientsin, and Shanghai. One can move down this hierarchy relatively easily, and parallel (to another urban place at the same administrative level) with some difficulty, but movement up, to a large urban place, is extremely difficult to arrange.[20] In the next two chapters we will see that this set of migration rules is backed up by a distribution system that makes it very hard to gain access to any of the necessities of life unless one is a permitted resident.

Families that are registered to live in a particular urban place all have household registration booklets (*hukou bu*) that are kept in the home. The household registration booklet has pages listing the various members of the household and their sexes, ages, marital status, class background, work units, and so forth. The local police station also maintains a register of each family in the neighborhood, and this contains information duplicating that in the household registration booklets (as well as other information police agencies like to collect). Changes in household composition through births, deaths, moves, and marriages must be reported to the police station, with the appropriate changes made in the household booklet and in the police station register. Visitors coming to stay with the family have to be reported to the police station as well, in order to receive "temporary household registrations" for the duration of their visit. The information in the family's household registration booklet is used in a variety of ways—to register a child for school, to collect rations, and so forth—and the police sometimes carry out surprise nighttime inspections

19. The nonagricultural/agricultural household distinction was formalized when the state took over the marketing of grain after 1954. The system is interpreted so as to minimize the nonagricultural population, which the state is obliged to provide with a steady flow of grain as well as other rations and privileges. Hence, normally one's household designation is inherited from one's mother, for it is fathers who are more likely to get a nonagricultural job in town.

20. That new urban workers should come almost entirely from the cities instead of the countryside was reaffirmed in 1980 (Zhang Qingwu, "Controlling Urban Population Growth," *People's Daily*, 21 August 1979, p. 3). In some new industrial cities this policy can be relaxed.

of homes or call in all household booklets in a locality to check the accuracy of the recorded information and to detect any people staying in the neighborhood without proper registration.[21] The one general exception to these procedures concerns individuals not living in family units, but by themselves in work unit or school dormitories. Such individuals do not have separate household registration booklets. Instead, the work unit or school maintains a collective household registration (*jiti hukou*) for all such individuals and monitors changes in their status and reports them to the local police station.

The control of city size has had another side to it, and this involves the relocation of urbanites. Household registration in a city is not an unrestricted right, but is in some sense a privilege. Over the years there have been several kinds of efforts to mobilize portions of the urban population to go and settle down in smaller cities or rural areas. Sometimes skilled personnel have been sent out to help establish new factories in the hinterlands; on other occasions "excess" bureaucrats and unemployed youths have been "sent down" to serve their country in lower levels of the hierarchy; and on other occasions political undesirables and their families have been forced to return to their native places.[22] The best-documented example of this kind of dispersal effort is the post-Cultural Revolution campaign to send urban educated youths to the countryside, which resulted in the decade after 1968 in the dispersal of more than 17 million youths from the cities (out of a total urban population of only a little over 100 million).

The consequences of this combined positive program of building interior cities and negative program of restricting urban access and dispersing population have been quite dramatic. Some of the largest cities have grown hardly at all. Metropolitan Shanghai, with an urban population of 6.2 million in 1953 had only slightly more than that in 1980. Some other major cities such as Peking, with its new administrative and industrial functions, grew quite rapidly. But, on the average, China's twenty-one cities of one million population and more grew by only 51 percent between 1953 and the 1970s while her next largest twenty-two cities of half-a-million population or more grew by 96 percent. Shanghai's share in total urban population dropped significantly while the share of interior cities grew, moving China back to the more even regional spread of cities typical of the pre-

21. For example, see "Residency Check," in Jo-hsi Chen, *The Execution of Mayor Yin* (Bloomington: Indiana University Press, 1978).

22. The Chinese concept of "native place" is particularly useful here. It refers to the place of origin of one's family (one's father, paternal grandfather, etc.), even if one has never lived there. Thus lifelong urban residents would still in most cases have a rural native place they could be sent to.

Western imperial period.[23] China reversed trends so typical of other developing societies and its own recent past, and in so doing kept the total urban population to 21 percent of the total population, while distributing urban centers relatively equally throughout the society.[24]

These policies had a radical influence on the internal structure of cities as well. By the 1960s, cities ceased to be bloated by rural migrants in search of nonexistent urban work. Our neighbor census sample statistics show the trends clearly. Through the early 1950s, Chinese cities continued to attract a large flow of migrants. We calculate that almost half of the urbanites who began work in these early years had been migrants. But then with effective enforcement of the 1958 migration controls, the reestablishment of rural order after the 1958–61 Great Leap Forward, and a cutback in urban jobs in the 1960s, migration to cities was sharply curtailed. By the 1970s, less than ten percent of those reaching age twenty and taking their first job were doing so in a city other than where they grew up.[25] And many of their siblings and former classmates were not taking urban jobs at all but instead were settling down in the countryside for varying lengths of stay. Chinese cities were beginning to have a residential stability that is unusual for cities anywhere in the world.

This stability extends to movement within cities as well as into them for reasons we will clarify later. Overall, in our weighted sample, only one-fifth of all urbanites had grown up outside their city of residence.

23. Clifton W. Pannell, "Recent Growth in China's Urban System," in *Urban Development in Modern China,* Laurence Ma and Edward Hanten, eds., table 2. Because of data problems, the figures are necessarily only approximate.

24. "1982 Census Results," *Beijing Review,* no. 45 (1982): 20–21. On difficulties with published urban population statistics, see John S. Aird, "Population Studies and Population Policy in China," *Population and Development Review* 8 (1982): 279–82. Currently 2,990 places are defined as urban, leaving out many rural market towns of less than 3,000 population.

Surprisingly, both China and India have followed very similar urban growth patterns. But in comparison to most developing societies, China's rate of urban growth has been much slower, particularly in its largest city. From 1964 to 1982, China's urban population grew at the rate of only 2.7 percent per annum while in other low income developing societies that rate averaged 5.4 percent over a similar time period. Also, Shanghai's share in China's total urban population dropped from 5 to 3 percent over the last two decades while the share of the largest city in other developing societies increased from an already high 25 percent to an even higher 28 percent. See "1982 Census Results," for China, and the World Bank, *World Development Report 1982* (New York: Oxford University Press, 1982), table 20, for other countries.

25. These calculations are based on adults born in China who held nonagricultural occupations in our census of neighbors (N = 913). The reconstruction of longitudinal trends from age data overstates the decline in migration—older people have had more opportunities to move. But the problem is a slight one, since with a system of lifetime employment in the nonagricultural sector, persons are quite unlikely to move once they have gotten a job in their early twenties. For details on our neighbor census sample see appendix 1.

Only ten percent had changed residence in the last five years, and only one percent had changed residence in the last year. The average residence in the same house or apartment was eighteen years. These are unusual figures for any society, whether China in the past, Third World societies, developed societies, or other socialist states. In the past China had considerable back and forth movement between city and countryside and among cities. In the United States, one of the most mobile of societies, two-fifths of all families change residence at least once in any five-year period and one-fifth move in a single year alone. Even in India, one of the most stationary of developing societies, about twenty-nine percent of the urban population changes residence at least once in five years, five to six percent move in a single year, and twenty-six percent live in cities other than where they were born. And in other socialist states such as the Soviet Union, which share China's goal of restricting the growth of large cities, there is only a rule against migration into the few largest cities (which is not that effectively enforced) rather than prohibitions affecting the entire urban hierarchy.[26]

In China the rules against migration are effectively enforced. A few people are able to use connections to get unorthodox moves into a city approved. There is also a small proportion of people living in cities without proper approval—about 2.5 percent of adults in our sample. But much of the illegal residence that persisted in the 1970s had to do with the special situation of urban youth who slipped back into the city to live with their parents after having been sent to the countryside, rather than true rural migrants. Among youths age 20–29 in our sample, illegal residents constituted at least 6 percent. Among people age 30 and above, they were no more than 1 percent. This fits the impression of most of our informants who reported it was virtually impossible for a peasant to slip into a city and live for long periods of time without being detected or running out of the rations so necessary for everyday existence.[27]

The effective restraint on migration has a number of social consequences. Unlike some cities in developing societies or in late imperial China, there are about as many females as males. Few people are isolated from their families. And there is an unusual opportunity for neighborhood familiarity

26. U.S. Bureau of the Census, *Statistical Abstract of the U.S.* (Washington: Government Printing Office, 1976), p. 29. Ashish Bose, *India's Urbanization, 1901–2001*, 2nd edition (New Delhi: Tata, 1978), pp. 432, 444. Robert J. Osborn, *Soviet Social Policies* (Homewood, Ill: Dorsey Press, 1970), chap. 6. There is considerable circular migration in India with migrants coming to the city for a time and then leaving—hence the more modest contrast in lifetime than in recent migration figures compared with China.

27. With the current relaxation in urban rationing and marketing, the number of illegals has increased somewhat in more recent years.

and solidarity to develop. In neighborhoods where people have often lived together for two decades, often sharing the same kitchen and toilet facilities, there is little reason for the anonymity often seen as typical of cities. This residential closeness and familiarity would seem to be an ideal breeding ground for social solidarity and peer pressure, features the urban authorities want to foster. There is some variation in residential stability among neighborhoods though. In cities such as Canton, the stable inner core is matched by outer suburbs where new housing has been built for factory workers. By comparing the more and less stable areas within Chinese cities in later chapters we hope to get a better sense of the role played by neighborhood cohesion and solidarity in social control and social change.

Bureaucratic Control

In the 1950s the new Communist government set out not only to redistribute the population of cities and limit their growth but also to rid them of the social ills which had become so common in the century since initial Western impact. In order to help eliminate crime, vagrancy, corruption, prostitution, and hunger and to help recreate the kind of political commitment known in Yanan, everyone was to be organized from the ground up. City residents were to live no longer in isolated families and alone but in cellular organizations, much as had been true in earlier times. Only this time the cells were not to be autonomous units operating on their own, like guilds and neighborhood associations of the past, but integral parts of the national bureaucracy extending all the way from Peking down to the local neighborhood and work group. Residential and production units provide the basic structures of the dual administration system that was worked out in the early 1950s.

The residential or neighborhood system varies somewhat from city to city, as well as over time, and we illustrate the system here by the terminology from Canton. At the apex is the city level of administration. Canton is divided on a geographic basis into six urban districts (as well as several rural counties), in each of which reside several hundred thousand people. These districts are then subdivided into units, usually wards or streets (*jiedao*), which are responsible for the 2,000–10,000 families living there. Since this is a formal administrative subdivision we will refer to these units as wards. Each ward is in turn subdivided into 4–12 residents' committee units, each of which supervises 100–800 families living in a smaller area within the ward. The residents' committee is finally subdivided into 5–20 residents' small group units, each of which looks after 15–40 families living in a single building or in several adjacent houses along a street or lane. In smaller towns, this structure is often less formalized and some of the intermediate levels may be absent, but the essential functions will still be performed by an analogous administrative structure.[28]

This structure is bureaucratic, not in that all its personnel are on the state payroll, but in that all levels are very much subject to appointment and control from above. In the upper reaches of the residential system we find several hierarchies of paid officials: the city administration proper, the Communist Party, the police, the courts, and so forth. At the level of the ward there is a ward affairs office, a ward Party committee or Party branch, and a ward police station. The people in these offices are paid officials who are appointed by higher authorities, and they do not all have to live in the neighborhood themselves. The two lowest levels, the residents' committee and the residents' small group, are slightly different. The residents' committee has four to ten officers running its affairs, but these are local residents, and they are not considered state officials. Most are unpaid, although the residents' committee chairman may receive a small stipend from the ward authorities. These petty leaders are generally appointed by ward leaders also, rather than being elected by the residents. Most residents' committee and residents' small group leaders are housewives or other middle-aged retired people, since these are the people who have the time to devote to neighborhood activities.

The top-down nature of this structure is further strengthened by its affiliation with the police. Indeed, there is some suggestion that much of the structure of urban administration had its original inspiration in the Japanese neighborhood police system adopted in some Chinese cities after 1911 and then during World War II and afterwards.[29] The ward affairs office typically adjoins the ward police station, which keeps the household registration records we have already talked about. It often designates a policeman to be in charge of one or two residents' committees, seeing that local household registers are kept up to date, that untrustworthy neighbors are kept under surveillance, that any other suspicious activities are regularly reported, and that citizen patrols are organized in times of disorder.

Several other potential functions help fill out the enveloping nature of the lowest three units of neighborhood administration. These functions vary from place to place and over time. We will simply list the sorts of

28. For a description of Peking's neighborhood organization, see *Beijing Review,* no. 44 (1980): 19–25. The 1954 regulations governing residents' committees and the neighborhood police apparatus are translated in Jerome Cohen, *The Criminal Process in the People's Republic of China 1949–1963* (Cambridge: Harvard University Press, 1968). These regulations were republished in China in 1980, thus indicating they continue to apply.

29. Buck, *Urban Change in China,* p. 148, Schurmann, *Ideology and Organization,* chap. 6.

activities they may engage in here, and in subsequent chapters we will describe their role in particular spheres of administration and distribution in more detail. Neighborhoods may run a variety of small factories and workshops employing local personnel; they may run a variety of small repair shops, paramedical stations, and other service facilities; they convene meetings of local residents to transmit messages from the government and organize study of indoctrination materials; they carry out local sanitation and cleanliness activities; they mobilize residents to practice birth control and send their children down to the countryside; they may organize reading rooms and post propaganda posters; they help administer rations and convene meetings to discuss major crime cases in the city; and they mediate disputes between and within families.

It is important to recognize how this residential part of the urban ad-· ministrative system differs from the territorial system of administration of American cities. Our cities, too, are subdivided into districts or boroughs, and sometimes below this into wards, although a ward may be an electoral district rather than a unit that actually administers programs and people. At this level our city administration proper generally stops. Insofar as there is leadership over individual neighborhoods or blocks it is generally organized from below or outside in the form of local citizens' groups, ethnic leaders, or political machines, and in many locales organizations and leadership are simply lacking. Americans tend to feel that it is illegitimate for city administrations to try to reach down into neighborhoods and formally organize them as part of the urban administrative system. The Chinese urban system, in contrast, has a hierarchy from the mayor's (and city Party secretary's) office right down to groups of a few dozen households, all organized according to a standard model. In fact the hierarchy reaches on upward to the capital in Peking, for this is not a federal system. The residents' committees and small groups are not voluntary associations or community advocacy groups; in fact, local interest and advocacy groups have been proscribed in the Chinese system. The entire structure is mandated by law and administered firmly from above, even though the lowest level leaders are not paid officials. So what looks on the surface like a territorial system of urban administration similar to our own is in fact quite a different system in its operation, particularly at the lowest levels.

It also differs from the Japanese and Soviet systems from which elements have been borrowed. The Japanese system has neighborhood police who keep registers on, and have an intimate knowledge of, local residents, but this policing function is not combined with the multitude of other economic, subsistence, sanitation, welfare, and political functions so vital to everyday life as in Chinese cities. The Soviet system has the ideal of multifunctional neighborhoods, but these tend to be very large units about the size of the Chinese ward and without the degree of internal organization found in China. If anything, Chinese neighborhood units harken back more to the multifunctional neighborhood and guild organizations of the past than to anything imported from abroad. But as noted earlier, these contemporary residential organizations are quite different from the past. Not only do they lack autonomy, but their members are not engaged in a common trade and may work elsewhere around the city.

For complete organization of the urban population, then, there has to be a production unit administrative system as well. In this second mode of organization we see the central stress in Chinese thinking on the work unit (danwei), which is seen not simply as a place to punch a time clock and earn wages but as an entity that plays a central role in organizing the lives of those employed there. Many programs and services are administered through work units rather than, or in addition to, being administered through the residential system just described. Again the details will become clearer in succeeding chapters, but work units may run nurseries, clinics, canteens, and recreational facilities; they convene employees to hear government decrees and for political study; they organize campaigns for birth control and to send down youths; they approve marriages and divorces and mediate disputes; they hold meetings to discuss crimes and misbehavior off the job by their members; they distribute rations and carry out cleanliness campaigns; they supervise untrustworthy employees and organize patrols to guard the area; and they may employ family members of employees in subsidiary small workshops or vegetable farms.

Work units vary in their size, their resources, their administrative level, and many other dimensions. These variations have consequences for employees, for they affect the extent to which they are dependent upon their unit or their ward for various goods and services, and how well those resources controlled by work units are supplied to them. For some individuals who work in large production units and are housed in dormitories right on the premises, there may be almost total dependence on the unit, and formal ward and residents' committees may be irrelevant. With work and residence combined, these settings approximate the living conditions in traditional Chinese cities. At the other extreme are those who are employed in small neighborhood workshops or service facilities, and those who are not employed. These individuals fall completely under the residential administrative system, and have no outside work unit to rely on. Many people fall somewhere in between, and turn to their work unit in dealing with some of their needs, and to their ward and residents' committees in dealing with others. Alternatively, they can be seen as moving between two sets of authorities regulating their lives. Things are more complex than this, however, for within a family some members will be mainly dependent on their work unit, while other members will be mainly dependent upon their ward. But just as individuals can be classified in this way, so can local residential areas be roughly classified according to whether most people living there are dependent mainly on work units or on wards. For shorthand purposes, in later chapters we will refer to the extreme cases as "work unit compounds" and "mixed neighborhoods." The former are most distinctive in comparison with our own urban experience, for they represent something like a company town complex within a diverse cityscape.[30]

Modern Chinese cities possess a structure which is distinctive compared with other societies and with traditional Chinese cities. As in the past, a highly centralized bureaucracy, unopposed by major interest groups, is in charge, only now the bureaucracy extends to much lower levels in the society. As in the past, there is a considerable emphasis on relatively self-contained, cohesive social units, though these are organized along new lines and connected to the centralized bureaucracy. As in the past there is a relatively even spread of cities across the Chinese landscape, but now instead of a vague and highly permeable boundary between city and countryside there is a very sharp one with little back and forth movement across it. This structure creates some very special opportunities, and some special dangers. The stability of residence, multifaceted involvement of neighbors with one another and the common joining of work and residence create the potential for high levels of social solidarity and cooperation, crime control, and social order, as well as a rapid remolding of the marriage customs, family patterns, fertility behavior, and other social and intellectual habits of the citizenry. The well-ordered distributive functions of the ward and work unit create the possibility of avoiding the inequalities of the market and distributing goods and services both equally and effectively. However, the joining of so many police, economic, welfare, and service functions into one massive bureaucracy also creates a potential for coercion, corruption, inefficiency, insensitivity to local needs, and personal vindictiveness by minor officials. One of the jobs of subsequent chapters is to assess in which of these directions the system has tilted in the past and what it is likely to do in the future.

30. In the Great Leap Forward an effort was mounted to reorganize cities into more integrated work and residence units, called urban communes, which was later abandoned. More recently, some new industrial cities and projects have taken a more integrated nature of this type, and an example would be the national model Daqing oilfield complex. However, the unusualness of this situation is one factor that has hindered other urban locales from seriously following the Daqing model. See Janet Salaff, "The Urban Communes and the Anti-City Experiment in Communist China," *China Quarterly* 29 (1967); and David Buck, "Urban Development: Beyond the Ta-ch'ing Model," *Contemporary China* 1 (1977).

3   The Quest
for Equality
and Security

W ere the ideals of the Chinese leadership to be realized, life in Chinese cities would differ from that in other societies not only because of greater stability of residence and more encompassing and tightly organized social units but also because of greater equality and security of living conditions, without sharp class divisions and inherited privileges.[1] To achieve this equality and security, Chinese leaders set out in the 1950s to introduce rational planning into the economy, to turn consumer into producer cities, to provide full employment, to narrow the range of urban (and rural) rewards, and to provide a stable floor in housing, health care, education, food, and the supply of other basic necessities. The question of this chapter and the next is the extent to which these goals have been achieved and whether the attempt to achieve them has produced unanticipated consequences.

State Planning

China's planned socialism developed in stages during the 1950s. Initially most employment remained in private firms, and cities had large pools of unemployed people. While economic expansion and dispersal of migrants to the countryside were supposed to relieve unemployment, transformation from private enterprise to public or socialist enterprise was designed to end the chaos of capitalism. Initially only selected firms were

1. For more details on the internal organization of work units, See William Parish, "The View from the Factory," in *The China Difference*, Ross Terrill, ed. (New York: Harper and Row, 1979); Andrew G. Walder, "Work and Authority in Chinese Industry: State Socialism and the Institutional Culture of Dependency" (Ph.D. dissertation, University of Michigan, 1981); Gail Henderson, "Danwei: The Chinese Work Unit" (Ph.D. thesis, University of Michigan, 1982); and Susan L. Shirk, "Recent Chinese Labor Policies and the Transformation of Industrial Organisation in China," *China Quarterly* 88 (1981): 575–93.

taken over by the government: large firms controlled by the former Nationalist government or leading figures within that government, many foreign-owned firms, particularly large and vital enterprises, banks, utilities, trade firms, and so forth. Private capitalism was allowed to continue into the 1950s, although increasing regulation and political organization within private firms gradually eliminated most of the decision-making freedom of the remaining capitalists. Then starting in 1955 (simultaneous with the drive to collectivize agriculture) the campaign to socialize the urban economy began. There were two main aspects of this. First, in 1955–57, the remaining capitalists were pressured to turn over their firms to the state, and were rewarded for their compliance with jobs within their firms at relatively high pay and with regular interest payments on the assessed valuation of their shares in the firm. These became the "joint state-private firms." Then in the second major stage in 1956–58, the authorities tried to organize all of the small peddlers, shopkeepers, noodle sellers, and repair workers into group enterprises in order to eliminate these petty capitalists. The resulting firms became known as "cooperative enterprises" and were collectively owned by those who worked in them. Thus, by early 1958, authorities could feel that the drive for socialist transformation and the elimination of capitalism was a success with virtually all urban employment in one of three kinds of socialist firm: state-run, joint state-private, and collective firms.[2]

Since that time further changes have taken place in the nature of urban work units, with many of the 1950s collective work units being brought under state ownership. In the Cultural Revolution the privileges enjoyed by former capitalists were criticized and eliminated, and the firms classified as "joint state-private" became indistinguishable from state-run firms. (The distinction had been nominal in the first place.) After 1958, cooperative stores were by and large amalgamated into the state trading network, thereby losing their collective character. Cooperative handicraft workshops were amalgamated into the Second Light Industrial Bureau even while technically remaining collective.[3] But while many of these

2. On this period of transition, see John Philip Emerson, *Nonagricultural Employment in Mainland China*, U.S. Bureau of the Census, International Population Statistics Reports, Series P-90, no. 21 (Washington, D.C.: U.S. Government Printing Office, 1965).

3. An example of the increasingly state character of "collective" units within the Second Light Industrial Bureau are the 1965–66 State Council regulations specifying retirement benefits in these units only slightly below those in full fledged state units and also specifying that any deficit in a unit's retirement fund would be supplemented from higher level state budgets—see Fujian Province, Revolutionary Committee Planning Commission, *Laodong Gongzi Wenjian Xuanbian* (Fujian, 1973), pp. 637–50. Besides our interviews, other references for this section include "Urban Collective Economy," *Beijing Review*, no. 35 (1979): 9–14; "On Collective and Individual Economy in Cities and Towns," *China Reconstructs*,

units were losing their collective character, other kinds of collective units were appearing. In the late 1950s and after, major efforts were made to mobilize housewives and others who were not employed to pool their talents and resources and set up small neighborhood factories and workshops. These neighborhood enterprises and others like them, providing work for people in smaller towns and for the unemployed children and spouses of employees of state factories, schools, and bureaus, became common by the 1970s. The resulting urban enterprise structure thus came to have two main sectors—the state and the collective—but with considerable variety in each sector. Among state-run enterprises there are some that are administered directly by the central government, some administered by provinces or counties, some administered by cities, and some administered by urban districts. Collective enterprises are generally smaller in scale, but they can also be administered by one of several levels: a state bureau, a state enterprise or office, a ward, or in smaller places directly by a town or commune.[4] Regardless of these complexities, the state has considerably advanced its control over the work force since the 1950s. In 1957, soon after the socialization of the urban economy, 69 percent of the nonprivate work force was in state enterprises. But by 1977 state control had expanded to 79 percent of this work force.[5]

Further evidence of the state's expanding control over the economy was the shrinkage of the private sector. By the 1970s only a few remnants survived. In 1957, perhaps ten percent of the nonagricultural work force was still private.[6] In the 1960s, large cities still licensed a modest number of individual street barbers, roaming knife sharpeners, mom-and-pop cigarette stands, and other individualist enterprises. But in the stricter at-

---

29 (January 1981): 293–94. In reading, distinguish cooperative (*hezuo*), which tells something about the history of an enterprise, and collective (*jiti*), which tells something about the legal ownership of an enterprise.

4. Collective enterprises under the Second Light Industrial Bureau contained 31 percent of all collective employees in 1978. There were 56,800 of these enterprises in 1978, each with an average of 110 employees. A year later, industrial (as opposed to service) enterprises run by neighborhoods (and probably including towns) numbered 36,412 while those run by dependents' organizations under state units numbered 6,766. Thus in collective industry alone, the Second Light Industrial Bureau was dominant, but in service enterprises, neighborhood and town units were dominant. Dependents' organizations ran a distant third, though they were increasing rapidly as they began to be used to provide jobs for the unemployed children of people working in the state unit that started them. See references in note 3.

5. State Statistical Bureau, "Communique on Fulfillment of China's 1978 National Economic Plan," *Beijing Review*, no. 27 (1979): 40.

6. Emerson, *Nonagricultural Employment*, table 3. But another source gives a lower figure of only three percent—*Zhongguo Jingji Nianjian, 1981* (Peking, 1981), p. VI-7.

mosphere after the Cultural Revolution, much of this licensing was eliminated.[7] The vestiges of capitalism and individual profit seeking these undertakings represented were seen as incompatible with the purer form of Chinese socialism the radicals were trying to promote. So too was the market activity of peasants which had previously been allowed in urban areas. In the 1970s some peasants still came in and covertly hawked their produce in urban neighborhoods. Illegally returned sent-down youths built furniture and sometimes trinkets in their homes to sell privately. In Canton, a few street barbers and other licensed artisans continued to operate. Some women took in private sewing jobs, and some men took jobs constructing and renovating housing without neighborhood supervision or taxation. A few old doctors saw patients privately and fortune tellers covertly received clients. People within the city and from outside engaged in black market exchanges of gold, watches, ration coupons, medicines, and other products. Within the urban economy these undertakings did not amount to much, however. In our weighted sample of neighbors (N = 1,031), only 3 percent were engaged in these kinds of activities for their major source of income. There was another in-between category, "putting-out workers," who got their cloth, straw, plastic parts, or other raw materials from an established factory and then made them into shirts, fans, toys, or other goods in their homes before selling them back to the factory. These too were but a small part of the urban economy, accounting for only 1 percent of our total sample of employed neighbors. Together, the independent workers doing private and putting-out work accounted for only 4 percent of the total nonagricultural labor force. Of the employed persons in our weighted sample, 73 percent were employed in state enterprises and 23 percent in collective enterprises.[8]

The distinctions among state, collective, and independent work are important for several reasons. State-run enterprises are supposed to have their production closely coordinated within the national economic plan; they are tightly regulated and are fairly standardized in terms of the wages they must pay, the fringe benefits accorded staff members, and the use made of profits and investment funds; if they operate at a loss the state

7. In 1966, independent workers are said to have still numbered two million. By 1978 there were only 150,000 registered (see "Collective and Individual Economy," and *Zhongguo Jingji Nianjian, 1981*, p. VII-7.) In the early 1960s, neighborhoods also helped supply day laborers to do hauling, construction, and other unskilled labor for state factories. This practice continued in small towns after the Cultural Revolution but generally not in large cities. It would appear from interviews that the practice may now be making a comeback even in large cities.

8. For additional published data on this distribution see appendix 1.

budget will cover the deficit; and they generally have more resources and amenities than the other types of enterprises.

The situation with collective enterprises is more variable. Some particularly large firms and those under state bureaus may not operate too much differently from state-run firms, and it is not uncommon for successful and large collective firms to be converted into state-run enterprises. But in principle, collective enterprises are not so closely planned and regulated and engage in production of less essential goods and services; they are to be responsible for their own profits and losses and can be reduced in scale or eliminated if they are not profitable; and a firm's success or failure determines the number of workers, the type of wage scales used, and the types of fringe benefits provided. So while workers in state enterprises are paid according to fixed wage scales that are centrally determined and enjoy a wide range of fringe benefits (health insurance, disability pay, paid maternity leave, subsidized preschool care, retirement pensions, etc.), in collective enterprises some people receive monthly wages, others receive daily wages for the number of days they worked, and others are paid by piecework or some other incentive device. Some workers in collective enterprises enjoy partial medical care benefits and disability insurance but usually not maternity leave or pensions, and some collective enterprises provide nothing in benefits at all, but only pay for the work done. (Fringe benefits will be discussed further in chapter 4.)

In theory, collective enterprises that are very profitable may be able to pay their employees wages that are higher than those earned in similar state enterprises, since sharing the fruits of success is supposed to be the essence of collective firms. However, in the radical atmosphere after the Cultural Revolution, it appears that taxation policies and administrative regulations were used to make sure that this would not happen, so that wages in collective firms would remain below those in comparable state enterprises. Thus in the 1970s and to some extent today employees in the collective sector were multiply disadvantaged—in job security, in wages, and in fringe benefits.

The distinction between the state sector on the one hand and the collective and independent sectors on the other is reminiscent of the distinction between the formal modern and informal bazaar sectors in the economies of many Third World cities (and primary and secondary sectors of the labor market in advanced capitalist societies). In China in the late 1970s, collective and independent workers made only about three-fourths as much as state employees (see table 1) and the differences in fringe benefits made the gaps even larger. As in other developing cities, education, sex, and age helped channel one into different types of jobs. Women and those with less education went disproportionately into collective and independent work. This was particularly true in metropolitan neighborhoods, where it was primarily those who were not fit for work in large state work units who were left behind to be employed by neighborhood enterprises. In smaller towns and commune seats there were not quite so many state jobs and the distinctions between state and collective jobs were not quite so great.[9] There females and those with less education were slightly less likely to be shunted into collective jobs. In both metropolitan areas and small towns, independent work tended to be reserved for older men and women who had few educational skills that could be used in the job market (table 1, last row).

This pattern of job allocation is strikingly similar to what one finds in other developing cities around the world. In China, this sectorial distinction is more clearly institutionalized than elsewhere. Nevertheless, the gap between the formal and the informal sectors of the labor market is in a number of ways smaller in China. Elsewhere, the informal sector may be more than half the economically active population.[10] In China, the informal sector is less than one-fourth of the economically active nonagricultural population. Elsewhere, informal sector incomes are often less than half those of the primary sector. In China, informal sector incomes are three-fourths those of the primary sector. Also, with regard to

Table 1   Income and Personal Characteristics
                                                         by Type of Occupation

Sector and Level of Ownership	Average Monthly Income (yuan)	Average Education (years)	Females (%)	Average Age (years)	Average N
State	46	8.3	45	35	(732)
Collective					
Town or commune	37*	7.0*	47	34	(107)
Metropolitan neighborhood	39*	5.6*	59*	36	(112)
Independent workers	35*	3.8*	50	47*	(33)

Source: Sample of neighbors.

*Difference with state sector would occur less than five times in a hundred by chance alone (p ≤ .05).

9. According to our neighbor census sample, 87–89 percent of those employed in national level cities and provincial capitals worked in state enterprises, compared with 75 percent of those in county seats and only 49 percent of those in commune towns (N = 1,260, counting only members of the nonagricultural labor force). However, our sample may exaggerate the distinction because many informants counted large collective factories under the Second Light Industrial Bureau as state enterprises.

10. The comparisons here and below are based on Dipak Mazumdar, "The Urban Informal Sector," World Development 4 (1976): 655–79.

age, sex, and educational composition, the sectorial differences in China are more modest.

Perhaps the most striking realm in which the state/collective distinction is less important than the formal/informal sectorial difference in other developing societies is in regard to job security. Even though in theory the employees of collective firms can be laid off or the firms can shut down entirely, throwing all of their personnel out of work, according to our informants, in practice this has rarely happened. So both sectors have shared to a considerable degree in a distinctive Chinese version of permanent employment. Once employed in an enterprise (or at least once past an initial probationary period) it has been almost impossible to be fired or laid off. At the same time, with a bureaucratic system of job assignments (to be discussed shortly) and no real labor market, it has been also almost impossible to leave and find another job. As a result, employed persons have had a reasonable degree of job security, but they also can be stuck forever in a very unpleasant work situation.[11] That both sectors of the urban economy share to a considerable degree in this permanent employment system can be seen in the popular terms used—state enterprise jobs provide an "iron rice bowl," while collective sector jobs provide an "earthen rice bowl." Both are hard to break and thus guarantee one's income and food, but the iron bowl is more durable. So in spite of some similarities with the situation in cities in other Third World countries, there does not appear to be as sharp a degree of economic dualism represented by the state/collective distinction in urban China.[12]

Producer Cities

Another type of problem that China's leaders wanted to avoid was the concentration of Chinese cities around consumption rather than production. Conspicuous consumption and tastes for foreign goods in treaty ports such as Shanghai provided prime examples of what was to be avoided in the call to change China's cities into producer cities, as noted in chapter 2. This call included an additional emphasis on industry as opposed to trade and the suppression of bourgeois "consumerism" and high life styles

11. After a period of purges, rehabilitations, and general turmoil, instances of individuals stuck as subordinates or colleagues with those who were formerly their chief tormenters have been the subject of press commentary and even drama in recent years. See the play by Xing Yixan, "Power versus Law," *Chinese Literature*, no. 6 (1980): 31–91.

12. Of course, there is a range of temporary and contract workers taken on by urban enterprises as well as individual putting-out workers who do not have this sort of job security. Under extreme circumstances, such as being arrested for a crime or political offense, even those in state enterprises could lose this security.

plus reorientation of city economies to serving the countryside with goods and services.[13] The statistics on the distribution of the work force by industry in 1957 and 1978 show that the first part of this call has been largely achieved (see table 2).[14] In two decades the proportion of workers in industry and construction has grown dramatically. Health and education have been big winners as well. At the same time, occupations associated with consumption and bourgeois life styles perceived as not contributing significantly to production were curtailed, at least in relative terms. Even while government duties and the complexity of the economy grew enormously, the proportion of the labor force in government administration, public utilities, and finance declined.[15] Transportation, food and drink, retailing, and other activities with the taint of bourgeois production for exchange rather than material production for use were sharply reduced relative to other occupations. Work as maids, barbers, and other service type jobs was reduced to a small fraction of former levels.

This situation contrasts sharply with that found in other developing states where the service sector, including trade and government services, is frequently among the fastest growing sectors in the total economy. In developed market states such as the U.S., the service sector grew gradually to its present level. But in many developing market states, the proportion of service personnel already approximates that found in the West (see table 3). Critics have taken this as evidence of how past colonial experience and world market forces have distorted development in currently developing cities. The urban middle classes clamor for government and professional posts and try to match the style of living of their former colonial masters and their present multinational corporation executives. The technologically sophisticated and capital intensive modern sector imported from abroad by the multinationals as well as local entrepreneurs lures migrants to the city but provides them with few jobs. Many in the lower classes end up hawking goods on the street, washing cars, sweeping

13. This interpretation borrows from Rhoads Murphey, *The Fading of the Maoist Vision* (New York: Methuen, 1980), p. 80.

14. For an alternate but still similar set of figures see *Zhongguo Jingji Nianjian, 1981*, pp. VI-7, 8.

15. Since in a socialist economy many of the personnel in industrial, education, and other enterprises are in essence government functionaries, the figures in table 2 for government administrators reveal less than we would like to know about the trends in this area. Nevertheless, the apparent decline in administrators relative to the rest of the labor force may be a true decline. Gur Ofer argues that socialist societies typically have rather few administrative personnel and are underadministered relative to their huge administrative needs—which is just the opposite of these countries (and China's) own analysis of having bloated bureaucracies. See *The Service Sector in Soviet Economic Growth* (Cambridge: Harvard University Press, 1973).

Table 2

The Nonagricultural Labor Force by Industry and Year

Industry	1957	1978	Change
Manufacturing and mining	34.5%	47.9	+39%
Construction	6.6	7.9	+20%
Health	1.7	4.1	+143%
Education, cultural, scientific affairs	8.1	12.0	+47%
Urban public utilities	0.4	0.3	-17%
Government administration and mass organization	8.7	6.1	-30%
Transport, post and telecommunications	12.9	8.4	-35%
Trade, restaurants, and hotels	23.7	12.4	-48%
Finance, banking, and insurance	1.9	0.7	-65%
Other services	1.5	0.4	-76%
	100.0%	100.0%	

Source: Adapted from John Philip Emerson, "The Labor Force in China, 1957-1980," in China under the Four Modernizations, U.S. Congress, Joint Economic Committee (Washington, D.C.: U.S. Government Printing Office, 1982), p. 247.

floors, and taking other marginal jobs in the urban informal sector. Both upper and lower classes help swell the service sector, and meaningful jobs in production that would help build a strong, balanced, autonomous economy fail to emerge.[16]

China, in contrast, has moved very rapidly to the pattern so characteristic of European socialist states (table 3, last two columns).[17] In China and in these other socialist economies, production is emphasized, while trade, government administration, and most other services are downplayed. These similarities with other socialist societies suggests that the human resources side of the Chinese economy had indeed been turned around by the end of the mid-1970s and Chinese cities had indeed become the producer cities desired in leadership policy.

This turnaround, plus the restrictions on urban growth and a freeze on urban salaries beginning in the late 1950s, gave the government ample resources for investment in the long-run growth of the economy. Government accumulation from earnings of state industry and taxes ran to

16. There is far from universal agreement on how damaging this early emergence of the service sector and its associated informal sector is to developing economies. For an introduction to the debate, see Robert A. Hackenberg, "New Patterns of Urbanization in Southeast Asia," Population and Development Review 6 (1980): 391–420; and Bryan Roberts, Cities of Peasants (Beverly Hills: Sage, 1978).

17. For an extended discussion of the parent model from which all these countries borrow, see Ofer, The Service Sector in Soviet Economic Growth.

Table 3   Nonagricultural Labor Force by
                                            Industry and Type of Economy[a]

| | Market Economies | | Socialist Economies | |
	U.S.	Developing Societies[b]	China	Eastern Europe[c]
Manufacturing and mining	28%	27%	48%	46%
Construction	5	8	8	10
Transport and public utilities	8	9	9	11
Finance	5	2	1	1
Trade, restaurants, and hotels	21	21	12	10
Government and other services	33	33	22	22
Total	100%	100%	100%	100%

Sources: China: table 2. U.S.: U.S. Bureau of the Census, Statistical Abstract of the U.S., 1976 (Washington: U.S. Government Printing Office, 1976), table 597. Others: United Nations, Demographic Yearbook, 1972 (New York, 1973), table 10, and Demographic Yearbook 1973 (New York, 1974), table 40.

[a]Except for China, all about 1970.

[b]Twelve societies with 1970 per capita GNP of less than $1,200, ranging from the poorest, India, to the richest, Argentina.

[c]East Germany, Hungary, Poland, and Romania.

about 25 percent in the 1950s and 33 percent in the 1970s.[18] With the greatest part of this being reinvested in machinery and other heavy industries, industrial output grew by a handsome 9 percent a year throughout the 1950s, 1960s, and 1970s. This record seems to demonstrate the production potential of socialist organization.

The shift to socialist producer cities had a dramatic impact on the visual appearance of Chinese urban areas. Traditional Chinese cities contained a jumble of sights and sounds, some of which are still visible today in cities like Hong Kong and Taipei. A variety of lacquered and, later, neon signs competed for customer attention; hawkers roamed the streets and alleys, each with a distinctive call or noise to signal potential customers; and streets and alleys were filled with small shops and stands, often no more than holes in the wall, with cut-rate garments, tasty morsels, gold trinkets, or other merchandise displayed to catch the eye. Coffin sellers, professional letter writers, incense salesmen, "spirit money" peddlers,

18. Special Commentator, "The Aim of Socialist Production Must Be Really Understood," People's Daily, 20 October 1979, pp. 1–2, translated in FBIS, 9 November 1979, pp. L3–10. For comparison, in other low income countries in 1978 (when China's accumulation rate was 36 percent), gross domestic savings averaged only 15 percent of gross domestic product and in industrialized countries savings averaged only 22 percent—World Bank, World Development Report, 1980 (New York: Oxford University Press, 1980), table 5.

ivory seal carvers, and vendors of other exotica could be located in various neighborhoods. The variety of open-air eating places was such that in a city like Shanghai it was said that one could take an olfactory tour through every province of China by walking a few blocks along the Bund. The appearance of cities in China in the 1970s was quite different. Signs were absent or small, rarely neon, and wares were not displayed to tempt the eye, for there is no need to compete for customers in a socialist economy. Most of the roving peddlers and hawkers were gone or had merged into larger cooperatives where the customers came to them. Some items were not for sale anymore at all (coffins, incense), and the variety of shops and restaurants had declined, as we will see in chapter 4. The process of socialist transformation and the emphasis on productive enterprises had produced fewer but larger and more standardized stores and shops selling goods distributed through the official commercial channels. Visually, then, Chinese cities were more sedate and drab, although whether this means that consumers were less well served is a topic we will reserve for later.

Employment

The goal of making China's cities producer cities rather than consumer cities also involved an attempt to increase the labor force and to reduce the share of urbanites who were dependent upon others for their support. Work and "production of material value" have an almost mystical evaluation in Marxist theory, but maximizing employment also had several practical benefits. Wages could be kept low but consumption standards could continue to improve as families began to have more of their members in the labor force. Fuller employment meant fewer members of the urban population who would end up as public charges and have to be supported by government welfare programs, diverting funds from "productive" investment. Employment of women on a wide scale could be expected, according to Marxist theory, to contribute to another official goal, sexual equality. And the economic security thereby provided would lessen the likelihood of many of the social evils—crime, prostitution, gambling—that the government wished to stamp out.

The goal of maximizing employment has been pursued over the years through a variety of measures—limiting migration to the cities, dispersing urbanites to the countryside, mobilizing women to work, holding down wages, and fostering birth control. The result has been quite dramatic. In the 1950s something on the order of 30 percent or less of the members of the urban population were employed; by the late 1970s between 50 and 55 percent were. In some cities the shift has been even more remarkable. Peking went from having 26 percent of its population employed in the early 1950s to more than 62 percent in 1979, and in Tientsin the shift over roughly the same period was from 27 percent to 63 percent employed.[19] Clearly these figures suggest a trend dramatically different from that in other parts of the Third World, where rapid urbanization has involved a decline of the proportion of urbanites usefully employed.

The problem of employment turned out to be much more complex than these figures imply, however. Unemployment proved difficult to eliminate in the 1950s and continued to be a problem for youth into the 1970s. In the 1950s, the socialization of work in state and collective units proved insufficient to rid cities of unemployment. Sterner measures were required. One was to restrict access to cities after 1958, as already noted. Another was to collect prostitutes, beggars, and other vagrants lacking regular work and send them to state farms and other rural places.[20] In 1962, peasants who had slipped into cities in the Great Leap Forward were shipped back to their home villages. But with state investment going largely to heavy industry, which generated only 94 jobs per 1,000 yuan investment compared to the 257 jobs that a similar investment in light industry could have generated, the state was doing little to maximize new employment opportunities.[21] By the early 1960s, newly expanded urban secondary schools were beginning to graduate more than two million new jobs seekers every year. At the same time, retirement rates were low within the young labor force that had flooded into the expanding state economy during the 1950s, and the urban economy was still recovering from the depression brought on by the failure of the Great Leap Forward. So prior to the Cultural Revolution a growing number of educated unemployed youths—"social youths"—had already appeared in China's cities. With no other solution at hand, the government tried to mobilize and induce them to go to the countryside to help develop China's agriculture.

This effort produced some volunteers then, but a much larger outflow in the subsequent drive after 1968, when it was made virtually mandatory. It was in the latter period that more than 17 million urban youths settled

19. *Zhongguo Jingji Nianjian, 1981*, p. VI-25. With increasingly fewer children per family, the proportion employed continued to change rapidly in the late 1970s. According to State Statistical Bureau surveys, about 49 percent were employed in 1978, and 56 percent in 1981. Li Chengrui and Zhang Zhongi, "Remarkable Improvement in Living Standards," *Beijing Review*, no. 17 (1982): 17. Based on surveys of employees in state-owned work units, these statistics must overstate employment slightly.

20. On continuing unemployment during this period, see Christopher Howe, *Employment and Economic Growth in Urban China, 1949–57* (Cambridge: Cambridge University Press, 1971). For later years, consult Thomas G. Rawski, *Economic Growth and Employment in China* (New York: Oxford University Press, 1979).

21. Zhao Lukan, "A Probe into Some Employment Problems," *Beijing Review*, no. 43 (1980): 20.

down in the countryside over the course of a decade. The "up to the mountains and down to the villages" campaign after 1968 was promoted largely as a measure to foster revolutionary fervor and class solidarity with peasants and to help build up the countryside. But, given the numbers involved—more than 10 percent of the total urban population—it is clear that easing the crisis situation of educated unemployed was a primary concern of the authorities as well.[22] The problem of unemployment among educated urban youths is of course widespread in other developing societies, and one may say that its appearance in China is due to some of the same factors as in other societies—overemphasis on capital-intensive enterprises in the urban economy and a "diploma disease" fostered by government expansion of secondary schools, for example. But the solution to this problem attempted during the radical atmosphere of the 1970s, shipping most urban school graduates off to the countryside, is clearly a novel one, and we will return at several points in our study to explore its consequences.

Through the 1970s, a complex system of providing employment existed. Its primary feature was its reliance on bureaucratic allocation, with no real labor market and little room for individual preferences and choice—less even than had been allowed during earlier periods. These characteristics again resulted from the radical policies then in vogue. In the views of Mao Zedong and his followers, youths should be trained to be willing to serve where society needed them, without regard for personal desires or material interests. Allowing people to pick the jobs they wanted to pursue and to change to a different job would encourage the kind of individualism and professional orientations that were seen as incompatible with a purer form of socialism.

As pieced together from our interviews, the employment system in the early 1970s worked roughly as follows. During their final year in school, students began to receive intensive "thought preparation" in support of going "up to the mountains and down to the villages." As this campaign became regularized during the 1970s, not all middle school graduates were required to go to the countryside. Exemptions were possible if one had a serious medical problem (attested in writing by doctors), if one was an

22. A tenth of our weighted urban sample were currently assigned to the countryside, and perhaps a fourth of those ever assigned had legally returned to a city. For not too dissimilar estimates, see Thomas P. Bernstein, *Up to the Mountains and Down to the Villages* (New Haven: Yale University Press, 1977), pp. 30–32; and Paul E. Ivory and William R. Lavely, "Rustication, Demographic Change and Development in Shanghai," *Asian Survey* 17 (1977): 445. On difficulties with these figures, see Leo Orleans, "China's Urban Population," in *China under the Four Modernizations*, U.S. Congress, Joint Economic Committee (Washington, D.C.: Government Printing Office, 1982).

only child, or if a certain percentage (or even all) of one's siblings had already accepted rural assignment. But outside such youths, the goal of school authorities was to get all students about to graduate to sign up for rural reassignment. We estimate that more than half of urban young people were sent to the countryside for some period or other during these years.[23] The decisions about actual allocations were coordinated between city labor bureaus, schools, urban wards and enterprises, rural communes, and state farms in a manner that is not entirely clear to us.

A small number of new urban jobs might be available each year as retirements and plant expansions produced official permission to recruit new staff members.[24] Some of these jobs would require people with special training who might have to be assigned or transferred from elsewhere in the country, and a portion of the slots might be reserved for youths who had already completed a stint in the countryside.[25] The remainder would in some fashion be allocated among the various schools in the city. For example, middle school number 26 might be told that there were jobs in state or large collective enterprises for 50 of its 300 graduates in a particular year. School authorities then had the task of evaluating students to pick which graduates would be assigned to these fifty jobs. Generally speaking, individual desires and interests seemed to have played little role in this sorting process. Many or all of the urban jobs might go to those eligible to be exempted from the sending-down mobilization, others might be assigned to the most deserving of those who had volunteered for village assignments. (Some informants felt that the most fervent in demanding rural assignments were those most likely to escape this fate and be given an urban job.) Some worthy youths might also escape rural assignments by being selected to join the People's Liberation Army, a highly desirable fate in the eyes of most students. Those not selected for an urban job or

23. Based on 16–17 million being sent to the countryside from an urban population of just over 100 million and an estimate of the age structure of that population. In our sample, 30 percent of the 20–24 year olds were currently in the countryside and some had returned to the city.

24. One interesting arrangement spread during these years, and that involved parents willing to retire (sometimes early) being able to pick one of their youngsters to succeed them in their jobs (or in some other job in their work unit). This practice of job inheritance, which was later formally institutionalized, was one effort to cope with the rigid restriction prohibiting state enterprises from taking on new permanent employees without special permission. It also seems to have appealed to the desire of parents to find ways to help their children avoid rural exile.

25. Initially the sending-down program was supposed to be for life, but in time it was softened to allow many youth to return to cities after a two to three year stint in the countryside.

for the army, if not exempted for health or family reasons, were expected to join the exodus into the countryside.

Those eligible to stay in the city but not assigned to jobs went home and became the responsibility of their ward and residents' committees. These bodies were supposed to help find jobs for such youths if they could, either by referring them to job openings in state or collective enterprises or by taking them on in the small workshops and service facilities run by the wards themselves. Most wards did not have that much to offer beyond introductions to a variety of temporary and largely menial jobs—unskilled construction work, transport jobs—what used to be called "coolie work."[26] But over a number of years a large share of such youths would eventually hook onto jobs, often in neighborhood repair shops, canteens, or putting-out workshops.

Very few of the urban middle school graduates who were supposed to go to the countryside could avoid doing so. The tight-knit organizational structure of Chinese cities made it possible to mobilize pressure on such youths in both their schools and their neighborhoods, and on their parents, in their work units, and also in their neighborhoods. It took unusual boldness to refuse. Once in the countryside, many urban youths without agricultural skills found it very difficult to adapt to rural living conditions, including the heavy physical labor, the low pay, the largely grain diet, and the strange customs of local peasants. Many began to drift back to the city for several months at a time and some just stayed back home permanently. Without a valid urban household registration, they were not supposed to be hired and had to remain unemployed or seek illegal sources of income. The numbers drifting back are difficult to estimate, though in our sample almost half of the males appear to have been spending more than six months a year back in the city. Females were in the same situation as males, though they tended to achieve urban assignment, generally to a collective enterprise, somewhat earlier than their male counterparts.

In the period since our interviews, the decision to curtail and eventually phase out the program of sending urban school graduates to the countryside and to rotate those already sent back to urban jobs swelled the number of youths remaining in cities legally and illegally, and it has also prompted

26. Some forms of temporary work were not so temporary, but in fact involved people hired for a long period, but at lower pay, than regular workers and without full fringe benefits. Such temporary workers were another way state enterprises used to get around the restrictions placed upon their number of permanent employees. Workers of this type protested their inferior positions during the Cultural Revolution, and in the early 1970s some of them were able to make the transition to the status of permanent employees. However, since that time new temporary workers have been taken on and this practice clearly remains important. In 1979 two million of the newly employed were said to be on temporary work arrangements. See *Zhongguo Baike Nianjian, 1980,* pp. 294, 628.

greater official candor about the unemployment problem. According to Chinese sources, by the start of 1979 there were five to twelve million unemployed persons, which translates into five to eleven percent of the nonagricultural labor force.[27] This is a fairly high rate for any society, and indicates that even with impressive controls on migration and labor allocation the battle against unemployment is not easily won.[28]

The Chinese employment system of the 1970s included several goals. It attempted to get as high a proportion of the urban population as possible employed in relatively secure jobs and in the process succeeded in increasing the proportion of the urban population that were "productive," even if not quite as much as the official figures imply. The jobs held by most urbanites involve a degree of economic security unknown to most employed persons in pre-1949 cities or in cities in other developing societies, even if we consider the "inferior" collective sector jobs. During this period further steps were taken to deemphasize individual undertakings and limit collective enterprises to foster the development of the more "advanced" state sector enterprises. Market forces and individual choice were deemphasized to an unusual degree, even for a socialist society, in an effort to subject all labor to a process of bureaucratic allocation to suit the state's needs.[29]

27. The low figure ignores urban youth still legally consigned to agricultural jobs in the countryside and is from Hu Mengzhou, "Solution to Employment Problems," *Beijing Review*, no. 39 (1982): 20. The higher figure includes urban youth who still were in the countryside but scheduled to legally return to the city in 1979–80. It is implicit in *Zhongguo Baike Nianjian, 1980*, pp. 627–28. There is a third and even higher estimate that may erroneously include all urban youth ever consigned to the countryside regardless of current residence and job status. This estimate of 20 million unemployed at the start of 1979 comes from a purported speech by Li Xiannian to the National People's Congress—"The Economy of the Whole Country Is Seriously out of Balance," *Ming Bao* (Hong Kong), 14 June 1979, p. 4, in *FBIS*, 19 June 1979, pp. L11–13.

28. To give some comparison, in our neighbor census sample 69 percent of the males aged 20–24 and 78 percent of those age 25–29 were employed in nonagricultural jobs. In eight developing societies (India, Indonesia, Thailand, the Philippines, El Salvador, Morocco, Malaysia, and South Korea), the average employed was 71 percent for males 20–24 and 90 percent for males 25–29 (sources same as in table 3). Thus we find evidence of a relatively low percentage of young urban males "plugged in" to urban jobs in China. With more recent efforts to provide employment, which will be described later, unemployment reportedly declined to 3 million by the start of 1982, or to less than 3 percent of the nonagricultural labor force—"Employment," *Beijing Review*, no. 16 (1982): 16.

29. In the Soviet Union and other East European socialist societies a labor market exists, as do hiring bureaus and other related institutions and cash incentives for accepting jobs in areas with harsh climate. Only during wartime was an effort made in the Soviet Union to forbid changing jobs. Today college graduates are assigned to jobs by the Soviet state, but they are able to switch jobs after they have fulfilled their period of state obligation (often two years). In China individuals are of course subject to transfers at the whim of higher authorities, and have little power to initiate job changes themselves. They have to request a transfer through the proper channels, and the obstacles are so severe (sometimes requiring

Equality of Income

In Yanan, the Communist leadership and the army had used an egalitarian supply system which provided only a basic ration of food and clothing and a small living allowance for everyone, with only slight variations by rank. That system did not long survive the takeover of cities. Capitalists and merchants lost the property which would give them extra income. But under Soviet guidance, the new leadership also moved to institutionalize a differentiated, Soviet-type wage system. This new system, formalized in 1956, provided for the strict grading of administrative personnel into thirty salary grades, technicians into eighteen grades, industrial workers into eight grades, and so forth, with prizes and bonuses for exceptional performance.[30]

The Chinese were never very happy with this imported system, and began to soften some of its harder material aspects soon after its adoption. By the late 1950s, in the Great Leap Forward, the use of piece rates in industry was sharply curtailed. During 1963–65, seasonal bonuses for managerial personnel were eliminated and the salaries of top military officers were cut back.[31] Yet, this imported system remained essentially intact until the Cultural Revolution, when radicals gained control and tried to promote a more egalitarian system. In the Cultural Revolution, all piece rates, bonuses, and prizes were eliminated, as were interest payments to former merchants and capitalists. Higher and middle salaries were frozen, and some managers and administrators were demoted for a time. The only general promotions after 1963 were around 1971–72, and they were given only to a minority of low-wage, high seniority workers. There were no merit raises. A few political activists moved into leadership positions, but in theory even they were to retain their old worker salaries. In general the pursuit of individual material gain that the variety of incentive payment schemes had fostered was seen as incompatible with the radicals' goals. Thus, the system captured in our mid-1970s census of neighbors is one resulting from the effort to promote a more egalitarian society.

---

the person to find an individual in the other unit willing to exchange jobs with him) that informants marvelled at people who were able to arrange such individually initiated transfers. How this system of direct allocation and elimination of the labor market was developed in China after 1949 remains somewhat of a mystery, since it has no clear precedent in either Chinese or Soviet experience.

30. These groups are now classified into twenty-four, seventeen, and eight ranks, respectively, *Zhongguo Jingji Nianjian, 1981,* p. IV-180.

31. See Michel Korzec and Martin K. Whyte, "Reading Notes: The Chinese Wage System," *China Quarterly* 86 (1981): 257–58.

What was the net result of this system for income equality? Our census suggests that Chinese urban incomes had become considerably more equal than in the average developing society (table 4). The poorest 40 percent of China's urban households received 25 percent of the total income distributed in cities; while in twenty-four developing market states, the poorest 40 percent received only 15 percent of urban incomes. These are average figures, around which there is considerable variation. Among market societies, the most equal is found in Taiwan, but, in comparison, mainland Chinese urban incomes were still slightly more equally distributed.

Compared with other socialist states as well, Chinese urban incomes were quite equal. Comparative data were gathered on earnings by workers and staff at the highest paid ninetieth percentile and on earnings of the lowest paid tenth percentile. Around 1970, in the Soviet Union, Rumania, and four other European socialist states, the higher paid group averaged 2.7 times more income than the lower paid group. In our sample of Chinese neighbors, in contrast, the higher paid earned only 2.3 times more than those below. This was about the same as in Rumania, the most equal socialist state on this scale, and considerably more equal than the Soviet Union, the most unequal, with a ratio of 3.2:1 between higher and lower paid workers and staff.[32] Given that economic development tends to increase equality eventually and that the European socialist states used for

Table 4		Income Inequality by Household Group and Society	
Urban Households	Gini Coefficient	Income Earned by Richest 10% of Households	Income Earned by Poorest 40% of Households
China	.25	21%	25%
Developing market societies[a]			
Average (mean)	.43	33%	15%
Range (Taiwan-Ecuador)	.27-.53	22-40%	23-10%

Sources: China: Sample of neighbor households. Other societies: Shail Jain, Size Distribution of Income (Washington, D.C.: International Bank for Reconstruction and Development, 1975).

Note: The data for the other countries is for the urban population while the Chinese figures are for the nonagricultural population, but this should make little difference in the results judging from nonagricultural data in Jain. All figures describe the distribution of households by total household income in each country or set of countries.

[a]Twenty-four market societies with a 1970 per capita gross national product of less than U.S. $1,200 and population greater than one million.

32. For detailed figures, see William L. Parish, "Egalitarianism in China," *Problems of Communism,* no. 1 (1981): 72; and Peter Wiles, "Recent Data on Soviet Income Distribution," *Survey* 21 (1975): 33.

comparison are all much more highly developed, the Chinese urban accomplishment is impressive. China is not a copy of the Soviet Union,
which it mimicked for a time in the mid-1950s. The Soviet Union itself
became more equal in the 1960s, but during this time China's cities moved
even faster to abandon the more inegalitarian aspects of the Soviet model
and to adopt reforms to provide one of the most egalitarian of socialist
urban settings.

That equality came to apply not only to current income but also to the
manner in which income, as well as education and jobs, was passed from
generation to generation. While in Marxist theory the transformation from
capitalism to socialism eliminates classes and class privileges, in reality
matters are not so simple. Classes may no longer exist in the sense of a
property-owning bourgeoisie and a propertyless proletariat; but insofar
as people have differing incomes, amounts of political power, and access
to resources, there is inequality, and insofar as those who are advantaged
in these regards tend to retain their advantages and have children who
obtain similar advantages, there is a system of stratification. Whether the
strata that are formed in socialist society—groups like "high cadres,"
intellectuals, industrial workers, service workers—should be called classes
is a contentious issue. But the evidence for the Soviet Union and socialist
Eastern Europe is quite clear—a well-institutionalized system of stratification and inherited advantages exists, even in societies that are theoretically classless.[33] This sort of society was not good enough for China's
radicals. They wanted to create a society in which the pre-1949 class order
was inverted and old elites could not regain their former advantages, and
in which access to mobility opportunities would depend upon proper
political commitment. To a considerable extent they succeeded, if only
temporarily.

In China, from the early 1950s to the late 1970s, it was not too hard to
tell whether the old class order was being inverted, since everyone carried
a class label marking their class origin. In cities, the process of class
labeling was never completely systematic, but in a series of political campaigns in the early 1950s, families gradually began to be identified with a
label such as capitalist, merchant, peddler, worker, or poor peasant.
Professionals, minor bureaucrats, and other intellectuals took the nebu-
lous label of "staff," which remained a relatively neutral label through
the early 1960s. Other labels were more highly charged. Worker and poor
peasant were among the more esteemed labels while capitalist, landlord,
and "bogus staff" (for higher level bureaucrats in the previous govern-

33. The most comprehensive discussion of the evidence is in Walter Connor, *Socialism,
Politics, and Equality* (New York: Columbia University Press, 1979).

ment) labels were officially despised. Some labels could be earned, including the positive one of "revolutionary cadre" (if one or one's father became a substantial administrative official in the new order) and the negative ones such as "counterrevolutionary" or "rightist" (if one was found in error in one of the myriad political campaigns of the 1950s). The precise emphasis on these labels ebbed and flowed with the political wind, but as a result of Mao Zedong's 1962 injunction to "never forget class struggle," they remained important.[34]

From the radicals' point of view, one's class label should affect all of one's life chances, from education through occupation, to rate of pay and promotion.[35] In the early years of the regime, the educational differences among urbanites of different class labels did narrow quite rapidly (figure 1).[36] Continuing a process begun by the 1930s and slowed only by the Japanese invasion in the 1940s, urban residents of peddler, worker, and peasant origin began to approach the educational level of the formerly dominant capitalists, staff, and similar classes. By the early 1960s, in the next generation, class was even less of an indicator of educational achievement. Yet, while the gaps between people of different class origins were narrowing, the rank order of educational accomplishment remained, with one major exception, the same. By the early 1960s, the children of the new elite administrative cadres began to get the most education, in some cases, attending elite boarding schools which later in the Cultural Revolution came to be attacked as "little treasure pagodas." With admission as much by rigid academic exams as by recommendation, the cadre children were often joined in these and other "keypoint" schools by the offspring of old professionals and other intellectuals as well as by the sons and daughters of former capitalists. China was falling short of the goal of inverting the old class order and was in danger of adding a new elite class on top of the old. Children of worker, peasant, and peddler origin continued to get fewer years of education and tended to be relegated to lower quality schools, which often combined work with study and had smaller budgets than the elite schools.

34. For a discussion of shifts in emphasis in class label policy, see Richard Kraus, "Class Conflict and the Vocabulary of Social Analysis in China," *China Quarterly* 69 (1977): 54–74.

35. Strictly speaking, the class standpoint expressed in one's behavior should be judged more than one's class background label. In practice, and particularly during the Cultural Revolution decade, class labels were often given primary emphasis in determining life chances and assumed to indicate thinking and behavior. See Kraus, "Class Conflict."

36. Figure 1 combines negative labels such as counterrevolutionary and landlord under the capitalist label, middling labels such as middle peasant under the staff label, and so on. "Peasants" here means former peasants and their offspring. What is referenced is class origin or class label rather than current occupation.

The issue of educational sorting came to a head in the 1960s as the state began to run out of urban jobs for new school graduates. Those jobs which continued to be given were again given to a considerable extent on the basis of academic merit and recommendations from one's middle school. As we might expect, the children of the old elite, who were doing the best in school, continued to get the best jobs (see figure 2).[37] The pre-1949 order was never thoroughly inverted even in the first years of the regime. Capitalist parents from the 1930–49 generation were hindered in getting and keeping the best jobs. But their children regained part of their lost advantage in the 1950s and continued it into the 1960s (figure 2).[38]

Meanwhile the children of workers and former peasants got poorer jobs or no jobs at all. With increasing urban unemployment in the early 1960s, when the administration turned to sending youth to the countryside, it was often the children of worker and peasant-origins with poor academic records who were sent first. Under these circumstances, there was ever more serious debate over the proper emphasis on academic achievement, political commitment, and class origin. Emphasis on political commitment or on the need to "serve the people" might be ideal, but it was hard to measure, and the children of intellectuals and capitalists, it was feared, were good at feigning proper attitudes. Class origin had its drawbacks as well, as some very committed people would be left behind.[39]

The answer of the Cultural Revolution was that academic excellence was to be abandoned as a determinant of life chances, since it selected careerists and people of bad class origin. In other words, the function of schools in sorting talent and determining mobility opportunities should be deemphasized if not eliminated. Class origin was to be a principal screening device; staff children were to be declared suspect along with capitalist and other bad class children. After initial screening on class origin, mobility opportunities were to be based on political commitment which would be measured partly by how one performed in lengthy stints of factory and farm work both during one's school years and for a number of years afterwards. Work periods during school were increased, and the

37. Throughout, occupations are ranked into 32 groups on the basis of the average monthly income of each group, giving a scale which runs from 22 to 103, thereby approximating Western occupational prestige scores which cover a similar range.

38. The major disadvantage that persisted is that those of capitalist backgrounds tended to be excluded from defense related and other sensitive areas. According to our informants, when candidates had equal qualifications one from a proletarian or cadre background would tend to be picked first even in the early years.

39. See Susan L. Shirk, *Communist Competition: Career Incentives and Student Behavior in China* (Berkeley: University of California Press, 1982); and Jonathan Unger, *Education under Mao* (New York: Columbia University, East Asian Institute, 1982).

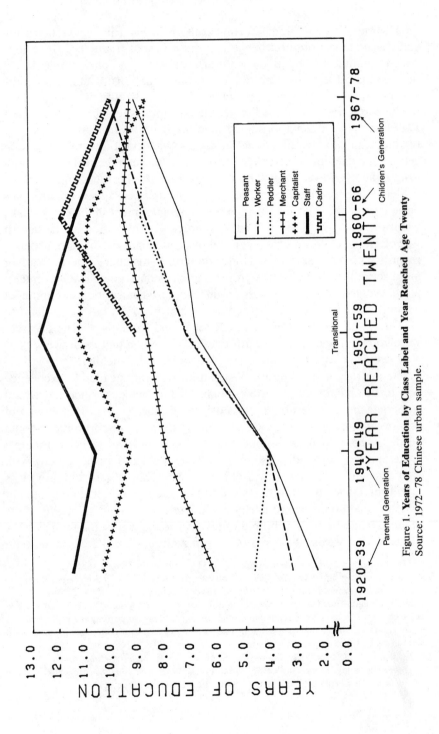

Figure 1. **Years of Education by Class Label and Year Reached Age Twenty**
Source: 1972–78 Chinese urban sample.

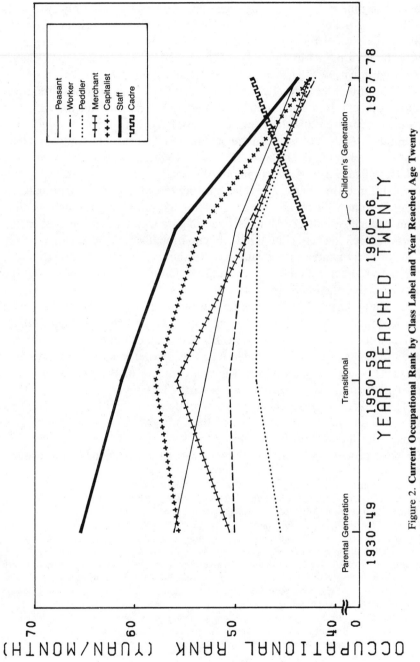

Figure 2. **Current Occupational Rank by Class Label and Year Reached Age Twenty**
Source: 1972–78 Chinese urban sample.

total number of years of precollegiate education were abbreviated from twelve to nine or ten years. College enrollment was drastically curtailed.

The new policy had much of its intended effect. Almost everyone in the 1970s moved rapidly toward the new norm of nine years education (see the final points in figure 1). With special schools closed, and exams watered down, worker, peasant, and other "good class" children simply passed through the school system for their allotted number of years. Staff and cadre children continued to do somewhat better than the rest, but capitalist children lost their former favored position.

Similar trends took place in the occupational world. The few urban jobs that were open tended to be worker jobs or similar ones with low average salaries (figure 2).[40] As was intended, capitalist and other bad class children suffered the sharpest reversal, losing their favored occupational position to others. Staff and other intellectuals' children got jobs no better than peasant children. And, as unanticipated, but later signaled in the press, cadre children gained in the occupational world the advantage they had formerly gained in education. With the exception of cadre children, the new radical policies were having their intended effect of narrowing and inverting the class order.

Urban children have been influenced not only by the class label which marked their fathers' positions as of about 1949, but also by their fathers' current occupation and education. Examination of fathers' current status and the status attainment of children age 16–39 (the generation that reached maturity since 1949) provides a better estimate of the extent to which post-1949 status groups were reproducing themselves.

The data from our neighbor census sample are divided between children who reached age 20 by the start of the Cultural Revolution in 1966 and those who did so afterwards. Prior to 1966, even if in muted form, the Chinese process of status attainment resembled patterns found around

40. Cautious readers may complain that the historical trend lines in figures 1 and 2 are reconstructed from age data alone and that while this may tell one a great deal about career patterns by age it tells one little about the experience of different historical cohorts. Note, however, that in figure 1, education at age 20 was largely fixed for life—it was only after 1978 that 20 year olds had much hope of competing for college. And in figure 2, with little job mobility, the job one entered at age 20 was likely to be the job from which one retired, even if one's exact rank and income increased within that job. Finally, comparisons with Korea and the U.S. show that China was exceptional in both the decline and the narrowing of the range of education, occupation, and income attainment among younger as opposed to older age groups, suggesting that cohort effects were stronger than simple age effects on these variables. For the details of the U.S. comparison, see William Parish, "Destratification in the People's Republic of China," *Select Papers*, no. 4 (Chicago: University of Chicago, Center for Far Eastern Studies, 1981), pp. 143–87.

the world (table 5).[41] Fathers in high paying positions with much education produced children who tended to get far in the educational system. Higher status fathers produced sons who got better jobs, and, as we have already seen, those with negative class labels continued to do well in the occupational world. Better education and better jobs were turned into higher incomes for high status families. The patterns are familiar. Familial influence over the education and status attainment of children is difficult to erase.

After 1966, however, the Chinese came very close to doing just that. The numbers confirm what informants often report—that after 1967 there was very little that a well-educated father could do to help his children succeed in school or find a better job once they were out. Education was no guarantee of occupational success (table 5, row 4). Government policy to break the reproduction of status groups was indeed effective, and it had the side effect of reducing male advantages in education, occupation, and income as well.[42]

However, our figures show that there was one crucial respect in which the Cultural Revolution reforms were less successful. The radicals were concerned not only to make sure that pre-1949 elites were not be able to pass their advantages on to their children. They also launched attacks on "people in power taking the capitalist road" and were concerned that a "new bureaucratic stratum" represented by state cadre and party elites not consolidate its position and pass on privileges to its children. In other words they wanted to find ways to forestall the emergence of what Djilas termed "the new class" in socialist societies.[43] However, our data in

41. Metric regression coefficients show the influence of a unit's change in each of the variables along the top of table 5. To illustrate, the top left coefficient says that for each extra year a father was in school his son or daughter got .22 years more education. The next coefficient says that for each extra jump in father's occupational rank (ranks = 22 to 103) the son or daughter got almost half a year's more education. The asterisk indicates that coefficients this large could have occurred from sampling error alone no more than 5 times in a 100. The R^2 at the end of each row shows how well we have done in explaining variation in the variable at the left. Prior to 1967, one could explain 38 percent of the variation in children's educational achievement, which is a pretty successful explanation as these things go. After 1967, we could explain 10 percent, which is rather low—illustrating again the post-1967 unpredictability of the society.

42. Because of the regularity of this pattern of familial influence in all kinds of societies, James Coleman has suggested that status inheritance could not be broken unless children were taken away from their parents at birth. The Chinese case shows that strict political control of job access alone can have the same effects. See Coleman's review of John Rawls' book, *A Theory of Justice*, in *American Journal of Sociology* 80 (1974): 751.

43. See Milovan Djilas, *The New Class* (New York: Praeger, 1957). One very Djilas-like formulation from one of the dominant Chinese radicals is Yao Wenyuan, "On the Social Origins of the Lin Piao Anti-Party Clique," *Peking Review*, no. 10 (1975): 5–10.

Table 5

Determinants of Educational Achievement and Income by Year Reached Age Twenty (Metric Regression Coefficients)

Dependent Variables	Father's		Class Label[a]	Child's				R^2	N
	Education	Occupation		Age	Sex	Education	Occupation		
Education[b]									
Pre-1966 cohort	.22*	.46*	1.09	.10	1.12*	--	--	.38	(117)
Post-1967 cohort	.05	.00	.09	.12*	-.23	--	--	.10	(165)
Occupation[b]									
Pre-1966 cohort	-.41	.29*	7.79*	.55	5.95*	1.30*	--	.31	(117)
Post-1967 cohort	-.20	.16*	-.54	.92	1.52	.60	--	.16	(165)
Income[b]									
Pre-1966 cohort	-.28	-.03	.93	.65*	2.16	-.06	.42*	.37	(117)
Post-1967 cohort	.05	-.07	2.08	.71*	-.13	-.29	.33*	.22	(165)

Source: Sample of urban neighbors, economically active nonagricultural population age 16-39.

[a] Class dichotomized with the old high status labels of "staff," merchant, and capitalist = 1, the others = 0.

[b] Education = years of education. Occupation = mean income of 32 occupational groups. Income = yuan per month.

*$p \leq .05$.

figures 1 and 2 indicate that offspring of cadres increased their advantages over youths from other families during the Cultural Revolution decade. These data are reinforced by informant reports and by later Chinese press charges that when academic performance and test scores gave way to judgments of revolutionary virtue in determining life chances, it was often not the virtuous but those who had parents or other patrons in high places who were able to escape the uncertainties and rigors of rural exile.[44] So for the bulk of the urban population the link between parental status and children's success may have been broken, but for the "new class" of bureaucrats it apparently was not.

Still, in general Chinese cities in the 1970s were distinctive in respect to both equality of condition and equality of opportunity. This discussion would not be complete, however, without noting how Chinese cities related to their rural hinterlands, for one other goal of the radical leadership in converting cities from consumption to production centers was to make them serve rural needs and decrease the "gap between town and country." The prices paid to farmers had taken an adverse turn during World War II and in the late 1940s. The new Communist government tried to correct this situation by raising farm prices for agricultural goods throughout the 1950s and early 1960s. In the Cultural Revolution there was considerable rhetoric as well as some concrete attempts to shift additional health care and educational resources to the countryside. Nevertheless, investment in agriculture continued to take a back seat to investment in heavy industry—averaging only a little over ten percent of the state investment through most of the 1970s.[45] It is true that the freeze on urban wages helped keep urban incomes from skyrocketing above incomes in the countryside. But rural prices were frozen as well between 1965 and 1975, and the radical emphasis on restricting private plots, free rural markets, and other parts of the private rural economy plus the emphasis on growing basic grain rather than higher priced commercial crops continued to restrict peasant incomes.

The net result was that the gap between agricultural and nonagricultural sectors failed to be erased. With more urban women going to work, the

44. It is well to remember that, while reliance on things like scores on academic tests may work to the advantage of youths from homes where parents have high education, the development of objective tests was originally seen as a way to detect and reward promising youths from lower classes and prevent elite children from having as much advantage as they would have if only wealth and connections mattered. In view of the small size of the number of cases with cadre backgrounds in our sample—7 before 1966 and 18 afterwards—the evidence here on the advantages enjoyed by their offspring cannot be regarded as too reliable, even if it does coincide with other kinds of evidence.

45. Commentator, "The Aim of Socialist Production Must Be Really Understood," *People's Daily*, 20 October 1979, pp. 1–2, in *FBIS*, 9 November 1979, p. L5.

gap in per capita incomes actually increased over time. Taking official income reports at face value and adding 30 percent for rural income estimated earned in the private sector gives a per capita income gap of about three to one in 1977. This is as large or larger than the gap in most other parts of Asia, and larger than the estimates available for China in the mid 1950s.[46] There are also considerable gaps in income among different villages in China, and when these are added in, the total income distribution in China is probably only slightly better than the average for developing countries. The poorest 40 percent of Chinese households are virtually all peasant households. Our rural and urban censuses of neighbors suggest such peasant households got only 14 percent of all income in the mid-1970s in China, which compares with a developing world average of 14 percent.[47] Thus, as in many other socialist societies, the rural sector has proved difficult to deal with in a planned economy.

Conclusions

By the 1970s a fairly distinctive economic system had developed in Chinese cities providing a relatively high degree of equality, high levels of labor force participation, and economic security for those employed. The state had gained firm control over the economy and employment opportunities, reoriented the pattern of employment to stress production rather than services or consumption, and provided a sober and relatively spartan work environment and urban landscape. In the 1966–76 radical decade a number of additional goals were pursued with considerable success—eliminating private enterprises and peasant marketing in urban areas, fostering the development of state enterprises, enhancing the state's control over labor allocation and reducing the role of individual preference, reducing the income inequalities within urban areas, and impeding the transmission of high status from one generation to the next.

In spite of what may be seen as considerable successes, the system had a number of serious problems during the period we studied it. Urban policies had actually enhanced the economic advantages of urbanites in relation to peasants and thus had reinforced the effects of the official migration restrictions, even while the goal of reducing the "gap between town and country" was being championed. The producer-city and state-enterprises emphases proved unable to generate enough jobs to soak up the increasing numbers of young people of the "baby boom" of the 1950s.

46. See evidence in Parish, "Egalitarianism in China." Following the adoption of new agriculture policies after 1978, the rural urban gap narrowed to about 2:9 in 1981. But large gaps in income among different villages in the countryside remained, so the overall distribution of income in China may have changed only slightly.

47. See Parish, "Egalitarianism in China," for sources for this calculation.

The method adopted to deal with the resulting unemployment problem—sending urban youths to live in the countryside—proved both unpopular and in the long run ineffective, since a good share of those sent returned to the cities illegally. The egalitarian income policies, combined with the official wage freeze and high job security, meant that problems of absenteeism, shoddy work, and simple laziness mushroomed in work units.[48] The resulting low productivity and unprofitability of many firms in turn made it more difficult to expand enterprises and create more jobs. Finally, the frustrated aspirations and anxieties produced by the elimination of the link between background and education on the one hand and careers and incomes on the other was reflected in growing anger at the advantages still being enjoyed by the offspring of China's "new class" of leading bureaucrats; this, combined with the other problems, threatened to undermine the legitimacy of the political system.

China's post-Mao leadership has responded to these problems by introducing a whole range of policy changes that represent a repudiation of much of the radical program of the Cultural Revolution decade and has even made some effort to reexamine the basic economic principles established during the 1950s. The program of sending youth to the countryside is being phased out, and vigorous efforts are being made to find ways to accommodate returnees from the countryside and new middle school graduates within the urban system. Some youths may be accepted in the expanding higher educational enrollments, but most will need urban jobs. To accommodate them the authorities are calling for a shift in emphasis away from capital intensive state enterprises to more labor intensive collective enterprises and neighborhood service facilities, and in 1979–81 fully 75 percent of the new jobs in urban areas were reported to be in these more informal sectors.[49] Liberalization of rules on private enterprises has also been undertaken to allow more unemployed youths (and some older people) to be licensed as individual workers engaged in repair work, sewing, snack selling, and other petty trades. These new employment policies of course have the advantage to the state of requiring a smaller financial outlay than would be required to provide jobs in state enterprises. In 1981, authorities also sought to lessen the burden on the state by announcing that the government could no longer be presumed to have an obligation to find employment for all urban middle school graduates, thus shifting more of the responsibility to the youths themselves.

48. See Parish, "The View from the Factory"; and Walder, "Work and Authority in Chinese Industry." The poor productivity of state firms meant that the state had to keep the level of investment at the very high levels already noted in order to sustain high industrial growth rates, a fairly costly way to pursue growth.

49. Hu Mengzhou, "Solution to Employment Problems," Beijing Review, no. 39 (1982): 21.

In the long run the strict enforcement of the official birth control program (which began during the radical period) is expected to ease the problem of providing urban jobs for the graduates of city schools.

Worker motivation has been addressed by implementing raises and promotions and by restoring piece rates, bonuses, cash prizes, and other material incentive devices. At the same time the system of permanent employment is being questioned, with work unit authorities encouraged in some cases to break the "iron rice bowl" and discharge employees who are creating serious problems. Meritocracy is the order of the day now, with exam scores used not only to pick entrants to schools and universities, but also on a trial basis to select new employees in some firms and to decide whom to promote (and demote). The official concern over job performance has also promoted increasing efforts to fit individual talents to particular jobs. Individual preferences are once again being sought and considered in school and job assignments, and technically trained personnel working in unsuitable jobs (an all too common phenomenon in any bureaucratic assignment system) are being allowed to request transfers to more appropriate jobs. However, in the early 1980s the idea of permitting a real labor market to exist so that individuals can seek and change jobs on their own was still not being seriously considered.

These recent measures are designed to address some of the problems of the previous period (unemployment and poor work morale) more than others (the rural-urban gap, cadre privileges). It remains to be seen how far the new reforms will be pushed, and how much they will alter the basic nature of the urban economic system as we have sketched it in the preceding pages. What is clear is that although an urban economic system that was in many ways quite distinctive and successful was built after 1949, the effort to improve this system in order to produce a purer form of socialism produced not the sought after sober and contented egalitarianism, but a growing sense of crisis. Other dimensions of that crisis, and the implications of current attempts to deal with it, will be explored further in subsequent chapters.

4 Social Services
and Supplies

The Chinese attempt to bring new patterns of equality to urban life involved not only the redistribution of income but also an effort to change the system of distributing supplies and services to urbanites. The negative features of pre-1949 urban life helped to shape the system that emerged. The Chinese Communist leaders had developed strong animosities toward the conspicuous consumption and privileged life styles of the pre-1949 urban elite and foreign residents, and toward the hoarding, inflation, and other disturbances of urban markets that wreaked havoc on living conditions. Begging, starvation, and other symbols of the breakdown of the pre-1949 supply system were vivid reminders of what the new system had to eliminate. Redistribution of incomes was not enough, for in the last analysis what mattered was not so much income but consumption. To be specific, China's new rulers saw their legitimacy as depending to a considerable extent on their ability to devise a system of distribution that would enable even poorer urban families to get reliable access to the food, housing, schooling, health care, and other resources needed for a decent life. The socialist (and bureaucratic) inclinations of the new leaders convinced them that the solution to this problem lay in reducing the role of market forces and using direct allocation of goods and services to ensure the desired equity.

This statement of the problem leaves a number of issues unclear. If access to basic supplies and services for all the population is the goal, there is still ambiguity about which supplies and services are most important and what constitutes a minimum or acceptable level of supply. Characteristically, in East European socialist societies increasing popular access to education, health care, and basic food items has been emphasized, while access to improved housing and consumer goods has not been stressed. A related issue is whether to stress present consumption versus future consumption. Again the inclination in other socialist states, following the Stalinist model, has been to sacrifice current consumption in favor of investment in industrial growth, with improved consumption standards promised for the future.[1]

Then there are the issues raised by critics about whether the costs of delivering social services by bureaucratic means are not too high. They note that keeping prices artificially low only creates pent-up demand, long lines, frustration, and corruption. In addition, with no financial incentives, those who deliver the services, be they doctors, teachers, store clerks, or house repairmen, lose a major incentive for giving their all. The multiplying of red tape simply makes bureaucracies much slower to respond to changing tastes and needs than would be true in a market system. Perhaps worst of all, the critics argue, the bureaucratic distribution system of socialist countries does as much to instill hidden privileges for a new class of bureaucrats as it does to create equality or guarantee basic services.[2] These are the sorts of issues we must face in assessing the delivery of education, health care, social security, housing, as well as consumer goods and services.

Education

Education has typically been heavily stressed in socialist systems. In China as well, basic education has expanded rapidly over the last three decades. This was particularly true in the 1966–76 decade, when radical leaders tried to provide a highly egalitarian education for both urban and rural children. As we have already noted, much of the competitive and hierarchical system inherited from the Soviet Union and from pre-1949 Chinese practice was dismantled then. Education was abbreviated, simplified, politicized, combined with labor, and made available to many who had been previously excluded. With only five years each for urban primary

1. Recent references which refer back to a considerable literature on these trends include Vic George and Nick Manning, *Socialism, Social Welfare and the Soviet Union* (London: Routledge and Kegan Paul, 1980); Gertrude E. Schroeder and Barbara S. Severin, "Soviet Consumption and Income Policies in Perspective," in *Soviet Economy in a New Perspective,* U.S. Congress, Joint Economic Committee (Washington, D.C.: U.S. Government Printing Office, 1976); Bogdan Mieczkowski, *Personal and Social Consumption in Eastern Europe* (New York: Praeger, 1975); Michael Ellman, *Socialist Planning* (Cambridge: Cambridge University Press, 1979).

2. Selected references on these issues include D. Gale Johnson, "Food and Agriculture in Centrally Planned Economies," Agricultural Economics Research Paper no. 81 (University of Chicago 1981, mimeo), p. 13; Charles E. Lindblom, *Politics and Markets* (New York: Basic Books, 1977); Arthur M. Okun, *Equality and Efficiency: The Big Tradeoff* (Washington, D.C.: Brookings Institution, 1975); Milovan Djilas, *The New Class* (New York: Praeger, 1957).

school and middle school, and with reduced enrollments and shortened periods of study in universities, educational resources could be spread more evenly in both cities and villages. Most villages came to run their own primary schools and many ran two-year lower-middle schools as well. In cities exams no longer controlled the flow of high achievers into elite keypoint schools, nor were low achievers shunted into second class vocational or neighborhood schools. All were required to attend more or less uniform quality neighborhood schools. In primary school and middle school, tuition continued to be charged as a rule, but with government pressures for higher enrollments, more tuition waivers were given to encourage students to stay in school. The result in the early 1970s was that advantaged parents in urban areas generally would not gain much preference for their children in comparison with children from poorer families, as our data in chapter 3 showed. With academics combined with labor during the school year, the school curriculum was supposed to become more relevant to the needs of worker and peasant careers.[3]

To some foreign observers, the Chinese experiment in educational reform seemed to avoid many of the problems of the urban-based, top-heavy educational systems of the rest of the developing world—systems that turn out unemployed B.A.'s with little knowledge relevant to their own society. In China one's job would not be based just on the credentials earned in the formal education system but on demonstrated skills more likely to be relevant for careers in a developing society. The countryside would not be neglected in order to overtrain children of urban elites, just to see these expensive intellectuals join a westward-flowing brain drain. Since every attempt would be made to avoid a dual economy with a large gap between traditional and modern sectors, urban elite parents would not be pressuring the government to provide more elite schools as ladders into the modern sector.[4]

Many of these goals were achieved, and these achievements continued to be obvious through 1979, even as many aspects of China's egalitarian experiment were being rescinded (see table 6). Nationwide, in villages as well as cities, Chinese adult literacy was far greater than one would expect from its level of economic development (row 1). With most rural and many urban children attended by grandmother or other older kinsmen, kindergarten enrollments remained low (row 2a). But primary and secondary schools still provided basic education for a very large proportion of the

3. For more detail on these reforms and subsequent changes, see Suzanne Pepper's two articles: "Education and Revolution: The 'Chinese Model' Revised," *Asian Survey* 19 (1978): 852–74, and "Chinese Education after Mao: Two Steps Forward, Two Steps Back and Begin Again?" *China Quarterly* 81 (1980): 1–65.

4. Ronald Dore, *The Diploma Disease* (Berkeley: University of California Press, 1976).

relevant age groups (rows 2a–b). Since many small villages had their own primary school and lower-middle school, the number of pupils per teacher continued to remain low (rows 3a–b).[5] At higher levels, the situation was quite different. Though universities, technical institutes, and other higher level schools were growing rapidly in the late 1970s, the proportions enrolled at these levels were still far below those in other developing societies (row 2d). Unlike some of these other societies, China's college graduates fell short of demand and were in no danger of unemployment.

The combination of the socialist reforms of the early years and the more radical policies of the Cultural Revolution decade produced a high-enrollment but geared-down system of schooling that matched official desires. However, there is not much question that in pursuit of relatively equal access to schooling other things were sacrificed. These sacrifices have led to a very negative view of education among many Chinese. From our interviews, and from later press critiques, it seems clear that the quality of schooling suffered during this period. The rapid expansion of education meant, as it does elsewhere around the globe, that poorly trained

Table 6   **Chinese and Developing Country Education** (National Averages)

	China	Developing Countries	
		Middle Income	Low Income
	(1979)	(1977)	(1977)
1. Adult literacy	70%	71%	38%
2. Enrollment ratios:			
a. Kindergarten	10%	--	--
b. Primary school	101%	97%	77%
c. Secondary school	56%	40%	24%
d. Higher education	1%	11%	4%
3. Pupil-teacher ratios:			
a. Primary school	27	34	38
b. Secondary school	19	24	21
4. Vocational as a % of all secondary school education	2%	12%	5%

Sources: China: Zhongguo Baike Nianjian, 1980, p. 536. Age distribution adapted from John Aird, "Reconstruction of an Official Data Model of the Population of China," (Washington: Bureau of the Census, Foreign Demographic Analysis Division, 1980, mimeo). Others: World Bank, World Development Report, 1980 (Washington, D.C., 1980), table 23, and World Tables, 2d ed. (Baltimore: Johns Hopkins University Press, 1980), p. 454.

5. The advantages of having so many teachers was offset in part by their poor quality and by the small number of classes that each teacher taught. Because of the last factor, average class sizes tend to be somewhat larger than the figures in table 6 suggest.

teachers had to be pressed into service. The experience of one of our research assistants who had studied Russian in an urban middle school and then was assigned to teach English in a commune middle school is indicative. The narrowing of all to a common denominator may have helped village youths who would have dropped out of school, but in the cities it prevented talented young people from acquiring skills and knowledge that would have contributed to development. With the closing of vocational schools as well as colleges, both the lower and higher level technical workers needed for China's modernization were not trained.

Another factor in the quality problems of these years was the change in atmosphere and motivation within the schools. In urban schools, attacks on intellectual elitism were mounted and the authority of teachers declined. Stories of teachers getting into trouble for disciplining a working class child circulated. Students also felt they had little reason to study hard. With schools no longer serving as a primary mechanism for determining mobility chances, and with most graduates expected to go to the countryside and adopt the life of a peasant, students lost motivation. With no rigorous examinations and with all students promoted automatically from grade to grade, there was also little fear of failing and bringing dishonor on one's family, and in this situation students increasingly took to fooling around and playing hooky. As noted above, anxious parents became increasingly frustrated at the capriciousness of the system and their inability to find compelling reasons to persuade their children to study hard and stay out of trouble. Parents and their offspring came to feel that such opportunities for urban jobs and college enrollment as did exist were being monopolized by the children of powerful cadres, who were using their personal connections to "go by the back door" to secure their children's futures.[6]

Finally, as we have already stressed, this geared-down system of schooling did not avoid the problem of the educated unemployed. Or rather, it avoided unemployment among college graduates, whose small numbers and scarce skills could easily be accommodated in the labor allocation system, but not among middle school graduates. The increasing numbers of unemployed urban middle school graduates, many with high expectations and aspirations encouraged by the more competitive system that existed before the Cultural Revolution, became a primary source of social problems in the 1970s and remain so today.

On balance, then, the Chinese Communists can be credited with a great deal of success in increasing attainment levels, universalizing access, and reducing status-related disparities in schooling (see figure 2 in chapter 3).

6. These observations are based on widespread themes in our interview accounts.

However, these quantitative successes have produced unanticipated problems of poor quality, inadequate technical training, and unemployment among middle school graduates that continue to plague China's leadership.

Health Care

Health care is also among those social goods which socialist states have typically felt should be provided in ample quantities to everyone in society at relatively low costs. China shares this goal. In the first three decades of Communist rule, health care expanded rapidly with the training of many new doctors and other medical personnel, the opening of many new hospitals, and many new public health efforts.[7] As a result, on a national level, China's health care system came to compare quite favorably with other developing societies. By 1979, China exceeded the levels of most other societies in its numbers of Western-style doctors.[8] In the middle income developing countries, citizens had to share a Western-trained doctor with almost twice as many people as in China. And in low income countries, with which China is more comparable, citizens had to share a Western-trained doctor with four times as many others (see table 7, row 1).[9] In addition, China trained secondary school doctors (similar to the Russian *feldsher*) to help with first line medical care and thereby diminished the number of people competing to see more highly trained physicians (row 2). New Chinese-style doctors were trained and the skill of old herbalists and acupuncturists upgraded to provide even more care (row 3). This medical corps, many of whom served in towns and cities, were beginning to be trained even before the 1966 Cultural Revolution.

7. There are many accounts of the Chinese health care system to complement the one presented here, including the travelers' account by Victor W. Sidel and Ruth Sidel, *Serve the People* (New York: Josiah Macy Foundation, 1973), and the documentary accounts by David M. Lampton, *The Politics of Medicine in China* (Boulder: Westview Press, 1977), and by AnElissa Lucas, "Changing Medical Models in China," *China Quarterly* 83 (1980): 461–89.

8. Western-style doctors are not, for the most part, doctors actually trained in the West but trained in China in medical care as it is practiced in the West, as opposed to being trained in traditional Chinese forms of medicine, which include such elements as acupuncture and herbal medicine.

9. For an additional perspective, the 1977 U.S. population per physician was 580 and per nurse it was 150 according to the World Bank's 1980 *World Development Report*. Such indicators are closely tied to a country's level of economic development, but socialist states tend to be somewhat better supplied than other societies at comparable economic levels. There are some issues of comparability in these figures—for example, doctors in China are trained in regular college programs and nurses in secondary school programs, unlike the postgraduate and college level programs favored in the United States.

After the Cultural Revolution the curriculum was shortened in order to speed the training of Western- and Chinese-style doctors as well as of 1.57 million rural, "barefoot" paramedics. The growing supply of doctors was complemented by a supply of nurses and hospital beds which was more typical of middle income than low income countries (rows 4 and 5).[10]

The supply of medical personnel, facilities, public health efforts, and other factors such as nutrition appear to have had a distinct effect. The statistics are shaky for China, as they are for many other developing societies. But to the extent that they represent general trends, China's decline in infant mortality and increasing life expectancy already approximate the more developed middle income countries and surpass by far

Table 7   Medical Care

	China 1979	Developing Market Societies, c.1978 Middle Income	Low Income
A. Population per:			
1. Western doctor[a]	2,470	4,310	9,900
2. Secondary doctor[a]	1,172	---	---
3. Chinese herbal doctor[a]	872	---	---
4. Nursing personnel	2,306	1,860	8,790
5. Hospital bed	503	570	1,730
B. Performance			
6. Infant mortality per 1,000 live births	49[c]	48	134[b]
7. Life expectancy at birth	68[c]	60	50

Sources: World Bank, World Development Report, 1980 (New York: Oxford University Press, 1980). World Bank, World Tables, 1980 (Baltimore: Johns Hopkins Press, 1980). Zhongguo Baike Nianjian, 1980 (Peking: Chinese Encyclopedia Press, 1980), p. 559. FBIS, 30 April 1980, p. 19.

[a]Including the doctors in preceding rows. "Barefoot" paramedics excluded from all figures.

[b]Figure only for India, 1970.

[c]Official figures. With correction for the underreporting of births and infant deaths these two figures might change to 56 and 64, but this would still compare favorably with most countries at China's level of economic development.

10. Of course, cities had much better medical care than rural areas. By the early 1970s in the Peking and Shanghai metropolitan areas (which encompass several rural counties, it should be noted) the population per Western-style physician was only 1,040 and 700, respectively; per physician of any type only 550 and 400; and per nurse only 520 and 600. Nationwide in the late 1970s there were only 176 urban people per hospital bed. See Sidel and Sidel, Serve the People, p. 43, and Beijing Review, no. 25 (1980): p. 20.

the experience of the average poor income country (table 7, rows 6, 7).[11] Dedication of new resources to health care (as well as nutrition), then, has had a dramatic impact on life spans.

How has the urban health care system been organized to deliver medical care? In a socialist-bureaucratic manner aligned to the organizational system described in chapter 2. By the 1970s, the various kinds of doctors and medical facilities were typically organized in a three-tier system, although there were levels within the tiers, and the details varied somewhat from city to city. At the lowest level were small clinics maintained in individual work units and "red medical stations" as well as some small clinics maintained in urban neighborhoods. These tended to be staffed by only secondary level Western and Chinese doctors and sometimes only by minimally trained paramedics or by nurses. At the middle level were hospitals spread throughout the city, taking patients from neighborhoods and work units within their assigned areas. These would have doctors with a variety of training. Finally, there were city or provincial hospitals to which cases were referred from the ordinary hospitals. These were staffed by the most highly trained doctors. In a large city, there might be several of these, some general hospitals, and other specialized (e.g., maternity, mental) hospitals, and some facilities designated to handle referrals from surrounding rural areas or from smaller towns that had only middle level hospitals.

Only relatively large and well-established work units had their own clinics, although some smaller units had minimal facilities (e.g., first-aid office, one nurse). Those in units with clinics were expected to go there for treatment when problems arose, particularly during work hours. If they lived elsewhere in the city or their unit had no clinic, then they were expected to take medical problems arising at home to their neighborhood clinic. If the problem couldn't be dealt with at this lower level, then it would generally be referred upward, usually to an ordinary city hospital. Work units and neighborhoods were each assigned to a particular middle level hospital, and the people there were not supposed to go to a different district hospital or directly to a higher level hospital.[12] This system is even more complex when looked at from the point of view of the family, since a family might have its various members falling under different units in

11. The infant mortality figures for China are unreliable, as many infants who die do not get counted (See William Lavely, "China's Rural Population Statistics at the Local Level," *Population Index* 49 [1983].) However, since the same problem affects this statistic in many other developing societies, comparisons may still be valid.

12. Some large or important work units may refer people directly to one of the higher level hospitals, rather than having to go through the intermediate level first. Their own well-endowed clinics represent, in effect, a middle level medical care unit.

the medical hierarchy. The husband might work in one unit and refer his medical problems to its clinic, and then to the hospital it is subordinate to; the wife might work in another unit and take her medical problems to its clinic and superior hospital; while the grandmother and the children might be taken to the neighborhood clinic and in some cases to the clinic of the husband or wife.

Besides providing ample personnel and facilities, socialist states have wanted to keep costs low so that even the poorest have ready access to medical care. The simplest procedure might be to nationalize all medical care and then to provide care to everyone free of cost. However, China has chosen a more mixed system. Not only factories and stores, but also doctors and hospitals were nationalized in the mid-1950s, so that the private practice of medicine was essentially eliminated. But although virtually all services are nationalized, fees are charged and only certain parts of the population have these fees covered by public insurance programs. Those in the countryside are excluded—they must organize their own group insurance programs if they are to have any coverage at all. In cities, those in state work units have almost all their medical expenses covered (except for things like hospital food, crutches, eyeglasses, expensive Chinese tonics, and ambulance fees). They pay only a nominal registration fee (usually 5–10 cents) to initiate treatment. Workers in state economic enterprises also get half of most medical expenses for their dependents covered.

Others have not fared so well. For example, teachers, government clerks, and other workers in noneconomic units have to pay for their own dependents—though in a few cities some people are now beginning to get dependent coverage as well.[13] Individuals working in collective enterprises may have similar coverage, partial coverage, or no coverage at all depending upon the history and resources of the local unit and neighborhood. Those who have never worked and who have no family member in an enterprise with dependent medical support can sometimes join neighborhood or unit organized cooperative insurance programs providing partial support at 2–4 yuan per month per person, although these programs do

13. On basic coverage rules for people in state enterprises see "People's Republic of China Labor Insurance Regulations," 2 January 1953, article 13. This document and subsequent elaborations and modifications appear in the collection edited by the Fujian Provincial Revolutionary Committee, Planning Commission, *Laodong Gongzi Wenjian Xuanbian* (Compendium of labor remuneration documents) (Fuzhou: Fujian Provincial Revolutionary Committee, 1973), pp. 275–406, and passim. On recent increases in coverage of dependents of workers in some other kinds of state units in Shanghai and Canton (but not elsewhere), see *Beijing Review*, no. 25 (1980): p. 25. Informants report that in the 1970s, a few state enterprises provided 100 percent coverage for dependents even though the labor insurance regulations call for only 50 percent.

not seem very common. Otherwise, they must pay all medical expenses themselves. As a ballpark figure, we estimate that in the nonagricultural population, about 40 percent have full coverage, 30 percent have only partial state coverage, and another 30 percent have no state coverage. An additional unknown proportion of the last two groups have joined cooperative programs to get some protection.[14]

For those who have no coverage or only partial coverage, the state has tried to reduce many costs. Western pharmaceuticals are said to be priced at only 18 percent of what they were three decades ago, while Chinese herbal pharmaceuticals are only 60 percent of what they used to be.[15] The registration fee of 5–10 cents for an initial consultation is only nominal. Longer hospital stays for more serious illnesses may still become a severe burden. They can cost 200–300 yuan in many cases, a severe burden in terms of urban wage levels. But even then a family may be able to apply to their neighborhood or a member's work unit for exceptional relief.[16] By and large, then, the goal of widely available, cheap medical care seems to have been achieved in cities.

Does this cheap medical care have some of the negative consequences people have predicted for socialized medicine elsewhere? Do patients have to trade waiting time for price, quantity for quality, and security for choice, and are malingering and other misuses of medical resources common in China? These problems do appear, even though their full severity is difficult to measure. Judging from our informants' reports of conditions in the 1970s, the problem of waiting was severest in outpatient care in middle

14. The estimate of 40 percent full coverage comes from reports of 50 percent employment, not quite 80 percent of those employed being in the state sector which usually has full benefits, and then a few retirees and collective workers who have full benefits. The 30 percent half-covered estimate comes from 85 percent of the households in our sample of neighbors having at least one family member in the state sector, about 70 percent (possible range is 64–77 percent) being in "productive" enterprise parts of the state sector that provide dependent benefits, and 50 percent of the nonagricultural population being unemployed (i.e., 85% × 70% × 50% = 30%). The remaining 30 percent includes the 10 percent employed and the 20 percent nonemployed population who remain uncovered. For some perspective, in the U.S. in the 1970s, 75 to 80 percent of the population had partial to full hospital coverage. Thus at least as many were covered in the U.S. as in Chinese cities. A comparison to other developing countries would of course be more favorable to China. See U.S. Commerce Department, Bureau of the Census, *U.S. Statistical Abstract* (Washington, D.C.: U.S. Government Printing Office, 1976), p. 75.

15. *Zhongguo Baike Nianjian, 1980,* p. 559.

16. For example, a visitor reports that in "the Wuhan Steel Factory Hospital, hospitalization only costs 5 yuan or twice the daily wage of an average worker. However, if a family gets into real financial trouble, the Labor Insurance Fund or the hospital may bear the cost instead." Eduard B. Vermeer, "Social Provisions and the Limits of Inequality in Contemporary China," *Asian Survey* 19 (1979): 867.

level hospitals in large cities. It is to these that workers with full medical coverage would first report if they had other than a minor complaint. In these hospitals, no advance appointments could be made. Unless one had a serious condition that would warrant immediate access to the emergency room, one had to go to the hospital in the morning to get an appointment number for the day. Generally there was a central registration desk that handed out numbers separately for each department in the hospital according to the number of patients that the staff in that department could see during that day. For example, they might have had 80 appointment numbers to hand out for department X and 300 for department Y, if the latter had a larger number of staff members. Once patients had appointment numbers, they then proceeded to the department concerned where they would be seen in numerical order during the day. Some with high numbers might go home and then come back at about the time they expected their number to come up. A prospective patient who arrived after all the numbers for the department had been given out would simply have to come back another day. Informants report that in many large city hospitals in the 1970s patients had to start lining up an hour or two before the hospital opened, sometimes even before daybreak, in order to get a number for the day. Then, once given a number, patients had no choice over which doctor they saw, and they were often concerned about the variable quality of the personnel that might treat them.[17] Experienced doctors trained in earlier years were generally respected, but graduates of the much-abbreviated Cultural Revolution era programs were seen as poorly prepared and were not trusted. For a period during the Cultural Revolution decade the egalitarian enthusiasm of China's radicals produced status reversals and changed work routines in many hospitals that affected the quality of the care given. Doctors were required to give inoculations and empty bedpans and nurses and orderlies were in some cases promoted to do work as doctors and nurses, all with the aim of breaking down the "feudal" status barriers between ranks. In this period patients feared being assigned to the care of these newly promoted people rather than to real doctors, or being assigned doctors and finding them exhausted by the new duties taken on. The enthusiasm for these status reversals waned even before the end of the radical period—by 1973 or so in most hospitals—but even then the crowds awaiting outpatient care meant that most consultations tended to be very brief ("two minutes," one informant grumbled).

17. However, patients could generally indicate whether they preferred to be seen by a Western-style or a Chinese-style doctor.

With these high rates of usage, shortages in medicine were also common. Doctors were reported to have to check a list of exactly which medicines were in stock, and even then patients sometimes couldn't get their prescriptions filled at the hospital pharmacy. Some of this grumbling about the doctor not being willing to assign valuable herbal remedies, tonics, and more exotic antibiotics was doubtlessly unjustified. But some was justified, as is indicated by some doctors' suggesting that patients use overseas connections to get both Chinese herbal and Western-style drugs mailed to them.

With cheap medical care, there has also been malingering by state workers. Some young workers are reported to have used the excuse of seeing the doctor to get a half day off. Informants report occasional instances of "5-29" workers—workers who would draw sick pay for five months and twenty-nine days until they had a miraculous cure on the day just before their six-month sick-leave benefits ran out.[18]

Both patients and the government have taken a number of steps to get around these kinds of problems. Patients report attempts to build personal connections with doctors in order to avoid early morning queues, to see doctors they trust, and to get scarcer medicines prescribed. In the early 1960s, the government began to require that workers in state enterprises pay their own 5–10 cents registration fee and more hospital costs for themselves and family members in order to reduce both the burden on doctors and the waste of medicine.[19] And in the 1970s, our informants report, some work units became more restrictive, paying only for benefits at work unit–linked clinics and hospitals that would ration access to higher level units in the three-tier system.[20]

18. The Chinese mass media provide some additional evidence of many of the points made by informants. For example, *Xinhua* (Peking), 17 November 1979, in *FBIS*, 20 November 1979, p. 15, notes that "Hospitals and out-patient clinics are always overcrowded." The recent discussion on needing to control bogus drug production as well as illegal imports gives a hint of pent-up demand—see Beijing Radio, 4 June 1981, in *FBIS*, 5 June 1981, p. K15. From similar sources, Lynn White documents the sharp rise in demand and overcrowding with the introduction of cheaper state supported medical care in the mid-1950s— *Careers in Shanghai* (Berkeley: University of California Press, 1978), pp. 117–18. *Beijing Review*, no. 25 (1980): 19 speaks of 40 percent of the nation's health workers as undertrained, in part because of the lowering of standards during the Cultural Revolution.

19. The demand control rationale is explicitly stated. See "Announcement on Resolving Several Problems in the Enterprise Personnel's Labor Insurance Medical Care System," Central Labor Compensation Document no. 60 (1966) in Fujian Province, *Laodong Gongzi Wenjian*, pp. 396–97.

20. If one goes to a standard referral hospital with the required form, one does not need to pay anything but the registration fee, and billing is handled directly between the hospital and one's work unit. If one goes to a different hospital one has to pay the hospital and then use the receipt to seek reimbursement from one's work unit. In this case the unit may balk or delay repayment.

There are some problems in the system, then. However, the investment in human and physical resources has been so massive that basic medical care is available to essentially everyone in cities. At the lower end, those completely outside state work units and without any insurance coverage suffer somewhat. At the top, high-ranking cadres have special rooms and sometimes whole wings in hospitals.[21] Also, some informants complain that high level cadres get medicines that are denied the common individual. Yet, overall, the provision of medical services seems remarkably equal, and on the whole, quite effective. The Cultural Revolution reforms do not appear to have been as disruptive in the case of health care as they were in education. The bureaucratic system of referrals may be exasperating and time consuming, but it does seem to insulate the best medical facilities and personnel from the overload potential of public demands for medical services so that they can concentrate on the most serious problems.

The Chinese health care system puts a major emphasis on prevention as well as curing. It is in the area of prevention that the less professional medical staff and the neighborhood apparatus come into full play. It is this use of nonprofessionals, along with the training of less-skilled doctors and paramedics, that helps set the Chinese health care system apart. The program of prevention emphasizes both inoculation and public sanitation. In periodic inoculation campaigns against measles, encephalitis, tuberculosis, and other infectious diseases, work units, neighborhoods, and schools notify those for whom they are responsible that it is time for a certain injection, checking up on who has and has not yet come to the local clinic or red medical station. Work units and neighborhoods also periodically post announcements of the health hazards of the season, advising their members when to wear gauze face masks to halt the spread of germs, when to drink certain tonics and soups to stay healthy, and so on. At several points in the 1950s, the authorities mobilized much of the urban population in an effort to eliminate flies, mosquitos, rats, and sparrows.[22] In general our informants felt that this sort of preventive medical work was diligently and regularly carried out.

Urban sanitation is also a source of constant concern. China's cities do not have centralized sewage treatment plants, and human sewage (night

21. Interviews, and Gail Henderson, *Danwei: A Chinese Work Unit* (Ph.D. dissertation, University of Michigan, 1982). When under attack in the Cultural Revolution, some high cadres sought refuge in private hospital rooms.

22. This "four pests" campaign involved having urbanites compete to turn in the most flies, discover the most mosquito breeding places, and stand on roofs and walls clanging pots and sticks to leave sparrows no place to alight. In the case of sparrows it was later determined that the masses that fell to their deaths exhausted had deprived urban areas of a valuable predator of other vermin, and bedbugs belatedly replaced sparrows on the extermination list.

soil) is a valuable commodity for use as a fertilizer in the fields of suburban communes. But removing night soil from homes and getting it out to the communes without creating health hazards is a fairly complex matter. In larger cities some buildings, particularly new, multistory ones, have flush toilet systems emptying into external cess pits. The city sanitation department periodically pumps these out into trucks and delivers the product to contracting suburban areas. But much older housing has no flush toilets or no internal plumbing at all. In some homes the family has wooden buckets in which excreta are deposited, and these are put out at night to be collected, again usually by the urban sanitation department. (The latter collects garbage and coal ash separately as well.) In other locales people simply use a nearby public latrine, and these are periodically cleaned out by the sanitation department and their contents delivered to rural areas. In smaller cities and towns there may be direct contracting with suburban communes, which send teams with wagons into the city to collect night soil from particular neighborhoods and public toilets.[23] These procedures give many Chinese neighborhoods a rather pungent aroma at certain times of day, even if no serious health hazards are created.

Collection procedures for night soil (and garbage) are accompanied by a wide variety of other sanitation efforts, particularly in the larger cities. The city sanitation department is responsible for sweeping the main streets regularly. But most cities are a beehive of small lanes and alleys, and sweeping them is the responsibility of those who live there. Usually local residents' committees find a person to take care of the day-to-day sweeping, and they collect a fee from each local household in order to pay that person. Periodically, though, they mobilize all families in the neighborhood for a general sweep-up effort. Authorities are also concerned about controlling insects and vermin, and they periodically distribute fumigation chemicals to each household with instructions on their use. Citywide cleanup campaigns are regularly carried out, often once each season. Families are notified that such a campaign is beginning and they are expected to make an especially thorough housecleaning. Then residents' committee cadres (or work unit cadres, in the case of those living in work unit housing complexes) come around from door to door and inspect each apartment to see how clean it is. The results are made public in the form of colored stickers placed on front doors of those who pass muster, which say something like "Clean Household." Those who do not measure up either have a bare door or a sticker saying the house is not clean, and they know they have to do better to pass the next inspection. All of these

23. "Night soil" contracts are no small matter to suburban communes and can sometimes lead to poaching and outright conflict between competing villages. On poaching, see Qinghai Radio, 11 April 1979, in *FBIS*, 16 April 1979, p. T2.

health and sanitation activities are reinforced by posters and banners made up by residents' committees and work units announcing the nature of the current cleanliness drives and exhorting local people to participate in the effort. In public health and sanitation work, then, matters are not left to medical personnel and paid sanitation workers, and major roles are played by the lowest levels of the urban administrative system in mobilizing individuals and families to keep the city clean. These efforts have not always been well done or uniformly successful. Informants claimed there was a fair amount of spitting and littering on the street despite efforts to get people to be neater and more sanitary. Also, efforts tend to be better organized in larger, high level administrative seats than in smaller county towns and commune seats. Three-fourths of our sample neighborhoods in the national municipalities of Peking, Shanghai, and Tianjin have neighborhood health stations seeing to inoculations, first aid, and other primary health care needs. Only 40 percent of the sample of neighborhoods in county and commune seats have such neighborhood health stations—they must rely instead on the local clinic or hospital which oversees a much larger area, including the surrounding countryside. According to informants' reports, there is a similar tendency for smaller, lower level cities to be less well served in other areas as well, be these inoculations, fumigations, and other health care efforts; the frequency and diligence of household cleanliness inspections; or the general cleanliness of the neighborhood as a result of frequent street sweeping, trash collection, and housecleaning campaigns. Chinese cities probably do better than many other developing cities in the world, but standards are clearly conditioned by the size and administrative importance of the city.

Social Security
and Other Welfare Benefits

China's well-developed education and health care systems are designed to prepare people for useful work in society as well as to keep them at work once they have started. However, not everyone is able to work—some are too old or are physically impaired—and that is where the welfare system enters in. The regulations that established China's welfare system in the 1950s and informant accounts about how this system works today indicate three distinguishing characteristics.

First, pensions, disability benefits, and several other social security programs exist not as rights for everyone but as privileges to be earned. These privileges are earned by accumulating seniority in state work units— fifteen to twenty years for a full pension, three years for full disability benefits, and so on.[24] People who do not work, and many if not most of those in collective industry, have no right to even partial benefits under the major social security programs. This principle is, of course, not confined to socialist societies.

Second, when benefits have not been earned, direct public assistance is to be given only as a last resort after all efforts to find a person a job or to find kin obliged to give support have been exhausted. The state does play a role in providing some jobs to certain kinds of handicapped persons who cannot work in normal jobs. But it is assumed that the family, including grandparents, will bear most of the burden. Indeed, the 1950 Marriage Law requires that parents support their children and children their parents, so that neither should become needless charges of the state. The attitude of dependence on the state is to be avoided.[25]

Third, the management of welfare benefits is decentralized down to work units and neighborhoods. As a consequence, the manner in which welfare benefits are dispersed can be highly variable. This is not so true for those on mandated pension and disability programs in state work units as it is for people who fall outside these programs. Variability is also promoted by the absence of a social work profession. To the extent that benefits are standardized, they depend on people such as accountants and other clerical workers and on trade union representatives. When they are not standardized, then the goodwill and sensibility of one's foreman, ward leaders, fellow workers, and ordinary neighbors can be all important.

24. For a compilation of labor insurance regulations current in the 1970s, including the central 1950s documents, see Fujian Province, *Laodong Gongzi Wenjian Xuanbian*. Revised retirement regulations issued in 1978 lowered the minimum years of service for a pension to ten years. See Culture and Education Administration and Finance Division, Ministry of Finance, *Shehui Wenjiao Xingzheng Caiwu Zhidu Zhaibian* (Excerpts on the system of social, cultural, and educational administration and finance) (Peking: Chinese Finance and Economics Publishing House, 1979), pp. 432–33. On current welfare practice, see John Dixon, *The Chinese Welfare System, 1949–1979* (New York: Praeger, 1981).

25. Besides our interviews, these points are substantiated in 1950s and 1960s discussions of the scope of welfare benefits. See, for example, "State Council Personnel Bureau Report on Improving Welfare Work for Workers and Staff in Government, Mass Organizations, and Enterprises," *Zhonghua Renmin Gonghe Guo Fagui Huibian* (Compilation of laws and regulations of the PRC), vol. 7 (Peking Law Press, 1958), pp. 413–16; "Management and Use Methods for Relief and Aid Work," *Zhonghua Renmin Gonghe Guo Fagui Huibian*, vol. 13 (Peking Law Press, 1964), pp. 70–75; *Dagong Bao* (Peking), 26 September 1959, p. 3; *Anhui Daily*, 19 October 1959, p. 3; *Liaoning Daily*, 7 January 1959; *Fujian Daily*, 8 October 1959, p. 3. The last four articles emphasize how people were taken off aid and put to work in newly created "social welfare production" factories. In 1969, each of the thirteen districts in Shanghai municipality had one of these factories for the blind, deaf, mute, and crippled. See Rewi Alley, *Travels in China, 1966–1971* (Peking: New World Press, 1973), p. 77.

In state work units, funds set aside for welfare benefits are said to have totaled 17 percent of the wage bill in the 1970s.[26] (Pensions are not included in this sum and represent an additional expense.) Normally, retirement is at the age of sixty for men and fifty or fifty-five for women, depending on whether they have engaged in manual work. However, the retirement ages are not compulsory and many skilled blue collar workers and even more technicians and managers and most intellectuals and cadres have continued working into their sixties and seventies. Benefits range from 40 to 85 percent of preretirement salary, depending on seniority and type of service. The most common benefit is 70 percent, and to this has been added the same medical insurance benefits and other supplements received before retirement.[27] Most retired workers return to their work unit to pick up their pension payment in cash each month.

Then there are a number of preretirement benefits. Married women workers get fifty-six days' paid maternity leave. Other workers get sick leave of 60 to 100 percent of their salary during the first six months of illness and then at 40 to 60 percent for subsequent periods, the exact percentage depending on years of seniority. Disabled workers get 40 to 100 percent of their pay, depending on years and type of service, with the more common payments being in the 60 to 75 percent range. Survivor benefits are more limited, normally being just a lump sum equivalent to six to twelve months' salary plus the expenses of cremation or burial. It is assumed that the spouse will have support in his or her own work unit, and that any dependent children of workers who have died young will be tended to by the spouse's work unit or neighborhood.[28]

Besides benefits for retirees, the sick, the disabled, and some dependents, work units provide a number of other benefits that do not fall within the normal range of social security benefits in other societies. State factories typically provide a free blue cotton work suit to manual workers annually. Monthly, these factories provide cash allowances sometimes totaling several yuan. These include transportation allowances to most

26. *A Glance at China's Economy* (Peking: Foreign Languages Press, 1974), cited in Vermeer, "Social Welfare Provisions," p. 869n. From other data, Vermeer suggests that perhaps only 10 percent is for labor insurance provisions while the remaining 7 percent is for food, transportation, and other kinds of salary supplements.

27. The 1978 pension regulation revisions raised the pension range to 60–90 percent of one's final wage and made 75 percent the common figure. See *Shehui Wenjiao*, pp. 432–43.

28. However, dependents of workers killed on the job will get 25 percent to 60 percent of their spouse's or parent's salary until they die or reach maturity. For an example, in a non-job death, of dependents having to turn to the neighborhood for support, see *People's Daily*, 11 January 1964, p. 5.

commuters.[29] In provinces with grain price increases in the 1960s, they provided a "grain differential" allowance for at least those workers employed at the time of the increase, and they provided a similar five yuan subsistence allowance for those employed when other food prices were raised in 1979.[30] In southern provinces some state factories provide a summer cool-drink allowance of a few cents a month, if not directly providing liquid refreshment. (The same is true for those working in high temperature jobs.) For workers with immediate kin living in a distant city or village, there is an annual two-week leave with pay.[31] Only those with a spouse elsewhere or, if unmarried, with parents elsewhere, can partake of this benefit. All other workers work six days a week year-round except for the seven national holidays scattered throughout the year.

Besides the above benefits that are earned, there are a few benefits that anyone may request once family resources have been exhausted. One of these is a hardship allowance for families that fall below certain minimum subsistence levels. State workers can apply to their work unit. Collective workers or the unemployed can apply to their ward. This can be a one-time request to meet an immediate crisis (e.g., death in the family, medical bills) or an application for a regular monthly supplement. While detailed regulations on the administration of this program are not available, a common practice in the 1970s was to define families in large cities with a total per capita income of less than 12 yuan per month and families in small towns with less than 8 yuan as being below the poverty level.[32] If below this level, and if not there because of violating birth control regulations by having too many children, the work unit or ward could choose to give an allowance to bring families up to the subsistence level. Primary and high schools could waive tuition, as noted earlier, and help find free or cheap books. Our informants agree that the number of families needing

29. In Peking, the travel subsidy has been available to those who commuted two kilometers or more, with commuters still being left to pay 1.5 yuan a month, or about 3 percent of the average wage, for public transport. *Xinhua* (Peking), 27 October 1979, in *FBIS,* 1 November 1979, p. R1.

30. On grain allowances, see *Laodong Gongzi Wenjian,* pp. 219–24; *People's Daily,* 1 November 1979, p. 1.

31. Additional time is added for travel, but travel expenses are excluded. Three weeks or more are allowed for those only able to return once in two years. See *Shehui Wenjiao,* p. 30. In 1981 these regulations were liberalized to allow twenty to thirty days' annual leave, plus travel time, and to have work units help pay travel expenses—*Xinhua* (Peking), 6 March 1981, in *FBIS,* 12 March 1981, p. L14.

32. For a more complicated payment formula for the city of Tientsin, see Tientsin Radio, 1 January 1980, in *FBIS,* 31 January 1980, p. R2. The bare bones of the hardship system are given in "State Council Personnel Bureau Report," *Fagui Huibian* 7 (1958): 413–16.

this allowance has declined sharply since the 1950s, when families had more children and fewer wives were at work. In our 1970s sample, only 2 percent of all families were below this poverty line. That much of this improvement had to do with wives going to work can be seen by noting that had wives not been working 25 percent would have been below the poverty line.

There are other less regular forms of assistance for these poorer families as well. Some work units and neighborhoods periodically distribute winter clothing, bedding, and other free goods to families classified as particularly needy. In factories, the work group may be asked whether one of their number needs this extra aid. In neighborhoods, there are fewer resources to provide extra aid even for those who regularly fall below the subsistence minima. Childless old people who never worked in a state factory and therefore get no pension or very little pension are the ones most likely to need help by the neighborhood. Some neighborhoods will have funds to provide assistance, but many others will try first to find a job sweeping the street, tending a nursery, or some other task for old people to help earn their keep.

Even without children, very few old people will leave their neighborhood for care in old-age homes. Indeed, throughout urban China in the late 1970s there were but 200 homes for the aged caring for only 60,000 people.[33] Also, handicapped and retarded children as well as mentally ill adults tend to be cared for at home and in their community rather than in institutions. A family may get a hardship allowance to help support a handicapped, retarded, or mentally ill family member, but it is only those without families or very severe problems who enter public facilities for more than short periods of time.[34]

In addition, there are sometimes ad hoc arrangements to help people cope with adversity. In factories and some other work units, workers sometimes participate in New Year's savings clubs, with perhaps three yuan being deducted from the paycheck each month to be deposited in a mutual savings account. Participants can then borrow from the account for emergencies such as a wedding, a funeral, or an illness, or they withdraw the full amount in time for Chinese New Year. These administered arrangements seem to have replaced revolving credit groupings that were

33. *Beijing Review*, no. 45 (1979).

34. Conclusions based on interviews and the press. There are but 254 mental hospitals for all of China, with not quite 5,000 beds. In the U.S. in the 1970s, there were over 7,000 mental hospitals with over 1.5 million beds. See *Beijing Review*, no. 25 (1980); *Beijing Review*, no. 41 (1980): 28–29; *Zhongguo Baike Nianjian, 1980*, p. 560; and *U.S. Statistical Abstract, 1976*, p. 81.

the informal means used by many pre-1949 workers to cope with special financial needs.[35]

Also, given the low levels of job turnover and residential mobility, work mates and neighbors tend to have rich supportive networks among themselves. There are a few examples in our interviews of people passing the hat to collect as much as 150 yuan to help a fellow worker or neighbor in need. There is one example in our interviews of lending a room to an old person without a family or home, and many other examples of neighbors preparing food and saving old clothes for those in need. Ward officers sometimes get into the act, helping to mobilize informal support networks to see that old people's daily needs are met, but much of this aid occurs spontaneously and informally.

In sum, this socialist system has not produced a major welfare bureaucracy. Labor insurance for those who earn their benefits in state industry is quite well developed. But for the rest of the population, the emphasis is still on family and community care and the avoidance of dependence on the state or social care professionals.[36] Social critics such as Christopher Lasch who see modern Western culture threatened by the excessive intrusion of the professions into community and family life should be pleased with the Chinese example.[37] Most of the time, this system appears to work well. However, there are examples in our interviews where people of the wrong class or background, or with poor interpersonal relations with neighbors and local officials, were neglected much longer than might have occurred in a more standardized system. Instances such as these make one a bit less sanguine about the operation of deprofessionalized welfare systems.

Housing

Education and medical care are considered to be fundamental human needs in socialist states, and all socialist states spend heavily and devote considerable personnel to see that these services are widely available. Welfare benefits are slightly less favored. When it comes to housing, however, socialist states typically have a much more ambivalent attitude.

35. Some older retired and unemployed residents continue to use the informal revolving credit groups.

36. The same tendencies are apparent in most other socialist states. For some of these reasons and also because of high levels of employment, socialist expenditures on social security tend to be less than in capitalist states at the same level of development. The same would certainly be true of China as well. See George and Manning, *Socialism, Social Welfare and the Soviet Union*, p. 32.

37. Christopher Lasch, *Haven in a Heartless World* (New York: Basic Books, 1977).

The urban citizenry are felt to deserve basic housing at minimal cost. But better housing is often seen as a luxury or consumption good that detracts from the greater goal of national productivity and growth. In practice, socialist states have skimped on housing, providing only minimal floor space per person, spartan plumbing, and long waiting lists for new housing.[38]

China is no exception to this typical socialist pattern. In the 1950s, soon after the revolution, the state moved quickly to clear some of the largest slums in Shanghai, Canton, and other large cities. Yet, even in the early 1950s new housing failed to keep pace with the influx of new residents into cities. And by the mid-1950s, national leaders began to have doubts about heavy investment in housing. The pace of residential building declined sharply and remained at a snail's pace through the mid-1970s except in the capital, Peking, and in budding industrial centers.[39] Nevertheless, Chinese urban housing still does not compare all that unfavorably with housing in many other developing cities where large squatter tracts mar the urban landscape. In our mid-1970s sample, the number of rooms per dwelling in China was only slightly below the average of that in other developing cities (line 1 of table 8). But in Chinese cities there were fewer dwellings with just one room (line 2). And with birth control taking effect and fewer persons per household, the number of persons per room and the percentage of dwellings with three or more people crowded into a single room were no worse than in other developing societies (lines 3, 4a, 5).

Moreover, some of the housing amenities in Chinese cities were considerably better than those in other developing cities (lines 6–11). Chinese urbanites were much more likely to have piped water and electric lighting. Though they didn't always have a kitchen for their exclusive use, by sharing with other families in the same building they did better than residents in most developing cities. Toilet and bathing facilities were not so close at hand as in other societies. But in large cities, by going a distance down the street, the Chinese urban dweller could usually find a public facility readily—if somewhat busily—available.

These housing comparisons are not nearly so favorable as the earlier health and education comparisons. And they would be even less favorable were the comparisons with the U.S., where dwellings average only half

38. James H. Bater, *The Soviet City* (Beverly Hills: Sage, 1980), pp. 97–111; Karel Joseph Kansky, *Urbanization under Socialism* (New York: Praeger, 1976), chap. 4; George and Manning, *Socialism, Social Welfare and the Soviet Union*, chap. 5.

39. Zhou Jin, "Housing China's 900 Million People," *Beijing Review*, no. 48 (1979): 17–27; Christopher Howe, "The Supply and Administration of Housing in Mainland China: The Case of Shanghai," *China Quarterly* 10 (1968): 73–97; White, *Careers in Shanghai*, pp. 176–96.

Table 8   Urban Housing Conditions in
                                 Selected Countries

	China (Mean)	Other Developing Countries[a] (Mean)	(Range)
Size and Density			
1. Average rooms per dwelling	2.5	2.9	2.0-3.3
2. Dwellings with only one room	18%	31%	9-52%
3. Persons per room	1.6	2.0	2.8-1.4
4a. Dwellings with 3 or more persons per room	24%	27%	50-16%
b. Dwellings with less than 1 person per room	18%	31%	9-52%
5. Persons per household	4.4	5.3	4.0-6.5
Amenities			
6. Piped water inside house	62%	43%	4-88%
7. Piped water inside house or within 100 meters	79%	67%	23-94%
8. Electric lighting	99%	64%	4-96%
9. Kitchen	72/93%[b]	79%	61-100%
10. Toilets	18/29%[b]	88%	67-99%
11. Fixed bath or shower	23%	40%	4-85%
Ownership			
12. Owner-occupied	42%	56%	47-74%

Source: China: Weighted neighbor sample, N=274. Others: United Nations Statistical Office, Compendium of Housing Statistics, 1972-74.

[a]Sixteen countries with a per capita gross national product in 1976 U.S. dollars of $130 to $600, which brackets China's 1976 figure of $200-300.

[b]The percentage with a private facility is shown to the left of the slash. The percentage including those sharing facilities with other households in the same building is to the right.

a person per room and where well over ninety percent of all dwellings have their own plumbing. Yet Chinese housing must be judged adequate by world standards. This is particularly true when one considers not just the average housing situation but also the situation for the poorest urban dwellers in these cities. There are few slums in Chinese cities. Brick and concrete structures predominate (89 percent in our sample), with few of the wood and tin shantytowns of other developing cities.[40]

40. Weighted sample. Because of repair problems, some Chinese writers are less sanguine, arguing that "20 percent of urban residents are slum dwellers." See Zhou Shulian and Lin Senmu, "On the Question of Housing," *People's Daily*, 5 August 1980, p. 5, in *FBIS*, 20 August 1980, p. L15. Neighborhoods such as Jaibei and Nanshi in Shanghai, Daobei in Xian, and Daowei in Harbin provide examples of remaining problems.

This uniformity was possible in part because Chinese urbanites have tended to share rather equally in the available housing stock, particularly during the mid-1970s. For example, while Chinese urbanites were no more likely than people in other developing societies to be crowded three to a room, the more fortunate of them were considerably less likely to be spread out one to a room. Their housing situation was much more tightly clustered about the average of two to a room (table 8, lines 4a–b). This equality is special even compared with the socialist states of Hungary and Poland. Rooms, toilet, and bath facilities in these two societies are less equally distributed than in China. And the lower level bureaucrats in our sample got only slightly better housing than the average Chinese citizen in the 1970s.[41] Chinese urbanites also pay relatively little of their income for housing. For those who live in rental housing, rent is said to average only 2–3 percent of total family income, with additional water and electricity expenditures raising total housing expenditures to only 5 percent of total family income.[42] This compares with an average in many other developing countries of about 10 percent of family income for housing.[43]

Despite these favorable comparisons, housing has been a frequent source of complaints among informants, among American Chinese who have gone back to visit their kin, and in more recent Chinese press and radio reports. One press report states that 35 percent of the families in Chinese cities live in overcrowded conditions and that 5 to 6 percent of them do not have proper houses at all. In many places, it is reported, floor space per person has been less than 2 square meters—about the space of a twin bed per person.[44] In the largest 192 cities in 1978, it was reported that the average floor space per person was only 3.6 square meters, about 40 square feet, or slightly less than the space of a king-sized bed per person.[45] Because of the small national investment in housing, there was a steady decline in space after 1952, when there was a reported average of 4.5 square meters per person in the major cities. (The current construction standard for new worker housing is only 4 square meters per person.) Thus the relevant comparison for many people must be the space available

41. See William L. Parish, "Destratification in the People's Republic of China," *Select Papers*, no. 4 (University of Chicago: Center for Far Eastern Studies, 1981), pp. 143–87.

42. Zhou Jin, "Housing China's 900 Million," p. 17. Our sample of neighbors produces a not quite so favorable rent expenditure figure of just over 5 percent of family income in large cities and 3.7 percent in cities and towns of all sizes.

43. Constantino Lluch et al., *Patterns in Household Demand and Saving* (New York: Oxford University Press, 1977), p. 40.

44. Summary of *Guangming Daily* article in *Xinhua* (Peking), 17 November 1979, in *FBIS*, 20 November 1979, p. L5.

45. Zhou Jin, "Housing China's 900 Million People," p. 18. The floor space figure excludes kitchen, lavatory, and public corridors. For 1979 the statistic cited had risen slightly to 3.7 square meters. See *Zhongguo Baike Nianjian, 1981*, p. 540.

to them in the past rather than what is available in distant developing countries. In this respect urbanites have serious complaints.

Our statistics also ignore a number of other problems. There is a rising demand for housing among young adults, and it is from them that many of the complaints come. In the mid-1970s, the problem in housing would have been even worse had not many young people been assigned to the countryside. Were they accounted for in the figures in table 8, average household size would rise to 4.5 and the number of persons per room to 2.3, which is distinctly worse than in the average developing city. Also, these additional people are adults, which makes the crowding situation more severe than in other developing cities where many of the extra family members are young children.

The Chinese architectural standard is that children will sleep in the same room with their parents through age twelve. After that teenagers of each sex should have separate rooms, though a grandparent may share a room with teenagers of either sex. By this standard, one-fifth of the families in our sample were overcrowded in the mid-1970s, which seems to agree with some of the surveys reported in the Chinese *Architecture Journal* for about the same time.[46] Some families have tried to cope with this situation by building a loft in a room and by putting up temporary partitions, but these are only halfway measures. The situation is most difficult of all for young adults who wish to get married but find that no housing is available. This accounts for much of the five to six percent of the urban population who are reported to be without proper houses at all. With the return of increasing numbers of youths from the countryside after 1974 this situation grew worse.

We have also failed to note some of the less favorable implications in our statistics. The small proportion of dwellings with fewer than one person per room indicates that very few of the professionals and administrators who would live in better housing in other societies have been able to do so in China. For them, the last two decades has often meant a rapid decline in space standards and privacy. This was particularly true at the height of the Cultural Revolution when intellectuals and former capitalists and merchants could not object as workers and others of good class background moved in to share their houses. In some cases cadres or intellectuals had to move out of spacious housing and into cramped hovels while several families of workers or janitorial personnel occupied

46. See the following issues of the *Architecture Journal* (*Jianju Xuebao*) 1, no. 134 (1978): 1–3; 136 (1978): 26; 2 (1973): 1–3; 2 (1974): 33–35. This figure is lower than the 35 percent of overcrowded households given in the Chinese press for 1979. Some of the difference may reflect deterioration through the 1970s, but the rest is probably due to using rooms per member versus square meters per member to judge overcrowding.

their former quarters—another manifestation of the attack on "feudal" status barriers at the time. Sharing common facilities sometimes separated only by a partition running part way to the ceiling, informants tell sometimes funny, but often sad, stories of mutual misunderstandings and suspicions. As in the case of people stuck in unpleasant work situations, there is no easy escape from the conflicts generated, since in China's administered housing system one cannot simply decide to move elsewhere (residential moves will be discussed shortly). Again we see that an egalitarian program can generate human conflicts.

We have also failed to note the difficulties of sharing a kitchen and toilet. In our figures, 21 percent of all dwellings require the sharing of a kitchen and 11 percent the sharing of a toilet in the building (see table 8, lines 10–11, noting the difference between percentages on each side of the slash mark). This situation is tightest in large cities where almost half of all families have to share a kitchen. Sharing is the most frequent source of conflict between families. Kitchens are typically so small that only one family can cook at a time. In some buildings built for other purposes and later transformed into housing, people have to use makeshift kitchens erected outside or in the hallways. In the evening when everyone returns home at roughly the same time there is competition for the use of this small space and there is a potential for conflict over who is using whose supplies and whose garbage is being left lying on the counter and floor. Urbanites desire not only more housing space but less sharing of facilities.

Finally, we have not considered the many problems of bureaucratic control of housing. Already in the 1950s and early 1960s, a considerable proportion of housing had passed into public hands. Some was left behind or confiscated from losers in the revolution. After the mid-1950s, urban landlords were pressured to turn over their rental houses to the state, while individual homeowners were mobilized to allow portions of their homes to be made over into multiple dwelling units to ease the overall housing shortage. New housing estates were built by factories, bureaus, and urban housing offices. Except for special dispensations to overseas Chinese and special loans to poor workers in some cities, permits and building materials for new private houses were seldom allowed. These processes continued into the 1960s and resulted in a growing share of public housing in China's large cities. In the Cultural Revolution there were attempts in some of the largest cities to completely eliminate private housing as yet another vestige of bourgeois society. Red Guards stormed into private homes and forced owners to turn over their deeds and, in some cases, to begin to pay rent on their own homes to the public housing authorities. Some people had more rooms taken away from them and given to others to live in, and a few were even completely displaced by new residents or organizations.

By the mid-1970s, while over two-thirds of housing in small towns remained in private hands, perhaps no more than 10 percent of housing in the largest cities remained under private control.[47] As long as the annual property tax was paid, these private houses could theoretically be both bought and sold and rented to others. But by the mid-1970s virtually all private homes were simply inherited from parents rather than purchased on the open market. And what little space was rented out tended to be restricted to close friends and kin. In the political atmosphere of the time, people were afraid of being accused of being landlords or they were afraid of new tenants claiming space and refusing to leave. In any event, through both direct supervision by the district housing offices and general fear of being criticized, rents remained so low that there was little economic incentive to open one's house to others.

Public housing in large cities fell under both direct city and work unit control. City-owned housing, administered by district housing management offices, includes buildings taken over from former private owners and newer housing built by the city. Work unit–controlled housing includes both large estates or compounds adjoining a factory, bureau, or school and detached housing units scattered throughout the city often at some distance from the resident's place of work. In older cities like Canton, where pre-1949 housing still predominates, most people live in city-run housing. In these cities, those who live in work unit housing are often scattered about the city rather than clustered next to their work unit. In cities like Peking which have grown more rapidly, people are more likely to live in work unit housing, often of the newer clustered or work unit compound type. In other cities that have grown more slowly, the Canton situation is still the predominant one, with most people living in old city-run housing or in small work unit buildings separated from the place of work. This all helps account for the very crowded public transport system and the press of bicycles on the major thoroughfares during rush hours.[48]

47. In our census of nonagricultural neighbors, 66 percent (63 percent owner occupied, 3 percent rented out) of commune seat housing was private—were agricultural households at the commune seat included, the percentage would be much higher. In this same census, 15 percent (all owner occupied, no renters) of housing in Peking, Tientsen, and Shanghai was private.

48. Nationwide, the pattern is moving slowly from the Canton type situation towards that in Peking. In China's largest 200 cities, fully 54 percent of all rental living space is unit owned, 29 percent city owned, and 18 percent privately owned—*Beijing Review,* no. 41 (1982): 28. And in recent years, over half of all housing construction funds have come from work units—*Zhongguo Baike Nianjian, 1981,* p. 540. A report on Qingdao City in Shandong

Whether old or new, city or work unit, clustered or scattered, most housing in China's cities is allocated and maintained not by impersonal market forces but by bureaucratic hands. This is an additional source of complaints about housing. If one works for a large and prosperous factory or powerful bureau that can afford to build ample housing for its workers, then one may have one's housing needs satisfied. But if one works for a resource-poor or insignificant work unit with little or no housing of its own, then one is thrown at the mercy of an overburdened housing system which, in the absence of market incentives, is very slow to move. With insufficient housing to distribute, the district housing management office has long waiting lists of newlyweds without housing, of older families with too many growing children for their current space, and of other families who wish to move nearer to work, escape an unpleasant neighbor, or otherwise improve their environment. Some prospective or newly married couples are lucky and get new housing in a few months, but instances of couples having to wait several years for housing are not uncommon. This is a familiar story in other socialist states.

Given the difficulties of finding housing directly through the district housing office and work unit, people sometimes arrange housing exchanges. They may post notices on street corners and utility poles. Many housing management offices provide a room or a space out front for posting notices and negotiating exchanges. The initiative here rests with the families involved. If a family is able to locate another family that is willing to exchange housing with them then they simply have to process the required forms through their local housing management offices and police stations to get the transfer completed. A second procedure is an illegitimate one: squatting. One hears of people hard-pressed for extra space keeping an eye out for housing left vacant in their vicinity, or even for utility rooms or other space not meant for residential use, and then moving into these premises when nobody is looking. When a family "squats" in this manner the housing office or work unit authorities generally come and try to get them out. But if their political record is clean and their need for housing is genuine they may adamantly refuse to move. In such cases the authorities either may have to let them stay or find them alternative housing to move into.[49]

Province further confirms the trend—*Beijing Review*, no. 48 (1979): 17. On the ideal of employee housing clustered around work units, and the difficulty of attaining this ideal in other socialist societies, see R. A. French and F. E. I. Hamilton, eds. *The Socialist City* (New York: John Wiley, 1979).

49. For one account of the difficulty of evicting such squatters, see "My Neighborhood," in M. Bernard Frolic, *Mao's People* (Cambridge: Harvard University Press, 1980).

Housing upkeep can also be complicated. Renters are supposed to see to whitewashing the interior walls and other interior decorating. More serious matters, such as window pane replacement, roof leaks, and plumbing repairs, are reported to the district housing offices or work unit, and these organizations employ repair workers who are in charge of housing repairs. Work unit housing tends to be relatively well maintained and speedily repaired, as the unit has both resources and an incentive to see that its personnel are satisfied. In city-owned housing, however, the rents are insufficient to provide for more than minimal maintenance budgets— a situation common to other socialist states as well. (In fact maintenance expenses are estimated to be more than double rent payments.) This, coupled with the lack of incentives for fixed-salary repair workers, means that most minor repairs are slow to be made.[50] Informants often expressed exasperation at waiting months for the repair workers to come, and they also report occasional rumors that speedy and good repair would be done if the workers were tipped or bribed for their services with a dinner or cash. Some exasperated renters try to get materials and do the repairs themselves.

The bureaucratic administration of housing has a number of significant impacts on the social organization of large cities. First, stable neighborhoods persist. With such a cramped housing supply and allocation through slow-moving bureaucratic channels, the rate of residential mobility within Chinese cities has remained low. Second, local areas within Chinese cities do not take on the class- and ethnic-segregated characteristics common in cities in other societies. Rents are so low and so minimally differentiated by income that they play only a minor role in sorting people across neighborhoods by income.[51] Personal preferences, as indicated, have a very small role, while bureaucratic criteria emphasize things like the type of work unit, seniority, and family size, rather than income, ethnicity, or similar criteria. The resulting pattern is not one of completely homogeneous neighborhoods and housing, but the differences that are visible tend to be more related to work units than to class or ethnicity. Chinese cities have in effect working class neighborhoods where large industrial en-

50. And perhaps not so minor as well. In our interviews, there is multiple confirmation of a three-story building collapsing in the early 1970s in Canton, killing quite a few residents in their sleep. Word-of-mouth had it that the residents had already complained to their local housing office to no avail. One media source complains, "It is estimated that more than 50 percent of the houses in the urban areas in China are in a bad state of repair and need maintenance, of which more than 10 percent are in dangerous condition." See Zhou and Lin, "On the Question of Housing." On the inability to pay for maintenance out of rents, see *Zhongquo Baike Nianjian, 1981*, p. 5l.

51. In our census of neighbors, rents range from only one to ten yuan a month per family and all occupational groups pay a more or less constant 3.5–4.0 percent for their housing.

terprises (with their attached employee housing) are located; they have distinctive and generally nicer than average housing in areas where universities, large administrative and party offices, and military units are located; and they have the mixed neighborhoods which house people from a variety of work units. Some of the latter are quite old and decrepit.[52] Many cities have special "Overseas Chinese New Villages," which are urban neighborhoods set aside for the detached privately owned homes financed by overseas remittances. So some classlike distinctions among neighborhoods exist. Still, on balance, most urban areas are fairly mixed. For example, a factory party secretary, factory engineer, and factory canteen cook may all live side by side in the same building. The mixing of status was particularly pronounced during the Cultural Revolution decade when, as already noted, special advantages in housing space and buildings were taken away from many high status people. Thus, we would still judge the housing conditions in the 1970s to be more equal, and the neighborhoods more heterogeneous in social status, than they would have been in a society where market forces and personal preferences predominated. This distinction also means that a deteriorating neighborhood or building cannot lead to fear about falling property values, flight to the suburbs, and slum creation and residential succession, which are the common patterns in American society.[53] The contrast is not a total one, but generally Chinese urban neighborhoods are both unusually stable and unusually heterogeneous.

Consumer Goods and Services

As with housing, socialist states have typically been quite ambivalent about the supply of consumer goods and services. They are committed to providing basic food staples and clothing to everyone free of fluctuating prices and other market constraints. This is part of the guarantee of equality and a floor under living conditions which each socialist state has attempted to provide. But socialist states tend to look askance at

52. A number of characteristics are associated with these differences. The living areas of urban elite units typically have well-built apartments surrounded by lawns and then walls, with relatively few of the neighborhood workshops, beehive coal pressing shops, and similar facilities in evidence. Factory housing tends to consist of large standardized block apartments which are less often graced by lawn or yards, but which also have few of the miscellaneous neighborhood shops and service facilities interspersed. In most mixed neighborhoods the buildings stand directly on the street and have many of these facilities occupying the ground floors.

53. For similar observations on housing heterogeneity and the centrality of work organizations in other socialist societies, see French and Hamilton, *The Socialist City*, pp. 97, 229.

nonessentials, not only because they are in potential conflict with egalitarian goals, but also because they can detract from the rapid economic growth that these states have pursued. In line with this thinking, socialist states tend to invest more heavily in steel, coal, machinery, and other producer goods than in consumer goods. And they tend to downplay marketing, which has often been seen as a largely useless process.[54]

Let us examine how the effort to distribute basic necessities relatively equally has been attempted in urban China and how successful this effort has been. To ensure that basic necessities are distributed equitably, China has controlled prices, subsidized the sale of grain, oil, and other basic commodities, and constructed a highly elaborate rationing system. The Chinese system of rationing surpasses in complexity any used in socialist Eastern Europe.

Though there is variation in other products, the three staples of grain, cooking oil, and cotton cloth have been consistently rationed in Chinese cities since the mid-1950s. The procedure is slightly different for single workers and students resident in their factory or school dormitory, but once a year ordinary residents are asked to present their household registration booklet to officers in their ward. Legal residence in the neighborhood entitles each family to a new grain booklet which provides rations calibrated according to the age, sex, and work of household members. For example, a child might be eligible for 9–10 kilograms of grain a month, an adult with a white collar job 14–15 kilograms, a person in a heavy manual job 20–25 kilograms or more, and a retired person 13–14 kilograms (with many gradations in between).[55] The family then deals with a designated neighborhood grain shop. When making purchases directly from the shop, for rice in the south or wheat, corn, or millet flour in the north, one presents both cash and the booklet. Each time a purchase is made the shop records how much of the monthly grain allotment has been used.

Alternatively, one can ask the shop for coupons to be charged against the booklet, and these coupons can then be used to purchase many different items made with grain (including even some liquors) in shops and

54. On Soviet consumer problems see Marshall I. Goldman, *Soviet Marketing* (New York: Free Press, 1963); Gur Ofer, *The Service Sector in Soviet Economic Growth* (Cambridge: Harvard University Press, 1973); and the delightful popular account by Hedrick Smith, *The Russians* (New York: Quadrangle Books, 1976), chaps. 1–3.

55. For more detail on these and other rations, see "Provisional Measures Governing Rationing in Cities and Towns, 25 August 1955," in *The People's Republic of China, 1949–1979*, Harold C. Hinton, ed. (Wilmington: Scholarly Resources, 1980), pp. 223–40; Dennis L. Chinn, "Basic Commodity Distribution in the People's Republic of China," *China Quarterly* 84 (1980): 744–54; Lynn White, "Deviance, Modernization, Rations, and Household Registers in Urban China," in *Deviance and Social Control in Chinese Society*, Amy Wilson et al., eds. (New York: Praeger, 1977).

restaurants throughout the city. Though in recent years these coupons could be used beyond the month in which they were issued, they cannot be used outside the city. Therefore if one is going on a trip to visit kin or to conduct approved business, one must provide the grain station with a certificate from one's work unit or ward attesting to the reasons for the trip. Provincial or national coupons (depending on where one is going) can then be charged against one's grain booklet. This, along with the other goods rationed, has provided one of the major constraints on migration into and among Chinese cities. There is a limited informal market in coupons, and more recently (since 1979) peasants have been able to sell some grain privately on their own. But the supply of coupons has been too small to support many illegal residents in the city for long periods of time. The former black market price for direct purchases of grain was about three times the state price, and even today with legalization, privately sold peasant grain remains high because it is not subsidized like the grain sold in state grain shops.

Cooking oil is distributed much the same as grain, using the grain booklet and the assigned grain station to get oil and coupons. However, oil rations are not graded by age or type of work, but are received on an equal per capita basis.

Cotton cloth and cotton products are similarly distributed according to a nationwide rationing system, but it is not as complex to administer. In this case rations are distributed on an equal basis per capita, and they have a one-year duration rather than monthly limits. These cloth coupons are distributed to families once a year, either through the ward authorities or through the work unit, and are also only valid locally. The procedures for rationing other items are variable. A fairly typical list of rationed items for a Chinese city in the 1970s would include pork, fish, sugar, eggs, chicken, soybean curd (*doufu*), soap, coal, kindling, toilet paper, bicycles, sewing machines, television sets, and wristwatches. Some synthetic fabrics might be rationed, as are certain brands of cigarettes and kinds of wine and liquor. Peanuts were generally not available in state-run shops at all, but were distributed in small, rationed amounts before Chinese New Year. Powdered milk generally could be purchased only with a new baby's birth certificate. Clothing wardrobes and some other furniture items were only sold in some cities upon presentation of a new marriage certificate. Some industrial items, such as nails and wire, were rationed at times, and in general, construction materials were not sold to private individuals unless they had some sort of work unit or neighborhood certificate. Items like light bulbs and toothpaste did not require ration coupons, but in many locales were only sold on a one-to-one basis as discarded bulbs and tubes were turned in.

The type of ration coupons needed for various items in our list, and how they were distributed, varied from item to item (as well as from place to place and over time). For items like pork and sugar people usually received coupons through their work unit or ward authorities which were valid for a month (generally .5–1.0 kilogram per month per person for pork and .2–.3 kilogram per month per person for sugar, but in some cities as much as .5–1 kilogram of sugar). These coupons were used individually along with cash to make purchases in stores. Sometimes for auxiliary food items like bean curd or fish, people received numbered and perforated sheets of paper. Stores posted, and only collected, the numbers of the slips that could be used during the designated time period (often ten days). In some cases the amount people would be allowed to buy in return for their perforated slips varied over time, depending on the level of supplies of these food items. In other instances, people received cards or small booklets for these auxiliary foods and for other items like coal and soap on which store personnel were supposed to record purchases as they were made. For most of the items discussed here, rations were valid for one month, and they were distributed on an equal per capita basis. In the case of coal and kindling not the individual but the family was the unit of computation, and families of under four, of four to six, and more than six members received different ration allotments. It was also possible for people to have valid ration coupons but find none of an item in the shops. Work units, wards, police stations, as well as commerce bureaus and commodity companies, were all involved in administering this maze of rations, and all required at a minimum that one be properly registered in the city.

The procedure of bicycles, wristwatches, and sewing machines was somewhat different. In recent years, at least for the better brands, these required work unit purchasing certificates in most cities. Rights to purchase these items were allotted to various work units throughout the city, presumably in some rough proportion to the number of people employed in each. Each work unit then had to decide how to distribute these purchasing certificates among its staff. In some cases a portion were reserved for managerial and technical personnel. The rest seemed to be distributed by one of two methods: either by having work groups discuss and nominate those most needy or by a simple lottery. Those fortunate ones who received the certificates could then go to the store to make the actual purchase (with the cash required as well, of course). Finally, we should state that not everything was rationed. Prominent among unrationed items were vegetables, fruit, candy, many synthetic fabric products, most brands of cigarettes, toys, stationery, radios, and dishes.

Besides trying to guarantee fairly equal distribution of goods through rationing, China tried to maintain access through controlled prices, subsidies, and special allowances. Prices for food and cotton cloth were kept essentially stable from the mid-1950s through the mid-1970s. Even though the prices paid to farmers for grain and oil rose several times during this period, eventually exceeding the urban selling price, the state chose to subsidize the loss. By 1979, this subsidy provided a hidden ten percent addition to every nonagricultural person's living standard.[56] Consumer prices for pork, vegetables, and other nonstaple foods took major jumps only in 1979. But even then, each person on a monthly salary as well as each retiree was given a monthly allowance of 5 yuan to offset the one-third price rise. Living standards were to be maintained at existing levels.[57]

Because incomes had not risen much, food as a proportion of family income was not cheap. In our sample of neighbors and in official studies as well, food costs hovered around 55 percent of total family income.[58] This was no lower than in the 1920s and 1930s.[59] Nor does it compare

56. Calculated on the basis of a stated annual per capita subsidy of 35 yuan and an estimated per capita income of 294 yuan. (Assuming 50 percent of nonagriculturists employed and using the figures from Peking Radio, 5 November 1979, in *FBIS*, 21 November 1979, p. T9, and "Communique on Fulfillment of China's 1978 National Economic Plan," *Beijing Review*, no. 27 [1979]: 40.) Including similar subsidies for pork and vegetables, the total 1979 subsidy may have added as much as 30 percent to nonagricultural household incomes. This assumes that virtually all the reported 20 billion yuan supplement went to nonagriculturists, and that the total per capita nonagricultural income was about 331 yuan. See "Interview with Wang Renshong, Secretary of the CCP Central Committee," *Politika* (Belgrade), 5 October 1980, in *FBIS*, 14 October 1980, p. L1, and "Communique on Fulfillment of China's 1979 National Economic Plan," *Beijing Review*, no. 19 (1980): 23.

57. It is unclear whether collective workers shared in this allowance. Most did not share in the grain differential allowance (*liangshi chae*) which was used to compensate for a slight increase in consumer rice prices in Guangdong in 1965. If the 1965 practice is followed, workers hired after 1979 will not receive a cost of living allowance either. Living standards will be maintained only for old workers.

58. In a late 1980 study of 7,962 households in forty-four cities, food costs totaled 60.6 percent of disposable income and, judging from other studies comparing total and disposable family income, the 60.6 percent figure implies that food costs were 55 percent of total family income—which is exactly the figure given in our sample of neighbors. The 1980 study also reports that food costs were down from 1957 when they totaled 68 percent of disposable income. See State Statistical Bureau, "Investigation of Worker and Staff Livelihood," *Banyuetan* 28 (25 June 1981): 28; and *Zhongquo Baike Nianjian, 1981*, p. 543.

59. Actually, compared to total income, including the many hidden subsidies for food, housing, medical care, and other services, the percentage spent on food most certainly has gone down—though this will not always be apparent to the family which is sensitive only to its cash income and not the income it gets in services and hidden subsidies. The figures for earlier decades are from forty-eight studies reported in L. K. Tao, *The Standard of Living among Chinese Workers* (Shanghai: China Institute of Pacific Relations, 1931), pp.

particularly favorably with market states at the same level of development where food costs are in the same range.[60] With prices for grain kept so low, families may have begun to consume more vegetables and meat than would otherwise have been expected. But the major change in food consumption has been less in total expenditures than in the provision of basic staples at low cost to poor families. With the poorest families in our sample spending only 64 percent on food, as compared to over 70 percent in some studies from the 1920s, the poor may have had more left over to spend on clothing, recreation, and other nonessentials than in the past.[61]

Though many items were rationed and controlled in price, they need not have been distributed completely equally. More could have been given to some regions than others. More could have been given to people of higher administrative rank, as in the Soviet Union. Since goods were distributed in large part by bureaucratic decision rather than supply and demand, there was ample opportunity for personal favoritism and corruption.

Distribution is clearly not equal across all kinds of cities. In the most general terms, we found that supplies and ration levels of most goods, both food and consumer items, were more abundant in the largest cities and tended to decrease with each step down the administrative hierarchy of cities. Peking, as the national capital, seemed to enjoy advantages even in comparison with the other national level cities, Shanghai and Tientsin. But there were variations from this pattern. Items like coal and cloth were more abundantly supplied in northern cities because of the colder climate. Commune and county towns in Guangdong were better supplied with

---

31–37, and four other studies cited in Charles R. Roll, "Population Control in China," (Paper presented at the Conference on the Lessons of China's Development Experience, Puerto Rico, 1976).

60. In 1965 in urban India, food expenditures averaged 60 percent of total family expenditures, which is very similar to Chinese figures for disposable income. Around 1960, in Korea, Thailand, the Philippines, and Taiwan, food expenditures were again in a similar range, constituting 56 to 60 percent of total family expenditures. That the proportion spent on food declines steadily with increasing development and rising income is well known and bears the title "Engel's law." To illustrate, in the 1970s, the average American family spent less than a fourth of its posttax, postsavings budget on food. See U.S. Bureau of the Census, *Statistical Abstract of the U.S.* (Washington: U.S. Government Printing Office, 1976), p. 396.

61. Arranging families by per capita incomes, the poorest fifth of families in our sample spent 64 percent and the richest fifth 40 percent of total income on food. In a 1929–30 survey of Shanghai workers, the poorest fifth spent 72 percent of their total income on food. They could spend this much only by most of them going in debt—a phenomenon which is rare today. Calculated from Shanghai City Government, Bureau of Social Affairs, *Standard of Living of Shanghai Laborers, 1934*, pp. 102, 107.

perishable food items like fish than Peking, reflecting the abundance of fishponds and a well-developed fishing industry in that province. Small towns were also less affected by the radicals' attempt to ban all peasant marketing from urban areas than were large cities like Peking. On balance, though, consumers were still best off in China's largest cities and perhaps worst off in medium-sized cities.[62] People in middle-range cities looked upon business trips to Peking or Shanghai as providing shopping sprees (for unrationed items). It was also in these small cities that long queues at shops seemed most common.

Deviations from equality in consumption also applies to different occupations in the same city. This fits what we know from other socialist societies. Central leaders in Peking do not stand in line with their fellow citizens. They have special bureaus to supply their daily needs and special stores in Peking at which they are allowed to shop. Throughout China, it is only higher officials that have regular access to chauffeured cars (with the type of car carefully graded by rank of the official). Also, higher level officials are supplied cooks and housekeepers, and many can sightsee and eat better food on official trips and at official banquets.[63] Dissidents and foreign journalists have begun to call attention to some of these privileges, and even the official press has begun to lash out at the frequent abuse of official position.[64] So clearly some of the tendencies present in the Soviet Union are also present in China. Nevertheless, the situation in China seems less extreme than in some other socialist societies.

The institutionalized privileges are restricted to a narrow band of the very top elite who are above rank thirteen in the official hierarchy of twenty-four ranks. In 1981, we are told, these officials, leading and helping lead ministries and departments in the capital, the provinces, and major cities, totaled some 80,000 in number.[65] There were thus fewer than one high level official (*gaoji ganbu*) for every 1,000 people in the nonagricul-

---

62. These conclusions are based upon comparison of the ration amounts for a variety of items claimed to exist in cities at different levels in the urban hierarchy by informants from those cities, figures which were collected during our interviews in special, standardized forms. The detailed evidence, not reproduced here, can be found in Parish, "Destratification in the People's Republic of China," p. 160.

63. For a list of cars, cooks, and other perquisites to which higher levels are entitled see "Regulations on Benefits for High-ranking Cadres," Radio Lhasa, 3 November 1980, in *FBIS,* 4 November 1980, p. Q1.

64. For example, see Fox Butterfield, *China: Alive in the Bitter Sea* (New York: Times Books, 1982), chap. 3.

65. The source for this figure gives 80,000 plus as the number of officials with at least the post of vice-head of a bureau (*ju*), department (*si*), or military division (shi)—which suggests ranks 1–12 in the official hierarchy. See, *Workers Daily,* 27 March 1981, p. 3, and the list of ranks by office in *Zhongyang Caizheng Fagui Huibian, 1956* (Peking, 1956), p. 228.

tural labor force and only about one high level official for every 225 officials (*ganbu*) of any rank. Even if their perquisites were worth some multiple of their salaries, they are such a small proportion of all income earners that the addition of their hidden income would have only a marginal impact on the total distribution of income.

Much of the official press criticism and the anger against special privileges that one finds in talking with people from China is not against these institutionalized privileges. Rather, it is against the noninstitutionalized forms—getting a son into college, getting access to special meals without paying or paying only a nominal sum, having children avoid criminal punishment, demanding gifts before performing a service, and so on. It was against these kinds of special privileges, particularly in the economic area, that many court prosecutions were launched in 1982. These privileges are not restricted to high level cadres but are available for anyone who has control over some scarce resource that is distributed by bureaucratic means. This includes not only the official who allocates steel but also the butcher who keeps some extra meat under the counter. These sorts of privileges do less to increase the income of high officials than simply to distribute hidden income more randomly up and down much of the service hierarchy.

Our data on middle and lower level cadres suggests that the institutionalized access to special consumption goods did not extend very far down the official hierarchy in the mid-1970s. As would be expected from a survey of about 1,600 employed individuals, we have only one high level official in our sample. Most of the officials in our sample are in the more modest ranks of sixteen to twenty-two in the hierarchy of twenty-four ranks. Nevertheless, these officials being the most numerous, a study of how their consumption compares with others' gives some indication of the pervasiveness of institutionalized privilege.

Income per capita does not rise as sharply for administrators and professionals as does individual income (figure 3). Professionals and administrators often had spouses and children who made low salaries and therefore reduced the total average income of the household. What differences in per capita incomes remained were only modestly reflected in consumption and not tied to administrative rank (figure 4). In the 1970s, some goods were much easier to buy and more widely distributed than others. Though still rationed, bicycles were common, as were watches and radios. Ninety-two percent of all households in our sample had at least one watch, and 76 percent had a bicycle. Variations among households showed up more in numbers of bicycles and watches owned than in the presence or total absence of these goods (see the right hand scale of figure 4). Sewing machines, electric fans, cameras, and televisions were scarcer.[66]

Simple visual inspection of the raw data in figure 4 suggests that the distribution of goods has not departed radically from the distribution of incomes. There are certain irregularities in the table having to do in part with random fluctuations in a small sample. And there are some more consistent patterns with consumption regularizing with occupation. The scarce items such as electric fans, cameras, and televisions have been more regularly available to those in higher level than to those in lower level occupations. However, to the extent that this bias in distribution exists, it has been slanted as much to doctors, professors, and other higher professionals as it has been to the majority of middle-ranking administrative cadres. Through the mid-1970s, then, these middle rank cadres were unable to intervene in the distribution system in any systematic way that would have given them consistent material advantages and a large hidden income. Our earlier description of cash income alone, then, has given us a fairly representative picture of the distribution of total material advantages.[67]

Also of concern is whether sufficient quantities of goods, both rationed and unrationed, are produced to meet consumer demands. By the 1970s there were some serious problems, since for the first three decades of the new regime, the emphasis had been on production rather than consump-

66. By 1980, ownership of electric fans and televisions had increased significantly, but all the other items were distributed much as we found them in the mid-1970s. In a national sample from the forty-four largest cities, each 100 families had 224 wristwatches, 127 bicycles, 85 radios, 66 sewing machines, 32 televisions, 22 electric fans, 6 tape recorders, and 3 cameras. See State Statistical Bureau, "Investigation of Worker and Staff Livelihood," *Banyuetan* 28 (1981): 29.

In the pre-Cultural Revolution period a system of "industrial item coupons" (*gongye juan*) was used to distribute many manufactured consumer goods, and the number of such coupons one received was proportional to one's salary. This particular part of the rationing system, then, favored the highly paid. By the 1970s this system had apparently been discontinued, although our informants were uncertain of the details—some claimed that such coupons were still in use for a few items but that new coupons were no longer being issued regularly.

67. The points made here are further substantiated by regression equations. In these equations, the items in figure 4 were more common in higher level administrative centers, in larger households with more potential consumers, and in households with higher per capita incomes. Once these conditions were controlled, higher professionals and administrators were special only in owning slightly more of the fans, cameras, and televisions. Lower professionals (teachers, nurses, etc.) were special in owning more of the rationed bicycles and sewing machines.

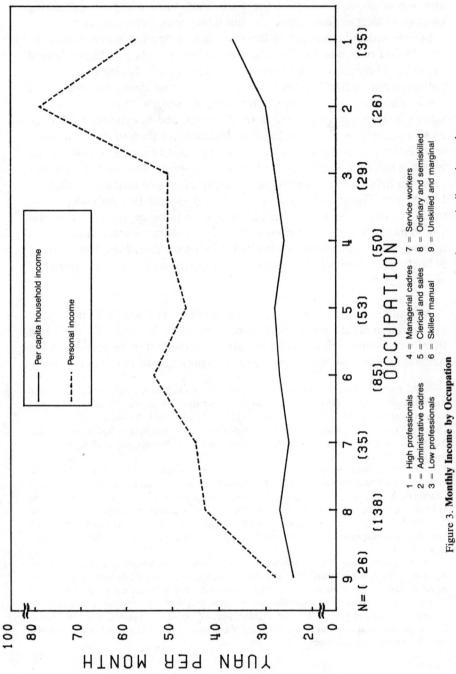

Figure 3. **Monthly Income by Occupation**
Source: 1972–78 Chinese urban sample, weighted subsample of economically active males.

1 = High professionals   4 = Managerial cadres   7 = Service workers
2 = Administrative cadres   5 = Clerical and sales   8 = Ordinary and semiskilled
3 = Low professionals   6 = Skilled manual   9 = Unskilled and marginal

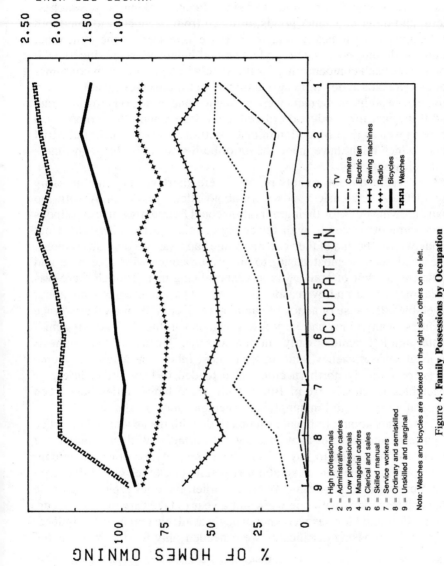

NUMBER PER HOME

2.50
2.00
1.50
1.00

% OF HOMES OWNING

100
75
50
25
0

OCCUPATION

1 = High professionals
2 = Administrative cadres
3 = Low professionals
4 = Managerial cadres
5 = Clerical and sales
6 = Skilled manual
7 = Service workers
8 = Ordinary and semiskilled
9 = Unskilled and marginal

——— TV
– – – Camera
·········· Electric fan
+++ Sewing machines
+++ Radio
▬▬▬ Bicycles
⌐⌐⌐⌐ Watches

Note: Watches and bicycles are indexed on the right side, others on the left.

Figure 4. **Family Possessions by Occupation**
Source: 1972–78 Chinese urban sample, economically active males.

tion. In line with this emphasis, investment grew to over one-third of gross national product. The major investment funds went to heavy industry, making steel, coal, lathes, locomotives, and other producer goods. The share of investment funds to light industry, making pots, watches, cloth, and other consumer goods, dropped from one-eighth to one-tenth of the investment in heavy industry.[68] As we have seen, at the same time, many small and independent collective and independent producers who could have been compensating for the state's lack of interest in consumer goods were closed down. In agriculture as well state investment remained minimal. In addition, farmers were forced to concentrate on growing grain and to neglect the production of edible oil, fruits, and other commercial crops as well as the production of mats, buttons, and other light industrial goods which might have made the lot of both rural and urban consumers more pleasant.

As a result, our informants report severe shortages in some areas by the 1970s. A few basic goods were about adequate. A family with too many growing boys for their grain ration could frequently borrow coupons from some other family with fewer big eaters. Most families came out about even at the end of the year, and some had a surplus of grain coupons. The need seen as most basic, to supply urbanites with a reliable and sufficient amount of grain, was in general being met. Though there was variation by year and by season, there were few major complaints about vegetables. Because of a lack of canning, refrigeration, and other storage facilities, many cities had very few vegetables in the slow growing midwinter and late summer/early autumn seasons. Because of the emphasis on local self-sufficiency, and on lower cost tubers and cabbages, some cities, particularly northern cities, also tended to have little variety of vegetables to choose from. But outside these limits, cities have been moderately successful in supplying vegetables most of the time.[69]

Complaints about cloth had as much to do with the absence of varieties of patterns and textures as with absolute shortages. With care and in the absence of any need to buy towels, handkerchiefs, or other items containing cotton, one can make about two suits of clothes out of one's 4.5 to 5.5 meters of cloth a year. As noted earlier, factories typically provide blue collar workers with one work suit a year to take care of work needs. Both radios and bicycles were increasingly available in the 1970s. Indeed, by 1978, purchasing certificates were needed only for the more highly

68. Li Dingzhong, "Some Problems Concerning Accumulation," *People's Daily,* 22 October 1979.

69. Also see G. William Skinner, "Vegetable Supply and Marketing in Chinese Cities," *China Quarterly* 78 (1978): 733–93. More recently, in 1981, there were recurring press complaints about urban vegetable shortages.

desired Shanghai and Tientsin brands of wristwatches in some cities. In Canton, local brands were unrationed.

However, many other products were much scarcer, and hence more tightly rationed or more likely to draw a crowd once they came on the market. Meat, oil, fish, and bean curd were almost universally perceived to be insufficient, except in Peking, Shanghai, and Tientsin, where some of these goods were at times unrationed. In the major cities, a family of four would be restricted to about one and one-quarter quarts of cooking oil per month.[70] This was a major constraint on the preferred form of stir-fry cooking, even when meat coupons could be used to buy lard to help make up part of the difference. Eggs and chickens were rare in the market, and outside of Peking and Shanghai (where it was illegal), many urban residents raised chickens in a small cage in a kitchen or some other room.[71] Fruit was only sporadically available and then of poor quality. Many traditional processed foods were simply not available because the street hawkers and small stores who used to make them had been driven out of business.

Consumer durables were often scarce as well. Given the timber shortage throughout China, furniture was in scarce supply and often of shoddy quality.[72] Idle youth turned to making furniture out of scrap pieces of wood, but they only filled part of the need. Synthetic textiles were only barely beginning to meet demand for a greater variety of cloths and clothes. Sewing machines remained below demand. What televisions were available during the mid-1970s usually had only a small black and white screen and sold for as much as a year's salary for the average worker. Many other goods of better or more novel quality remained only as "display goods" in the store window or on a shelf out of reach and were not for ordinary customer purchase.[73]

Given these shortages, customers tried to cope in whatever way they could. One way was to form special relationships with persons in the distribution network. Informants report a saying in the city of Canton that

70. Based on .25 kilogram per person per month. Smaller places would have less.

71. In our weighted Lingnan sample, 69 percent of all homes raised chickens while 32 percent raised rabbits or other animals as well. In 1981, urban residents in the northeastern province of Heilongjiang were still being encouraged to raise more chickens to compensate for market shortfalls. See Harbin Radio, 14 May 1981, in *FBIS,* 19 May 1981, p. S1.

72. According to our informants. See also more recently Peking Radio, 10 October 1979, in *FBIS,* 12 October 1979, p. L7. At that time, timber shortages were so severe that even those with purchase rights could not pick up their furniture.

73. For vivid accounts of the frustration caused by such display items, see "The Big Fish" and "Nixon's Press Corps," in Jo-hsi Chen, *The Execution of Mayor Yin* (Bloomington: Indiana University Press, 1978). More recently color television sets—even more extravagantly priced—have become available.

one should maintain relations with "three valuables" (*sanbao*)—a doctor, a truck driver, and a sales clerk. The doctor would help one beat the lines and medical shortages at hospitals. The truck driver could get one cheap goods from markets outside the city. The sales clerk could notify one when scarce goods like electric fans, televisions, and better clothing were about to appear on the market and might "forget" to check purchases off on one's ration book. The Chinese press repeats similar themes. Recent accounts complain of truck drivers buying goods here and there for family and friends and even for strangers at a profit. They complain of factories falsely declaring consumer goods damaged and selling them at a discount, and of sales clerks selling televisions "through the back door."[74] Foreigners, including one of us, also report goods being brought from under the counter when it is discovered that the visitor is not just an ordinary customer. Thus, many of the tendencies toward finagling the system had begun to appear in China by the 1970s as they had appeared in the socialist societies of Eastern Europe in earlier years.

Customers suffered not only from shortages and lack of variety but also from poor quality and service. In spite of the radicals' emphasis on Mao's slogan "serve the people," poor service standards had become a major problem by the 1970s—with many former stores closed and many open stores understaffed or staffed by sullen clerks. This was in part a consequence of the three-decade drive to change Chinese cities from consumer into producer cities. The change can be seen in statistics for the number of service centers and stores that remained open. Throughout the country, the number of retail service centers is said to have been reduced from 1 million in 1957 to 219,000 in late 1979, even as the population to be served was getting larger and larger.[75] Including small snack stands, the city of Peking had 10,200 restaurants in 1949 when the population was less than 2 million. But by the 1970s, when the total urban population was almost 5 million and incomes were higher and far more out-of-town visitors arrived on official business, there were only 656 restaurants to serve everyone. The number of shops in Peking had declined from 70,000 in the early 1950s to 10,000 in 1980. Similarly, in Peking, the number of bicycle repair centers declined from the 780 of 1957 to only

74. *People's Daily,* 8 April 1978, p. 4; 20 May 1978, p. 3; 5 April 1978, p. 1; and *Da Gong Bao* (Hong Kong) 16 November 1977, p. 1.

75. "Interview with Commerce Minister Wang Lei," Peking Radio, 31 December 1980, in *FBIS,* 5 January 1981, p. L13.

169 in 1973, while the population of bicycles was exploding.[76] Knife sharpeners, pot menders, carters, and others who used to roam the street offering services virtually disappeared from some cities.

The results were obvious. For the Chinese urbanite it began to mean long treks to the market, standing in line, or simply going without. Restaurants were packed, with new customers guarding their hoped for place by standing behind previous customers while they ate. People who needed special services such as clothes making had to "rush all over the city." Those needing their cotton quilts refluffed often had "to get up well before daybreak and stand in line." In the absence of washing machines and the closing of public laundries, washing clothes was said to have become "a burden only second to cooking." Indeed, cooking was a major problem in a land without refrigeration, where marketing had to be done almost daily, and where there were long lines in front of the fish counter and for other popular but scarce items. As one worker reported, "If we have any spare time, we are so busy eating, drinking, and attending to household duties that we go through the whole day with aching heads. How can we possibly have the strength to think of the four modernizations, or carry them out?"[77] In an interview by a journalist from the *Workers' Daily,* this worker and others elaborate on how members of each family set forth into the streets on their one day off in the week according to a carefully worked out battle plan. "One goes out to buy rice, another coal, another vegetables, another meat. . . . And if all goes well, the tasks are completed in half a day."[78] The result in some places was for people to "become more tired on Sundays than on working days."[79] This kind of situation was particularly severe in new working class districts in the suburbs, where factories have skimped on facilities in order to save money for production or where factory housing plans ran ahead of city commerce bureau plans for urban service.[80] Thus what might seem admirable at first—the emphasis on production rather than the emphasis on the make-

76. *People's Daily,* 27 April 1978, p. 3; *Xinhua* (Peking), 28 May 1980, in *FBIS,* 2 June 1980, p. R2. The restaurant example is so drastic as to be only slightly misrepresented by the exclusion of new canteens at places of work. The same can be said for the figures on shops, where the 1980 versions tended to be larger than those in the 1950s.

77. See, on these complaints, editorial, *Beijing Daily,* 25 July 1979, p. 1, in *FBIS,* 9 August 1979, p. R2; and Peking Radio, 18 July 1979, in *FBIS,* 23 July 1979, p. L12.

78. *Workers' Daily,* 13 November 1979, cited in the *Christian Science Monitor,* 14 November 1979, p. 3.

79. Peking Radio, 18 July 1979.

80. On the same tendencies, in the Soviet Union, see James H. Bater, *The Soviet City* (Beverly Hills: Sage, 1980), pp. 117–22, 130–33.

work service jobs of other developing cities—turns out to have been a severe drain on the energies and pleasures of urban workers at all levels.

Consumers also suffer the increased sullenness and unresponsiveness of many service personnel. Chinese patterns were beginning to repeat those of the Soviet Union. Recent Chinese analyses pointed to the "iron rice bowl" problem in shops as in factories, whereby workers suffered no threat of demotion or firing because of poor service. There was no extra income for good service. Chinese sources note that urban youth particularly shun service jobs. With unified assignment by the labor bureau, young people have to accept the work they are given.[81] But not all of them took their assigned jobs. There are examples in our interviews of youth sent to the countryside refusing to come back to the city when the only opportunity offered them was to be a waiter in a restaurant, conductor on a bus, or a clerk in a store. Youth, particularly those with good education from intellectual family backgrounds, were often not content with lesser service jobs.

What is more difficult to interpret is why these service jobs are seen as having such low status. There seems to be an element here that is common to socialist societies. Interviews in other socialist societies show that people accord different occupations about the same prestige levels as in the capitalist West, except that service occupations tend to be ranked somewhat lower and skilled blue collar jobs somewhat higher.[82] The labeling of service work as nonproductive, and the according of such high prestige to the productive proletariat may have had a more pervasive effect than most people imagined.

Conclusions

The distinctive urban policies and organizational strategies sketched in chapters 2–3 have also been applied to the distribution of supplies and services to urbanites, and the radical policies of the Cultural Revolution decade had their effect in this realm as well. The distribution system as it existed in the early 1970s had several basic goals. Goods and services were to be distributed to a considerable extent by bureaucratic allocation rather than by market forces. Rational planning by the authorities was supposed to prevail over consumer preference, and this would ensure that

81. Xue Muqiao, "Noted Economist on Employment," *Beijing Review,* no. 33 (1979): 14. The term "service jobs" has a more restricted meaning than that implied by "service sector." It involves personal service trades such as barbers and waiters, but does not include such jobs as bank tellers or nurses.

82. On the interpretation of European socialist prestige studies, see Connor, *Socialism, Politics, and Equality,* pp. 259–66.

an adequate supply of needed goods and services was available to all urbanites. In line with the emphasis on production rather than consumption, a supply of goods above the level of "an adequate supply" was not of great concern. The authorities did not want to expend scarce resources catering to consumer whims, and they did not want status differences within urban society to lead to disparities in consumption standards and differentiated life styles. The relative uniformity of dress and living standards so often commented upon by foreign visitors during these years was not the product simply of poverty and necessity, but of a conscious, egalitarian policy of the government. In addition to these primary goals in distribution and consumption, the authorities also wanted to achieve a positive service atmosphere, minimal corruption, and a decentralized system for coping with special welfare needs.

During this period, bureaucratic controls triumphed to an extent unusual even in other socialist societies. During the Cultural Revolution decade, relative equality of consumption was also obtained to an unusual degree, and the separate consumption styles and perquisites of intellectuals and bureaucrats one sees in other socialist societies were largely suppressed (although our sample of neighbors does not allow us to examine the situation of the highest-ranking cadres). As to whether basic needs were being met and an adequate amount of various goods and services was being supplied, there is much more room for debate. The evidence seems fairly clear to us that urban medical and public health needs were being provided for fairly well, especially in comparison with other developing countries. Urban schooling had been universalized, minimal needs of grain and cotton and some other items were being assured, and a system of fringe benefits and welfare assistance that is fairly extensive in comparison with other Third World societies had developed. But at the same time many items that are not consumer frills—pork, cooking oil, fish, fruits, and so forth—were scarce and unreliably supplied and were felt to be quite insufficient. Housing was very cramped, even in relation to many other developing societies, and the bureaucratic rigidities in housing allocation were the source of frequent and bitter complaints. Certain groups, such as those with bad class or political labels or simply those not in with the bureaucratic gatekeepers of the distribution system, were particularly discriminated against.

Overall, our informants felt that their needs, at least for food items and housing, were not being as well supplied as they had been before the Cultural Revolution or even, for those with longer memories, back in the years 1956–58. Of course, it is hard to know how much faith to place on claims of a bygone "golden age" for consumers, and we know that some items, such as wristwatches, bicycles, and radios, were increasingly avail-

able during the 1970s. But official figures on the decline in housing and
the fact that an increasing number of items became subject to rationing
during the 1970s suggest there was some truth to the popular impression
that the urban supply system was not meeting needs, or at least demand,
as well as it had in the past. It is true that urbanites did not face the
specter of starvation or the need to sell daughters or go begging on the
street to make ends meet, as had occurred at times before 1949. But the
attempt by families to meet their basic consumption needs, particularly
in regard to food items, was seen as an increasingly complex and frus-
trating business. In a culture where food and its preparation and consumption are such central concerns, stressed even while clothing and
material possessions may be neglected, this was a serious problem point
in the distribution system.[83]

So although the urban distribution system of the 1970s was successful
in reaching its goals to a considerable extent, it nonetheless spawned
problems that could not easily be ignored. Urban schools were providing
a basic education for all, but that education appeared to be of increasingly
poor quality and to be unsuitable for detecting and training people to
acquire high level specialized skills. The geared-down schooling of the
Cultural Revolution decade produced frustration among the many urban
youth who had to join the exodus to the countryside after graduation.
Fewer serious problems were visible in the health field, but phenomena
such as excess demand for medical care and the dispensing of care by
unqualified personnel occasioned some concern.

Outside the educational realm, the most serious problems concerned
the distribution of housing and consumer goods. As we have just stressed,
urbanites perceived an environment in which their needs were not being
met as well as in the past and in which, had they money to spend, they
often could not purchase items they wanted to buy. Many urbanites felt
trapped in poor housing or housing inconveniently distant from their work
place. In this environment many began to lose faith in the distribution
system and to feel that one had to pursue special angles to get your needs
met. One had to cultivate special ties with gatekeepers guarding access
to various goods and services or with truckdrivers or others who were
able to go around the barriers in the system, or one had to engage in illicit
trade, black marketeering, and chicken raising. The time and energy required to take care of one's needs—whether legally or illegally—constituted a drain from the productive work that was supposed to be the focus
of the lives of socialist urbanites. Some who managed through various

83. On the significance of food in China traditionally, see K. C. Chang, ed., *Food in
Chinese Culture* (New Haven: Yale University Press, 1977).

devices to gain access to resources that were not readily available might feel quite pleased with themselves, but by the same token, their growing cynicism about the official system of distribution was confirmed. Some would feel increasingly that the ones in the best position to manipulate the system by "going by the back door" were the high-ranking cadres, who didn't have to face the frustrations and privations that ordinary urbanites did.

It could be argued that the popular support that the CCP developed in urban areas in the 1950s depended to a considerable extent on the ability of the new government to equitably and honestly distribute goods and services so that popular consumption needs would be met at low and stable prices. By the 1970s the neglect of consumption in favor of production had produced a supply situation that was not meeting popular demands. In the atmosphere of shortage that developed, equality in distribution was not sufficient comfort, and in fact urbanites began to doubt that equality of access and honesty in distribution were being preserved. If the potential political repercussions of consumer grievances were not already apparent to China's leaders in the period we are dealing with, they were brought home rather vividly by the events in Poland in 1980.

In the period since our interviews a number of changes have been initiated in the urban distribution system to deal with the problems that surfaced during the radical decade. Changes in the school system have been the most extensive. Almost all of the radical innovations in schooling have been repudiated. Equal access to neighborhood schools has given way once again to a hierarchy of schools of varying quality, entrance to which is governed primarily by scores young people achieve on entrance examinations. The "keypoint schools" that crown the system receive the most resources and the best teachers and receive as their students the top performers in the entrance examinations. Within the schools the emphasis on academics is back with a vengeance, political and labor activities have been cut back substantially, strict tests and grading are again in vogue, and the authority of the teachers is once again stressed. Those who do best in school and in college entrance examinations can once again go directly to the university, without any stint of labor in the countryside, and can expect assignment to a good job after they graduate. As one might anticipate, competition for university selections is particularly fierce, and a thriving business of home tutoring to prepare young aspirants has sprung up once again. So the role of schools in sorting and channeling talent is once again the order of the day, and urban youths have to prepare for rigorous competition in order to succeed. Considerable family energy and time is directed toward children's study and their success in school.

In health care, changes are less apparent, but the emphasis on medical standards and training has superseded the previous stress on breaking down status barriers between doctors and nurses. The provision of medical care for the urban population is more strongly emphasized. To cope with the excess demand for care, a minor liberalization has been adopted that allows some retired or unemployed medical personnel to see patients on a private, fee-paying basis in their homes.[84] Review procedures are also being instituted to check the competency of medical personnel trained during the Cultural Revolution with an eye to demoting or retraining those who cannot pass muster.

In the welfare system, some benefits, such as retirement pensions, have been increased, and discrimination based upon class origin labels is supposed to be eliminated. But overall the minimal changes in this realm suggest official satisfaction with the system adopted in the 1950s, which to a considerable extent survived the Cultural Revolution.

Several measures have been adopted in the realm of housing. Urban cadres, intellectuals, and former capitalists who lost their housing during the Cultural Revolution have had it (or comparable facilities) returned to them. (Actually this change began earlier, starting in about 1973, according to informants.) In accord with the new emphasis on stimulating work contributions via rewards, but contrary to the previous egalitarian emphasis, a set of policies is being implemented to reward intellectuals and other high status categories with more space and better housing than other urbanites.[85] In many large cities major drives to construct new housing began after 1978. The authorities recognize that this new construction will not be enough to meet pent-up demand, and they have encouraged some localities to experiment with allowing individuals to undertake construction of private housing in urban areas.[86] Still, in view of the very great scarcity of land, not to mention building materials, it seems unlikely that this last tactic will make much of a dent on housing needs in China's

84. See *Xinhua* (Peking), 5 September 1980, in *FBIS,* 9 September 1980, p. L32.

85. One list of criteria for allocating housing in Canton ranks the deserving into eight categories. Deserving intellectuals and army personnel end up near the top of the list (along with overseas Chinese), while families who simply live in very overcrowded conditions rank eighth. See Guangdong Radio, 8 May 1980, in *FBIS,* 13 May 1980, p. P2.

86. See Peking Radio, 23 July 1979, in *FBIS,* 26 July 1979, p. O1. The city of Fuzhou (Foochow) in Fujian Province has been publicized as a leading city in promoting new private housing construction. Some cities have also undertaken to build housing that is in turn sold to private families, using that bourgeois device, the installment plan. (See *Xinhua* (Peking), 15 April 1980, in *FBIS,* 15 April 1980, p. L1.) The numbers involved seem quite small in most places, however. One set of figures lists only 780 plus housing units sold to families in fifty different cities—*Zhongguo Baike Nianjian, 1981,* p. 540.

large cities, where queuing up for an officially allocated apartment is likely to remain dominant.[87]

On the consumer goods front as well, a series of reforms have been instituted. Peasants are once again allowed to sell their produce privately in specially designated market areas within cities, and by 1980 there were two thousand such markets in China's largest cities. The thirteen peasant markets in Peking were in 1979 supplying about one-tenth as many vegetables as supplied by the state vegetable markets in the city. In the countryside the policy of local grain self-sufficiency was relaxed to encourage growing vegetables and other cash crops, procurement prices were raised in 1979, and the level of state investment in agriculture was modestly increased in an effort to increase the amount of food supplies available for marketing in cities. More consumer items have begun to be imported from abroad. As noted in chapter 3, restrictions on collective and private employment have been relaxed, and the authorities hope that the new shops, repair facilities, and service facilities of these types that spring up will not only relieve unemployment but reduce consumer complaints about shortages and service. These and other measures seem to have produced some success in improving urban food supplies and easing consumer grievances. For example, pork began to be sold without ration coupons once again in some cities in 1979. But shortages of a number of items remained fairly serious in the early 1980s—of tea, cooking oil, bean curd, fish, eggs, sugar, soap powder, and leather goods, for example.[88] The state's decision to raise the cost of certain food items to cover some of the costs of paying the peasants more, combined with the relaxation of controls over commerce and employment that has taken place, also meant an upsurge of inflation after 1979, a new source of worry for both the government and consumers.

The measures adopted in regard to corruption and special privileges in distribution have a mixed character. On the one hand the authorities hope that by increasing supplies and by emphasizing legalism and rational bu-

87. The scarcity of land is illustrated by the fact that in 1980 it was revealed that in previous years about one-fifth of all urban park lands had been taken over for other uses (Peking Radio, 15 October 1980, in *FBIS*, 17 October 1980, p. L2), and that large areas in many college campuses throughout the country that had been taken over for use by the PLA during the Cultural Revolution were still being so occupied in 1980, in spite of government edicts that they be returned to university use (see, for example, *Xinhua* (Peking), 29 September 1980, in *FBIS*, 30 September 1980, pp. L18–19; *Xinhua* (Peking), 13 October 1979, in *FBIS*, 15 October 1979, p. L1).

88. See Timothy McNulty, "Chinese Just Can't Swallow Tea Shortage," *Chicago Tribune*, 14 June 1981, section 3, p. 13. However, a Chinese news report claims that the improved supply situation allowed the number of rationed items to be reduced from 73 in 1978 to 17 in 1982. See *Xinhua* (Peking), 9 January 1983, in *FBIS*, 11 January 1983, p. K2.

reaucratic procedures they can close the "back doors" that have been used to gain special access. There have also been a number of prominent examples of powerful people being exposed and criticized for grabbing special privileges—eating banquets at restaurants without paying full price, for example.[89] But on the other hand, the post-Mao policies represent a rejection of the extreme egalitarianism of the previous period and stress using consumption differentials to reward contributions to society. Insofar as the "new class" of leading bureaucrats can be argued (by themselves, of course) to make special contributions, does this mean that they now can obtain and increase their consumption advantages not by finagling, but by normal bureaucratic procedures? From press articles in the early 1980s it appeared that the authorities were having a difficult time convincing the public that no privileged bureaucratic situation existed in China.[90] Though small in number this group and its privileges continue to elicit moral reproach, and even jealousy, in a society emphasizing equality.

In many respects the distribution system developed in China seems to have more in common with other socialist societies than other Third World cities. Even in comparison with Eastern Europe, though, urban China in the 1970s was distinctive. Most notable were the unusually high development of bureaucratic allocation procedures rather than markets and an unusual degree of equality in consumption, at least for those below the very top of the political hierarchy. These distinctive features have now been modified somewhat by the post-Mao reforms, making the Chinese distribution system less unusual. But to date these reforms still seem to be mainly "at the edges" and do not fundamentally undermine the predominantly bureaucratic and egalitarian nature of the distribution system. This system was seen by the CCP as very successful in eliminating most of the evils of the prerevolutionary market system, but the problems that plague socialist distribution systems elsewhere—rigidity, low quality goods, poor service, frustrated consumer demands, red tape—arose to cause new problems, particularly during the radical decade. Whether minor tinkering will be seen as sufficient to alleviate these problems, or whether the authorities will eventually feel pressed to make more drastic shifts away from the system they have grown accustomed to, as Yugoslavia and Hungary have managed to do, remains an open question.

89. The Minister of Commerce, Wang Lei, was disciplined for such behavior in a widely publicized incident—*Beijing Review*, no. 44 (1980): 6–7.

90. See, for example, Kong Qian, "Correction of 'Oppose the Bureaucratic Class,' " *Liberation Daily*, 9 February 1981, in *FBIS*, 10 February 1981, p. L1; Lin Yoye and Shen Che, "Commenting on the So-Called Opposition to the Class of Bureaucrats," *Red Flag* 5 (1981): 12–18, in *FBIS*, 31 March 1981, pp. L1–8.

2 Family Behavior

In part 1 we described the political economy of Chinese cities as it developed in the 1950s and then was transformed under radical tutelage in the 1970s. The post-1949 Chinese urban political economy has a number of distinctive features, among which an unusual degree of bureaucratic control and allocation, a heavy stress on achieving equality and basic economic security, and the development of tight-knit and highly organized neighborhoods and work units stand out in particular. In the three chapters that follow we examine what impact the transformation to this distinctive form of urban organization has had on various aspects of Chinese family life.

Chinese rulers for centuries have recognized the importance of the proper functioning of family units for social harmony and stability, and Confucian philosophy was filled with familial metaphors used in describing the political realm, for example, in the term "father-mother officials" (*fumu guan*). Then, too, it would be hard to find another culture in which family loyalty and obligations have been so emphasized and successfully inculcated. While respecting part of these family traditions, the Chinese Communists were nonetheless heirs to the tradition of iconoclastic criticism of family customs of the May Fourth movement of 1919. Although they recognized that family changes had already occurred in Chinese cities as a result of economic changes and the influence of the May Fourth ideas, they were convinced that further major changes in family life would be needed to produce the kind of modern socialist society they envisioned. After 1949 they attempted to bring about such changes both by direct family policy edicts and propaganda and by changing the institutional environment in which families are formed and function. It is the task of the next three chapters to examine how the urban Chinese family has been affected by such efforts over the last thirty years.

The confrontation of the new government and institutional structure with the urban family raises several issues. To what extent have traditional family customs and relationships survived the revolutionary changes, and why? Insofar as changes have occurred, have they been due mostly to conscious government manipulation of family life or to urbanites' adapting to their changed institutional environment? Are the changes in family life that have occurred ones that are common with economic development in many other societies, or have the distinctive features of Chinese urbanism left their stamp? For example, has the unusual degree of economic equality achieved reduced the importance of social status differences in mate choice and family life? Are there signs that various kinds of family disorganization common in cities in other developing societies—marital instability, illegitimacy, neglect of the aged—are on the increase in China as well? Or have the novel features of the Chinese case produced a different and perhaps unanticipated set of family problems? These are some of the questions that will guide our discussion of contemporary urban family patterns in part 2. We begin this discussion by examining the institutions by which family units are formed: mate choice and marriage.

5　Mate Choice and Marriage

For the most part, the policies toward marriage implemented by the Chinese Communists are extensions of reform efforts initiated by earlier reformers and formalized in the Nationalist government's Civil Code of 1931.[1] Many of the major policies of the new government were codified in the Marriage Law of 1950, which was issued in modestly revised form in 1980. Other policies evolved over the years in the form of official statements and administrative regulations. The major emphases can be stated fairly simply. Marriages should be based upon the free choice of the young couple, rather than arranged by parents and marriage go-betweens. There should be no demands for gifts or material goods as a precondition for the match, although modest wedding presents are allowed. Press discussions have made it clear that certain criteria for picking a mate are seen as appropriate (personal compatibility, political attitudes, and character judgments) while others are seen as inappropriate (wealth, good looks, sexual attraction, family "connections").[2]

In the government's eyes, marriage begins when the couple carries out

1. For reviews of changing family policy in China, see Olga Lang, *Chinese Family and Society* (New Haven: Yale University Press, 1946); C. K. Yang, *The Chinese Family in the Communist Revolution* (Cambridge: MIT Press, 1959); and M. J. Meijer, *Marriage Law and Policy in the Chinese People's Republic* (Hong Kong: Hong Kong University Press, 1971). For descriptions of marriage customs in Chinese cities earlier in this century, see, in addition to Lang, Sidney Gamble, *How Chinese Families Live in Peiping* (New York: Funk and Wagnalls, 1933), chap. 10; and Sophie Sa, "Marriage among the Taiwanese of pre-1945 Taipei," unpublished paper.

2. See the discussion in Lu Yang, *The Correct Handling of Love, Marriage, and Family Problems* (Jinan: Shandong People's Publishing House, 1960), translated in *Chinese Sociology and Anthropology* 1, no. 3 (1969). The 1950 law gave the minimum marriage ages as 18 for females and 20 for males, and the 1980 version raised these figures to 20 and 22, respectively. However, since the early 1970s late marriage has been forcefully advocated. Often in urban areas the demand has been for the female to be at least 25 and the male 27 or 28, or for the ages of both partners to total at least 50.

the necessary paperwork at the ward marriage registration office. Civil registration of marriage is, of course, a twentieth-century innovation, for traditionally the family wedding feast was the event that signified a couple was married. The continuing desire for family celebrations is recognized, so while the government officially espouses a simple and secular tea party to announce the wedding, they do not object to modest wedding meals for the families and close friends. But elaborate feasts with traditional ritual activities are tabooed. No clear preferences have been stated by the government in regard to residence after marriage. The Marriage Law does include an obligation of children to help support their aged parents, and the lack of extensive investment in old-age homes rests on an official presumption that most old folks will end their days living with grown children. But whether they live with a son or a daughter, or indeed with one child or several together, has not been a subject of much debate or concern. A few articles have appeared in the press in recent years commenting on the advantages of the couple moving in with the bride's parents, but still the matter remains open for personal (and family) choice.[3]

These are only some of the most basic features of the government's policy toward mate choice and marriage, and we must now discuss various aspects of the marriage institution in contemporary Chinese cities. As we do so we will comment upon official policies in more detail and consider how these policies have interacted with other factors to shape the form of contemporary mate choice. At a number of points along the way we reinforce our general discussion of contemporary mate choice with data on a sample of marriages constructed from our interviews. All told, the sample includes 831 marriages formed over the years, but for many variables we have data on only a modest portion of this sample.[4] Still, this marriage case sample gives us an opportunity to check some ideas about trends in marriage behavior in urban China.

Age at Marriage

In table 9 we present figures on the trend in marriage ages over time, as shown by our sample of marriage cases. The trend shown in the table is unambiguous. Throughout the post-1949 period average marriage ages

3. The most specific articles advocating matrilocal residence that have appeared concern rural areas. See *People's Daily*, 14 March 1975; *Southern Daily*, 18 January 1975. We will not discuss one other requirement of official policy: monogamy. Taking extra wives has not been an option or issue in recent years, although there still remain a few cases of pre-1949 polygamous marriages.

4. On the construction of the sample, see appendix 1. No cases of bigamy turned up in our interviews although such cases are occasionally noted in the press. See Institute of Sociology "Report on an Investigation of the Marriage Situation in Metropolitan Shanghai," *Shehui Kexue*, no. 10 (1981): 78.

were rising for both urban men and women, so that by the 1970s the average marriage age for both sexes was about five years later than in the period before 1949. By the 1970s there were no cases in our sample of males marrying before the legal age of 20 and females before the age of 18, as there had been earlier. If we take 27 and 25 as the new preferred minima, then we find that 36 percent of males were still marrying below this figure in the 1970s, and 49 percent of women were marrying below, but on balance the drive for late marriage must be judged a considerable success.[5]

What remains uncertain is how much of a role government pressure played in bringing about these later marriage ages. The evidence on this point is mixed. On the one hand our informants did describe a number of cases to us of couples who wanted to marry being pressured into delaying for a year or more. Getting married is not always a simple matter in urban China. The male and female must first seek the approval of authorities in their respective work units (or wards) in order to marry. In large cities this step, rather than procedures in the marriage registration office, is the crucial obstacle. Unit authorities can object or cause delays on a variety of grounds. If one has chosen a person regarded as politically unreliable, the authorities may caution one to think it over and consider the risks to one's own future.[6] For those who avoid such unwise choices

Table 9				Change Over Time in Average Marriage Ages		
	Pre-1949	1949-1957	1958-1965	1966-1970	1971-1978	1974-1978
Male	22.6	24.1	25.4	26.4	27.7	28.5
(N)	(19)	(14)	(67)	(89)	(144)	(64)
Female	19.6	20.5	21.7	23.3	24.4	24.4
(N)	(20)	(15)	(74)	(98)	(149)	(63)

Source: Weighted Lingnan Region marriage sample, first marriages only.

5. A few other statistics help corroborate these trends. In a Shanghai study, female age at first marriage rose as follows: 1950–54, 20.9; 1955–59, 22.1; 1960–64, 23.3; 1965–69, 24.8; 1970–74, 25.5; 1975–79, 26.8—Gu Xingyuan et al., "Shanghai Family Planning," in *China's Population: Problems and Prospects,* Liu Zheng et al., eds. (Peking: New World Press, 1981), p. 140. In the pre-1949 surveys, female marriage age is typically between 18 and 20— Janet Salaff, "Youth, Family, and Political Control in Communist China" (Ph.D. dissertation, University of California, 1972), p. 221.

6. Political unreliability may involve past political mistakes of the intended partner, bad class background or political errors by his or her family, or in some periods even such things as relatives overseas. For most individuals persuasion is all that is applied in such cases, and if the couple persists they can still marry. However, Party members, people who work in high security work units, or individuals in the army may be forbidden to marry such a person, or told they will lose their privileged status if they do.

to begin with, the matter of age is more important. If a couple is regarded as too young the unit authorities will tell them so and try to persuade them to wait until they pass the required ages. If they do not acquire work unit approval, the local marriage registration office will not let them register the marriage.

A forced work unit delay is usually the end of the matter, but it need not be. In some cases the parents may come to the unit to protest the delay, explaining that they are old and in need of the aid of a daughter-in-law. Such family-oriented appeals are still highly respected, and sympathetic work unit authorities may be nudged into acquiescing. If the couple has been sexually involved and the female becomes pregnant, the authorities may also give approval for an "early" marriage, although in recent years they may instead demand that the woman get an abortion and that both male and female be subjected to criticism meetings. In cases where the unit does approve an early marriage, the marriage registration office usually seems to go along and permit registration, rather than acting as a second vetoing agency.[7] Finally, in a few cases determined couples may, with the support of their families, have a wedding ceremony at home and begin to live together without benefit of registration, and go back and procure the official registration once they come of age. Lax enforcement and these sorts of strategies help to explain the considerable minority of marriages that table 9 shows were still "early" in the mid-1970s. In recent years cases of determined couples who buck the authorities have become steadily rarer, however. Since couples depend on work unit authorities for so many things—often access to housing and nursery schools, as well as job opportunities—they know that making a fuss or disobeying may cost them later on. The general pattern is to accept delays as unavoidable.

It would appear, then, that pressure from authorities (especially in the work unit) is a major factor fostering later marriage ages. However, further reflection makes it clear that many other factors are involved. First, urban marriage ages have long been "later" than those in rural China and were on the rise even before 1949.[8] Second, a rise in the average marriage age

7. Some press discussions have argued that marriage registration offices are shirking their responsibility by relying too heavily on the certification by the work unit. The formal regulations for marriage registration are translated in *Survey of the China Mainland Press*, no. 1062 (1955): 32–34. For an early guidebook, see *How to Manage Marriage Registration Work Well* (Peking: Village Reader Publishing House, 1963), translated in *Chinese Sociology and Anthropology*, 1, no. 2 (1968–69). In our interviews there is one case of factory authorities inflating the age of a female employee by one year on their certificate to avoid hassles at the registration office (SSM2:11).

8. See Lang, *Chinese Family and Society*. Also compare the figures for 1970s rural Guangdong marriages in William Parish and Martin Whyte, *Village and Family in Contemporary China* (Chicago: University of Chicago Press, 1978), chap. 10.

tends to occur in all modernizing societies that possess the sort of arranged marriage/early marriage system that China did. In non-Communist Taiwan, for example, from 1940 to the 1970s the average marriage age for both males and females increased by about three years, so that it is about 26 and 23 today.[9] Furthermore, our figures for urban mainland China in table 9 show that the rise in marriage ages during the Communist period has been fairly constant, rather than being concentrated in the last decade, when the official late marriage campaign began to receive major emphasis. The gradual rise makes us look to other influences on marriage ages. We can see that the structure of opportunities facing young people has changed in ways that promote later marriage.

In the 1950s the urban economy was reviving and expanding, and there was a great demand for skilled personnel of all types. At that time much urban housing still remained in private hands or was only loosely controlled by the authorities. New wage systems and wage increases were also introduced, with procedures specified for subsequent promotions. At the same time efforts to increase school enrollments were vigorously promoted. In this situation increased school attendance began to delay entry into the work force for a large portion of urban youths and consequently also delayed the attainment of full adulthood. But once schooling was done urban youths seemed to have good prospects for employment and advancement, and could contemplate marriage as soon as they had found a willing partner.

Increasingly over the years this picture changed, as we have previously noted. Educational enrollments continued to expand, delaying work entry further, but in later years the opportunities facing school leavers were not so bright. Urban jobs became increasingly scarce, and many youths faced the prospect of being sent to the countryside in the 1960s and 1970s. Even those who managed to get assigned to jobs received low starting pay levels, with little prospect for raises that would allow them to plan for a wedding and support a family easily. The authorities added to this difficulty by trying to enforce a ban on courting during schooling and work ap-

9. For the worldwide trend, see William J. Goode, *World Revolution and Family Patterns* (New York: Free Press, 1963). For the trend in Taiwan, see John B. Casterline, "The Determinants of Rising Female Age at Marriage, 1905–1976" (Ph.D. dissertation, University of Michigan, 1980). American visitors to China are often surprised at what seems to be the unusually late ages of marriage of young people in China. Actually it should be noted that average marriage ages in the United States—roughly 21–22 for females and 24–25 for males in recent years—are unusually early, with averages in the late twenties the rule in most other developed societies and in Japan. In one Chinese city outside the Mainland—Singapore—the mean ages of marriage in 1970 were 24.3 for females and 27.8 for males. See Applied Research Corporation for Ministry of Social Affairs, *A Study of Non-Muslim Divorce in Singapore* (Singapore: mimeograph, 1979), p. 38.

prenticeships. We have seen that housing also became a serious problem as urban living space became increasingly tight and as a dominant share of housing (particularly in large cities) came under control of the authorities. This housing crunch meant that if neither set of parents had extra room, the new couple had to apply to their work units or to city housing offices, and they might have to wait for several years before an apartment would be assigned to them. In one case in the city of Kunming a couple delayed marriage for four years while waiting for unit housing, and when in 1973 the only new housing built was a collective dormitory for males to which the prospective groom was assigned, his sympathetic roommates moved out so that the desperate couple could use it as their bridal suite (over the protests of work unit officials).[10]

From a practical standpoint several things are required in order to contemplate marriage: a willing mate, funds to pay for wedding expenses and the expenses of equipping new housing, access to housing, and income or prospects of earning an income that can support a family. As most of these resources became increasingly scarce, marriages were inevitably delayed. The delay was particularly marked for those millions of urban educated young people who were sent to the countryside. Most remained unmarried in the villages in hopes of returning to the city, but even those who managed transfers back to an urban area had to start at the bottom in a work unit, often as apprentices, several years after they had finished their schooling and required several more years before they could establish themselves well enough to contemplate marriage. This changing urban opportunity structure in a sense made it "easy" for the authorities to call for late marriage as an explicit goal, since most urban youths were already having to adjust their behavior to accept later marriage ages as normal.

Over time urban youths have tended to marry at later and later ages, but still there is variation, with some individuals marrying in their mid- or even early twenties, and others not until their thirties. (The sentiment in favor of eventually marrying remains very strong; lifelong bachelorhood or spinsterhood is still not seen as an acceptable option.) What are the reasons behind the current variation in marriage ages? Traditionally there is evidence that youths in better-off families could often marry when quite young, while those from poor families often had to wait or even remain unmarried. Poor individuals could not so readily attract or support partners, and poor families were reluctant to part with the earnings of a working daughter if she married. By the 1930s observers argued that these patterns were changing, with children from well-to-do families delaying

10. Interview KUM2:10. There are also cases in our interviews of couples losing their patience and building a makeshift loft within the parents' apartment to use as their bridal suite (interview KSM6:23).

marriage later than poorer youths in order to pursue educational and other opportunities.[11] In other words, a pattern more familiar to the industrial societies, of earlier marriage in lower classes, was beginning to emerge.

In table 10 we examine the pattern of ages at marriage for our post-Cultural Revolution marriage cases. The pattern for male marriage age and female marriage age is quite similar. The major finding shown in these figures is that when either the male or the female (or both) has more education or a higher status job, then both will tend to marry at later ages. Only one other relationship stands up under statistical scrutiny besides this one. Males who live in large cities tend to marry somewhat later than males who live in small cities. It is interesting to note that Party membership and political leadership positions do not seem to have an independent effect in favor of later marriage ages, as we might have expected them to if political pressure for late marriage were the key change mechanism. We had also expected that, at least for men, bad class background or errors by the male and his family would lead to delayed marriage, but table 10 shows that when educational and job levels are partialed out, these variables also do not have an independent effect upon marriage ages.[12] When we examine who marries earlier and who later, we find that variables that are important in this context in other societies, particularly educational attainment and occupational status, are the most important factors. This analysis tends to reinforce our earlier conclusion: the rise in marriage ages in urban China cannot be attributed simply to the official late marriage campaign and the political pressures it has generated. The structure of urban careers and the willingness to delay marriage to take advantage of educational and occupational opportunities are at least as important.

Freedom of Mate Choice

Later marriage ages represent only one important type of change in this important social institution. The nature of mate choice has also changed in critical ways. Again, changes in this area were well underway before 1949, but there is little doubt they have accelerated in the Communist

11. For evidence on the tendency for males from well-off urban families to marry earlier than other males around the turn of the century, see Sa, "Marriage among the Taiwanese." For the subsequent change, see Lang, *Chinese Family and Society*, pp. 128–29.

12. We checked the relationships in the table by partialing out other variables not shown here, such as the gender of the informant, informant optimism, Lingnan Region, Canton residence and radical year, and they did not substantially affect the relationships shown here. The derivation of the various variables and scales used here and later in the chapter is described in appendix 2.

Table 10   Marriage Age by Selected Background
                                            Characteristics (Partial Correlations)

	Husband's Marriage Age		Wife's Marriage Age	
	Informant quality controlled	Socioeconomic status controlled[a]	Informant quality controlled	Socioeconomic status controlled[a]
Socioeconomic Status[b]				
Education	.28*	--	.31*	--
Occupation	.23*	--	.32*	--
Parent's social status	.07	-.01	.23	.09
Political Status[b]				
Good class label	-.10*	-.06	-.11*	.07
Party/League member	--	--	.09	.00
Leadership role	.12	.08	--	--
No personal error	-.03	-.02	.11	.07
No family error	-.24*	-.15	-.09	-.08
City Characteristics				
Administrative level	.16*	.13*	.11*	.04
Lingnan Region	-.02	-.07	.04	-.02
Median N	(221)	(181)	(232)	(181)

Source: Marriage sample, post-Cultural Revolution marriages only.

[a]Simultaneous partialling out of the effects of husband and wife's education level as well as husband and wife's occupational status.

[b]Background characteristics of husband in columns one and two and of wife in columns three and four.

-- = not relevant because of statistical controls or not computed.

*p ≤ .10

period. Traditionally marriages were based upon the decisions of the parents, using the aid of marriage go-betweens to find prospects and to aid in negotiations. The young male and female were not expected to have much say in the process, and in many cases they had not met at all. In interviews conducted by Olga Lang in the 1930s, out of a sample of 194 married male college students, 83 had never seen their brides before the wedding, and only 4 had chosen their brides themselves. Interviews with industrial workers convinced Lang that only 20–25 percent of their marriages involved the consent of the bride and groom.[13] But educated youths of the May Fourth generation were already rebelling against arranged marriages. One of the most famous modern Chinese novels, Ba Jin's *Family,* focused on conflict between the generations on matters such as marriage choice, and among Mao Zedong's earliest articles are vigorous

13. Lang, *Chinese Family and Society,* pp. 122, 124.

denunciations of the system of arranged marriage that drove an unhappy bride to commit suicide.[14]

By the 1950s the principle of freedom of mate choice had won general acceptance among urbanites of all classes. The marriage cases for which we have detailed information on aspects of parental or youth control do not go back much further than 1958, but in the cases since then there is no significant change in various indicators of the freedom of mate choice. This does not mean, however, that all marriages are made completely by the young people themselves, with no outside intervention or parental influence. The picture is more complex than one might expect, given the general support for freedom of mate choice. In our post-1958 marriage cases (N = 174), 56 percent of the couples met directly, while 44 percent had to rely on introductions from others. Of these latter cases almost half involved introductions arranged by parents, while the remainder were based upon introductions provided by friends or workmates.

If almost all young people believe in freedom of mate choice, why do so many of them end up relying upon go-betweens and even their own parents to find them a marital partner? In fact, the situation in urban China is not all that unusual in developing societies making a transition from arranged to free choice marriage.[15] In theory, for young people to make their own choices they need to be able to meet potential spouses and to be able to become familiar enough with some of those they meet to decide whether they would want to marry them. In America a "dating culture" provides opportunities for young males and females to mix fairly freely and to explore romantic relationships in a relatively casual atmosphere, with no long-term commitments expected, and this experience is seen as important in making possible eventual choice of a mate. In urban China as in many other developing societies freedom of mate choice has won acceptance without a dating culture having emerged, and so young people confront a number of obstacles in trying to find a spouse.

Young people can meet in China's coeducational secondary schools and universities, but as noted earlier there has been an official policy at least since the late 1950s that young people still in school should not pair off—

14. See Roxanne Witke, "Mao Tse-tung, Women and Suicide in the May Fourth Era," *China Quarterly* 31 (1967): 128–50.

15. On Japan in the 1950s, see Ezra Vogel, "The Go-Between in a Developing Society: The Case of the Japanese Marriage Arranger," *Human Organization* 20 (1961): 112–20; and Robert Blood, *Love Match and Arranged Marriage* (New York: Free Press, 1967). On Taiwan at roughly the same time, see Albert O'Hara, "Changing Attitudes toward Marriage and the Family in Free China," in his *Research on Changes of Chinese Society* (Taipei: Orient Cultural Service, 1971). On Hong Kong in 1967, see Robert Mitchell, *Family Life in Urban Hong Kong*, vol. 1 (Taipei: Orient Cultural Service, 1969), p. 210.

literally, "talk romance" (*tan lianai*)—and marriage is strictly forbidden. Even though the ban on romance cannot be effectively enforced, particularly at the university level, its existence does make it more difficult for youths attracted to each other to communicate their feelings and develop a romantic relationship. School authorities make a great effort to develop activities involving large groups of males and females in comradeship and to urge students to devote their energies to their studies rather than to romance. Youths with romantic impulses must also consider the implications of the state labor assignment system. A couple might, under this system, be assigned to jobs in different locales after graduation and be forced to choose between marrying and living separately or breaking off the relationship to look for a new partner. Whether this happens or not depends on the consideration shown by school authorities for romances that develop in spite of the ban, and this consideration seems to have varied over time. (As noted in chapter 3, during the radical period such personal preferences were largely ignored.) Given these uncertainties, it is not surprising that many young people hesitate to get romantically involved, although it seems fairly common for them to try to get to know desirable classmates well in order to file them away as future prospects in case circumstances should be more favorable to romance later. In one case in our interviews a male met a young female in middle school in 1962. He remembered her and began writing platonic letters to her during the Cultural Revolution. When he was assigned to a distant province in 1968 he began writing in a more direct fashion suggesting marriage. She at first resisted, but when he visited back home he worked at persuading her and her parents, and she finally relented and in 1969 agreed to marry him. They finally married only in 1973, eleven years after they first met.[16]

Given the constraints presented by the school romance ban, the official late marriage policy, the program of sending educated youths to the countryside, and the state labor assignment system, it is fairly common for young people to wait until they are assigned work before they begin to seriously consider finding a partner. Even then "talking romance," or at least marriage, is supposed to be forbidden for those serving as apprentices (a term that may last three years). Once one is promoted to a secure job as a regular employee it still may not be an easy matter to select a partner, for several reasons. First, there is a considerable amount of occupational segregation by sex and assignment of men and women to different kinds of jobs even within enterprises (discussed in detail in chapter 7). For those who are most segregated, such as women textile workers and nursery

16. Interview CWD1:13. On the anxieties about job placement and enforced separation from an intended, see Tung Chi-ping and Humphrey Evans, *The Thought Revolution* (London: Leslie Frewin, 1967), pp. 151–58.

school teachers or male coal miners, there are few prospects close at hand. The highly involved and inclusive nature of work units and their activities helps to reinforce this isolation, while the absence of facilities of a dating culture—dance halls, drive-in movies, and all the rest—means that individuals do not have lots of time and opportunities to meet eligible partners outside on their own. In the 1950s and early 1960s it was not uncommon for work units to hold dances and parties of various types, and even occasionally to hold what we would call "mixers," parties jointly sponsored by a unit with extra males and a unit with extra females that were aimed specifically at fostering romance. In later years such activities were seen as bourgeois and decadent, and they were rarely held after the Cultural Revolution.

Even those in mixed-sex work units have some difficulties in converting a fellow-worker tie into a romantic relationship. Here traditional mores and expectations enter in. Any public sign of pairing off is seen not as a preliminary and casual stage of romance, but as indicating a serious commitment that is expected to lead to marriage.[17] In this context it is not uncommon for a person to have a workmate in mind as a partner for some time before being able to find both the courage and the appropriate context for discussing their feelings. So direct contacts through work do not automatically allow romances to blossom. Young people do have some opportunities to meet prospects through outside activities—athletics, mass organization meetings—but here again the atmosphere tends to inhibit romance. In spite of these many obstacles more than half of our marriage cases did result from couples meeting directly, often getting to know each other first for an extended period of time as classmates, coworkers, or neighbors, and then developing the courage to declare feelings. But for the considerable number of urban youths who feel they have few chances to meet eligible mates or who are too timid to make a direct approach, assistance in finding a mate is needed. This assistance can come in several forms and need not mean leaving matters in the hands of one's parents. In about half of the cases of introduced marriage partners in our sample, the parents were not involved until relatively late in the day. Sometimes the young male or female sought the help of friends or coworkers to arrange introductions. Sometimes workmates or superiors became concerned about the lack of romantic success of a colleague and proceeded to seek out prospects for the individual on their own. There is much public support for this kind of informal matchmaking activity, and at times it can become almost a unit project, with various individuals providing intro-

17. A similar context involving the absence of approval for casual dating is described on Taiwan in O'Hara, "Changing Attitudes toward Marriage."

ductions until at last one succeeds and results in marriage. The mass media have more recently praised this sort of activity, particularly in regard to aiding young people who had their lives disrupted as a result of the Cultural Revolution. Indeed, in one speech in 1980 a secretary of the Central Committee of the Communist Youth League, Guo Zhanxiang, went so far as to argue, "We should mobilize the entire force of cadres of the Youth League to act as matchmakers for youths of marriageable age."[18] A good share of marriages in urban China involve introductions and go-betweens, but not the traditional kind of parental arrangement and professional matchmakers.

However, there remains an important minority of cases (21 percent in our sample) in which the parents take the initiative in finding a mate for their son or daughter. In some of these cases the parents are simply eager to settle the matter and see some grandchildren before they get too old; in others they intervened only after several attempts at introductions initiated by the younger generation failed to produce success. Even when the parents take the initiative, however, they are not all-powerful. Only in a very few cases (about 2 percent in our sample) do they use professional marriage arrangers, and even then they do not usually have the final say in the matter. Typically they use ties among their friends, neighbors, and coworkers to try to locate prospects. If a prospect is located they consult their son or daughter, providing personal details and perhaps showing a picture, and if they evoke some interest they will arrange a meeting so that the pair can become acquainted. It is still the general understanding, though, that it is up to the young couple to decide whether they want to marry or not. Informants could provide very few instances of "forced marriages," in which the young people had not exercised an independent judgment.

More is involved in courtship than simply being able to meet suitable prospects. If freedom of mate choice is to operate, young people need to be able to get to know prospects to decide whether they want to marry them or not. In the absence of a dating culture and given the seriousness usually assigned to pairing off, there is some danger that a couple will have to try to make a decision about marriage before they really get to know each other well.

Three general stages in marriage decisions in urban China can be distinguished: information gathering, a suitability-check stage, and "proto-dating." In the first stage each person tries to find out as much as possible about the prospect, often indirectly. If the couple have not yet met, each may pepper the introducers with a variety of questions in an effort to find

18. *FBIS*, 19 November 1980, p. L6.

out whether the prospect fits criteria for a mate they have in mind. If they are already acquainted, each may try to observe the prospect at a distance and in different contexts to try to learn as much as possible about each other and how each behaves in a variety of situations. Or each may even try to have long talks with the potential mate about aspirations and values, without romance ever being brought up. All of this effort at information gathering conveys the view that romance is not a matter to be entered into lightly, and that one must think carefully in order to avoid a mistake one will regret later.

In the second, suitability-check stage, the couple begin to directly discuss their feelings and to try to get to know each other at a deeper level. Usually there is nothing we would call dating at this stage, and their activities are often engaged in in secret. If they are being introduced it will often occur in a public park or at a friend's home, and if they know each other from work they will usually arrange to meet privately after work. Couples at this stage generally go for walks together and have long talks about their goals in life, their interests and hobbies, and what sort of things they are looking for in a mate. The secrecy is designed to prevent gossip from arising, and to permit the couple to see how suited they are to each other without feeling too much pressure one way or the other. Each partner may talk with closest friends at this stage, and in some cases also with parents, seeking advice on whether to get more involved or not. If they decide to break the relationship off at this stage hard feelings will not be too severe, and others outside the circle of their closest friends and family will be none the wiser.

If this stage has gone well and the partners feel romantic desires building up, they can "go public" and move into the third stage. In Chinese terminology they are regarded as having "established a relationship" (*kending guanxi*). There is rarely a formal engagement (*dinghun*) in urban China today as there was before 1949, but a couple who has entered the proto-dating stage is viewed as being tantamount to engaged. As our term suggests, it is only at this point that activities similar to Western-style dating begin—dating follows the commitment to marry, rather than pre-. ceding it. Couples commonly go for long walks in parks, go to movies together, go on shopping trips, and visit in each others' homes. The stage of proto-dating may continue for some time, even years. The average length of acquaintance before marriage of the cases on which we have information (N = 159) was about two years and nine months, and fully one-fourth of the cases involved a couple who knew each other for more than five years before marrying. Most couples do not rush into marriage, then, but delay until they have saved up and arranged for housing so that they can start their marriage on a satisfactory basis. This prolonged period of proto-dating gives the couple the opportunity to get to know each other much better, and also to establish closer ties with their future in-laws, ties that will continue to be important later on.

The deeper acquaintance achieved during this third stage may, of course, lead to problems if one or the other partner begins to regret their commitment and to want to back out of the marriage. Doing so is not an easy matter. If some action reveals a partner to be unworthy, or hidden details about the partner or the partner's family come to light that the other can use to justify breaking off the relationship, then others will understand. But it does not appear that simply "falling out of love" is readily accepted by public opinion. Faithfulness is one of the qualities most sought in a mate, and fickleness a trait that occasions much gossip and scorn, so that a person who breaks up a relationship at this stage may have trouble finding a new partner if others do not feel there was sufficient basis for having terminated the romance.

Love, Rational Criteria, and
Status Matching

Up to this point we have discussed Chinese mate choice practices without mentioning feelings of love. Do feelings of romantic love play an important role in mate choice in contemporary China? Clearly in the traditional system of arranged marriage they were not an important factor, and families tried quite hard-headedly to find suitable partners for their children to produce a match between status equals. Indeed, romantic attractions might have undermined the family effort to "match doors and households" (*mendang hudui*). With the gradual acceptance of freedom of mate choice, but without an institutionalized dating culture, what role do feelings of love play in mate choice today compared to more rational considerations? Do urban Chinese experience the same kinds of romantic emotions that, say, American youths in love do? We cannot hope to give any precise answer to this latter question, but we can present impressions from our interviews and generalizations about how mates are chosen.[19]

First, at least a significant portion of young people clearly experience emotional highs and intense preoccupation with their prospective partner that are indicative of romantic love, and they also feel that such feelings

19. For social science studies of the role of love in American mate choice, see William J. Goode, "The Theoretical Importance of Love," *American Sociological Review* 24 (1959): 38–47; Ira L. Reiss, "Toward a Sociology of the Heterosexual Love Relationship," *Marriage and Family Living* 22 (1960): 139–44; Bernard Murstein, ed., *Theories of Attraction and Love* (New York: Spring, 1971); and Zick Rubin, "The Social Psychology of Romantic Love" (Ph.D. dissertation, University of Michigan, 1969).

are a necessary prerequisite for marriage. In other words, there are lots of love stories in the contemporary Chinese marriage scene. Yet at the same time there seems to be more use of fairly explicit lists of rational criteria for picking a spouse than is generally the case in American society. This is of course particularly true of those couples who meet through an introduction. The many marriage introducers who operate in Chinese cities will inquire about the criteria the person they are trying to help has in mind and will survey their contacts and offer to make introductions specifically in terms of these criteria. When it comes time to make a commitment to marry a person, there is often an effort to weigh the merits and demerits of a particular prospect in a fairly rational manner. There are not a few cases in our interviews in which a person decided to reject a suitor with whom they were clearly in love because of some defect or flaw and ended up marrying someone more "suitable" in terms of rational criteria, although the feelings for the eventual mate were not as strong as for the rejected suitor. Finally, there are still a minority of cases of marriages that occur without a prolonged period of proto-dating or even acquaintance that could allow strong emotional attachments to develop. We could only code the intensity of courting activities for a small portion of our marriage sample (N = 76), but among these cases about 12 percent of the couples had little or no contact before marriage, and another 16 percent had only occasional meetings or visits. The remaining 72 percent experienced the sort of prolonged proto-dating period that we described above.

In general it seems to us we are dealing here with the same kinds of emotions and concerns we find in American mate choice; what differences exist are not of a qualitative sort. But differences there are, and these are represented by the greater penchant for explicitly using rational criteria, rather than simply one's feelings, in picking a mate in urban China. We don't mean to suggest that American youths don't have any rational criteria for a mate or that they never think about potential partners in a rational manner; only that they operate in a culture where it is assumed that "love is all that matters," where "love conquers all," and "love at first sight" is not out of the ordinary.[20]

What are the kinds of criteria used in screening potential marriage partners? The government has from time to time tried to discourage people

20. Research on dating and marriage in America indicates that status-related selection often takes place at least partly on an unconscious or semiconscious level, as segregated social life and differential values tend to screen out many prospects who come from discordant backgrounds. See Bernard Murstein, *Who Will Marry Whom?* (New York: Spring, 1976), and Ted Huston, *Theories of Interpersonal Attraction* (New York: Academic Press, 1974).

from thinking in materialistic terms of income and status and has tried to encourage people to pick partners according to their political thinking.[21] Our informants make it clear that the criteria used are considerably more complex than media stories indicate and that they have been altered over time in ways the government has not anticipated.

The story our informants tell about the evolution of mate choice criteria goes roughly as follows: In the 1950s and early 1960s picking a "promising" partner was important, particularly to women, and this involved betting on a person's future. Futures were to be made along two paths, one political and the other professional (i.e., the "red" and "expert" paths). Some individuals were eager to find a partner who was likely to have a bright political future, and this meant looking for political activists, individuals who held offices in the Communist Youth League or various youth and student organizations, or who had been able to join the Communist Party or the People's Liberation Army. Others might focus instead on diligent and intelligent individuals likely to go on to the university and to promising careers as skilled personnel and intellectuals.[22] In both "tracks" the class origins of the individual were seen as relatively unimportant, since many opportunities were available, and even youths from the "exploiting classes" could relatively easily disassociate themselves from their origins in order to qualify for such opportunities.

These patterns began to change during the 1960s, particularly with the advent of the Cultural Revolution. The most immediate impact of the Cultural Revolution, say our informants, was to stiffen the "class line," making individuals more anxious to avoid marriage with a person from an exploiting class background. A similar effect was produced by the attacks on Party leaders and intellectuals typical of that time. Since both high ranking "reds" and "experts" were getting into trouble, the issue of how to pick a promising mate became confused. In the 1970s the situation evolved further. Class labels remained important, and the situation stabilized enough for people to begin to have some basis for judging what a good prospect was again. But since most wage increases and promotions were frozen at this time, and the wages of most young people were all about the same (generally 30–35 yuan a month), wagering on a person's future no longer seemed so sensible. Instead criteria became more present oriented. What sort of spouse could provide immediately visible benefits? In part, this meant picking a person who already had a

21. See, for example, Lu Yang, *The Correct Handling of Love.*

22. The "two track" nature of the mate choice option parallels the way youths thought about their future careers in this period. See Michel Oksenberg, "The Institutionalization of the Chinese Communist Revolution: The Ladder of Success on the Eve of the Cultural Revolution," *China Quarterly* 36 (1968): 61–92.

good income or a trusted position, say, an older individual. One common saying describes how young women looked at monthly wages of a prospect: "If it is 30 yuan, don't consider it; if 50 yuan, examine his appearance; and if 100 yuan, run after him." Present-mindedness also might mean a sent-down female picking an urban male with some authority, a male who might be able to arrange to get her household registration transferred back to the city. In this frame of mind, the family and kinship network of the individual became increasingly important as well. Were his or her parents people with high positions, comfortable incomes, ample housing, overseas relatives and remittance income, or simply lots of connections? (And on the negative side, one had to avoid people whose parents were poor and perhaps disabled, who had other children still in the countryside that were a drain on resources, or who simply had few resources and connections.)

This increasing stress on the characteristics of the family rather than simply of the young prospect seems paradoxical, in view of the success of the egalitarian policies of the Cultural Revolution decade, as documented in chapters 3 and 4. If family income and occupational status were no longer good predictors of educational attainment and job opportunities for offspring, why not disregard characteristics of the family and focus exclusively on those of the young person being considered as a mate? The answer to the paradox has already been alluded to. For those concerned about improving their life chances and not just marrying a compatible person (i.e., presumably most urban youths), the wages and resources of even employed young people were so low and so similar, and their future prospects were so unpredictable as a result of the egalitarian policies, that there was little to choose among them. The status and resources of their families, on the other hand, were already established and provided a much more reliable basis upon which to discriminate among prospects.

Of course not everyone operates with the same criteria in mind. Some informants claimed that youths from intellectual background tended to pick mates more in terms of their personal qualities, while the offspring of workers tended to stress income and other material concerns. The criteria stressed by males and by females also differ somewhat. We list here a rough rank ordering of the criteria our informants said were most stressed by males and females in the 1970s:

Female considers:	Male considers:
1. job and income of male	1. class label and political record of female
2. class label and political record	2. good looks

3. family income, housing, connections
4. urban registration
5. overseas connections and remittances
6. pleasing personality, good character
7. good looks

3. family income, housing, connections
4. pleasing personality, good character
5. job and income of female
6. urban registration
7. overseas connections and remittances

Several things may be noted about these rough rank-ordered lists. First, there is evidence here of the same sort of sexual asymmetry that we find in other societies, even though almost all urban Chinese women work and the men are not "the sole breadwinners." The nature of the job and income is more important in picking a husband than a wife, while good looks and individual character traits are more important in picking a wife than a husband. Finding a partner with an urban registration is also more important to a female than a male, and probably more important to her than our list indicates. Many urban females would not even bother to consider marrying a male who lived out in a suburban village, and so might not bother to list this among their criteria for a mate. But some urban males are willing to consider marrying peasant females if they are having trouble finding an urban bride. Another point of interest is that educational level is not prominently listed among the criteria for a mate by either males or females. This reflects the present-orientation we have referred to. Educational level is particularly important when it helps one predict the future career prospects of an individual, but given the disruption of this route to mobility in the post-Cultural Revolution period, most individuals focused instead on what jobs people had already managed to obtain.

The two lists conceal some other differences in the precise criteria that the two sexes use. For example, many informants said that more was important about a job than simply its wage level. Women felt that men with jobs in state factories were relatively desirable, since they not only had good pay and fringe benefits but social prestige and access to the resources (housing, nursery schools, etc.) of their unit. They preferred to avoid marrying men working in service jobs, which have low prestige and generally provide lower pay and less access to resources. Some men, on the other hand, actually preferred wives with service sector jobs, since job prestige is not seen as so important for a wife, and these jobs tend to have more flexible schedules, with fewer demands, making it easier for women in such jobs to cope with domestic responsibilities. In terms of personality and character, the specific traits described also differ to some extent. Women particularly want a husband who is diligent, kind, and respected by his coworkers, while males often look for a wife who has a pleasant personality, a good moral reputation (virginity is usually essential), and ability to manage domestic affairs.[23]

In pre-1949 China it was generally thought that marriages should involve status matching. To achieve this parents and matchmakers carefully considered the social status of the family of the prospect and to some extent the status-related characteristics (education, occupation, and so forth) of the prospect. As we have seen, in the post-1949 period the authorities tried to discourage concern for the economic status of the family of origin in picking a spouse and encourage focusing on the characteristics of the prospect. They tried to discourage stressing the prospect's external status criteria, such as income, and encouraged consideration of personal character traits. But it is clear that official policies and trends since the Cultural Revolution have to a considerable extent worked against these professed goals. Then, too, in the highly bureaucratized distribution system that controls urban resources, people with political power or gatekeeper roles (or from families with parents in such roles) inevitably became desirable prospects, regardless of their personal qualities. The resulting situation is that matching according to status criteria remained extremely important during the Cultural Revolution decade. Children from high cadre families tended to marry others from such families, worker offspring usually married other worker offspring, and so forth. Indeed, some informants argue, and later press critiques charge, that a shift toward more emphasis on external status criteria occurred during the period we are concerned with.[24] The particular status criteria emphasis had clearly changed, with such things as property ownership and regional and ethnic origin more important in the pre-1949 period, and such traits as class

23. Other criteria mentioned less regularly are not included here, such as educational level, health, and regional origins of the prospect. We should also note that traditionally families took the "eight characters," the horoscopic data on the time of birth of the male and female, to a ritual specialist to check whether the couple was suited or not. In only a handful of cases in our sample was this step followed recently.

24. These tendencies are described and criticized in Shanghai Academy of Social Sciences, Institute of Sociology, "Investigation of the Marriage Situation," pp. 77–78. In our marriage sample these were correlations from .40 to .75 between the various status characteristics of the bride and groom (features such as education, wage level, occupation, class label, and so forth). However, the correlations were if anything lower, rather than higher, in the post-1966 marriage cases when compared with earlier cases. While this might be taken to indicate more focus on the personal qualities of the partner, it could also indicate the shift from selections based on poorly predictive status characteristics of the prospect to those of the parents. Unfortunately, we have parental characteristics for too few cases in our marriage sample to investigate whether matching in terms of these family characteristics increased.

labels and urban registration more important in recent years.[25] But in any case, in the 1970s there was clearly still a strong concern for "matching doors and households."

This continued importance of status matching should not be seen as very surprising, however. While some have supposed that status matching should be important in an arranged marriage system and should decline as free choice and romantic love come into play and lead to a more random pattern of mate selection, sociological evidence provides little support for such an idea. In societies with well-institutionalized free mate choice cultures, such as the United States and the Soviet Union, it is clear that most marriages bring together people from similar status backgrounds.[26] Wherever there are marked disparities in social status and life chances, as there are in socialist societies as well as capitalist ones, invariably a "marriage market" operates in which, through competition for partners, individuals tend to end up married to people who bring to that competition similar social resources. So status matching will predominate, no matter whether it is the parents or the young couple who dominate the decision. Whether in fact the extent of such status matching has changed in urban China in recent years, or whether it is more or less than in other societies, are questions we cannot answer conclusively.

Premarital Sex

The image the outside world has of China is of the ultimate in puritanism. The late marriage regulations, the taboos on "talking romance" in school, the tendency toward "unisex" loose-fitting clothing and lack of concern for cosmetics and personal appearance in the radical decade, and the publicity given to political criteria for mate choice all have often persuaded foreign observers that China remains one of the last bastions of premarital chastity. As with most stereotypes, there is both accuracy and error in these views. Unfortunately, we do not have very full information on this topic, as the interviewing setting did not allow us to inquire in detail about whether couples in our marriage cases had been sexually intimate or not. But from various pieces of evidence in our data a few generalizations can

25. We have noted that ethnic and regional origins do not figure prominently in the stated criteria for mates our informants give. When asked specifically, their views on the importance of this factor differed. Some felt, for example, that Cantonese did not like to marry Hakka, but were fairly amenable to marriage to people from northern provinces (which for Cantonese includes places like Shanghai). Others argued that such factors were not important anymore.

26. For the United States, see the sources cited in footnote 20 and A. C. Kerchoff, "Patterns of Homogamy and the Field of Eligibles," *Social Forces* 42 (1963–64): 289–97. For the Soviet Union, see Wesley Fisher, *The Soviet Marriage Market* (New York: Praeger, 1980).

be advanced. Many couples are still virgins when they marry, but the pattern is by no means universal. During the Cultural Revolution, some Red Guards received initiation into sex as well as politics. Even in the more controlled years that followed, most informants could describe cases of premarital pregnancies among people they knew, and so one must assume that the number of cases of couples who were sexually involved but avoided pregnancy must be even larger. Among the alienated and unemployed youths who disrupted social order in the 1970s (discussed in chapter 8), sexual activity seems to have been fairly common, and the official puritanism was rejected and ridiculed.

It has often been pointed out that the lack of privacy and facilities of a dating culture make it difficult for Chinese couples to find any place where they could have sex, but again the difficulties can be exaggerated. Chinese tend to be quite resourceful and ingenious, and it does not seem likely that a couple willing to engage in premarital sex could be deterred by this difficulty. Insofar as sexual frustration can be said to be a problem for young Chinese, it is mostly a problem of young people who have not had much luck in finding a romantic partner at all, and not so much an issue of couples who desire to begin sex but feel they must wait.[27] In general, then, we conclude that much courting activity in urban China is fairly restrained and chaste by Western standards, but that physical attractions do play some role in the courting process, and that in the fairly long period we have referred to as the "proto-dating" stage not a few couples manage to loose their virginity.

Variations in Freedom of Mate Choice

We have described earlier the evolving stages and expectations in urban mate choice in China, stressing the variety of obstacles that make freedom of mate choice difficult to realize. Here we want to provide some concluding observations on the role that parents now play in the mate choice process, and what the circumstances are that produce more or less freedom of choice.

Parents are still important in a number of ways, in spite of the general acceptance of free mate choice. As we noted earlier, about 21 percent of the marriages in our sample resulted from introductions arranged by parents, although parents generally have to get their offspring to agree even-

27. A Communist Youth League official has noted that some young people become mentally deranged due to frustrations over romance and marriage—*Shanxi Daily,* 22 October 1980, p. 3, in *FBIS,* 19 November 1980, p. L6. A Western journalist has described a rise in sexual offenses and rapes attributable to such frustration—Fox Butterfield, "Love and Sex in China," *New York Times Magazine,* 13 January 1980, pp. 15–17, 43–49.

tually or the marriage will not take place. Even if a couple has met on their own, the parental role is not unimportant. Couples are expected to seek the approval of their parents for the partner they have chosen. The proto-dating stage often involves mutual visiting in the homes of both families, so that the parents can have an opportunity to form an impression of the partner their son or daughter has chosen. Generally the visiting prospect tries to bring small gifts and perform tasks to earn the favor of the future in-laws, and clearly the views of the older generation are regarded as playing a important role in the matter.

In some cases, naturally enough, the parents do object to the prospect their son or daughter has chosen. If this happens considerable tension can occur, and there are no clear rules anymore on how the matter should be settled. Some young people will call the match off if their parents object, in deference to family feelings. Informants say simply that more docile and obedient youths are likely to do this, and that a really obedient offspring would consult with the parents early on, during the suitability-check stage, in order to be able to call the matter off before getting too emotionally involved. Parents are said to object on a whole variety of grounds—the prospect has a low status job, a bad political background, different regional or ethnic origins, the wrong age, or simply bad looks or an unsuitable personality.

If the parents object they often cannot prevent the marriage from occurring. Most informants agreed that if the young people were committed to each other, they could and would go ahead and marry even in the face of parental opposition. In urban China today parents do not control the sorts of resources they did in the past, and the bureaucratic gatekeepers guarding the marriage altar are not likely to be swayed by parental objections. Parents may take the extreme step of threatening to break off all family ties with the couple if they marry, but even this often fails to prevent the marriage. Our informants were able to supply quite a number of such cases, and usually the bold couple married, and after a child was born the grandparents softened and repaired the broken relations. Given the general inability of parents to prevent marriages they object to, most do not resort to such drastic tactics. Instead, it is more common for parents to voice their objections strongly, but if their son or daughter is not swayed they throw up their hands and reluctantly agree to accept the decision to marry. Of course, the fact that marriages are taking place at later ages makes it all the more possible for young people to stand up to parental opposition.

Several cases from our interviews illustrate the range of things that can occur when generations disagree on a marriage prospect. In one case a male from a Guangdong county capital worked as a temporary worker in a construction team. While doing some work in a neighboring county town he met a young woman who worked as a waitress there. They fell in love and in 1972 told her parents that they wanted to get married. The girl's parents opposed the relationship, arguing that he had no steady work, and they cursed their daughter for disregarding their wishes. When this conflict had gone on for some time she ran off and moved in with his family, who approved of the match. They married in 1973, and the groom offered to pay the bride's family 300 yuan from his savings as a bride price/peace offering, but they had still not cooled down enough to accept it by the time our informant left in 1974.[28]

Another case concerns a male worker in a district city in Guangdong. His parents had agreed when he was still young to have him marry a maternal cousin (an arrangement traditionally favored in some parts of China), and the two families often visited one another. But in 1972, when the male was 23, he fell in love with a female worker in his factory and told his parents he wanted to break off the betrothal to his cousin. His parents were angry, and they marched off to confront the factory director. They told him that their son was already married and that he should control the new girlfriend to keep her away from their son. The factory director replied that their son was not considered married in the eyes of the government or the unit, and that he could do nothing to interfere with the relationship with the new girlfriend. Not satisfied, the parents then went to the home of the girlfriend and told her parents that their son was spoken for and that they should keep better control over their daughter. With all the fuss caused by the male's parents, eventually the relationship with the girlfriend cooled, and the male worker was left without a prospect. Finally in 1975 he gave in to his parents' pleas and his feelings of obligation as an only son and agreed to marry the maternal cousin, although our informant felt his heart was not in it.[29]

Our final example concerns a couple from bad class origins who met during their middle school days in Canton. Their relationship as schoolmates blossomed into romance during the Cultural Revolution, but in 1968 they were sent to settle down in separate villages. Over the next few years they wrote letters to each other but could rarely meet, owing to the considerable distance between their villages. In 1971 a People's Liberation Army (PLA) veteran developed an interest in the girl and promised if she would marry him that he would arrange to get her household registration transferred back to Canton. She was sorely tempted, both because of her desire to escape the countryside and also because marriage to a PLA

28. Interview HHH1:7.
29. Interview SWP4:8.

veteran would help her to escape the political stigma of her family back-ground. Her parents wanted her to marry the army veteran and forsake the boyfriend in the village, but they did not force their views upon her. The girl wrote to her boyfriend telling him of her new suitor, and he rushed to see her. He managed to persuade her to remain true to him and marry him once they could get back to the city. In 1973 the boyfriend managed to get transferred back to a job in Canton while the girl was still stuck in her rural village. At this point her parents became anxious, and they went to visit the prospect they had once tried to discourage their daughter from marrying, using flattering words to try to make sure that he would not forget their daughter. Fortunately, the girl managed to get transferred back to a job in Canton in 1974, and the story ends happily with their marriage in 1975.[30]

Clearly there are variations in the extent of freedom of mate choice in urban China today, with young people more dominant in some matches, and parents relatively more influential in others. What characteristics help to explain this sort of variation? To examine this question, we constructed a scale composed of four separate codes: whether the couple met by introduction or directly, whether any introductions were provided by the parents or by contacts of the young people, how long the couple knew each other before marriage, and how extensive their proto-dating activities were. Matches that score high on this scale are viewed as the ones most removed from traditional modes of arranged marriage: matches in which the young couple met on their own or through their own contacts, got to know each other over an extended period of time, and often engaged in joint activities as a couple during the courting stage.

In table 11 we examine how scores on this scale are related to other characteristics, looking at the post-Cultural Revolution cases. The rela-tionships in the table are modest at best, but they suggest a few general patterns. First, for husbands there are fewer significant associations than for wives (only the finding that good class permitted males more free mate choice in the post-Cultural Revolution cases is statistically significant). Second, for wives there is a general pattern for women with good jobs and well-placed parents to exercise more freedom of mate choice than other females. (Curiously, female membership in the Youth League or Party is associated with less freedom of choice.) Third, there is evidence here that if the male and female grew up in the same community and if the female's parents reside in another city there is more free choice in-volved. Some expected patterns are not visible in table 11: There is no

30. Interview KSM27:20–21.

Table 11   **Freedom of Mate Choice by Selected**
                                   Characteristics (Correlations)

	Husband's Characteristics	Wife's Characteristics	Both
Socioeconomic Status			
Education	-.06	.12	
Occupation	-.05	.17*	
Parent's social status	.21	.41*	
Political Status			
Good class label	.18*	-.01	
Leadership role	.18	--	
Party/League member	--	-.33*	
No personal error	-.01	-.04	
No family error	-.19	.12	
Situational Factors			
Parents elsewhere	-.13	.25*	
Grew up in same city			.17*
City Characteristics			
Administrative level			-.06
Lingnan Region			.04

Source: Marriage sample, post-Cultural Revolution Cases only, median number of marriages in correlations = 125.

-- = not computed.

*p ≤ .10

evidence here of more free mate choice in larger cities, which may suggest that the conservative rural influences in small cities are counteracted by the lesser impersonality and greater ease of getting to know prospects in such communities. There is interestingly no strong evidence that the level of education of the male or female is the primary predictor of whether the match will be by free choice or not, which contrasts with Olga Lang's finding in the 1930s that this was the most important variable.[31]

The general situation conveyed by these figures is one in which the norm of free mate choice has been fairly widely diffused and accepted among the general population, rather than varying in clear ways in relation to educational level, political awareness, or occupational level. Certain situations can, however, give at least daughters more autonomy in mate choice, and these include having a good job, a well-off family, parents living elsewhere, and a prospect who has grown up within the same city.[32]

31. See Lang, *Chinese Family and Society.*

32. We note that this pattern is different from one commonly seen in other societies, in which upper class families tend to shelter and restrict their daughters, while working class women have more freedom in picking a mate.

Marriage Finance

In urban China as in rural China, the agreement to marry was traditionally contingent upon a marriage finance agreement and the negotiation of a written marriage contract between the two families. Commonly marriage finance involved what is technically called an "indirect dowry"—the male's family was required to deliver a bride price of cash and gifts to the bride's family, who might use part of this to hold their own celebration and the remainder, as well as funds of their own, to equip a dowry for the bride, which she would bring with her to the marriage.[33] Nowadays cases of such explicit interfamily negotiations over marriage finance are rare in large Chinese cities, although they persist in many rural areas and to some extent in smaller cities. There is also considerable flexibility and even ambiguity about the kinds of gifts and payments that may be expected in connection with a marriage. But many urban weddings still involve considerable expenditures, rather than the nominal gifts and frugal ceremonies the government would prefer. Here we will try to give a general picture of the range of practices that occurred in the 1970s.

First, it is clear that many marriages occur without any gift demands being made. In such cases the male may nonetheless decide to give a variety of presents to his future bride and her family during the period of courtship. A basic asymmetry is preserved, with presents originating from the male's side (although now often from the male himself, rather than from his parents), but their obligatory nature is gone. Sometimes gift demands are made, but even then they take a different form than in earlier times. The demand usually is not pressed in negotiations between the two families, but is made by the young woman to her suitor. The things that are demanded are quite modern in most cases, generally a set of expensive consumer durables. A number of informants refer to increasing requests in recent years for the "four big items," or the "three rounds and one sound" (a bicycle, sewing machine, wristwatch, and a radio), also for the "thirty legs" (of the bed, table, chairs, and other furniture the male is asked to supply).[34] The parents on each side will sometimes play some role in this gift exchange—the bride's by encouraging her to ask for certain

---

33. There might also be a separate, and earlier, engagement present from the groom's to the bride's family. The most detailed account of wedding expenditures before 1949, for Peking in 1926–27, is provided in Gamble, *How Chinese Families Live*, chap. 10. In ten marriage cases investigated by Gamble, the families involved spent from one and one half to nine times their family monthly income on celebrating a wedding, with the average being somewhat more than four months' income.

34. The cost of providing these items, and of celebrating a wedding in general, can be

items, and the groom's by helping him to pay for them if he is not able to do so himself. Still, these are not seen as an exchange between two families, but as a gift from the prospective groom to his intended. Such expensive gifts are meant to symbolize the male's seriousness about the match as well as to display that he is financially able to provide desirable items for his future family. We stress again, however, that such relatively expensive gifts were not demanded by many prospective brides in the period we are concerned with and that many marriages took place without them.

Whatever gifts are exchanged these days, they are not sufficient to equip a household for the new couple. The responsibility for providing whatever furniture, bedding, dishes, and other items are needed is again handled in different ways by different families, rather than according to a strict set of customary rules. If the new couple is to live with either set of parents, then that set of parents will play a major role in helping to furnish the new couple's room, but with the bride and groom usually chipping in to help pay for certain items. If the young couple lives separately, then in some cases a work unit will provide an apartment that is at least partly furnished, but if not, the couple is expected to do most of the furnishing out of their own savings, with parents helping out insofar as they are able. Many informants imply, though, that there remains a male bias in this regard as elsewhere in the marriage process, with the family of the groom or the groom himself expected to shoulder the main burden of furnishing the new apartment. For example, the male may purchase the bed and other furniture, the female the bedding. Finally, friends and workmates often chip in to buy wedding presents for the new couple or simply give them cash gifts that they can use to buy needed household items.

---

considerable. Our informants cited 500–800 as the "typical" range of expenditures by the male and his family on a wedding in the mid-1970s (including gifts supplied, furnishings, and the cost of the wedding banquets) and 300–500 yuan as the cost to the female side. Expenditure by the male side would represent something like three to five months' family income for the average urban family. If we go by these estimates and the fragmentary figures Gamble gives for Peking in the 1920s, we might conclude that fifty years later there has been little change in the economic burden weddings represent. However, we stress again that there was considerable variability during the period we are dealing with, and that some couples married with minimal expenditures. Chinese press reports in more recent years suggest that the post-Mao liberalizations may have led to wedding expenditures becoming higher and more obligatory. For example, one study in Peking in 1980 claimed an average wedding expenditure of 1,554 yuan, with most of this spent on gifts and furnishings. See *People's Daily,* 3 January 1981, p. 4.

The Wedding

The wedding itself has also changed in substantial ways compared with earlier generations. First, the selecting of a time for the wedding is generally handled differently. Traditionally, ritual specialists were consulted who used the horoscopes of the young couple to select a particularly auspicious wedding day. Nowadays few such specialists are left in urban areas, and in only a handful of marriage cases was there mention of this sort of date setting. Instead the date is usually set to fit the work schedules and personal convenience of the bride and groom and their families. This means that the most popular dates are just before official holidays, with the longest of these, the three-day Spring Festival (traditional Chinese New Year), the most popular time in the year for weddings. By this sort of scheduling couples can "piggyback" the paid leave they get for a wedding (generally three days) with the paid leave of the holiday, and use this time to get settled in their new home or even to take a honeymoon-like trip.

The issue of setting the date introduces a note of ambiguity about just what event constitutes the wedding. There is now a required civil marriage registration procedure, as we noted earlier. But in many cases there is also a family wedding celebration, whose central event is a banquet. Informants gave different views on which event "really" signifies when the couple is considered married. It is our impression that among intellectuals the registration is increasingly seen as the crucial moment, while among ordinary urbanites the wedding celebration is still seen as the moment of transition. The latter may occur right after the registration, or not until several days or weeks later. Some feel that conjugal relations can begin in the interim, but most do not.

The registration itself is devoid of any ceremonial activity. Here the Chinese have not followed the Soviet model of trying to elaborate civil registration into a ceremonial substitute for traditional weddings by providing music, flowers, fancy wedding garments, and so forth. Instead the couple goes in ordinary street clothes with their work unit approval certificates and proceeds to have the match registered in the marriage registration office within the neighborhood government office (either where the bride resides or where the groom resides).[35] In a small minority of our

35. In the 1950s a medical examination used to be required preliminary to marriage registration. Later on this requirement seems to have been dropped or ignored, and few of our informants mentioned this as a preliminary. However, in more recent years the government's advocacy of "one child families" and encouragement of eugenics to promote high quality offspring seemed to be leading to a revival of concern about premarital medical exams. See *Xinhua* (Peking), 18 February 1981, in *FBIS*, 18 February 1981, p. R3, and Shanghai Academy of Social Sciences, "Investigation," p. 79.

marriage cases (only 8 percent, N = 191) there were no other festivities to speak of. The couple simply moved into their new room and began life as man and wife, perhaps with a few close friends or relatives dropping by to have tea and eat candy, or with small gifts or candy being given out to close friends and coworkers the next day in order to announce that a wedding had taken place. This very simple and frugal style of wedding, which involves only 10 or 20 yuan or so to provide the small group of guests with tea and refreshments, is of course the sort of wedding that the authorities would like to promote. This style has given rise to new kinds of expressions and phrases. A colleague who jokingly wants to inquire when you are going to get married may ask, "When are you going to invite me to eat candy?" But we should underline that much more is involved in the majority of urban marriages besides sipping tea and eating candy with friends.

In the large majority of cases a wedding is focused around feasting activity, as it was traditionally. The nature of this activity has changed somewhat over the years, though. Traditionally the main activity was a feast in the home of the groom's family, or sometimes separate feasts in the homes of the bride's and groom's families. By the 1930s it became increasingly common to hold such wedding banquets in restaurants, and these meals formed an important part of the business of such establishments. Such banquets were continued into the 1950s, but since the end of that decade the government has tried to discourage wedding feasting and other extravagances, and during the Cultural Revolution decade a family could be subjected to public criticism for holding a lavish wedding feast. Nevertheless, the desire for a wedding feast is still quite strong. Some kind of wedding banquet was held in 92 percent of our marriage cases, and in 46 percent of the cases the feasting was fairly elaborate, with fifty or more people attending.

How do families manage to hold such feasts, if the authorities frown on them? Several strategies were utilized in the 1970s. First, very few families held wedding banquets in a restaurant, unless it was a very modest affair. Instead, wedding banquets have retreated back into the home. There both the cramped living conditions and the desire to avoid attracting attention led most families to break up wedding banquets into several modest meals, each attended by no more than 10 or 15 people. So in such cases guests ate in shifts and even came on successive days, with coworkers invited for one meal, family friends for another, and sometimes with simultaneous small banquets being held by both the bride's and groom's families. Finally, in some cases individuals were confident enough of their relations with their neighbors and work unit authorities that they could still hold a large banquet, with neighboring families cooperating by lending their apartments to accommodate additional tables, and in turn being invited to join in the banquet. Similarly, work unit leaders might be coopted by inviting them to attend a banquet and even serve as the master of ceremonies, giving a small speech.[36]

While wedding feasting activity is still seen as quite important, even if not absolutely obligatory, many of the ceremonial aspects of the wedding have been altered substantially. In traditional weddings the bride dressed in red, and later urbanites sometimes adopted the Western style of a white wedding gown and tuxedo, but now the general dress code for weddings involves simply new clothes of ordinary style.[37] Brides used to be fetched for the ceremonies in sedan chairs, and in later years often in a taxi or limousine, but only a minority of our marriage cases from the 1970s involved any formal bride-fetching rituals. Instead, she would usually arrive under her own steam and without ceremony. Most other traditional rituals are also gone: ritually cleansing the bride when she emerges from the sedan chair, bowing to parents, making offerings to the ancestors, reading the marriage contract, and making speeches about fertility and filial piety. Instead there is a minimum of ceremony. The guests feast, and the new couple goes around to toast the guests, and sometimes there will be a short speech about the obligations of the new couple to each other and to society. In some of our marriage cases a new ritual had been adopted in place of some of the old ones: during the ceremony the couple would bow to a portrait of Chairman Mao and make a pledge of devotion. However, this ritual was not generally followed, even during the headiest years of the Cultural Revolution.[38] In some cases younger guests stay on after

36. Traditionally wedding banquets were presided over by respected local figures as masters of ceremonies, who gave speeches of blessing to the new couple. See Lang, *Chinese Family and Society,* p. 132, and William Sewell, "The Banker Marries," in *The People of Wheelbarrow Lane* (London: Allen and Unwin, 1970). Putting a leading cadre from one's work unit in this role is simply an adaptation of the traditional custom. As to the willingness of such leaders to take part in such "feudal" weddings, informants often noted, "cadres have a different face outside of the work unit."

37. On 1920s and 1930s ceremonies, see Lang, *Chinese Family and Society,* pp. 130–33, and Gamble, *How Chinese Families Live,* pp. 204–5. Before the Cultural Revolution couples often rented Western-style wedding garments to have a formal wedding portrait taken, but wore more ordinary clothes at the meal itself. This sort of portrait fell out of favor in the Cultural Revolution, but appears to be making a comeback.

38. Bowing to Mao is again an adaption of traditional customs of bowing to ancestors and elders. This adaption is described as occurring in a rural village as early as 1955. See W. R. Geddes, *Peasant Life in China,* Society for Applied Anthropology Monograph no. 6 (Ithaca, 1963), p. 25. In some of our wedding cases discordant elements were combined—bowing to Mao along with elaborate bride fetching and feasting, for example. Group wedding ceremonies, in which several couples marry at the same time, were fostered in the 1950s but had gone out of style in the period we are concerned with.

the feasting is over to engage in continued toasting and teasing of the new couple, but this activity seems less boisterous than the "teasing of the new bride" that occurred traditionally and that is now seen as an optional element. The general picture, then, of wedding festivities is that they took more varied forms during the period we are concerned with and were somewhat simplified and secularized, but that there was still a minimum sort of feasting activity that most people feel is needed in order to begin married life.

If we look at the contemporary customs in regard to marriage finance and wedding celebrations, we can see that they symbolize important changes in the conceptions Chinese urbanites have of the meaning of marriage. Very clearly the role of the bride and groom as the focus has been heightened, and the stress on the interaction between the two families has been reduced. For example, even when an elaborate feast is held, many of those invited are friends and fellow workers selected by the bride and groom, rather than people who have ties with the parents. The gifts to the young couple, the ability of the bride to arrive on her own, rather than being fetched away from her family, the general absence of bowing to parents and ancestors—these and other elements all point to the increased importance of the conjugal relationship rather than the familial alliance formed by the wedding. The fact that marriage finance no longer involves demands for a bride price also symbolizes the fact that rights over the bride are not being transferred to the groom's family in the same way that this used to be seen, and is still seen in rural China. The fact that a feast of some kind, even if quite modest, is regarded as essential by most urbanites does indicate that marriage is still perceived as a vitally important transition in life, one whose passage cannot be properly marked by simply passing around a few pieces of candy and drinking some tea. Marriage remains an event to be elaborately celebrated, insofar as circumstances allow, but it is a celebration of a new conjugal unit, rather than of a new addition (the bride) to an existing family unit.

What characteristics influence whether a wedding is elaborate or simple? To answer this, we use a composite scale made up of seven separate codes: whether there were demands for gifts before the wedding, whether the expenditure on gifts was high or low, whether there were wedding celebrations in the unit, whether a wedding banquet of some size was held, whether some traditional rituals were observed at the wedding, and whether the cost of the wedding to the male side, and the total cost, were high (e.g., 1,000 yuan or more) or low. This we refer to as our Wedding Simplicity Scale, since a high score indicates the sort of simple wedding the authorities would prefer. In table 12 we present the results of looking at the correlates of wedding simplicity.

In terms of characteristics of individuals and families, table 12 makes clear that weddings tend to be simpler when the husband is more highly educated, when the husband has committed a political error, when his family has committed an error, when either set of parents lives elsewhere than in the city where the marriage occurs, and when either spouse carries a good class label. Several types of influences seem to be operating here. Husband's education might be seen as reflecting the influences of enlightenment, with the better educated more willing to dispense with "feudal" rituals. However, it should be noted that several other variables that might

Table 12   Simple Wedding Celebrations by
                                                Selected Characteristics (Partial
                                                Correlations)[a]

	Husband's Characteristics	Wife's Characteristics	Both
Socioeconomic Status			
Education	(.38*)[b]	−.06[c]	
Occupation	−.09[d]	−.09[d]	
Parent's social status	.01	.07	
Political Status			
Good class label	.15*	.12*	
Leadership role	.11	−−	
Party/League member	−−	.06	
No personal error	−.33*	.21	
No family error	−.29*	.07	
Situational Factors			
Parents elsewhere	.17*	.26*	
Grew up in same city			−.09
City and Neighborhood Characteristics			
Neighborhood stability			−.28*
Work unit compound			.38*
Household control scale			.32*
Neighborhood infrastructure			−.01
Political study			.30*
White collar neighbors			.31*
Ration and supply scale			.07
Low unemployment			−.24*
City administrative level			.08
Lingnan Region			.09

Source: Marriage sample, median sample size for city and neighborhood characteristics = 36 and for other characteristics = 89.

[a] Correlations controlled for husband's education.

[b] Simple correlation prior to control.

[c] Prior to control this correlation was .25.*

[d] Prior to control these correlations were each .10.

−− = not computed.

*p ≤ .10

be presumed to reflect enlightenment, such as husband's leadership, wife's Party membership, high occupational status of the couple and parents, and the level of the city, do not seem to have an independent effect upon the simplicity of the wedding. Perhaps more educated males also tend to end up in types of work units where the pressure for simple weddings is more directly felt. The relationships with male and female errors we assume to reflect a fear factor, with those who have been in trouble less willing to attract attention to themselves by engaging in "feudal" traditions. Finally, the fact that weddings are simple when the two sets of parents do not reside locally also makes a great deal of sense, since much of the impetus for elaborating the celebration and inviting more guests comes from the families of the couple. In some cases where the two sets of parents both live elsewhere, the couple may engage in one of the "model" simplified wedding tea parties and then take a few days for a trip to visit the parents, where they may find a belated wedding feast of some kind awaiting them.[39] Finally, we note here, in contrast to table 11, that characteristics of the husband and his family make more difference than those of the wife. This pattern is also understandable, since there is still a tendency for the wedding festivities to be seen as more the responsibility of the husband's side.

The kind of neighborhood in which the wedding takes place also influences wedding simplicity. From table 12 we can see that weddings tend to be simpler in newly built, white collar neighborhoods and work unit compounds where political study and household controls are well developed, and also in neighborhoods where private housing is rare and unemployment is a problem. Again we suggest that it is not simply education or class-related enlightenment that is important for promoting simple weddings. The figures in the last part of table 12 imply that when individuals are heavily dependent upon neighbors with whom they don't share long histories of cooperation, when they feel subject to fairly rigorous social control devices—conditions most common in the compounds of bureaucratic offices—they tend to hold fairly modest wedding celebrations. When their neighborhood has economic problems they will also feel less pressure to hold an elaborate wedding. In general the findings displayed in table 12 suggest that those most subject to pressure to hold simple weddings, and those least able to draw upon the support and pressure of nearby parents and lifelong neighbors in favor of elaborate feasting and expenditures, will tend to comply most closely with the official ideals of frugality.

39. We only coded for marriage ceremonies held within the city where the marriage occurred, so these later and more elaborate celebrations would not be included in our codes. These trips are facilitated by the few days of paid leave for weddings mentioned earlier.

Postmarital Residence

With the wedding concluded, normal marital relations can begin. The final issue we take up in this chapter is where those relations begin, i.e., where does the new couple live after marriage? As we have seen, there is no free market in housing in urban China, and housing is a very scarce commodity. Traditionally it was generally expected that the couple would move in with the groom's family, at last initially, in the customary arrangement referred to as patrilocal residence. When we asked informants where people tend to live after marriage today, many simply replied "wherever there is the most room" or "wherever they can get access to housing." These replies suggest that the housing shortage and bureaucratic controls over housing have eliminated any concern for traditional customs and have produced a high degree of flexibility in deciding where to live. To expand a bit on the "general preference" replies, informants say that the couple will consider first whether either set of parents has extra room and, if so, will move in with whoever has the most room. Only if neither set of parents has enough room to accommodate them will they be considered eligible for a waiting list for unit housing or city-run mixed public housing. In these latter cases, also, informants suggest that the couple will apply wherever their chances of success seem greatest. These comments all imply a fairly even distribution across different housing possibilities in recent years. Some informants even argue that, insofar as preference for a particular arrangement is felt, it is for one that is quite different from the traditional patrilocal pattern. They argue that a new preference for residence with the bride's parents has emerged, since fewer family conflicts arise this way than in the traditional patrilocal arrangement.

When we examine the actual places where the couples in our marriage cases lived, it turns out that these general responses are quite misleading. In our post-Cultural Revolution cases (N = 359), 38 percent moved in with the groom's parents and only 3 percent moved in with the bride's parents. Furthermore, there is no evidence in our sample that the frequency of residence with the bride's family has increased in recent years. These cases also make clear, though, that the most common pattern is for the new couple to set up a household separate from either set of parents—what anthropologists call neolocal residence. To be specific, in our post-Cultural Revolution cases, 29 percent of the couples lived in work unit quarters, 23 percent lived in a city-run apartment, and 7 percent lived separated from each other, because of household registrations and jobs in different locales. It might be noted that even within the neolocal arrangements there is a male bias—where males and females worked in different units it was about six times as common for them to end up living in unit housing of the male rather than unit housing of the female.[40] So not only do urbanites still generally feel that the male's family has greater responsibility than the female's for furnishing the new housing, but work unit and city housing authorities also tend to assume that preference should be given to male-oriented arrangements.[41] In any event, the clearest pattern is not a weakening of the male bias in housing arrangements but a shift toward neolocal residence. This shift is quite understandable in terms of the increasingly tight housing supply and decreasing family control over housing that we have described.

One final question concerns whether there is a general syndrome of marriage behavior in contemporary cities, such that some people tend to marry late, exercise freedom of choice, hold simple and frugal weddings, and perhaps live separately from the groom's parents while others follow more traditional patterns. An examination of this question using scales used in earlier tables revealed that there was no such general pattern. So, for example, males who marry late are more likely than men who marry early to hold fairly simple wedding ceremonies, but they turn out to be somewhat less likely than younger men to exercise freedom of choice. Couples who have met and fallen in love directly are not more likely than introduced couples to hold a simple wedding or to live separately from their parents. These findings reaffirm a point we have been stressing throughout this chapter. The marriage behavior of urbanites is not primarily reflective of some overall ideological state (modern versus traditional, or socialist versus bourgeois or feudal) or of some general propensity to comply with or ignore official marriage ideals. Instead, young people face a number of constraints, opportunities, and pressures that they react to and that affect different portions of the mate selection process in varying ways, and the outcome may be combinations that strike ideologues as odd—introduced couples bowing to a Mao portrait at the wedding, for

40. To be specific, 15 percent of the post-1966 marriage cases involved moves into housing supplied by the male's unit, as opposed to only 2.5 percent moving into housing supplied by the woman's unit. A further 12 percent were cases where the bride and groom worked in the same unit and secured housing there. Our figures can be compared with data collected in a single neighborhood in Tientsin in 1981 by Burton Pasternak and his Chinese collaborators. Of married women born after 1951, 26 percent moved in with the groom's family, 5 percent with the bride's family, 2 percent did not establish a common residence, and 67 percent adopted a neolocal residence. See Pan Yunkang and Pan Naigu, "Preliminary Views on Our Country's Urban Families and Family Structures," *Tianjin Shehui Kexue*, no. 3 (1982): 11.

41. This preference for allocating housing to male staff members has been criticized more recently in the Chinese press. See, for example, *Xinhua* (Peking), 22 March 1981, in *FBIS*, 23 March 1981, pp. L21–22.

example, or couples who meet directly and fall in love spending lavishly on wedding festivities.

Conclusions

Having examined the various stages in the contemporary mate selection process in urban China, we must now return to the questions with which we began this section. First we must discuss which aspects of marriage behavior have changed, and which traditional customs remain in effect.

A number of areas of change in marriage are quite clear. Both males and females are marrying considerably later than they did before 1949. Many more couples today meet without parental introduction, and young people have much more control over the final decision on whether to marry or not. Marriages usually do not involve the financial and gift negotiations between the two families that were common in the past, and the expenditures are more optional. For some families the relative cost of a son or daughter's marriage may be comparable to the burden felt by families in the 1920s and 1930s, but in a considerable number of cases weddings are now quite inexpensive affairs. Weddings are today shorn of most of their traditional ritual elements, and in some cases no wedding banquet is held at all. Finally, in a majority of cases of contemporary urban marriage the couple does not start their married life with the male's parents, but in a separate apartment provided by a work unit or city housing office.

While the changes in marriage customs are important, we also need to note that there are clear signs of continuity in the marriage process as we have described it. Nobody could mistake the patterns of courtship and marriage in contemporary China for those existing in advanced Western societies or the Soviet Union. For one thing, a dating culture is still largely absent, and this absence poses a number of obstacles to youths exercising free choice in choosing a mate. Public displays of affection and premarital sexual involvement are still strongly frowned upon, although engaged in by the hardy few. Even with young people tending to have the final say in marriage, the role of explicit status criteria in picking a mate continues to be very important, while the role of romantic feelings is variable. Public opinion still makes most weddings more expensive affairs than the simple tea parties that the government would like to popularize. In spite of the increasing educational access and employment of women, there are still very clear kinds of male bias reflected in marriage customs—in the greater desire to protect the virtue of daughters than sons, the heavier financial burden that marriage poses for the groom and his parents, and the continued preference for residence with the groom's parents for those not able to obtain new housing. All these aspects of continuity reflect the time when marriage was more of a family affair that brought an emotionally uninvolved female out of her own family and incorporated her into the family of her new husband. Can these traditional elements can expected to disappear in time? Perhaps, but we should note that our data don't show any marked evidence of change in most of these elements (except for marriage age) since the late 1950s. This suggests that a relatively stable compromise form of marriage, mixing old and new, emerged in socialist China fairly early on and has not changed markedly in recent years.

If we want to explain why changes in marriage have occurred, it is tempting to attribute them to government policies, for after all, in large part official policy in China has promoted most of the changes we noted. However, at several points in this chapter we have suggested that the change process is more complex. First, most of the changes were underway before 1949, even though the political scene was very different then. Second, the kinds of individuals who are most likely to comply with the official ideals of late, free choice, frugal marriages are not particularly those who are most "red"—Party members, leaders, and people with good class backgrounds—who might be expected to be most responsive to government pronouncements. Third, except for marriage age most aspects of the marriage process apparently have not changed markedly since the late 1950s, even though government pressure for more spartan and revolutionary weddings heightened considerably during the Cultural Revolution decade. Finally, there are places we have noted young people adapting to their changed environment by altering their marriage customs in ways the political authorities clearly disapprove of. The romantic and sexual experimentation of some Red Guards is one example, and the shift in favor of looking for immediate material benefits in marriage is another. All of these observations suggest that pressure from the government is only one element in a complicated change process. Also clearly important are alterations in the opportunity structure facing young people and the extent to which they can draw on resources independently of their parents. Clearly important as well are things that affect the urban "marriage market"—the supply of eligible and desirable spouses, ways young people can meet and pair off, and opportunities to get to know prospects well enough to be able to decide whether to marry them. It is unfortunately not possible to totally disentangle the several elements in the change process to be certain how important each is in affecting different aspects of marriage change.

A final reason not to attribute most of the changes visible to direct government pressure comes from considering our next question: How distinctive are the changes in marriage behavior that have taken place?

We must conclude that many of the changes parallel those in other developing societies, even though most of these other societies have very different political systems and family policies. In particular, the shift toward later marriage age, more freedom of choice, and separate residence, it has been argued by William Goode, is part of a "world revolution" taking place today which involves industrialization, urbanization, and other forms of modernization producing more of a "conjugal" emphasis in family life.[42] The conjugal family, as defined by Goode, is distinguished by the paramount importance of the husband-wife tie and by a weakened role of extended kin power and obligations. Earlier in this chapter we used this term and noted a variety of ways in which the contemporary marriage customs we have been describing involve such an increasing conjugal emphasis. We will have occasion to comment later on some limits in the extent of this shift toward the conjugal family in the Chinese case, but still it is important to stress that many of the changes we have observed are not unique to the Chinese scene.

The fact that many of the changes are familiar ones also leads us to doubt that they are primarily a product of the distinctive urban institutions operating in the Chinese case. For instance, in a number of other cultures a reversal of the relationship between class and marriage behavior has been commented upon. Before modern social changes have much effect, the middle and upper classes tend to be most strict about observing traditional marriage customs, and the lower classes, with far fewer resources, are less so. With modernization the advantaged classes participate more in modern education, employment and other change-inducing environments, with the result that eventually their marriage behavior becomes less traditional than in the lower classes. In urban China there is evidence of the same sort of reversal.[43] However, while the broad pattern of change is not unique to China, there still are some ways in which the distinctive nature of urban institutions in China has made its influence felt. For one thing, the changes in such things as marriage ages and wedding ceremonies seem to us to have been unusually rapid in the Chinese case, and it is plausible to suggest that the highly bureaucratized nature of Chinese cities has accelerated the process.[44] Simpler wedding ceremonies are not a nec-

42. Goode, *World Revolution and Family Patterns*.
43. We noted earlier that this trend for a reversal of class differences in marriage patterns began before 1949. Some of our informants felt that status differentials in the type and lavishness of wedding celebrations were less now than before 1949.
44. The fundamental structural mechanism underlying the modernization-induced shifts toward the conjugal family in other societies, as analyzed by Goode, is the decline in the control over property and economic opportunities by families and kin groups and the increase in such control by nonkin bureaucratic structures (schools, factories, and so forth) that modernization produces. Although it could be argued from China's economic level that it

essary part of Goode's conjugal syndrome and may be attributable in part to bureaucratic controls and coercion. Finally, although the concern for status matching in marriage remains important as before, the distinctive institutions and recent history of urban China have altered the status hierarchy and the mate criteria in important ways. So while the general pattern of change looks familiar, the speed and some of the details may be regarded as distinctive features of the Chinese case.

If we consider whether the pattern of change in marriage customs has produced disorganization and problems, the initial impulse is to answer negatively. Certainly the kinds of breakdown of moral consensus and control visible in urban areas in at least some developing countries, with rising illegitimacy, prostitution, and common-law marriages, seem virtually nonexistent in urban China in the period we are concerned with. Indeed, some would argue that a new puritanism was put into force, with the power of the state restoring and reinforcing the familial controls over sexuality and mating that were beginning to break down before 1949. To be sure, there are cases of premarital pregnancies, and even a few instances of cohabitation without marriage turned up in our interviews, but still there is very little evidence that marked changes in marriage behavior and the surrounding society have produced the sorts of problems visible on a large scale in some other developing societies. We do not wish to imply, however, that all is well with the marriage institution in urban China, for from the pattern of change that has occurred a distinctive set of problems and concerns has arisen.

For many if not most urban youths, the modified set of marriage customs today clearly "works"—they are able to find spouses and are satisfied with the choices they have made. But there are at least two major problem areas that have arisen as a consequence of the changes we have described. The first is that for a considerable number of youths in recent years, the difficulties of finding a suitable mate have become a source of much anxiety and frustration. In earlier chapters we noted how the disruption of the urban opportunity structure undermined school behavior and work discipline. Now we see that this disruption also interferes with the process of mate choice. Young people who have seen the way their older siblings and relatives were able to marry and establish families as well as careers despair of their own ability to do so. Disrupted education, years in the countryside, a late start in a poorly paid, low prestige urban job—these

---

has not yet modernized much (hence the need for pursuing the current "four modernizations" drive), the extensive bureaucratization of urban life described in previous chapters
has meant that this decline in family controls has occurred more rapidly and totally than in
other societies. In other words, the Chinese pattern of bureaucratic socialism accelerated
changes that could have been expected to occur more gradually with economic development.

common life experiences leave may urban youths in their late twenties and early thirties still agonizing about whether they can ever find and attract a suitable mate.[45] And in their anxiety and desperation to get their lives back on track, they may be led to enter into marriage with partners that they are not very well suited to.

The second problem is a related one. The notion of free mate choice presupposes that couples can get to know a prospective partner well enough to decide whether they want to marry them or not. However, the nature of the mate choice process in China places various obstacles in the way of the ability of youths to make this decision "wisely." First, a minority of young people not only rely on introductions but make very little attempt to get to know their prospective partners before marrying them. Second, some individuals clearly place status criteria of various kinds above romantic feelings and personal compatibility as the basis for choosing a spouse, while others may become anxious enough to accept the first willing prospect that comes along. Finally, even when couples engage in proto-dating for an extended period of time, if they have second thoughts and want to pull out before marriage, they may find that pressure from family and friends makes it difficult for them to do so. All of these circumstances result in couples marrying who are not deeply in love and not very compatible.[46] In the traditional marriage system the absence of love and failure to establish personal compatibility were not always sources of serious problems later on. Young people had low expectations of marital happiness and had overarching loyalties to parents and extended families that might make the difficulties of such a marriage tolerable. Of course a relationship that began with little feeling might blossom into an affectionate partnership. But in today's China the situation is different. As ideals of romantic love and personal compatibility have been accepted, and as larger numbers of couples have started off married life in an independent household, expectations about the quality of the marital relationship have risen. Substantial numbers of individuals, then, find themselves in marriages that they find unsatisfying. One additional element has made such feelings especially troublesome. This is the official policy of sternly discouraging divorce. Even couples who have severe conflicts and demand

45. See, for example, Xiao Cheng, "The Change in Marriage Concepts in the Mainland," *Zhengming* 42 (1981): 17–18; *Shanxi Daily,* 22 October 1980, p. 3, in *FBIS,* 19 November 1980, pp. L6–7; Butterfield, "Love and Sex"; and Liu Xinwu et al., *Come Let Us Talk of Love,* translated in *Chinese Sociology and Anthropology* 14, no. 2 (1981–82).

46. These problems are not unique to China, but occur in any society emphasizing freedom of mate choice—although we suspect that they are more common in a society like China where no real dating culture exists, where the constraints on premarital relationships are strong, and where disrupted opportunities upset the marriage market.

a divorce will generally receive "mediation" and be told to go back and try to solve their problems and stay married. This means that such couples may feel themselves stuck for life in an unsatisfying or conflictual marriage.[47] Thus, both difficulties in finding a spouse and dissatisfaction with the spouses chosen were causes for increasing emotional concern during the period we are concerned with.

More recently, the post-Mao leadership has begun to recognize these problems and has taken some initial steps to deal with them. Problems of romance and mate choice are no longer tabooed topics for discussion in the mass media, and stories of love and marriage difficulties have begun to appear with some regularity in newspapers and popular literature. The authorities have not only taken steps to try to restore the opportunity structure for urban youths, but also to make it easier for them to find potential spouses. Since 1980 public marriage introduction agencies have been opened in many Chinese cities and seem to have attracted a large number of customers.[48] At about the same time, new and as yet rather timid efforts have been been made to introduce sex education materials into the curricula of some urban middle schools.[49] There was also a slight revision of the divorce provisions in the 1980 version of the Marriage Law that seemed to reflect official recognition of the need for some liberalization of the policy against divorce.[50] The changes instituted so far seem modest, however, and 1981 press articles denouncing moral laxity among youths and the revival of lavish spending on weddings make it seem unlikely that the government will encourage any major liberalization in policy affecting marriage.

47. The inability to get out of an unhappy marriage is criticized in Shanghai Academy of Social Sciences, Institute of Sociology, "Investigation," p. 93. One other report (Xiao Cheng, "Change in Marriage Concepts," p. 18) claims that 52 percent of the cases of murder by women in southern Shaanxi Province involved husbands slain by women who had fallen out of love with them and in love with another man, but had been unable to get a divorce.

48. See, for example, Xiao Cheng, "Change in Marriage Concepts"; Xu Wulin, "Should Marriage Be Based upon Politics or on Love?" Xinhua Monthly Abstracts, no. 10 (1979): 34–35; and a letter to the editor, "What Should You Do If You Fall in Love with Two People?" Zhongguo Qingnian, no. 1 (1980): 46.

49. See the report in Ming Bao, 3 May 1980, p. 3.

50. The text of the 1950 law can be found in Meijer, Marriage Law and Policy, Appendix 8, and the 1980 revision in Xinhua (Peking), 15 September 1980, in FBIS, 19 September 1980, pp. L22–25.

6   The Organization of Urban Families

The Chinese family has long been known as a pervasively important and highly solidary institution. Indeed, one authority argues that, "family loyalty has been the overriding motive in Chinese life at every social level to an extent generally considered to have few if any parallels."[1] For some time there were recurring rumors in the West that the family in China was being destroyed by China's new rulers and replaced by a collective system oriented to loyalty to the father figure of Mao Zedong. It is now clear that such fears were unfounded, and that the Chinese family is alive and perhaps even thriving in contemporary China. Still, important changes have taken place in family organization whose nature we wish to understand better. As in chapter 5, we want to consider as we describe contemporary family patterns what evidence they provide in regard to our main orienting questions: How much of the traditional family patterns have survived or been changed and why? Have the changes that have occurred resulted from direct government efforts or simply from urbanites reacting to the altered social environment in which they now live? Are the changes that have occurred in urban family life occurring in many other developing societies, or are they unique products of the distinctive form of Chinese urbanism? Have the kinds of family disorganization and problems visible in many other Third World cities been serious, or are there a set of family problems occurring that are distinctive to urban China? In the pages that follow we will not be able to discuss all aspects of family life but will focus first on the structures into which Chinese families are organized and then on the internal relationships that prevail within such families. We rely heavily on data from our neighbor household census sample of 581 families (and the weighted version of this sample).

1. Charles Madge, "The Relevance of Family Patterns to the Process of Modernization in East Asia," in *Social Organization and the Application of Anthropology,* Robert J. Smith, ed. (Ithaca: Cornell University Press, 1974), p. 164.

Family Size and Structure

Early Western observers of Chinese family life, in keeping with the views of many Chinese commentators, stressed that China was distinct from the West in having a prevalence of "big families"—family compounds with several generations and a number of related married couples living together. They cited the Confucian ideal of having "five generations under one roof," and they noted the custom of sons marrying and bringing their brides to live in the homes of their parents.[2] Modernization theories would lead one to anticipate that such complex, extended families would decline in importance in modernizing Chinese cities. Although the Chinese Communists have not attacked extended family living per se, one might also anticipate that socialist reforms, and particularly the elimination of land and other property controlled by family heads, would similarly promote smaller and simpler family forms. But analyzing trends in Chinese family size is complicated by our awareness that few families in earlier periods realized the traditional ideals or remained "big families" for long. The sort of large family compound with dozens of members portrayed in China's classic novel *The Dream of the Red Chamber* may have had a powerful impact on popular thinking, but such families were decidedly unusual. So if we wish to examine changes in urban family life we must first seek some baseline data on what sorts of families were typical in earlier years.[3]

We have examined a number of sociological studies of Chinese family forms in urban areas, both studies from earlier decades in this century and ones of recent patterns in Taiwan. We summarize what these studies say about family size and structure in table 13. Family size is simply the total number of individuals who are members of the economic and residential unit that is the family, and as such, size can increase both by having more children or by expanding into an extended family—by having more adults or married couples than the one couple needed to form a nuclear family. Since family size is "contaminated" by differential fertility we will focus our discussion on the family structure figures in the table, and then take up the issue of the changing number of children in urban families. The family structure categories in the table are those commonly used in studies of this type. Nuclear families consist of a couple and

2. For a good general discussion of both traditional family ideals and their realization, see Hugh Baker, *Chinese Family and Kinship* (New York: Columbia University Press, 1979), chap. 1.

3. The modernization argument in regard to family forms is presented in William J. Goode, *World Revolution and Family Patterns* (New York: Free Press, 1963). For an application to Chinese data on family forms, see William L. Parish, "Modernization and Household Composition in Taiwan," in *Chinese Family Law and Social Change in Historical and Comparative Perspective,* David Buxbaum, ed. (Seattle: University of Washington Press, 1978).

Table 13

Family Size and Family Structure Distribution in Chinese Cities

	Sample	Year	Mean Family Size	% Nuclear Units	% Stem Units	% Joint Units	% Single, Other	N of Families
Contemporary China								
Lingnan cities	Weighted neighbor census	1972–1978	4.4	68	22	2	8	451
Pre-1949 China								
a. N. China/Shanghai	Various strata	1935–1937	5.1	55	34	10	--	1573
1. N. China/Shanghai	Working class	1935–1937	4.1	61	31	7	--	569
2. N. China/Shanghai	Lower middle class	1935–1937	4.4	53	35	12	--	293
3. N. China/Shanghai	Middle class	1935–1937	6.1	51	34	15	--	511
4. N. China/Shanghai	Upper class	1935–1937	6.4	52	29	19	--	200
b. Peking suburb	Town survey	1928–1929	4.9	82[a]		18	--	371
c. Nanking	Working class areas	ca. 1930	4.3	48		44[a]	7	2027
d. Various	College student families	1923	9.0	--	--	--	--	610
Contemporary Taiwan								
e. Taipei suburb	Neighborhood survey	1970	5.5	67	21	4	8	196
f. Tainan	Married male sample	1966–1967	--	58	29	14	3	358
g. Kaohsiung	Married male sample	1966–1967	--	79	15	2	4	148

Sources: Contemporary China: Weighted sample of neighbor households from Lingnan Region. a: Olga Lang, *Chinese Family and Society* (New Haven:Yale University Press, 1946), chap. 12. b: Leonard Hsu et al., Ching Ho: *A Sociological Analysis* (Peiping: Yenching University, 1930), pp. 38–42. c: L. S. C. Smythe, "The Composition of the Chinese Family," *Nanking Journal*, 5, no. 1: (1935): table 6. d: A. Milam, A Study of Student Homes of China (New York: Teachers College, 1930), p. 10. e: Mei-chun Tang, Urban Chinese Families (Taipei: National Taiwan University Press, 1978), pp. 66, 88–90. f: g: William Parish, "Modernization and Household Composition in Taiwan," in D. Buxbaum, ed., Chinese Family Law and Social Change in Historical Perspective (Seattle: University of Washington Press, 1978), p. 288.

a Percentages including families from both the adjacent columns.

unmarried children (although units with a single parent, or a couple without children, are also included under this type). The stem form contains an aged parent or parents, one married child and his or her spouse, and perhaps grandchildren as well. The joint form differs by having two or more married siblings living together with their children and often a grandparent or two. The stem and joint forms together are termed extended families to distinguish them from nuclear units. Finally, some studies include an additional category of single person households and other arrangements (e.g., an aunt living with a niece). The figures given in the table should be considered suitable only for a rough comparison, since there are a number of problems in the samples used, how family units were defined, and so forth, that make comparability problematic.[4]

Several general comments can be made about the figures shown in table 13. First, the average family size is not inordinately large in any of the studies except the 1923 Milam study. The averages computed for samples of the "ordinary population" range between four and five members generally, although it is clear that among the wealthy, larger units were more common. Lang's samples of middle and upper class families, for example, show an average of over six members, while Milam's data on the families of college students show about nine members. The largest family reported in Milam's survey was thirty-eight. So the average family size was not very large, but among wealthy urban families there were a few exceptionally large units.[5]

In terms of family structure, the nuclear family predominates in almost all studies, but by varying degrees. Smythe's study of Nanking laboring families circa 1930 shows an unusually low proportion of nuclear units (48 percent) and high frequency of extended units (37 percent), while Lang's interviews in Peking and Shanghai yield a figure of 55 percent nuclear units. Figures from more recent studies in cities in Taiwan suggest

4. For example, the studies differ on such things as whether a younger family member who lives elsewhere but is still considered part of the family economic unit should be included or not.

5. For comparison purposes, urban household size statistics computed on the basis of police reports rather than household surveys reveal the following picture: In the period 1928–35, the average household size in 19 of China's largest cities was said to range from 4.6 to 6.1 persons (median = 5.1). Similar reports for 17 large cities in 1948 put the range at from 4.2 to 6.0 (median = 5.0). See L. K. Tao and Shih-ta Wang, "Population," in *The Chinese Yearbook* (Shanghai: Commercial Press, 1937), pp. 41–45; *Tongji Yuebao* (Statistical monthly), no. 125–26 (Jan.–Feb. 1948):, 20–28. These figures are for households, and not families, and thus would include people like servants. Recent Chinese urban surveys yield family size estimates similar to our own: 4.3 persons (*Xinhua* [Peking], 22 August 1981, in *FBIS,* 24 April 1981, p. K3—a survey of 7,962 families in 44 cities) or 4.48 persons (*Xinhua* [Peking], 30 December 1980, in *FBIS,* 5 January 1981, p. L20—a survey of 86,955 families in 44 cities).

an even greater predominance of nuclear units there, with Kaohsiung having 79 percent of the families sampled of this type. In general these figures suggest that the proportion of extended families likely to be found in Chinese cities is quite variable in the range of 20–45 percent.

Before examining the figures from our interviews, we need to note that several complexities of family forms in pre-1949 Chinese cities are generally unobservable in these studies. For one thing we know that the sex ratio was often highly unbalanced in Chinese cities early in this century. There might be 70 percent more males than females living in a large city, for example.[6] Many of the extra people did not live in family units, but in group dormitories or other shared housing situations that did not lead them to be counted in studies of family units. Servants were also commonly found in middle and upper urban households, and they are also omitted from data on families.

We can now examine data from our weighted neighbor census sample to determine how the household structure in contemporary Chinese cities compares with that found in earlier studies. Our figures show an average of 4.4 family members and that more than two-thirds of the families take a nuclear form, while very few are joint in structure. In comparison with the other figures cited in table 13, then, family size looks quite similar or only slightly smaller, while families are now somewhat less likely to take extended form. (In comparison with the rapidly growing and highly migrant Kaohsiung on Taiwan, though, there are more extended families in our data.) The figures in the table do not reveal anything particularly surprising about the changes in household structure in urban China. Families do seem to be slightly smaller and simpler in form than was the case in the 1920s and 1930s, but we have already noted that this seems to fit trends observed in many other developing societies.[7]

6. For information on urban sex ratios, see Sidney Gamble, *Peking: A Social Survey* (New York: Doran, 1921), p. 99. In a study of Kunming, Yunnan, in 1942 males were only 27 percent more numerous than females. See Ernest Ni, "A Study of Urbanism and Population Structure in a Metropolitan Community in China," in *Contributions to Urban Sociology*, E. W. Burgess and D. Bogue, eds. (Chicago: University of Chicago Press, 1964), p. 423.

7. Family forms are also more standardized now. Migration restrictions effectively limit the unbalanced sex ratio, although a fair number of both young males and young females now live in collective dormitories between their school days and marriage (and are not reflected in our figures.) Family servants are much less common now, although some still exist among well-off families. One recent study of a working class neighborhood in Tientsin reveals an even greater preponderance of nuclear families than do the figures for Kaohsiung. In a sample of 452 families, 83 percent were found to be nuclear in form, 15 percent stem, 1 percent joint, and 1 percent "other." See Pan Yunkang and Pan Naigu, "Preliminary Views on Our Country's Urban Families and Family Structures," *Tianjin Shehui Kexue*, no. 3 (1982):12.

Several features of our contemporary family structures deserve special notice. As in the past, figures on household structure at any one point in time ignore variations that people experience over their life cycles. As a result, our figures on the predominance of nuclear units tend to understate how common the experience of living in an extended unit *at some point* actually is. We noted in chapter 5, for example, that about 40 percent of the couples in our recent marriage cases start out their married lives living with parents, even though after a few years of life in this setting they may succeed in moving to separate housing. If we look at the situation of old people we can see a similar pattern of prevalent family extension. In our weighted sample of all men over 60 (N = 64), only 4 percent lived alone or in some "other" structure, 46 percent lived in a nuclear unit, and 50 percent lived in extended families (47 percent of stem form, and 3 percent of joint form). For women over 60 this tendency was even more marked. Of a total of 89 such women, 12 percent lived alone or in other arrangements, only 28 percent lived in nuclear units, and fully 59 percent lived in extended arrangements (57 percent stem, and 2 percent joint). So for old people even more than for those in other life stages, extended family structures are the most common form. One might argue that this pattern of old people living with grown children is a departure from what we should expect in urban settings, and indeed it does contrast with the pattern of separate residence by the aged favored in America. However, a similar or even more pronounced tendency seems to exist in more highly developed Chinese cities in Taiwan and in Hong Kong, so it is not at all clear that the persistence of three generation families represents a distinctive trait of socialist China.[8] At most our data show that the Communist revolution has not been much more disruptive of ties between generations than the rampant capitalism of these other Chinese settings, a topic on which we will have more to say later in this chapter.

Why do some families even today take on extended forms, while others remain nuclear? In earlier times two patterns, at least, were fairly clear. First, and contrary to the pattern in developed societies, wealthier families tended to have more complex family structures than poorer families. Second, and more in keeping with worldwide patterns, in large cities the

8. In Ronald Freedman et al., "Household Composition and Extended Kinship in Taiwan," *Population Studies* 2 (1978): 65–80, it is calculated that among all Taiwanese families in 1973 (rural as well as urban) 83 percent of parents lived with a married son. A survey in Hong Kong concluded that 70 percent of the fathers and 87 percent of the mothers of married men lived with a married or unmarried child rather than alone or simply with a spouse. See Robert Mitchell, *Family Life in Urban Hong Kong*, vol. 2 (Taipei: Orient Cultural Service, 1972), chaps. 15–16.

average family size tended to be smaller than in small towns and rural areas. Our data in table 14 enable us to investigate whether similar patterns are still found today, and what other correlates of family extension might be. Our dependent variable is a dichotomous scale: nuclear, single person, or other households versus extended ones (stem and joint).

In table 14 we can see, first, that there is now no clear relationship between the administrative level of the city and the proportion of extended families. When we look elsewhere in the table we can see that the strongest effects visible involve situational factors: the age of the family head, the number of years the family has lived in their current residence, and whether or not they own their own home. Primarily what we see here is a sort of "rootedness" factor, in which families which are headed by old people and which have remained in one place and kept control over their own housing over a long period are more likely to be extended. Neither of

Table 14   Family Extension by Selected
                                             Characteristics

	Simple Correlations	Partial Correlations[a]
Social Status		
Education of head	-.11*	-.06
Income of head	.01	.04
Income per capita	-.18*	-.19*
Living standard	.03	.01
Consumption index	-.06	-.05
Remittances	.05	-.00
Head occupational status	.10*	.13*
Head seniority	.04	-.06
Head employed in state enterprise	.02	.07
Reside in work unit housing	-.13*	-.01
Head of good class	.11*	.14*
Head in Party or League	.02	.07*
Head committed error	-.06*	-.08*
Other Characteristics		
Age of head	.13*	--
Head a local native	.06*	.00
Years resident	.29*	.20*
Lived in own house	.23*	--
Administrative level of city	-.05	-.02
Populous city	-.05	-.02
Lingnan Region	.01	-.04
Median N	(436)	(383)

Source: Census of neighboring households.

[a]Correlations controlled for age of head and residence in own (private) home.

-- = Controlled characteristics.

*p ≤ .10

these patterns is surprising in view of the life cycle patterns described above and the severe housing shortage in urban China.

Once we control for private home ownership and the age of the family head (in the second column of the table), we can investigate whether social status variables also affect family structure. We noted earlier that there are difficulties in talking about social class under socialism, but there are still various dimensions of social status by which we can rank people and families. In the top panel of the table we see that many standard socioeconomic status variables are not significantly related to family extension—this is the case, for example, in regard to the education and income of the family head and indicators of the consumption standard of the family. Not only do families headed by men with high incomes not live in larger families, but extended families in our sample turn out to have significantly less income per capita than nuclear families. But there are weak but fairly consistent indications that families headed by people with high occupational or political status—cadres, Party members, males with good class background and no history of political errors—tend more than others to live in extended families. In other words there is at least a slight tendency for the traditional pattern to persist of high status males heading more complex families than low status males, but this involves high status in the "new class" sense, rather than high income or education. Given the negligible relationships with education and living standards, we do not assume that this persistence is explained by the factors noted in the traditional scene—a stronger sense of family obligation and the solidarity enforced by greater wealth of high status families. Instead we suspect more mundane influences are at work—the greater ability of high status males to command spacious housing and help arrange suitable and nearby jobs for at least one grown offspring. Still, the weakness of the correlations indicates that we might also draw another conclusion from these figures. The failure of social status variables to show a stronger relationship with family extension testifies to the homogenizing effect of bureaucratic control over housing and job placement commented upon in chapter 4.

Changes in Fertility

Family size depends not only on kinship extension, but also on fertility.[9] The traditional high fertility ideals of Chinese culture are well known.

9. One additional way of enlarging families will not concern us much here: concubinage. A minority of wealthy families (9–15 percent, according to the studies by Milam and Lang) but very few ordinary families included concubines and their children. Concubinage has been eliminated in contemporary Chinese cities, although a few cases of multiple wives

Aphorisms such as "the more children the better" and "bearing sons to guard against old age" convey the importance attached to childbearing. A relatively high infant mortality rate (184 per 1,000 according to a Peking study published in 1919) also motivated parents to bear more children than they wanted, on the assumption that some would not survive.[10] Studies in Chinese cities early in this century leave us with some uncertainty about what number of children the average woman could be expected to bear in her lifetime. Lamson's study of Shanghai families in the 1920s yielded a figure of 4.81 surviving children in the average family, but the sample was of relatively well-off families of schoolchildren, and it is unclear whether children of concubines are included or not.[11] Lang calculated that the 68 urban women over age 45 that she interviewed had given birth to an average of 4.9 children (including those who died?), with upper class women in this group having higher fertility than lower class women.[12] This suggests we are not unjustified in concluding that an average of more than four children born was typical for urban women earlier in this century.

Since 1949 there have been a number of trends fostering reductions in urban fertility. The most widely known are the official birth control campaigns. For a period in the mid-1950s, and then with ever-increasing vigor since the early 1960s, the government has been trying to get the entire population to have fewer children. This effort involves campaigns and propaganda designed to lower childbearing aspirations (two children was the ideal promoted during most of this period, but since 1979 a vigorous campaign has been mounted to foster one child families), making contraceptive devices and procedures widely known and available at no cost, and a system of sanctions for rewarding those who comply with the small family ideal and punishing those who have too many children.

By the end of the Cultural Revolution, a highly organized, and some would say Draconian, system of enforcing the birth control policies had been developed. In both work units and neighborhoods married men and women (especially the latter) had to fill out and periodically update forms describing the number of children they already had, the contraceptive

---

from the period before 1949 remain, as noted in chapter 5. This represents a minor but important change in Chinese family life.

10. The infant mortality figure is from a study by Dr. W. G. Lennox cited in Gamble, *Peking: A Social Survey*, p. 348.

11. H. D. Lamson, "A Study of the Relationship of Education to Family Size," *The China Critic* 3 (1930): 799–802.

12. Olga Lang, *Chinese Family and Society* (New Haven: Yale University Press, 1946), p. 152.

devices they were using, and any desires they might have for bearing more children. Periodic group meetings were held to drum the government's birth control message into all married couples and, in some work organizations, to discuss which members of the group would be allowed to bear one of the children permitted under the annual "quota" established for the work unit or neighborhood. In a few cases, organizations even established what might be called a "menstrual monitor," a woman responsible for keeping track of the periods of the women under her supervision and inquiring whether they were "on schedule" so that a pregnancy could be detected at the start. In the mid-1970s women who became pregnant after a second child, who became pregnant too soon (within four years, according to a common formula) after a first child, or simply out of turn in terms of the organization's birth quota system would be subjected to incessant individual chats and group meetings designed to get them to agree to abortions. If a woman went ahead and insisted on giving birth, the infant would often not be registered for a number of months or even years, thus depriving the family of the ration increments that would normally have been theirs. (Since 1979, with the "one child" policy, more detailed cash awards and deductions from wages and other sanctions have been used to enforce compliance.)

These official efforts are not the only forces working toward fewer children, however. Many other influences in urban areas foster reduced fertility. Most married women of childbearing ages work full time outside of the home now (detailed figures are provided in chapter 7), and as in other societies we should expect working women to have lower fertility than housewives. As noted in chapters 3 and 4, the state has made minimal investments in services, production of labor-saving appliances, and housing, and therefore families are faced with life in cramped quarters and an exhausting round of chores. As women continue to be the ones who perform most of those chores, it is understandable that they don't welcome the prospect of having to cope with a large number of children. These conditions by themselves should be enough to bring down urban fertility, even without official incentives. Indeed, women in urban Russia who face many of the same burdens have sharply reduced their fertility, even though in the USSR there is a pronatal policy with the government offering awards to women who bear large numbers of children.

Finally, a number of other influences operate in urban China in favor of government policy. An increasing share of urbanites are entitled to pensions these days, so they do not anticipate having to be so dependent upon the earnings of their grown offspring in their old age. Infant mortality has been drastically reduced as noted in chapter 4, so that families now have a high assurance that the children they do bear will survive into adulthood. Urban children also cannot do much in the way of contributing income to the family until they are at least 16, in contrast to the past or to the situation in rural China today. Furthermore, the official campaign to send urban youths to the countryside in the 1970s may have fostered lower childbearing ideals as well. Recall that under the regulations of this campaign one child could remain in the city, but any others might be assigned to a rural area, where they could become an economic burden to their families. Finally, the freezing of most urban wages during the years 1963–77 made families very doubtful they could support many children. Together these many forces created an environment that was decidedly hostile to high fertility.

There is no doubt that sharp reductions in fertility have taken place in urban China. Official figures and our own data both lead to that conclusion. Crude birth rates for Chinese cities early in this century were not particularly high—for example, estimates of 12–20 per 1,000 in Peking in the teens—but such figures are misleading because of the large number of single adults and the unbalanced sex ratio in such cities, as well as a severe underreporting of births. Gamble used a sample of family units to calculate a more realistic crude birth rate estimate for the period of 26.5 per 1,000. Contemporary Chinese cities have much more closely balanced sex ratios as well as birth rates that are much lower (and a much more thorough reporting system for births and deaths). A number of major Chinese cities dropped below a crude birth rate figure of 10 per 1,000 even before the one child policy was implemented.[13]

Evidence from our interviews confirms the general trend. Few of our informants could think of cases among the people they knew of women who had given birth to more than two children in recent years, and those who could provide examples viewed these as isolated cases—mostly couples with only daughters who had either very traditional ideas or a lot of pressure from grandparents. Many informants volunteered that no pressure was really needed to enforce the limit of two children then in effect, particularly among educated urbanites, since couples realized it would be very difficult to try to raise more than that number. We can examine the trend in a more systematic way by looking at the number of surviving children born to women in different cohorts in our neighbor household census. These figures are presented in table 15, and they show a reduction from about 3.5 children for women married before 1949 to less than 2.5

13. The Peking figures come from Gamble, *Peking: A Social Survey*, p. 31. For figures on Chinese cities in recent years, see Pi-chao Chen and Ann Miller, "Lessons from the Chinese Experience," *Studies in Family Planning*, 6 (1975): 354–66; and Judith Banister, "Mortality, Fertility, and Contraceptive Use in Shanghai," *China Quarterly* 70 (1977): 255–95.

for the final cohort.[14] All signs, then, point to a dramatic reduction in urban fertility levels over the past generation.

While we are certain that dramatic reductions in urban fertility have taken place, we can't say with confidence why they have taken place. Were the official birth campaigns the main factor? Or perhaps the tight housing situation or the many burdens women face? We cannot answer these questions definitively, but we can provide some clues by examining which sorts of families and women tend to have smaller or larger numbers of children these days. If political pressure is the most important influence we might anticipate that Party members or people who live in the most tightly organized neighborhoods would have lowest fertility. If housing shortages and difficult living conditions are the main factor then we might expect people living in more crowded and anxious surroundings would bear fewer children. Finally, if it is a question of a shift away from traditional attitudes and a balancing of family with career orientations that is most important, then we might expect women with more education and with more demanding jobs to have the smallest number of children.

In table 16 we examine the socioeconomic correlates of the number of surviving children of women in our neighbor sample, and in tables 17 and 18 we look at further relationships with political control and urban amenities measures. (One notion we cannot test with these figures is the simple effect of women working, since there are too few housewives in our figures to make an adequate comparison.) In general, only a few of the ideas

Table 15   Surviving Children by Year Married

| | Year Married | | | |
	Pre-1949	1949–1953	1954–1958	1959–1963
Mean number of surviving children	3.52	3.03	3.32	2.45
(N)	(36)	(34)	(41)	(68)

Source: Weighted sample of currently married female neighbors, age 15–49.

14. Note that if these figures and earlier estimates are correct, they indicate that urban fertility was already declining modestly before 1949. The final cohort included in the table have not completely passed out of their childbearing period (they had been married 15–20 years by the time of the interviews, but were not all over 45), so the completed fertility figure for this cohort might be slightly higher. However, because there is a clear tendency to bear children soon after marriage and then stop, and in view of the official pressure for small families, we do not feel much inaccuracy is involved. Still younger cohorts in our sample have given birth to fewer than two children, on the average, but in those cases we really can't be so sure that childbearing has been completed. There is every reason to believe, however, that this fertility reduction trend is continuing.

Table 16   Surviving Children by Socioeconomic
                                            Status (Correlations)[a]

Socioeconomic Status	Women Married 1963-1975	Women Married 1950-1975
1. Wife		
Income	-.14*	-.09
Occupation	-.08	-.15*
Education	-.40*	-.30*
2. Husband		
Income	-.13	-.06
Occupation	-.29*	-.16*
Education	-.37*	-.24*
3. Household income per nucleus	-.23*	-.18*

Source: Sample of neighbors, currently married women, married at least three years and age 49 or less. N = 183 for 1963-75 and 320 for 1950-75.

[a]The dependent variable is surviving children per currently married woman net of years of marriage.

*p $\leq$ .10

advanced in the hypotheses above receive support from the figures in these tables. It appears that couples with high socioeconomic levels do have fewer children than others, with the effects of the woman's educational level the most noticeable. Once one controls for this factor, which we do by using the wife's educational level and the husband's occupational level, none of the other variables used show strong associations with the number of surviving children. (The few significant associations noted in tables 17 and 18 could be attributable to chance alone.) We are not entirely surprised that the political control variables do not seem to count for much, since in much of our research we have arrived at similar findings, indicating that the influence of these variables is often overrated. We had expected problems of tight housing and poor services to show some effects, but they are not visible in table 18.

These findings suggest that the influences promoting lowered fertility are not so different, after all, from other developing societies.[15] In urban China and commonly in other societies as well, higher education and more

15. This conclusion is also reinforced by the similarity of the fertility reduction trend in Taiwan, where modernization is more advanced but the family planning campaign is much less coercive. Overall in Taiwan (for both urban and rural areas) the crude birth rate dropped from about 45 per 1,000 in the early 1950s to slightly over 25 per 1,000 in the 1970s. See Republic of China, *Demographic Fact Book* (Taipei: Ministry of Interior, various years). In Hong Kong the crude birth rate had dropped from 30 per 1,000 before 1970 to only 18 per 1,000 in 1975. See *Hong Kong Monthly Digest of Statistics,* January 1976, p. 2. The reduction in urban fertility in China does appear to be unusually rapid, however.

Table 17   **Surviving Children by Political and Administrative Control** (Partial Correlations)[a]

	Women Married 1963-1975	Women Married 1950-1975
Political Control		
1. Wife		
a. A Party member	.04	.04
b. In League or Party	.07	.02
c. An administrative cadre	.03	.02
2. Husband a Party member	.00	.07
3. Frequent neighborhood political study	.34*	.13
Administrative Control		
4. Wife a state employee	-.03	-.06
5. Family resides in unit quarters	.08	-.03
6. Neighborhood		
a. Supervision	.07	.06
b. Tightness	-.11	.01
c. A unit compound	.17	.02

Source: See table 16.

[a]Correlation controlled for wife's education and husband's occupation; dependent variable the same as in table 16.

*$p \leq .10$

Table 18   **Surviving Children by Urban Amenities** (Partial Correlations)[a]

	Women Married 1963-1975	Women Married 1950-1975
Housing		
1a. Nuclei per room	-.07	-.18*
b. Ideal rooms - actual	-.07	-.11
c. Households per kitchen	-.03	-.06
d. Households per toilet	.02	.01
e. No piped water in home	.05	-.02
2. Neighborhood housing scarcity	.11	.15
Neighborhood Services		
3. Infrastructure weak	.07	-.04
4. Lines common in markets	-.14	.01
City		
5. Administrative level	-.09	-.10

Source: See table 16.

[a]Correlation controlled for wife's education and husband's occupation; dependent variable the same as in table 16.

*$p \leq .10$

absorbing jobs tend to promote lower childbearing aspirations, often leading to a negative association between social status and fertility. A variety
of explanations have been advanced in the literature for this pattern.
Higher education may foster receptivity to modern ideas, and having few
children is one of those modern ideas. (Education may also promote
awareness of contraceptive technology, but that doesn't appear to be a
consideration in the Chinese case today, with knowledge of birth control
very widely dispersed.) High education and high status jobs may also
promote involvement in work and a desire to limit the burdens of family
life, including childbearing. High education and high status may also lead
to high aspirations for one's children and a desire to concentrate one's
efforts and hopes on a smaller number so that their chances of success
will be maximized. No doubt a number of such considerations are operating, and informants provide anecdotal support for these motivations.
They note, for example, that working class families are less willing to
comply with the official small family ideals than intellectuals, and that
well-educated families are more sensitive to the problems of finding "good
jobs" for their children. With these findings we have not proved that birth
control campaigns and difficult living conditions have had nothing to do
with reducing urban fertility, for it may simply be that these influences
affect urban families too uniformly, so that there are no differential effects
strong enough for our variables to detect. With the distinctive pressures
experienced by Chinese urbanites, it is still the same kinds of well-educated, career-involved people as in many other societies who are likely
to lead the way in reducing their fertility.

So far in this chapter we have examined both family structure and
fertility, and several conclusions have emerged. In general the same sorts
of trends in family organization that are taking place in urban areas in
many other parts of the developing world are visible in China as well.
These trends can be summarized as leading to simpler family structures
and fewer children. In the Chinese case, the second change has been
much more dramatic than the first. Nuclear families seem to have increased somewhat, but extended families (very predominantly the stem
form) make up quite a common alternative and appear to be more numerous than in the most industrialized cities of Taiwan, for example. The
reductions in fertility, in comparison, have been quite rapid, and have
resulted in levels that are unusually low for cities in developing societies
and more comparable to the levels in more economically developed socialist countries in Eastern Europe, where many of the same kinds of
living conditions prevail. As in other developing societies it appears to
be well-educated people who lead the way in forming simpler families

with fewer children, but perhaps one trace of traditional patterns remains in the more complex families that urban bureaucrats are likely to maintain. In sum, the types of changes in family size and structure are not too different from those occurring in other societies, but the speed of these changes does appear to be affected by the particular nature of urban institutions.

Family Relationships

When we shift from examining family organization to looking at internal family relationships, we are inevitably dealing with more complex and subtle phenomena difficult to describe on the basis of interviews or even after prolonged observation. There is a considerable amount of debate among experts, for example, about what sorts of family relationships were typical in Chinese cities before 1949. Perhaps the predominant image of urban as well as rural families in imperial and republican China is that they were "patriarchal," a term which conveys the image of a male family head ruling over a unit that was strictly and hierarchically ordered in terms of generation and sex, with younger members subordinate to older members and females subordinate to all males. But there is debate over just how patriarchal families generally were. Did family heads rule with an iron hand and make decisions unilaterally, or was there, in fact, considerable mutual influence and consultation? Some evidence exists to qualify the strictly patriarchal view. Lang tells us, for instance, that 24 out of the 60 working class wives she interviewed claimed they were regularly consulted by their husbands on business matters. She also interviewed 46 wives who worked in factories or had formerly done so, and of this number only 10 were never consulted by their husbands and had no control over their earnings, while at the other end of the scale 22 of them were judged to have power equal to, or greater than, their husbands'.[16] A study in a town on the outskirts of Peking in 1928–29 found that in 38 percent of the families a woman served as the family manager (who managed the daily finances and other matters—distinct from the family head, virtually always a male.)[17] In Smythe's study in Nanking circa 1930, of 288 families that took a patrilineal stem or joint form, 16 percent had family headship exercised by a son rather than by the senior male in the household.[18] On the same point, Lang classified from her sample 126 families in which there were employed, married sons, and she

16. Lang, *Chinese Family and Society,* pp. 194–95, 206.
17. Leonard Hsu et al, *Ching Ho: A Sociological Analysis* (Peking: Yenching University, 1930), p. 44.
18. Computed from Smythe, "Composition of the Chinese Family," chart 3.

found that in 47 percent of these the father was still in complete control, while in 33 percent there was consultation between generations, with the son in more or less complete control in the remaining 20 percent.[19] These fragments from various studies do not of course show a picture of familial equality, but they do qualify the picture of patriarchal family life to some extent and show that at least in a considerable minority of pre-1949 urban families there was some sharing of power by wives and grown sons.

We could say that since 1949 the government has formulated a clearer official policy in regard to family relations than in regard to family structure, but has enforced this policy much less vigorously than the campaign on birth control. In general this policy involves advocating more egalitarian relationships within the family and attacking the old patriarchal forms. The official ideals include something close to equality between males and females within the family, somewhat tempered authority of the aged, criticism of corporal punishment as a means of discipline, and concern to promote family solidarity as long as it does not interfere with the obligations of family members to society. More concrete policies include an obligation of parents to discipline and be responsible for the acts of their children, equal property rights for male and female family members, and a firm preference for mediating marital problems and preventing divorce. In the pages that follow we cannot hope to deal with all aspects of family relationships, now and in the past. Instead we will focus on relations between old and young and between husbands and wives. In doing so we will be trying to give capsule pictures of what family relationships are like in contemporary cities and how much change from the past is apparent.[20] We begin by considering selected aspects of childrearing.

Some things about childrearing have clearly changed dramatically, while others remain much the same as in the past. The clearest change concerns who does the caretaking. As noted before, most married women as well as men work full time outside the home. For those in state enterprises a 56–day paid maternity leave is provided, but after that period most women have to resume work and make alternative arrangements for caring for their infants. Several options are available. Many large work units and some neighborhoods provide crèches and nurseries, although in large cities there are not enough spaces in these to meet the demand for them. The child can be left in care of grandma (or, less often, grandpa) in the home, if the family is an extended unit. A relatively well-off family may hire a nursemaid to live in their home or may hire a babysitter to watch their child in her home. Others may send their children to be tended by

19. Lang, *Chinese Family and Society,* pp. 229–30.
20. Relationships with kin outside the family are not dealt with here but in chapter 11.

grandparents or other relatives living elsewhere. The first two options are most frequently resorted to, as the figures in table 19 show, and nursery schools share equal place with family care only in the largest cites. In contemporary cities, in contrast with the past, during waking hours a child is likely to be cared for by somebody other than its parents. But these others are most often other family members, and it is important to note that the view that Chinese children are reared collectively from birth by the state is an exaggeration.[21]

There is considerable debate both by observers outside China and parents within about exactly what the consequences of this shift to "other" caretakers are. The official media promote a view of nurseries as being preferable because of the way that their collective upbringing may train the child to be less selfish and fit into the group; care by grandma may result in making the child spoiled and self-centered. Parents we interviewed sometimes agreed with this view, but tended to be more critical of collective child care. None of them voiced concern that life in nurseries would "subvert" their children and turn them against the family. Rather, the most common complaint was that many nurseries are crowded and unsanitary and that children often contract illnesses there and bring them home. Many also noted the cost factor, saying it didn't make sense to spend 8–15 yuan a month to send a child to a nursery when a grandmother could do the same job for no fee and have something to keep occupied

Table 19   Care of Children by Type of City

Children Cared for by	National/ Provincial Capitals	Prefectural Capitals	County/ Commune Seats and Small Towns
Nursery/kindergarten	47%	24%	20%
Family member	49	71	59
Other person	4	5	22
Total %	100%	100%	101%
Number of children	(98)	(41)	(41)

Source: Sample of neighbors, children age 0–6.

21. The kindergarten enrollment rates shown in table 19 are considerably higher than the 10 percent noted in table 6 in chapter 4. The data in table 6 are national and thus include rural areas, where nurseries and kindergartens are often absent or not heavily utilized. Recent Chinese press articles have claimed kindergarten attendance rates of 25–30 percent. (See for example, *Xinhua* [Peking], 31 December 1980 in *FBIS*, 31 December 1980, p. L9; *Beijing Review*, no. 10 [1981]: 29–30). We assume that these latter figures refer only to urban areas.

with in the process. (The nursery fee does include lunch, however, making the contrast in costs less extreme than it appears.) Some interviewees did not see home care as leading to the child being spoiled, and in fact they argued that the child could receive more consistent attention and discipline in the home.

While a number of differences were observed, in general informants did not feel that a choice of home care versus nursery care would have a major impact on the way their children developed. They saw much the same sorts of discipline and similar values being stressed in both these settings. So the choice was generally decided by issues of cost and convenience, rather than feelings about what sort of personality was desirable for the child.[22]

What are the primary emphases in urban childrearing? In this realm the changes from traditional patterns are much less marked. Informants noted primary concern with training children to be obedient, diligent, respectful of others, helpful, and cooperative rather than aggressive, all values that were stressed by parents of an earlier era. We asked informants whether parents were more concerned about teaching obedience or teaching their children right or wrong, and overwhelmingly they responded that obedience was most stressed (although some noted that obedience was more stressed in working class families than by intellectuals, as has been found to be the case in studies in the West and in Taiwan).[23] Parents train their children to be obedient in helping around the house, in avoiding conflicts and fights with siblings and children outside, in being respectful to their elders, and in other realms. The discipline techniques used to instill these behaviors are varied—spankings, scolding, bribes and threats, inducing fear, and explaining and lecturing. Some informants feel that there has been some shift toward more use of verbal techniques and less use of beatings, but without systematic data it is hard to know how accurate this is. One informant from a Guangdong county town notes,

> Cadres or intellectuals usually resorted to persuasion when their children were naughty or lazy, but common people resorted to

22. A similar judgment about the general congruence between childrearing in the home and in collective nurseries is reached in William Kessen, ed., *Childhood in China* (New Haven: Yale University Press, 1975). It should be noted that there is considerable variety in the types of nursery schools and kindergartens available in urban China, ranging from makeshift babysitting facilities run by neighborhoods to high quality institutions with professionally trained staff, some of which are boarding facilities keeping children for an entire week.

23. For studies on this point in the U.S., see Melvin Kohn, *Class and Conformity* (Homewood, Ill.: Dorsey Press, 1969). For Taiwan, see Nancy Olsen, "Social Class and Rural-Urban Patterning in Socialization in Taiwan," *Journal of Asian Studies* 34 (1975): 659–74.

scolding or beating to teach their children. What all wanted, though, was for their children to be 100 percent obedient to them no matter whether they were right or wrong. In fact parents considered that they were always right.[24]

A Canton informant chimes in with a similar view:

Parents vary in discipline, but 70 percent of the time they use hitting, and if the child steals or fights and they find out they will certainly hit the child. They also may scold, but if the family is educated they may do things in a different way, for example bribing the child to perform properly with the promise of a toy or snack. But if the parents are getting dressed in the morning and the child keeps changing clothes until they are late for work they will certainly hit the child. They hit the child with a feather duster, or more often with their hand, and only in the most serious cases with a stick.[25]

On the other hand, an intellectual from Tientsin presents his approach:

I emphasized honesty with my children as the most important thing, rather than obedience. Perhaps because my father was Westernized he influenced me to do this. If the children were naughty I did not care too much or think it was bad, since Chinese are used to suppressing their feelings until they can't bear it, and so I feel it is better if children develop more freely. I would even let my children argue with me, which even my father had not done.[26]

There is substantial agreement about what constitutes a well-behaved child, and it seems to be fairly widely shared in different social strata and by nursery and kindergarten teachers as well as parents. What is less clear is how successful socialization agencies are in producing well-behaved children. Informants seem to feel that raising a child properly requires constant supervision and attention and an ability to use a broad variety of disciplinary techniques to shape the child's behavior. Conditions for realizing this situation are difficult, however, particularly as the child gets older. Work schedules do not match school schedules—in fact, in some cities schools have had to operate on half-day sessions—and many families do not have grandparents at home to watch the children. Thus there are many "latch-key" children in Chinese cities, a phenomenon of concern in American society as well. In some locales schools organize after-school supervisory activities, and a few neighborhoods try to organize activities to keep children occupied after school. However, these

24. Interview HNH1:15
25. Interview KSM9:36.
26. Interview TIM1:18

efforts have been too intermittent to cope with the problem. Some of the unsupervised children go home and do homework and perform household chores, but some play unattended in the streets. This lack of supervision is of some concern to parents, but many feel fatalistically that there is little they can do about it other than relying on neighbors to informally keep an eye out, since they cannot shirk their work obligations.

A number of elements of parent-child relationships seem distinctive in comparison with the patterns we are familiar with in the West. Infants are frequently fondled and held, but there is not much concern with stimulating the child to enhance its development. The infant is not felt capable of learning much until it is at least two to three years old. Young children are treated quite indulgently, but at about the time they enter school they begin to be treated less affectionately and to have more strict demands placed on them to behave and to help out around the home. Many parents do not play or "joke around" much with children after age seven or so, and fathers, in particular, increasingly appear remote and severe to their children. These are all traditional patterns, but some informants argued that minor changes were visible—for instance, with some fathers not acting so stern and domineering as in the past.

By age nine or ten many children are expected to help out in major ways around the home, including in some cases helping with marketing and cooking the meals. Many school-aged children do spend much of their free time around the home or in the near vicinity, and in the evenings and on days off they often discuss problems and concerns with their parents. Both sons and daughters more readily go to their mothers with things they want to discuss, as is the case in other societies, and mother-daughter ties are described as particularly close and warm. Informants claim that few children are openly naughty or disrespectful around the home, but that unruliness outside is a problem in some families. Parents recognize that the outside society is a realm in which they have few controls, even if they can maintain respect and obedience within the home. Young people recognize the same important dichotomy, pointing to Red Guards during the Cultural Revolution who struggled against bureaucratic officials during the day but remained solicitous of parental needs when they were at home at night. Thus although there is still relatively little overt generational conflict visible in Chinese families, urban parents have a growing feeling of loss of control over their children as they grow up. The outside world is a realm that is hard to control and predict, and official campaigns, youth gangs (discussed in chapter 8), uncertain career prospects, and other phenomena orient young people away from whatever demands the parents might make on them, even if the home remains an island of relative calm.

We can examine one aspect of this mixture of continuity and change in the role of the aged in the family. Clearly aged family members have less power than in the past. They do not usually control important inheritable property or have the power to provide careers for their children, and we noted in chapter 5 that they have less control now than in the past over whom their children will marry. At the same time, they are often more burdened with family chores, since there are very few daughter-in-law/housewives these days to take over the main burden.

Still, on balance, the main stress should probably be on continuities with the past. As we saw in the first part of this chapter, a majority of old people do live in extended households with a grown child, usually a son, and in chapter 4 we drew attention to the fact that very few old people end up in old-age homes or similar institutions. Furthermore, not all old people in extended family units are powerless dependents. Among men over 60 in our neighbor household sample who live in patrilineal extended units, twenty percent have turned over the headship to their to their sons (N = 44). The rest remain in at least nominal command. This figure is not much different from the statistics cited above from studies by Smythe and Lang in the 1930s, although family headship may not have quite the importance today it did then. It is by no means clear that family power is ceded to the next generation more readily than in the past.

Several features of the urban scene favor retention of power by the older generation. Of particular importance in this regard is their economic contribution. Informants noted that family headship usually passes to the son when the main burden of supporting the family falls to his generation (or when physical or mental incapacity prevents the old man from taking charge). We have noted elsewhere that a good share of the aged, particularly among cadres and intellectuals, have not been required to retire from work and have been able to keep on earning their regular salaries until they die. Personnel who do retire may have had such high wages that even with a pension of 70–80 percent of their final wages they continue to bring in more money than their grown children, whose earnings have been hurt by the wage freezes of the last two decades. In cases in our interviews in which the old couple jointly earned 150–300 yuan and the young couple only 60–100 yuan there was little question about which generation had the most power in the family. As in traditional times, one may assume that for the younger generation in such families the material advantages of sharing the home with resourceful parents more than compensates for the added tensions and conflicts that may occur. In three generation units there still tends to be a fair amount of respect and usually an understanding that the young couple will give over a major share of their earnings to be managed in the common family pot, usually by the mother.

In many families, though, headship eventually passes to the younger generation. This happens most frequently when the older man dies, for, as in earlier times, few widows are motivated and feel capable of retaining control. Health problems of the aged can hasten this process of relinquishing control, even if the father remains alive. Even if the son does take over the leadership of the family, there are rarely signs of overt conflict between him and his parents (conflicts between his wife and his parents are another matter, to which we will turn later). Acceptance of the obligation to support aged parents seems virtually universal and is not much begrudged. Only a few informants had heard of cases in which sanctions had to be taken by authorities to get children to live up to their obligation.[27] The burden of providing such support is now generally shared among all grown children. Daughters often contribute some of their earnings, in a departure from past custom, under which only sons were so obligated. A number of informants drew attention to cases of grown children living elsewhere sending at least token amounts from their earnings to parents with high salaries or pensions as a sign of respect, or what used to be called filial duty.

Old folks who do not enjoy high earnings or pensions generally still have a secure place in the family. Unless they are disabled they can perform very useful roles that will ease the burden on the younger generation of employed family members. As we have seen, many couples prefer to have their children cared for by grandparents than in a nursery school, and the burden of household chores is such that they weigh very heavily on couples who do not have an old person around the home to help out. Thus, even if grandparents become financial dependents they can usually still perform functions that are absolutely vital to the smooth functioning of the family. Care of aged parents who are disabled is a more difficult matter. In such cases younger family members are faced with a triple burden—working, performing household chores, and tending to the needs of the old person. This combination can be extraordinarily stressful, and informants did note instances of conflict and complaints in such cases. Still, in most cases the obligation to care for aged and infirm family members is borne, even if grudgingly, and there is strong public sentiment that only death can release the younger generation from their duty to repay

27. As noted earlier, the obligation to support parents is written into the marriage laws of 1950 and 1980. If a son or daughter shirks this responsibility, the neglected parents can complain to his or her work unit. After investigation, the unit may decide to automatically dock the employee's pay each month and send the funds to the parent.

the parents for the years of care and effort they experienced to raise the family.

In sum, major social changes have occurred in Chinese cities since 1949 without destabilizing relations between the generations in major ways. The power of the aged has clearly softened somewhat, but strong feelings of respect and mutual obligation remain to bind the generations together. While foreign observers have sometimes feared that the Party was trying to turn children against their parents, a strong case could be made for the opposite notion—that the kind of socialist distribution policies pursued in China, including seniority-based wages and pensions, minimal investment in housing, low levels of provision of appliances and services, and other factors, help to maintain the importance of the roles old people can play in families and maintain the strength of intergenerational bonds.[28] As a result, even highly educated urbanites continue to see such strong familial bonds as natural and important and scoff at suggestions by some foreign sociologists that such bonds may not be very "modern."

To penetrate still further into the lives of urban families requires us to give a more detailed account of a theme we have touched upon at a number of points in this study: the heavy time and task burdens faced by families. We pursue that topic here by considering the sort of daily schedule that is common for urban families. Here we present only a general picture which does not try to deal with all of the kinds of variations among families.

Most urban Chinese follow Benjamin Franklin's dictum "early to bed and early to rise." Common times of getting up are 5:30–7:00, and bedtimes are usually 9–10. Work units have varying schedules, but 8 A.M. is a not uncommon hour for work to begin and, particularly for those who have to bike or take long bus rides to work, an early wake-up is mandatory. Many families feel so pressed for time in the morning that no breakfast is cooked; instead, cold leftovers are eaten, or family members grab a snack from a street food stall or in a work unit canteen just before work. Early morning is also the time when the best supply of fresh produce is available in the markets, but usually only families with retired old folks at home are able to send someone to stand in line to take advantage of this supply. Typically, even those who do eat breakfast at home do not do so together; instead family members rise at various times and eat hurriedly before setting off to meet their different work and school schedules. By 9 A.M. or so only old folks and small children are left at home, except for a few adults who have staggered days off during the week.

28. Similar conclusions are reached in Deborah Davis-Friedmann, "Old People and Their Families in the People's Republic of China" (Ph.D. dissertation, Boston University, 1979).

Patterns of taking the noon meal vary, depending upon family circumstances. If people live near their work they may come home for lunch, and most schoolchildren do so as well. But employed people who have a decent canteen in their work unit sometimes prefer the convenience of eating there, particularly if there is nobody else left at home to prepare the meal in advance. Work units also vary in the amount of time they give off for lunch, with factories often allowing a half hour, while some offices provide up to one and one-half hours, providing time for a nap or some shopping. From our weighted neighbor household chore subsample (N = 403), we estimate that 80 percent of adults eat at home rather than at work or in a restaurant.

The end of the work day does not usually mean leisure time for most family members. On one or more days a week there are generally meetings after work. In factories these typically take place right after the shift, but in some offices employees may have to return in the evening. Then there may be a commute back home, with stops on the way to shop for groceries. (Without refrigerators, shopping remains a daily or almost daily chore.) Most families do try to eat their evening meal together, with the laborious tasks required—lighting and tending the fire, slicing and dicing the ingredients—sometimes shared by several members of the family.[29] But with some members arriving back late from work and the time-consuming nature of meal preparation, it is understandable that some informants would say that many families have no leisure time to speak of during the week. After dinner there may only be a little while to perform chores or sit and relax before it is bedtime. When some time is left before bed, it is common for fathers to sit and listen to the radio or talk and play cards with neighboring friends, for mothers to tackle household chores, and for youngsters to do homework or play in the neighborhood before turning in. Some informants argue that in intellectual families the activities of the husband and wife are not so distinct, and that both may read academic journals and discuss professional concerns in the short time remaining before bed.

Most leisure-time pursuits are reserved for days off. Whether the family can do things together then depends on whether their days off coincide. In factories around a city days off are staggered, but still a large share of

29. Few urban families have gas or electric stoves to cook with. Even in 1979 only 15 percent of the urban population in large and medium sized cities was served by gas (*Xinhua* [Peking], 26 May 1980, in *FBIS,* 2 July 1980, p. L7). In large cities urbanites not only heat but cook with "beehive coal," which are cylinders stamped from coal dust and mud which have beehivelike holes punched through them. These are lit with kindling and burned in special burners for cooking. In small towns people may make do with kindling and straw.

the urban population will have Sunday off, so on that day the streets are filled with people. Even on Sunday, however, families may have to spend at least half the day dealing with chores that they have not been able to take care of during the week, particularly the laborious hand washing of the family bedding and other laundry. Commonly there is only half a day left for walking in parks, going to movies, window shopping, or simply socializing with friends.

From the responses of many informants one might assume that the pressures under which families live help to foster the sort of general equality and flexible sharing of roles that the government would like to foster. When asked about how families generally divide chores, they often claim that whoever is available, young or old, male or female, will step in and take charge of the chores that need doing. When we collected information on the actual division in some of the households in our neighbor census, however, it became clear that these general answers distort reality. Families in China, as elsewhere, tend to fall into fairly regular divisions of labor. Even if the work and other outside burdens family members face are similar, the task of performing household chores is not borne equally.

In figure 5 we display the average scores of members of these families in performing a set of household chores, broken down by age and sex. The patterns visible in the figure are for the most part ones very similar to those found in studies on other societies. Although the sex differences in chores performed by youngsters are minimal, it is quite clear that adult women are more burdened with household chores than adult men. Men mostly take charge only of tasks that involve heavy lifting, such as buying and carting home grain and coal. Age is also important, with older women taking over more and more of the less strenuous chores and younger women the more strenuous ones and the management of family finances. Perhaps the most surprising pattern here is that women are so predominant in the management of family funds. Such evidence as we have from earlier studies indicates that only a minority of women managed the family money in pre-1949 cities. Even if we allow that today men may have more say over major purchases than is revealed by our simple question on money management, this seems like a clear instance of change in family relations. We may speculate that the socialization of the economy, and the consequent change of urban families from being production units to units of consumption, means that family money management is now a less complex matter, one men are willing to leave in the hands of their wives. On balance, though, the evidence in figure 5 indicates the continued importance of generational and sex differences in shaping the division of family roles.[30]

Some power differentials between spouses are apparent, although informants differ somewhat on how marked they are, and whether they have been reduced. The most common situation is illustrated by the following comments:

> Some women complain about their husbands not doing enough of the chores, but it doesn't do any good. The husband's authority is still greater than the wife's authority. It is occasionally mentioned during political study meetings that this should change, but nothing ever comes of this.

> Most couples get along well, but in most the female does more chores, and the male rarely does any, and the wife is accustomed to this, so she willingly bears it. Generally the daily expenditures are decided by the wife, but when buying a large thing, like a bike, a watch, or furniture, then they have the male decide.

> The man is the main power in the family. If he objects to something, then 95 percent of the time it won't happen. If the wife objects and he insists, then they quarrel, but more than likely the man will get his way.

> When the father speaks the children obey, even though the mother does more of the daily disciplining. The children see that the mother obeys the father, so they know that he has more power, even though they are not openly taught that. The father has the main voice in disputes on starting school, discipline, and other matters, but things are more equal today. The wife can reason and try to persuade the husband. They consult, and he is not always that stubborn. They try to agree.[31]

The predominant trend is still toward a modest amount of male dominance in family life, but informants argue that among both more educated and younger couples, and in couples where the wife earns more, the relationship is more equal.

It is clear that the pressures under which families live have consequences for family relations. These pressures include not only time and chore burdens, but also cramped living quarters, the need to share kitchen

30. This finding is hardly surprising, and a number of studies have argued that flexible switching of roles does not make economic sense, since it is less efficient than forming a stable division of labor. In fact, time and economic constraints may make a stable division of labor more important, while leisure and affluence may make it easier to ignore efficiency and experiment with flexibility. For the economic arguments, see Gary Becker, *A Treatise on the Family* (Cambridge: Harvard University Press, 1981).

31. In succession, from interviews HNH2:8; CSH4:18; CWD1:11.

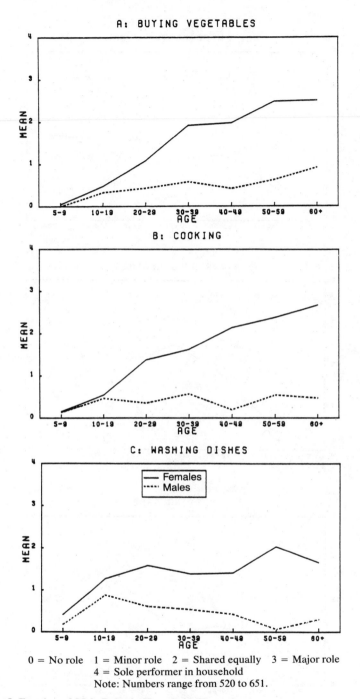

Figure 5. **Female and Male Roles in Household Chores by Age**
Source: 1972–78 Chinese urban chores subsample.

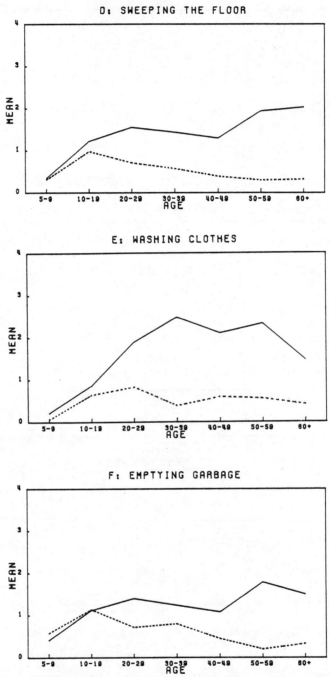

(Figure 5, continued)

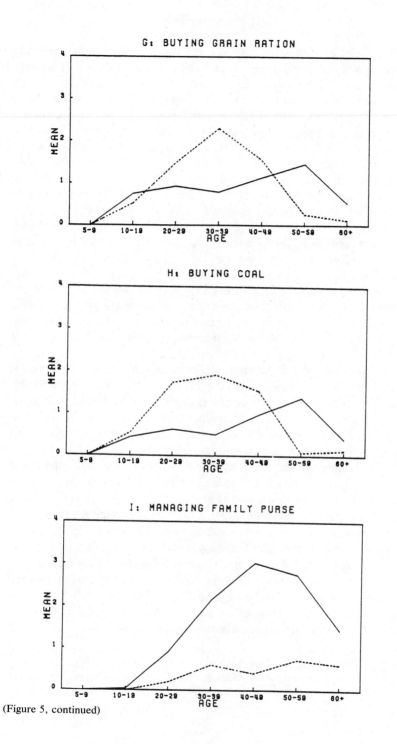

(Figure 5, continued)

and toilet facilities with other families, the difficulties of raising growing children on low and frozen wages, and the political buffeting of government campaigns. The family is not a cozy nest where members can find a haven from these pressures. To some degree the family is penetrated by them. Characteristically, Chinese families tend to emphasize the instrumental side of family life—task performance—and to underplay the affective or emotional side. Members are encouraged to see themselves as working together to cope with a difficult situation, rather than simply enjoying one another's company. All recognize the importance of keeping emotions under control if conflicts are to be avoided. In this setting there tends to be a certain amount of reserve and lack of demonstrativeness in comparison with Western family life, even within the confines of the home. Family members show their concern for each other mainly by the acts they perform for each other and the family, rather than by outpourings of sentiment. Even between spouses there is generally no open display of affection outside the bedroom, even in cases of couples known to get along very well. This emphasis on keeping emotions bottled up is of course not a novelty of Chinese socialism, since it readily fits within the Confucian emphasis on self-control and has been commented on in capitalist Chinese cities as well.[32]

In spite of this emphasis on emotional control, family conflicts do occur and can sometimes escalate into severe fights. It is very hard to say whether the frequency of such conflicts is much different from the past, but we can describe the types of conflict that are most common. Informants focus on two central conflicts, between husbands and wives and between mothers-in-law and daughters-in-law. The latter has long been seen by the Chinese as the most volatile relation in family life, and many informants claim that much the same is true today. Relations between mothers-in-law and daughters-in-law are so rarely harmonious that many accept conflict as a matter of course in any patrilocal extended family and comment on harmonious cases as exceptional and admirable. The main ways to solve the problem are for the young couple to live separately or to have the old woman live with a married daughter rather than a son. This new, matrilocal arrangement is felt by all to be largely free of tension, since a son-in-law seems to be able to live in harmony with his wife's parents. But we noted in chapter 5 that the matrilocal arrangement is still not widely followed, despite recognition of its virtues.

32. See E. Anderson, "Some Chinese Methods of Dealing with Crowding," *Urban Anthropology* 1 (1972): 141–50. Another Hong Kong study notes, "We Chinese don't show our love for each other, but keep it instead in our hearts." See Sherry Rosen, *Mei Foo Sun Chuen: Middle-Class Chinese Families in Transition* (Taipei: Orient Cultural Service, 1976), p. 165.

While conflict between mothers-in-law and daughters-in-law seems to be endemic, as in the past, the form it now takes is often different. In the past the younger woman chafed under the bossiness of the family matriarch. Nowadays the situation in some families has almost reversed. A daughter-in-law may regularly criticize her mother-in-law for not keeping the house and tending the children the way she thinks these should be done. The older woman may complain in turn that her daughter-in-law is sending too much money off to her own mother and not providing the mother-in-law with funds enough to meet her daily needs. The husband in such cases usually tries to remain neutral, and with no resolution this kind of conflict can smolder for years, sometimes leading the couple to arrange separate housing or the older woman to live with a different son or a daughter. One informant from Canton describes the following case:

> Nearby there is a woman who had two sons. The one son and daughter-in-law live with her, while the other daughter-in-law is in a suburban village and has an agricultural household registration, but visits once a week. The grandmother takes care of the children of both daughters-in-law. She is a very severe woman and is very displeased with the second daughter-in-law due to her rural registration and the fact that she earns little money and brings few gifts when she comes. She is very nice to the other daughter-in-law she lives with because she works in a food stall and often brings home tasty things to eat. So it appears as if the difference is completely due to economics.[33]

Another Canton informant supplies a more complex case:

> This mother-in-law/daughter-in-law conflict has both economic and personality causes. The older woman complains that her daughter-in-law doesn't help enough with the chores and that she and the son give her too little money to spend. The man fluctuates between supporting his wife and supporting his mother, and the result is that neither of them listens to him. The younger couple have different days off, and when they are off they both go off and do things with their friends outside rather than helping out the older woman around the home. The husband demands that his wife stay home on her day off, but she won't listen to him.[34]

For the majority of families that are nuclear units, the husband-wife relationship is the most subject to conflict. The causes of such conflicts are numerous. According to informants, economic problems are the most frequent cause. In one common pattern the wife complains that the hus-

33. KSM4:8
34. KSM30:9

band earns little and spends too much on himself, leaving too little money to meet his obligations to his family. Or the couple will squabble over whether to make a particular large purchase or not, or over funds to be sent to his parents versus hers. In the difficult economic circumstances in which many families live, even a small issue, like spending too much on a particular item, can lead to spats.

A number of other causes of marital conflicts are also fairly common. Couples may argue over how to discipline their children, or over the fact that the husband does not help out much with family chores. Sexual conflicts also occur, and infidelity will often lead to major fights. However, nobody mentioned to us conflicts over how to meet the sexual needs of the partner, and it is apparent that expectations are not very high in this realm. Political problems are a final important cause of marital disputes. The common pattern is for the husband to be denounced in a political campaign or arrested and sent to a forced labor camp, creating a strong stigma for the wife and children. In some cases the wife will self-righteously reject the husband and demand a divorce, while in others she will continue to remain devoted to him but agree to seek a divorce for the sake of the children.[35] In the Cultural Revolution a few husbands and wives ended up in opposing factions, although in these cases divorce was not the usual result, and most couples smoothed over their relations after the heat of the campaign had died down.

Informants describe a variety of concrete cases of conflicts between spouses:

> This husband and wife used to call each other names a lot and argue over money. In this case the male used to gamble, and he lost a lot of money, and the family's budget was severely affected. The wife criticized him and they quarrelled a lot, and at one point he threatened to commit suicide. Later on friends talked him out of it and they continued living unhappily together.

> There was a woman married to a very skilled lathe worker. She had married him in 1967, and in so doing she rejected a man she was in love with for the practical suggestion of her mother that she marry this worker. They had one child, and their relationship was stormy from the start. The husband wanted a second child,

35. See an example of the latter in Bao Ruo-wang, *Prisoner of Mao*, (Baltimore: Penguin, 1973). More recently, the wave of political rehabilitations since 1976 has fostered a considerable number of remarriages of such couples (half of one percent of all marriages in 1979 were rejoined couples, according to one source). See Shanghai Academy of Social Sciences, Institute of Sociology, "Report on an Investigation of the Marriage Situation in Metropolitan Shanghai," *Shehui Kexue* no. 12 (1981): 78; *Zhongguo Baike Nianjian, 1981* (Chinese encyclopedia yearbook 1981) (Peking: Chinese Encyclopedia Press, 1981), p. 543.

but she kept refusing. Later on she started an affair with a former army man. The leaders in the factory found out about it and notified the husband. Before this she had quarrelled with her husband and had run away from home four times because of these quarrels. Her husband had hit her because of her refusal to have a second child. The factory told her that she could not have a divorce because of her affair, and she and the former army man were criticized in the factory and received demerits. Later on the couple still lived together and the woman eventually did have a second child.

There was a couple who had married in about 1965. The wife had been in music school and played the violin, but she dropped out in order to marry her husband. He worked in a state factory, but she could only get assigned to a poorly paid job in a neighborhood workshop. They had a daughter during the Cultural Revolution, and the daughter had some sort of medical problem. The mother had to take one year off after the birth to tend the child, and later on she often had to take more time off for the same reason, which meant that she lost even the 80 cents a day the neighborhood shop paid. She often argued with her husband from about the time the daughter was born. She complained that he returned home late from work, took no responsibility around the house or with the daughter, and gave her very little money while he spent a lot on drinking and other things for himself. Usually they just argued and even hit each other and neighbors would try to ignore the matter, but once she came out and started hollering on the street how her husband was beating her, and the neighborhood patrol came along and took them to the ward police station. They turned the matter over to the work units of the couple, and the authorities there told the male he had to change his ways and that the couple had to calm down and work out their problems. Things would settle down for awhile but then flare up again, and the mediation would start again. After several rounds of this the female finally began demanding a divorce in about 1969. After several more rounds of mediation by both work units and the court, the divorce was finally granted in 1972.[36]

One particular factor that may promote conflict between spouses should be noted. A significant number of couples are not able to live together. In some cases marriage takes place across the barriers created by the household registration system (say, between an urban male and a suburban female), and this prevents the couple from living together. In other cases the bureaucratic job allocation system results in a husband and wife being

36. In succession from interviews CSH2:8; KSP14:18; SSM3:22.

assigned to work in different locales. We noted in chapter 5 that seven percent of the post-Cultural Revolution cases in our marriage sample had to live separately after marriage for one of these reasons. For those living on opposite sides of the administrative city wall, there can be regular visits back and forth, but for those separated by larger distances there are only the annual paid leaves of two weeks (more recently 20–30 days) during which they can be together. The tensions created by this situation can be imagined. Assuming there are children, in the usual arrangement the mother has to care for them in addition to job and other duties without even the minimal help that a husband sometimes provides. In spite of the generally prudish nature of work units, the loneliness and vulnerability created by prolonged separation creates the potential for extramarital affairs to develop. In this divided state perhaps most couples manage to grimly persevere, but a portion of them end up breaking apart.

Very few marital disputes end up in divorce in urban China, though. If minor conflicts occur within the family they will generally be ignored by outsiders, but if things get more serious there are a number of levels of mediation, informal and formal, that are brought to bear on the situation. Neighbors may informally mediate at first, but if there are frequent shouting matches or physical fights, residents' small group heads, work unit cadres, residents' committee leaders, or even local police are likely to step in to try to calm things down. There are even a few cases in our interviews of an aggrieved wife requesting the authorities in her husband's work unit to investigate and sanction him for beating her or having an extramarital affair. When outsiders step in their goal is clear: to get each side to agree to calm down and try to do better in order to keep the marriage together. This tactic is often effective only temporarily, and as in our example above, there are some couples who have been through the mediation mill on repeated occasions.[37] There is a traditional phrase that captures public feelings about such cases: "even an honest official finds it hard to settle a family quarrel (*qingguan nanduan jiawu shi*)." But at least the knowledge that a severe argument will likely become the focus

---

37. Officially there are supposed to be mediation officers formally designated within each residents' committee. At the time of our interviews most committees had no such officer, but instead various neighborhood cadres stepped in as needed. Since that time efforts have begun to try to revive the system of formal mediation officers, even though it is recognized as a thankless job. A recent source claims that 39 percent of the divorce cases referred to local Civil Affairs offices in 1979 were successfully mediated and that about 37 percent of the divorce cases referred to the courts in that same year were either successfully mediated, sent back to work units for handling, or withdrawn. See *Zhongguo Baike Nianjien, 1981*, p. 543. For an example of forced reconciliation by the court see Felix Greene, *Awakened Giant* (Garden City: Doubleday, 1981), chap. 9.

of embarrassing outside mediation efforts must act as an inhibiting factor, reinforcing the tendency to keep conflicts bottled up.

Even when disputes get quite severe, they rarely result in divorce. How much this is due to the official policy which discourages divorce and how much to traditional attitudes that divorce is shameful and that marriages should be for life is difficult to say. It is clear, at least, that most of our informants felt it was very difficult to get divorced in urban China, even if relations between the couple were miserable. Some interviewees stated flatly that they knew of no cases of divorce in their social environment, while others could mention only one or two. All told, we could collect information on only sixty-six divorce cases, not a very sizable sample upon which to base conclusions. But the following characteristics may be noted. While informants commonly felt that economic conflicts were the most common cause of marital disputes, when we look at divorce cases we find that sexual infidelity and political problems are the most common primary causes (32 percent and 29 percent, respectively), with economic problems running a distant third (at 9 percent). Evidently it is felt that economic problems are normal and do not normally constitute grounds for terminating a marriage, while adultery and political errors are more serious matters.[38] Another pattern in these cases is that in 74 percent of them the initiative for requesting the divorce came from the woman. While this fits the pattern common in the U.S. and in many other societies, it does not fit the traditional pattern in China, where the husband had more rights than the wife to seek a divorce.

We have argued that divorces were fairly rare and difficult to procure in urban China during the 1970s. We still have to try to provide some comparative evidence on this point. Unfortunately we cannot do this in the most desirable way, since we don't have the sort of comprehensive statistics on urban divorce rates in China or comparable figures for other

38. One recent study of a district in Shanghai (in Shanghai Academy, "Investigation," pp. 78–79) found that of 281 divorce cases, the problem in 27 percent was the incompatible natures of the spouses, in 16 percent infidelity, in 15 percent rash marriage decisions, and in 10 percent economic problems. In that district infidelity was said to be increasing as a cause and to constitute 41 percent of the cases couples submitted to a novel marriage counselling service run in the years 1978–80. Political problems are not mentioned among the top four reasons of divorce cases in this survey, which may reflect the changed political atmosphere of the late 1970s (see chapter 9 on this point) or the inability to speak openly about such problems (e.g., "incompatible natures" could include political problems) or both. Another study of Peking district in 1979 found that of 397 divorce suits initiated, 29 percent were due to mother-in-law conflicts or economic problems, 19 percent were due to lack of mutual understanding, 17 percent involved infidelity, 13 percent concerned mistreatment, 12 percent involved mental or physiological defects of a spouse, and 8 percent were due to political reasons. See *Xinhua* (Peking), 5 October 1980, in *FBIS*, 16 October 1980, p. L12.

societies to rely on. In table 20 we present the best approximation we can make. There we present figures given by a recent Chinese source on the crude divorce rate and divorce/new marriage ratio for all of China, rural and urban in 1979. The computed figures we compare with ones for a number of other Asian societies, with East European socialist societies, and with the United States. The following observations can be made about these figures. On the one hand, divorce is clearly far less prevalent in China than in the United States, and considerably less than in European socialist states. If the comparison is with other Asian societies, on the other hand, the contrast is not so marked: China has a relatively low rate, but not extraordinarily so. Since these other societies do not put such extreme obstacles in the way of divorce, we conclude that China's low rate is not simply the product of restrictive government policy. That may be a factor, but traditional family orientations and other factors may play a role as well.[39]

Marital conflicts do occur in urban families, and in a very few cases they may lead to divorce. But we do not wish to imply that Chinese marriages are generally conflict-ridden or that most people would like to discard their spouses if only the government would let them. Most informants felt that the majority of marriages of people they knew were satisfactory and devoid of sharp conflicts. In part it is our impression that this satisfaction is related to the fact that expectations of marital happiness are not that high. In a society that has only recently made a transition away from strictly arranged marriages, many people continue to see marriage, in the terms of sociologist E. W. Burgess, more as an institution than in terms of companionship. Whether further experience with free

39. We do feel that there is some pent-up demand for divorce in urban China. There were even wall posters protesting against restrictions in 1979 (see Agence France Press, Hong Kong, 5 December 1979, in *FBIS*, 6 December 1979, p. L12). When modest liberalizations of the divorce provisions were incorporated into the revised Marriage Law in 1980 it was reported that in Shanghai the number of divorce applications received by the courts almost doubled. *Zhongguo Baike Nianjian, 1981*, p. 543). But it should be obvious that government restrictions are not the only reason to stay married. Inspection of the figures in table 20 suggests that other factors such as the level of economic development and the prevailing religion affect the prevalence of divorce. It should be noted that in the initial years after 1949, offical policy stimulated divorces as part of an effort to free people (largely women) from unhappy forced marriages. In the five years after 1950 an average of 500,000 or more requests for divorce were received per year. Subsequently official policy turned sharply in favor of marital stability, and this in turn was rationalized by arguing that those who had not divorced, and who entered marriage after 1950 under socialist "free choice" conditions rather than via arranged marriages, should be able to achieve enduring marriages. The number of divorce applications fell off sharply, and in 1979 was only about one-third the level of divorce requests in 1953 relative to population. See *Zhongguo Baike Nianjian, 1981*, p. 543, and Meijer, *Marriage Law and Policy*.

Table 20   The Chinese Divorce Rate in
                                        Comparative Perspective

Country	Divorces per 1,000 population	Divorces per 100 marriages in same year	Year
China	.33	4.9	1979
Peking District	.44	2.1	1979
Singapore[a]	.19	1.8	1975
Taiwan[b]	.47	5.2	1975
Japan	1.07	12.6	1975
Eastern Europe (mean)	1.77	19.5	1975
(range)	(1.18–2.44)	(14.0–29.3)	
USSR	3.08	28.8	1975
U.S.A.	4.82	48.3	1975

Sources: China: Zhongguo Baike Nianjian, 1981 (Peking: Chinese Encyclopedia Press, 1981). Peking District: Xinhua (Peking), 5 February 1980, in FBIS, 7 Feb. 1980, p. Rl. Singapore: Applied Research Corporation for the Ministry of Social Affairs, A Study of Non-Muslim Divorce in Singapore (Singapore: mimeo, 1979). Taiwan: Republic of China, 1976 Taiwan-Fukien Demographic Fact Book, (Taipei: Ministry of Interior, 1977). U.S.: U.S. Department of Commerce, Bureau of the Census, 1976 Statistical Abstract of the U.S. (Washington: U.S. Government Printing Office, 1976). Others: United Nations Demographic Yearbook, 1977 (New York: United Nations, 1978).

[a]Non-Muslims only.

[b]Five year average around the listed year.

choice marriages and small family living will contribute to a heightening of expectations and perhaps more open discord in marriages only time will tell.

Conclusions

In our examination of urban family patterns we have found a mixed pattern of change and of continuity. In terms of family structure, Chinese families are only modestly smaller and more nuclear in form than were families in pre-1949 cities, and where extended patterns arise, they are still usually based on patrilineal lines. However, a number of features of earlier families are much less in evidence today—for example, concubines, servants, and an uneven sex ratio brought about by excess migration of single males into the cities. In some sense family life has become more "standardized." However, one fairly prevalent form of nonstandard arrangement has been promoted by the state's bureaucratic job allocation system—a significant number of couples that are not able to live together and must content themselves with occasional visits, often only once a year. The modest reduction in family size is the product of a number of conflicting influences.

The baby boom of the 1950s and increasing longevity for the urban population promoted larger families, while bureaucratic restrictions on housing, the campaign to send urban youths to the countryside, and the birth control campaign vigorously enforced since the 1970s have worked in favor of smaller families.[40]

In terms of family relationships, the most striking change is for a significant minority of urban preschoolers to be cared for outside the home, and for very few of them to be tended during the day by their own mothers. The relationship between generations has also clearly changed in important ways, with old people in many families not controlling as much power and resources as used to be the case and having to cope with domestic chores so that the younger generation can meet their work obligations. Parents also tend to feel their ability to control their children has declined over the years. While the age hierarchy seems to have softened, the evidence in regard to sexual inequality within the family is more mixed. Females do have some rights to family property, more control over the family purse than in the past, and some sharing in the obligation to support aging parents, but on the other hand the tedious burdens of household chores are still mostly borne by women. The equal sharing of family chores that the government advocates is not closely followed; instead a fairly traditional division predominates. Some informants feel that changes have occurred in both childrearing and husband-wife relations to reduce the level of physical violence, but there is enough anecdotal evidence in our interviews of violence continuing to leave the "reality" of this purported trend uncertain. In regard to divorce one can probably argue that, while marital breakup was traditionally discouraged in Chinese culture, the official obstacles of today make divorce even less likely than before, and certainly less common than it would be if easy access to divorce were allowed.[41]

40. The countervailing nature of these influences can be seen by considering the fact that in 1964 (after the baby boom but before strict birth control and the campaign to send youths to the countryside) the average urban family had reportedly reached 5.3 people, and then was reduced by a full member, to 4.3, by 1980. See *Xinhua,* Peking, 22 April 1981, in *FBIS,* 24 April 1981, p. K13.

41. This observation is supported by the increase in divorce applications that occurred following the modest liberalization of the divorce provisions of the Marriage Law in 1980. Also the history of divorce rates and divorce laws in the Soviet Union might be noted. The divorce rate was relatively high in the USSR during the period of the liberal family policy in the 1920s, but in the mid-1930s a sharp change in favor of a very restrictive divorce law produced a cutting of divorces by about two-thirds. The backlog of de facto dissolutions and marital tensions that was apparent in the 1950s led to a series of liberalizations in divorce law and procedures in the 1960s, and the Soviet divorce rate shot up to become one of the highest in the world. See Peter Juviler, "Family Reforms on the Road to Communism," in *Soviet Policy-Making,* Peter Juviler and Henry Morton, eds. (New York: Praeger, 1967).

The obligation to support aged parents is still felt very strongly, and a majority of old people still live with a married child even if their relationship with that child is no longer so autocratic. Generational conflict does not seem to be a prevalent phenomenon within families, in spite of the conflict between young and old fostered during the Cultural Revolution. Parents continue to place a strong emphasis on obedience and family loyalty in their childrearing, and from the available evidence this is done with considerable success. Families continue to restrict emotional expressiveness and try to avoid conflict in order for all to be able to get along in the highly constrained circumstances in which they live. There are hints in our data of social status related distinctions in family patterns still existing, with wealthy or powerful parents maintaining more control over their offspring than others, and with well-educated parents having fewer children and using less physical punishment in disciplining their children than parents who are less educated. On balance, then, the changes in urban family life seem more evolutionary than revolutionary.

In regard to the issue of what forces have caused the changes, our conclusions are similar to those in chapter 5. Official family policies cannot by themselves explain the pattern of changes observed in urban family organization. Some of them, to be sure—the end of concubinage, the reduction in the servant class, cutting off of much rural immigration, and divided couples—can be attributed in large measure to official policies. Others—the reduction in fertility, the modest decline in extended families, the low divorce rate, and the patrilineal bias in family formation—are the result of an interaction between official policies, the changed urban environment, and underlying cultural predispositions. In many respects the changes are similar to those in other cultures. The tendency to form nuclear families, the decline in fertility, and the decreasing power of the aged are common trends toward more "conjugal" family forms occurring worldwide.[42] So we might again argue that to a considerable extent official policies and the distinctive urban environment created by the Chinese Communists have simply accelerated changes that could have been expected to occur as a result of industrialization, urbanization, and other forms of modern social change.

Our claim that family changes in urban China are neither so revolutionary or so distinctive as some have supposed can be highlighted by considering the predictions about family change in socialist theory. About a century ago, Engels wrote a controversial book on the evolution of family life in human history.[43] In that work he described the distortions

42. See Goode, World Revolution.
43. Friedrich Engels, On the Origins of the Family, Private Property, and the State (1884; Chicago: Charles Kerr, 1902).

of family life that capitalism tended to produce and the improvements that could be expected under socialism. Very briefly, he argued that under capitalism concern for material wealth tended to corrupt family life and make it impossible for families to be formed simply on the basis of personal attraction and human feelings. Under socialism, with the abolition of private property, Engels felt that these distortions could be eliminated, and that family life based on human feelings rather than economics could emerge.

In Chinese socialism these hopes are still far from being fully realized. We saw in chapter 5 that economic status and prospects remain a predominant concern in picking a spouse, and in this chapter we have argued that material concerns still form central problems with which urban families have to cope, while personal feelings often have to be held in check. A considerable number of our informants saw the division of power within families as almost mechanically reflecting the economic contributions made by each member. If a husband earns much more than his wife he will tend to boss her around, whereas if she earns as much as he does she will have more of an equal say. Similarly, they claim that the role of an old person in the family can range from autocrat to powerless dependent, in relation primarily to size of their salary or pension. We doubt that the relationship is really that automatic, but the fact that many informants see it so is an interesting testimonial to the continuing predominance of material concerns in family life, contra Engels. The era of family life based upon simple human feelings has not yet arrived, and this suggests that socialism does not have as dramatic an impact on life as Engels supposed.

At the same time, we do not wish to carry the argument on the familiarity of the family change process in China too far. In certain respects trends in other societies do not seem to be duplicated in China. This is apparent if we consider the realm of family problems. It has been argued that in a considerable number of other countries a "culture of poverty" tends to develop among the swelling ranks of the urban poor, that their family life is characterized by early sexual initiation, common-law marriages, illegitimacy, brittle marriages, mother-centered families, and low family solidarity.[44] We have seen that these phenomena are absent or of minor importance in urban China, even among the poor. Indeed, urban family life in China is characterized to a considerable extent by the opposite traits: late sexual initiation, conventional marriages, low illegitimacy, stable marriages, moderately male-dominated families, and high family sol-

44. The culture of poverty thesis is elaborated in Oscar Lewis, *La Vida* (New York: Random House, 1965), Introduction. For a critique of the thesis, see Charles A. Valentine, *Culture and Poverty* (Chicago: University of Chicago Press, 1968).

idarity. The problems that plague urban families in China today are things of a different order—for example, anxiety about the future of the children, feelings of being stuck in unhappy marriages, tensions of close living arrangements, and the difficulties of "divided" spouses.[45]

Why is there no "culture of poverty" in China today? In part—perhaps in large part—the difference may be attributable to Chinese culture and family traditions. There is not very much evidence of a culture of poverty in Singapore, Hong Kong, or Taipei today, or for that matter in mainland Chinese cities of an earlier era. So one may suppose that the Chinese kinship system and cultural mores provide some barriers to its development.[46] But we would argue that features of the distinctive urban environment of contemporary China also prevent such a culture of poverty from emerging. The migration restrictions, high employment policy, and solidary neighborhoods and work units give families security that is lacking in most developing societies, security that may foster family stability. While the highly bureaucratized nature of the urban system might be expected to destabilize family life by depriving families of the resources and authority they once enjoyed, paradoxically the effect is quite the opposite. Because families have lost resources and power, they confront a bureaucratic machine that controls their destinies. Success in life requires being able to cope with this machine, and that necessitates that family members subordinate individual interests and desires to the struggle on behalf of the entire family. The complexity of this struggle, and the knowledge that bureaucratic barriers can be short-cut if one has the right connections, encourages families to make use of the kinship ties they have in their effort to satisfy their needs. When family difficulties and problems occur, they can often be externalized and blamed on the arbitrariness of

45. In the post-1976 period the government has made some efforts to deal with family problems such as these. In addition to the modest liberalizations in the divorce provisions in the Marriage Law, there has been some effort to reunite married cadres who have been working in separate locales. (So far the effort only applies to cadres and military officers though, and not to other kinds of separated couples.) Chinese sources report that in the three years after 1977, 200,000 such couples were reunited (out of an estimated 500,000 or more) and that as a result the proportion of cadres living apart from their spouses was reduced from 7 percent to 4 percent. See *Zhongguo Baike Nianjian, 1981*, p. 542; and *Xinhua* (Peking), 22 October 1980, in *FBIS,* 24 October 1980, p. L1–2.

46. Lewis notes that one of the factors required for the culture of poverty to develop is bilateral kinship, so on this count alone China, with its patrilineal descent system, might be expected to be different. What special role Latin American culture plays in fostering cultures of poverty in the particular cases he considered (Mexico, Puerto Rico) remains uncertain.

bureaucracy, rather than blamed on the failings of the family members.[47] The continued importance of a strong sense of corporate family interests and obligations is one important respect in which Chinese urban families do not yet appear all that "conjugal," and at least in part this family solidarity is sustained by the bureaucratic nature of the urban system. Families may not provide a peaceful haven or a warm nest of human feelings for their members, but they are still the primary resources urbanites turn to for the cooperative efforts needed to cope with urban life.

47. Another factor Lewis saw as necessary for a culture of poverty to develop was a stress on personal failure as an explanation for lack of social mobility, and here also the Chinese case would be different. Lewis felt that socialist societies in general should be immune to the culture of poverty, and he was engaged in research on this point in Cuba at the time of his death. In regard to China we agree with his conclusion, although we differ over the reasons. Socialist China, for instance, has not been able to avoid some of the causative forces Lewis sees behind cultures of poverty, such as high unemployment and low wages, and we argue that not simply socialism, but a particular bureaucratic form that in China is combined with a patrilineal and highly familistic tradition helped to minimize the family phenomena Lewis was concerned with.

7 The Position of Women

The consequences of modern social and economic changes for women have been widely debated. From the perspective of advanced industrial societies, it is often obvious that development benefits women, providing them not only with increasing legal status (voting, property, divorce, and other rights), but also with a more equal position within the family. In developing countries, however, the issue often is less clear. Some scholars have argued that economic development improves the status of women in the Third World, but others find evidence that development may actually promote sexual inequality.[1] In regions of the world where women have important roles in the traditional economy, for instance, new opportunities provided by development may accrue primarily to men, and women may be reduced to a more extreme dependency.

In China, of course, we have a developing society with a government that not only claims to be in favor of fostering sexual equality but that also feels it is guided by an ideology that provides the answers to how equality can be realized. The cultural context in which this effort is being carried out, however, is one most observers would argue is quite challenging to any quest for sexual equality. China for centuries has been a patrilineal and patriarchal culture in which women at all stages of their lives were expected to be subordinate to men—to their fathers, husbands, and sons. Men dominated positions of authority and received most of the schooling, and most women did not have important economic roles outside of the home. Even within the family their position was clearly inferior, and customs such as foot-binding and concubinage, as well as instances

1. See William Goode, *World Revolution and Family Patterns* (New York: Free Press, 1963), but contrast the arguments in Ester Boserup, *Woman's Role in Economic Development* (New York: St. Martin's Press, 1970); and Irene Tinker, "The Adverse Impact of Development on Women," *Women and World Development*, I. Tinker et al., eds. (New York: Praeger, 1975).

of female infanticide, give testimony to the pervasive male bias in Chinese culture.[2] In this chapter we wish to examine how, in the most developed parts of contemporary China—the urban areas—the effort to promote sexual equality has fared. As in previous chapters, we wish to focus on whether the pattern of change reflects distinctive features of Chinese urbanism or parallels that in other developing societies.

Before looking at the contemporary evidence, we need to spell out the ideological sources of the official effort to promote sexual equality in China. The basic text is the one discussed in chapter 6, Engels's *The Origins of the Family, Private Property, and the State*. Put briefly, Engels felt that sexual inequality under capitalism was rooted in the system of private property ownership and male monopolization of control over property, and in the female dependence upon males that was thereby produced. Socialism could be expected to alter this situation fundamentally. With private property ownership eliminated, men would no longer control the means to oppress women, and with women regularly involved in jobs, they would meet men as equals. In China it was expected, then, that socialist transformation combined with full labor force participation by women would provide the basic conditions needed for full sexual equality to emerge. The "feudal legacy" of patriarchal ideas would still have to be fought through propaganda campaigns and organizational efforts by the National Women's Federation, and achieving sexual equality might take some time. But in the cities, where agitation for sexual equality predated the Communist period, and where the distance from village traditionalism and lineage influences provided fertile soil for egalitarian ideals, the quest for sexual equality was likely to be most successful.[3]

Let us examine, then, how accurate these expectations about the preconditions of sexual equality were by considering the extent of sexual equality and inequality in urban China in the 1970s. In the pages that follow we draw together material introduced in earlier chapters and weave it together with other data, much of it derived from our neighbor household census. How successful has the effort to promote equality for those who "hold up half the sky" been?

2. For accounts of various aspects of women's lot in Chinese society, consult Margery Wolf and Roxanne Witke, eds., *Women in Chinese Society* (Stanford: Stanford University Press, 1975); and Marilyn Young, ed. *Women in China* (Ann Arbor: University of Michigan Center for Chinese Studies, 1973).

3. Denunciation of the evils caused by sexual inequality was one of the prominent themes of the May Fourth movement of 1919 and later years, and we have already noted that in that year a young intellectual named Mao Zedong wrote a series of attacks on a celebrated case of a woman driven to suicide by unhappiness with an arranged marriage. This series, one of the earliest appearances in print by Mao, testifies to his strong feelings on the issue. See Roxanne Witke, "Mao Tse-tung, Women, and Suicide," in Young, *Women in China*.

Education

We know that in imperial China education was highly valued, not only as a means to social mobility, but also as an end in itself as a sign of culture and enlightenment. But we also know that most opportunities for schooling were concentrated on males at least through the end of the nineteenth century.[4] In the twentieth century, with the ending of the exclusively male system of imperial examinations and the adoption of new models of schooling from the West and Japan, girls began to enter formal schooling in large numbers for the first time. This trend has continued since 1949. If we look at our weighted household neighbor census we find that twenty-two percent of all females over age 20 had no education at all, while for males the figure is only 2 percent. But in the younger age cohorts this substantial gap has been largely eliminated, as universalization of at least primary schooling (and often lower-middle schooling as well, in larger cities) has been approached. In our data we find only 4 percent of the females in the 20–39 age bracket having had no education, and none of the males, illustrating the dramatic reduction of urban illiteracy, formerly a predominantly female phenomenon.[5]

Do urban women now receive as much schooling as men? Before 1949 it might have made some sense to send a daughter to school for a few years, so that she would be able to get a good job and help the family before she married, and so that she would be a more attractive marital prospect. But education was usually costly, and since women were not expected to contribute materially to their families after marriage, parents often chose not to send their daughters to school for as long as their sons. Has the logic of the situation now changed?

We can get a rough idea about trends over time in urban schooling by examining the average years of schooling attained by males and females in different cohorts in our weighted neighbor census sample.[6] The relevant

4. On literacy in general, and of females in particular, see Evelyn Rawski, *Education and Popular Literacy in Ch'ing China* (Ann Arbor: University of Michigan Press, 1979), esp. pp. 6–8.

5. One pre-Communist source states that in 1946, 26 percent of the pupils in primary schools nationwide were females, as were 20 percent of the secondary school students. See *Tongji Yuebao,* no. 127–28 (1948): 63–64.

6. We wish to caution the reader, however, that the nature of our data may exaggerate this trend somewhat. Our data refer to members of current urban populations of various ages, and not to the urban populations that existed earlier. A good share of the older members of the current population originated in rural areas and moved into the cities as adults in the 1950s when such migration was still relatively easy. Insofar as the underrepresentation of females in school was more serious in rural areas than in urban areas, this may make the margin between males and females in the earliest cohorts in the figure larger than it would have actually been for the urban population at the time.

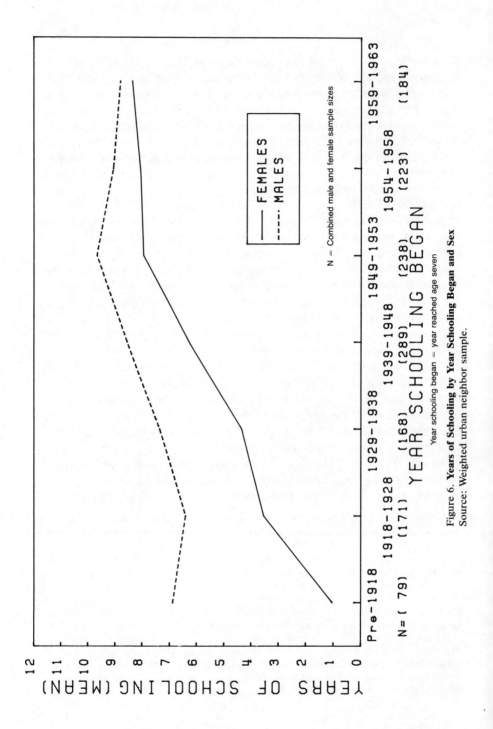

Figure 6. **Years of Schooling by Year Schooling Began and Sex**
Source: Weighted urban neighbor sample.

N = Combined male and female sample sizes

Year schooling began = year reached age seven

YEAR SCHOOLING BEGAN

| Pre-1918 | 1918-1928 | 1929-1938 | 1939-1948 | 1949-1953 | 1954-1958 | 1959-1963 |

N=(79)   (171)   (168)   (289)   (238)   (223)   (184)

FEMALES
MALES

YEARS OF SCHOOLING (MEAN)

data are displayed in figure 6. Several things are clear. The dominant trend has been toward a closing of the gap between males and females. From about six years difference in educational attainment for the cohort that began schooling prior to 1918, the figure shrinks to less than half a year for the youngest cohort. The difference is still significant, and it favors males, but it has come close to being eliminated entirely. We might also note that of the 67 individuals in our weighted sample who had attended college, 30 percent were females. Again this shows that women are still underrepresented, but not so severely as in earlier times.

There are several other notable features of the data in figure 6. First, much of the increase in overall enrollments and the narrowing of the gap took place during the Nationalist period, not simply during the post-1949 years. Second, the figure provides clear evidence of the "gearing down" of schooling in the Cultural Revolution, which produced a noticeable drop in the growth of education so constant in earlier years. The immediate consequence visible here is that males in the youngest cohort in the figure received only about as much schooling as their "fathers" who entered during those war years, and considerably less than their "older brothers."

How does the current situation in regard to relative female educational attainment in urban China compare with that in other societies? Unfortunately, we cannot provide a firm answer to this question, because we have been unable to assemble systematic data on school enrollments in urban areas in other countries. There are some national figures (i.e., for both urban and rural areas) that allow us to put China into comparative context. The results of this exercise are presented in table 21. The figures in the table indicate that China does not do as well as either advanced capitalist or East European socialist societies in achieving female parity in school enrollments, but this might be expected, given China's lower level of economic development. If we use a more appropriate reference group, developing societies in Asia, we would judge China's performance to be only average. Females have better access to schools than in countries like India and Bangladesh, but poorer access than in places like Sri Lanka and the Philippines. China's performance in promoting equal access at the lower levels looks better than at the university level, where women are clearly still severely underrepresented.[7]

7. The underrepresentation of Chinese women in university enrollments is worse now than in some earlier periods. According to official figures, female college enrollment rose from 20 percent in 1949 to 23 percent in the mid-1950s, to 27 percent in 1965, and 33 percent in 1976. But since 1978, female enrollment has again fallen to 23 percent. See Gao Yi, et. al., eds., *Zhongguo Gaodeng Xuexiao Jianjie* (*A Brief Introduction to Chinese Universities*) (Peking: Education and Science Publishers, 1982), p. 9. The comparison with other Asian societies reflects kinship as well as economic and political factors. Women are best represented in colleges in Southeast Asian countries with bilateral kinship systems, ranged around

Work and Wages

Engels's description of the preconditions for sexual equality stressed women participating in the labor force, and we wish to consider here how successful the Chinese Communists have been in realizing this. More generally, we wish to see here how much of the urban labor force is female and whether women work in similar jobs and earn incomes comparable to men.[8] Over the years, and particularly during the period of the Great Leap Forward (1958–60), propaganda campaigns and other efforts have been mounted to try to get women out of their homes and into the work force. The official low wage policy and difficult living conditions have also provided a strong incentive for women to work, since most males do not earn a sufficient wage to support a family. The rising rates of female labor force participation that trends such as these produced are the primary reason for the shift in Chinese cities toward the more favorable earner/dependent ratio we noted earlier in our study. The results can be seen more directly in table 22. The data in the table make clear that levels of work participation by urban women are now almost equal to those of men. Overall, about 93 percent of the women in the 20–49 age range in our sample were employed, compared with 96 percent of the comparable

Table 21   National Data on Percentage of School
                                    Enrollments Female

	Primary (%)		Secondary (%)		Tertiary (%)	
	Median	(Range)	Median	(Range)	Median	(Range)
China (1978)	45	---	41	---	24	---
9 European socialist states	48	(47–50)	48	(38–58)	41	(32–51)
19 Euro/American capitalist states	49	(48–50)	44	(41–52)	34	(23–48)
15 Asian developing states	46	(27–51)	39	(15–51)	29	(10–55)

Sources: China: Beijing Review, no. 1 (1980): 18. Others: UNESCO Statistical Yearbook, 1977 (Paris: UNESCO, 1978), pp. 194–212, 252–313, 325–87 (Data circa 1970).

_____

the median in other East Asian patrilineal societies, and worst represented in the patrilineal cultures of South Asia (India, Pakistan, Bangladesh). Compared with other East Asian developing countries, China's figure of 24 percent for female enrollment in universities is only moderately below par.

8. Theoretically, at least, these are independent issues. It is possible for women to work in large numbers, but at very low wages relative to men. Or few women might work, but they might hold similar jobs to those men hold.

men. In general young women in Chinese cities do not even consider the role of homemaker as an option, and only in unusual circumstances (e.g., women with health problems or without an urban registration) will they stay out of the labor force. It is only after age fifty, when retirement regulations allow women to retire earlier than men (45–55 versus 50–60), and among women who were never employed, that we find a substantial difference in the rates of labor force participation by sex.

Again we can examine how the rates of female labor force participation in our data compare with other societies. In this case we can approximate a more direct comparison with our urban data by using figures derived from International Labor Organization Yearbooks on the proportion of the nonagricultural labor force that is female.[9] The relevant figures are displayed in table 23. There we can see that in regard to female labor force participation our figure for urban China looks very high indeed. None of the advanced capitalist or developing Asian countries approaches the rate we have computed for China, and only the most advanced East European socialist societies show comparable rates.[10]

Women participate in labor almost on the same level with men, but do they work in the same kind of jobs and earn comparable incomes? Studies in other societies indicate that relatively low pay and occupational segregation by sex are pervasive phenomena, even when women participate in work in large numbers. Our data provide several ways to examine whether the same patterns occur in China. In table 24 we use our neighbor

Table 22			Proportion of Women and Men Employed
Age	Female(%)	Male(%)	N
10–19	21	19	362
20–29	93	93	461
30–39	94	97	355
40–49	89	98	223
50–59	73	99	175
60–64	20	38	151

Source: Weighted sample of neighbors.

9. The comparison is approximate because some portion of the nonagricultural labor force in each country resides in rural areas, and our data are for the nonagricultural labor force in cities alone. However, note in appendix 1 how our data correspond closely to other data on the nonagricultural labor force for all of China.

10. Among the other Asian developing societies there is a tendency for South Asian countries to rank lowest, East Asian near the median, and Southeast Asian ones highest, in terms of female labor force participation. But in this case, in contrast to what we found in the educational realm, social changes since 1949 have made urban China distinctive from other East Asian cultures and, indeed, even in comparison with those of Southeast Asia.

Table 23   Percentage of Labor Force Female

Countries	Median	(Range)
China	48%	---
8 European socialist states	44%	(29–50%)
16 Euro/American capitalist states	33%	(22–44%)
10 Asian developing states	28%	(10–44%)

Sources: China: Weighted sample of employed neighbors, N = 1,727.
Others: Computed from nonagricultural labor force data in 1977 Yearbook of Labor Statistics (Geneva: International Labor Organization, 1977).

census data to examine women's income by different occupational groups and the proportion of each group that is female. The pattern that is so common in other societies is clearly visible here. Generally, women tend to be underrepresented in occupations that receive the highest pay and overrepresented in low-paying jobs. Even the detailed kinds of jobs in which women are heavily concentrated—light industry, services, clerical work, health care, lower level education—are similar to those seen as "female jobs" in other societies. The jobs in which they are underrepresented are familiar as well—heavy industry, police work, skilled work and foremen, and travelling salespeople (our expediters and procurers).

In chapter 3 we noted another factor relevant to economic inequality between the sexes: the formally institutionalized distinction between state enterprises and collective enterprises. The distinction is somewhat similar to the division between primary and secondary sectors of the labor force in advanced capitalist societies and between formal and informal sectors of the urban economy in developing societies. Although the disparities do not seem to be as sharp in China as in many other developing societies, in each instance those employed in the lower status sector of the economy tend to earn less, to have fewer fringe benefits, and to enjoy less job security and opportunity for advancement. In any case, we find in our weighted sample that women are somewhat underrepresented in the labor force in state enterprises (45%) and overrepresented among those employed in collective enterprises (59%).[11] The channeling of women into such collective enterprises is clearly one factor producing relative disadvantages.

11. It should also be noted that there are differences within the state sector that may be related to "peripherality." For example, state primary school teachers and shop clerks are

We can delve further into the question of relative earnings of women by examining data on the mean wages earned by males and females in different age cohorts. We present the appropriate data in figure 7. It would appear that women and men start out with fairly similar wage levels, but at later ages men are able to progress into higher wage brackets, while women do not continue to make equal progress. Overall, the average female in our weighted household census sample earns about 77 percent of what her male counterpart earns. We should mention that our data in figure 7 are cross-sectional and not longitudinal. Women in older cohorts in the figure are likely to have less of the important determinants of wage levels (e.g., education, skill, and seniority) than do younger women, and these data do not show that as younger women age they will follow the same earnings trajectory. Is this earnings difference a temporary phenomenon that will pass as the less career-committed older women pass out of the labor force? Some light on this question is provided by performing a regression analysis on our reported earnings data. Table 25 presents the results of such an analysis, for the whole sample and for men and women separately. Regression analysis is a multivariate statistical technique designed to help us to separate out the "pure" influence of gender from other factors, such as educational attainment or seniority.

The figures in table 25 reveal several things. The metric regression coefficients show that men benefit slightly more than women from each step up the occupational ladder, and considerably more than women from each added year of seniority (see the top rows in panels A and B of the table). These patterns are important because, as the standardized regression coefficients in the panels show, occupational placement and seniority have stronger independent effects upon income than does educational attainment. The bottom panel in the table reveals another important fact. When one controls for other variables, the independent influence of gender is considerably reduced, although not totally eliminated. The metric regression coefficient for sex in panel C (4.38) is considerably reduced from the 14.6 yuan gap in mean incomes that existed before the other variables were taken into account. This means that when Chinese authorities say they are providing women with equal pay for equal work they are not distorting reality too much. The main sources of the lower incomes women receive are attributable more to their being placed in lower wage jobs where they benefit less from seniority than to their earning

---

generally regarded as underpaid, and wage scales in light industry (where women are more commonly found) tend to be lower than those in heavy industry.

Table 24

Average Wage Levels and Female Representation in Occupational Groups

Occupational group	Average wage (yuan)	%	Occupational Group	Average wage (yuan)	%
College professor, school principal	103	39	Construction workers	53	18
Engineers, technicians	90	29	Accountants	53	47
Doctors, pharmacists	81	31	Expediter/Procurer	53	0
Government administrators	75	22	Teacher, unclassified	51	57
Other cadres, military officials	74	30	Sales superviser	50	33
Managers, shop heads, etc.	67	23	Other clerical	48	66
Other professionals	63	33	Nurses	45	97
Foremen	63	0	Primary school teachers	44	80
Secondary school teachers	62	67	Cashiers, sales clerks	42	68
Drivers, transport workers	60	13	Cooks, waiters, barbers	42	48
Skilled production workers	60	7	Ordinary workers	41	54
Independent sales workers	57	33	Street cleaners	38	86
Artists and authors	56	71	Preschool teachers	37	100
Policeman and soldiers	56	7	Nursemaids, servants	29	93
Transportation conductors, postal workers	55	55	Temporary workers	27	75
Rank and file government employees	54	53	Apprentices	22	55

Source: Sample of employed neighbors, N = 1,232.

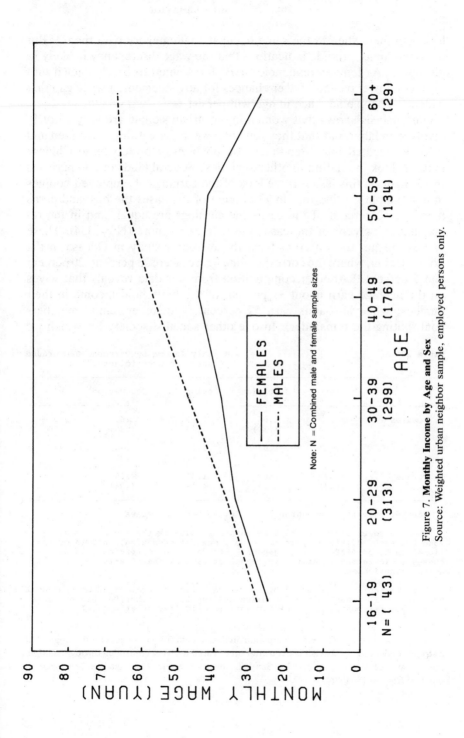

Figure 7. **Monthly Income by Age and Sex**
Source: Weighted urban neighbor sample, employed persons only.

less than men when in the same occupational category with them.[12] But our data do not provide indications that the wage discrepancy is likely to disappear. As long as tendencies exist for women to be channeled into jobs with lower pay and fewer chances for advancement, a wage gap that widens as people advance in age will persist.

Our analysis shows that women in our urban sample are very actively involved in labor, but that they tend to have lower earnings than men and to be segregated into "feminine" occupations. How do these Chinese patterns look in relation to other societies? Several kinds of comparisons throw light on this issue. If we look at the earnings of employed couples in our sample we find that in 73 percent of the cases the husband earns more, in 12 percent of the cases the earnings are equal, and in the remaining 16 percent of the cases the wife earns more (N = 354). These figures are not too different from those from a study in Odessa in the Soviet Union, where the corresponding figures were 73 percent, 20 percent and 7 percent.[13] Another computation from our data reveals that wives on the average earn about 37 percent of the household income in their families, while husbands earn 57 percent (with other family members contributing the remainder). In one other socialist society for which we

Table 25   Monthly Income by Personal Background (Regression Coefficients)[a]

	Sex	Education	Seniority	Occupation[b]	R^2
A. Females		1.05 (.20)	1.19 (.43)	.62 (.38)	.50
B. Males		1.03 (.11)	1.81 (.47)	.72 (.32)	.43
C. Totals	4.38 (.07)	1.00 (.13)	1.57 (.44)	.69 (.34)	.47

Source: Sample of neighbors, 302 females and 364 males.

[a]Metric coefficients without parentheses indicate the monthly return in yuan for each additional year in school, year of education, unit in occupational rank, or difference in gender. Standardized coefficients in parentheses indicate the relative importance of each of these variables in determining income.

[b]Occupation is represented by the average income level of 32 occupational groupings. The mean income for males and females together in this analysis is 50 yuan per month. All coefficients are significant at p ≤ .01.

12. We note that one study of occupation and wage data from a Soviet city did argue that a strong gender effect was visible even after other variables were controlled through multiple regression. See Michael Swafford, "Sex Differences in Soviet Earnings," *American Sociological Review* 43 (1978): 657–73.

13. Ibid.

have comparable figures, Czechoslovakia, wives contributed somewhat less, 18–20 percent of household income on the average.[14] In the United States in 1974 the average married woman earned 26 percent of her family's income if she worked, again somewhat lower than our Chinese figure.[15] To look most systematically at the question of female relative incomes it would of course be desirable to have systematic data on the ratio of the average female wage to the average male wage for a large range of countries. Unfortunately such data are not generally available, and even where they exist they are subject to serious problems of comparability. For what it is worth, various surveys show a range of about 50 to 80 percent for advanced capitalist societies, with a median of about 60 percent (which is about the figure for the United States), and a range in East European socialist societies of 63 to 84 percent, with a median value around 66 percent.[16] The only developing society for which we have located a comparable figure is Egypt, where in 1970 it was claimed that women in the nonagricultural sectors of the economy earned on the average 61 percent of what men earned.[17] Since we compute from our sample that urban Chinese women earn about 77 percent of what men do, our general conclusion is that in comparative terms they are doing quite well, although they are not "off the scale."

The problems of making comparisons are even more complex if we consider the question of occupational segregation by sex. The methodology for making such comparisons is still in its infancy. One measure that has been developed is called the index of dissimilarity. This statistic can be interpreted as the percentage of females that would have to change jobs in order for women to have the same occupational distribution as men.[18] One problem with this measure is that its size depends strongly on how occupations are categorized. For the same set of data, a finer occupational breakdown will yield a larger index value. It is difficult to make comparisons, then, unless one can be sure that one has truly com-

14. Barbara Jancar, *Women under Communism* (Baltimore: Johns Hopkins University Press, 1978), p. 27.

15. L. Suter and H. Miller, "Income Differences between Men and Career Women," *American Journal of Sociology* 78 (1973): 657–73.

16. Miscellaneous figures leading to these computations are cited in Martin King Whyte, "Sexual Inequality under Socialism: The Chinese Case in Perspective" (Paper for Conference on Inequality and Class in Socialist China, Cumberland Lodge, England, July 1980), and in International Labor Organization, *1977 Yearbook of Labor Statistics* (Geneva: ILO, 1977), pp. 632–39.

17. ILO, *1977 Yearbook of Labor Statistics,* p. 632.

18. The formula used is $ID = 1/2$ of the sum over $|Fi - Mi|$, where Fi and Mi are the proportion of the total of employed females and males that are employed in the ith category of the occupational distribution.

parable occupational breakdowns, and for any broad-ranging comparison this means one has to use very crude breakdowns.[19]

The most detailed occupational breakdown we developed with our data, involving a fifty-category occupational code, provides an index of dissimilarity (ID) of .34. This means that about a third of the women (or men) would have to shift categories in order to end up with the same distribution for both sexes. If we use a reduced set of ten categories (high professional, administrative cadres, managerial cadres, low professional, clerical and sales, skilled manual, service workers, ordinary and semiskilled manual workers, unskilled and marginal workers, and other), we compute an ID of .31, only slightly less. For the purposes of international comparisons even this is too detailed, and instead we collapsed our data into a standard six-category breakdown of nonagricultural occupations used in International Labor Organization (ILO) data: professional and technical, managerial and administrative, clerical, sales, service, and production workers. With these categories our data yield a substantially lower ID for urban China of .15, meaning that only about one out of six women would have to shift among these gross categories in order to make the distribution for both sexes parallel. In table 26 we display this figure along with similar indexes computed for other countries. The conclusion we reach is similar to that we arrived at in regard to the relative wages question. The degree of occupational segregation by sex in urban China appears to be more moderate than that found in most other societies, although there are other places with still lower figures. In this case it is also interesting to note that occupational segregation by sex seems to be more marked in the most developed societies. However, what exactly socialism may do to influence this form of occupational segregation is not very clear. The highest ID values occur for advanced capitalist countries (Norway, to be specific), but the lowest value was computed for Hong Kong (ID = .09), which happens to be highly capitalistic as well as Chinese.[20] In general we conclude that urban Chinese women are doing relatively well, but that we are still a long way from understanding the factors responsible for this

19. One can compute standardized indexes of dissimilarity to eliminate some of these problems. This index is computed the same as the unstandardized version, except that each country is assumed to have the same overall occupational distribution (say, with 1,000 employed persons in each of six categories). When we did this it yielded a pattern not very different from that shown in table 26 using the unstandardized index. For example, the standardized index of dissimilarity for our urban China sample is .27, which compares with the median value of .30 (and minimum of .22 and maximum of .36) for the other ten Asian developing societies on which we have data.

20. Overall, there is no tendency among the Asian developing societies used in table 26 for the degree of occupational segregation to be consistently associated with kinship form or region.

favorable picture. China's socialism does not seem to be the primary explanation, except in regard to the high rate of labor force participation by women.

We can advance one explanation about the causes of the fairly high relative wages and low occupational segregation of women. We saw in figure 7 that the wage gap for young men and women is very small, and in a separate analysis we found that occupational segregation by sex is also lowest in the youngest cohort of employed people.[21] We speculate that at least part of this age difference is attributable to the urban employment crisis of recent years and the effects the Cultural Revolution had on job opportunities for the young. Essentially the educational ladder to relatively well-paid, nonmanual jobs was pulled out from under our youngest cohort, and only a limited range of jobs, mostly in industry and the service and sales sectors, was available for those lucky enough to remain in the city and be eligible for an urban job. In other words, the range of job opportunities that had existed was sharply truncated, and young males and females scrambled to get whatever jobs were available. They were then stuck at fairly uniform beginning wage levels (generally of 30–35 yuan) until the wage adjustments which began in 1977 (whose effects are not reflected in our data). We are suggesting, then, that these factors to some degree short-circuited the "natural" tendency for male and female job destinations (and wages) to differentiate. The Cultural Revolution reforms had a "real" effect promoting equality between the sexes as well as among different social strata. This short-circuiting and

Table 26

Countries	Occupational Segregation by Sex (Indexes of Dissimilarity)	
	Median	(Range)
China	.15	---
7 European socialist states	.34	(.25–.45)
17 Euro/American capitalist states	.38	(.22–.51)
10 Asian developing states	.22	(.09–.26)

Sources: China: Weighted sample of employed neighbors. Others: Computed from nonagricultural labor force data in 1977 Yearbook of Labor Statistics (Geneva: International Labor Organization, 1977).

21. Our ten-category occupational breakdown has an ID of .31. Broken down by age cohorts, the ID is .20 for the cohort aged 20–29, and then .34 for those 30–39, .43 for those 40–49, .35 for those 50–59, and finally .55 for those 60–94.

the effects of this younger cohort on the overall wage and occupational distribution may help to explain the relatively favorable conclusion we have drawn from our data on Chinese working women. One implication of this hypothesis is that, as the policies of the pre-Cultural Revolution years are restored and a broader range of urban job prospects appears, with some allowances even made for individual job preferences, we might expect the job prospects of males and females to diverge more noticeably and for the distinctiveness of the Chinese case to be reduced. (The over-representation of males in current Chinese university enrollment will also promote such a tendency.)

Politics

In the realm of politics there are some limited national figures to cite. We have not been able to find a current figure on the percentage of all Communist Party members who are women. However, 19 percent of the 1,510 delegates of the Eleventh Party Congress in 1977 were women, and women constituted 11 percent of the membership of the Central Committee selected at the congress (7% of the full, as opposed to alternate, members of the CC), and only one out of twenty-eight members of the politburo (or 4%), that one being only an alternate member. These figures do not represent any clear increase over previous Party congresses.[22] If we switch our attention to the state organs, we find that one out of fourteen (7%) vice-premiers chosen at the Fifth National People's Congress in 1978 was a female, as was one out of the thirty-seven ministers designated then (3%). (Actually the one female here is also the single politburo member, Chen Muhua, who is doing double duty in these figures.) Women do somewhat better in the more honorary, and less powerful, positions in the state hierarchy. They constitute 14 percent of the chairmen and vice-chairmen and 20 percent of the members of the standing committee of the NPC who were named in 1978.[23] Women also make up 26 percent of the more than 18 million state cadres in China, but only 3–6 percent of

22. Figures computed from *Peking Review,* no. 34 (1977): 7, 14–17. The Ninth Congress of the CCP in 1969 chose a Central Committee that was 8 percent female, and the Tenth Congress in 1973 chose a Central Committee that was 13 percent female. Figures cited in James Seymour, *China: The Politics of Revolutionary Reintegration* (New York: Thomas Crowell, 1976), p. 233. Subsequently, at the Twelfth Party Congress in 1982, female representation fell off further with women representing only 7 percent of the members of the new Central Committee elected then (and only 5 percent of the full members). See *FBIS,* 10 September 1982, p. K1 and 17 September 1982, p. W1.

23. Figures from *Peking Review,* no. 10 (1978): 41–42.

the high-ranking state cadres (those above rank 13 in the official system of 24 cadre ranks).[24]

While these figures show that women in China are underrepresented in political leadership positions, and particularly so at the highest levels, they again do not speak to how China looks in comparative terms. Here the data are quite spotty, but what we have been able to assemble is presented in table 27. Comparisons are also difficult because the importance of particular political organs is not the same in various countries. It is clear, for example, that parliaments in many countries have more power than does China's National People's Congress, while Party leadership positions are more important in China than in pluralist systems. Given these problems of comparison, we may still observe that the figures in table 27 again present China as doing fairly well in representing women in political leadership, and about average compared to other socialist states, although another conclusion would be that in no society are they represented very well (the few female prime ministers notwithstanding).

We can also examine women's political representation in our weighted urban sample. In doing so we find that overall, women make up 62 percent of the members of the Communist Youth League, but only 12 percent of the members of the more selective Chinese Communist Party. In figure 8 we display the pattern of membership by gender in both organizations, broken down by age cohorts. There we can see that at the peak in the 40–49 age cohort, almost a quarter of all the men in our sample were Party members, but only 8 percent of the women were, in spite of the

Table 27   Female Representation in National Elites

Countries	Party (%) Median	(Range)	Party CC (%) Median	(Range)	National Legislature (%) Median	(Range)
China (1977–78)	---	---	11	---	20	---
9 European socialist states	23	(20–27)	9	(3–15)	20	(8–32)
19 Euro/American capitalist states	---	---	---	---	6	(2–22)
5 Asian developing states	---	---	---	---	5	(0–14)

Sources: China: see text. Others: Janet Giele and Audrey Smock, eds., Women: Roles and Status in Eight Countries (New York: John Wiley, 1977), p. 17; and Sharon Wolchik, "Politics, Ideology and Equality: The Status of Women in Eastern Europe" (Ph.D dissertation, University of Michigan, 1978), pp. 116, 131, 133, 153.

24. See Beijing Review, no. 11 (1981): 6, and no. 12 (1981): 5.

advantage women have at younger ages in Communist Youth League membership. If we look at the other end of the leadership scale the picture is different. The most menial positions of general leadership in urban China are the residents' committee and residents' small group leaders in local neighborhoods. According to data supplied by our informants, fully 70 percent of the residents' committee chairpersons and 88 percent of the residents' small group heads in their neighborhoods were women.[25] Our findings in general conform to a pattern that seems universal in societies: the higher one gets in political power and leadership status, the more likely men will have the monopoly.[26]

Family Relations

A further area of sexual inequality was introduced in chapter 6: the division of labor within the home. There we saw that a general pattern exists within urban China, as in other societies, for women to do more around the home than men. In particular, women do most of the shopping, cooking, dishwashing, cleaning, and laundering, and more often than not they are also the ones to empty the garbage and manage the household purse. Men in their prime years are more likely than women to perform particularly heavy chores, such as carting home the family grain and coal rations, and they also predominate in making household repairs.

Under what circumstances are men or women more likely to perform various chores? A number of patterns have been suggested. Perhaps men who are well educated or politically conscious help out more around the home than other men. Or perhaps men with more resources (high incomes and positions) help out less than other men. Perhaps in larger, more cosmopolitan cities men help out more, or help out more in families that are especially pressed for time. We examine these and a number of other possibilities in table 28. Our measure of chore performance there is a mean of the scores of individuals on the five "feminine chores"—shop-

25. A vivid account of the duties of these lowly offices is presented in M. Bernard Frolic, "My Neighborhood," in *Mao's People* (Cambridge: Harvard University Press, 1980). However, we should note that having women as formal neighborhood leaders is an innovation, one initially difficult for some urbanites to accept. On this point see Franz Schurmann, *Ideology and Organization in Communist China,* 2d ed. (Berkeley: University of California Press, 1968), p. 377.

26. It might be objected that we are ignoring the National Women's Federation, a political organ that parallels the Party and is exclusively a female organization. We feel justified in doing so because the Women's Federation functions as a mass association under the domination of the CCP, rather than having any independent power in its own right. While this organization may perform useful services and promote the interests of its members, in no way does it alter the male monopoly of authority in the larger society.

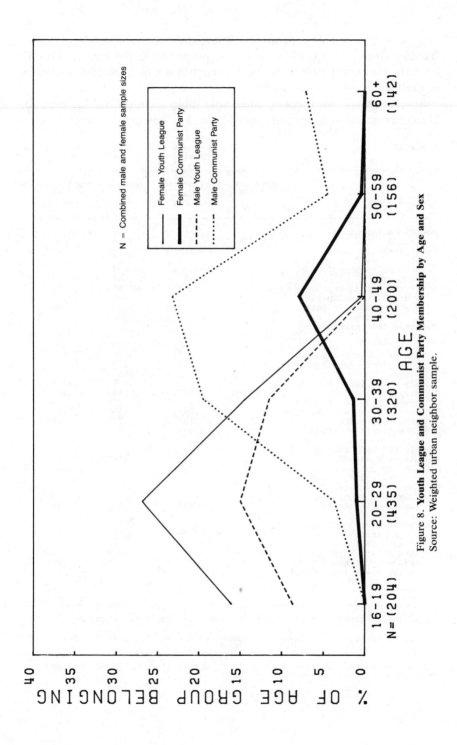

N = Combined male and female sample sizes

Female Youth League
Female Communist Party
Male Youth League
Male Communist Party

Figure 8. **Youth League and Communist Party Membership by Age and Sex**
Source: Weighted urban neighbor sample.

ping, cooking, washing dishes, sweeping the floor, and washing clothes (ranging from 0 = no role to 4 = sole performer in the household). We examine the correlation between this mean score and selected attributes of individuals and their families.

Several things can be concluded from table 28. First, having high socioeconomic standing or personal resources does not seem to be con-

Table 28   Factors Affecting Participation in
                                            "Feminine" Household Chores

	Wife's Participation Correlations		Husband's Participation Correlations	
	Simple	Partial[a]	Simple	Partial[a]
Job Characteristics[b]				
Income	-.27*	--	-.14*	--
% of family income contributed	-.18*	-.11	-.14*	-.10
Whether employed	-.22*	-.19*	-.04	.00
Seniority	-.29*	-.10	.01	.11
Tertiary industry	-.17*	-.26*	-.10	-.06
Prestigious occupation	-.14*	-.05	-.07	-.09
State-owned work unit	-.25*	-.11	-.06	.04
Personal Characteristics[b]				
Age	.01	.06	-.13*	-.07
Education	-.03	.14*	.08	.10
CYL or CCP membership	.05	.12	.00	-.01
Good class background	-.02	.03	.00	-.00
Family Situation				
Extended family	-.39*	-.32*	-.16*	.01
Unemployed females at home	-.21*	--	-.27*	--
Eat lunch at work unit	.06	.09	.16*	.15
Long work hours	.13	.10	.31*	.26*
Many evening meetings	-.19	-.03	.24*	.40*
Family Living Standard				
Living standard	.11	.24*	.14*	.17*
Consumption index (bike, radio, watch, sewing machine)	.33*	.41*	-.02	.01
Household amenities	-.01	.05	.13	.19*
Own home lived in	.11	.13*	.05	.06
Characteristics of City				
Administrative level	-.30*	.27*	.08	.17*
Lingnan Region	.10	.09	-.16*	-.20*
Rations and supplies	.05	.01	-.22*	-.26*
Frequency of household cleanliness inspections	.15*	.26*	.15*	.24*
Median N	(111)	(108)	(120)	(111)

Source: Currently married men and women in sample of neighbors.

[a]Coefficients, controlled for income and presence of unemployed females at home.

[b]Wife's characteristics used in left pair of statistical columns and husband's characteristics in right pair.

-- = controlled characteristics. *p ≤ .10

sistently related to chore performance for either sex. For women various aspects of high status jobs are associated with low household chore performance, but having high education, membership in the Communist Party, or favorable class label does not show the same pattern. (For husbands only the negative relationship with income holds up.) For the same reason, the notion that men who are more "enlightened" or politically conscious will help out more around the home does not stand up to scrutiny. Nor is there clear support for the notion that when family members are more pressed for time others will help out more. In fact, we find a puzzling pattern in which husbands who eat lunch away from home, work late, and have many evening meetings are significantly more likely to help out around the home than other husbands.

Nonetheless, there are several consistent patterns in the table. Wives do fewer chores when they are employed in high income, high prestige, high seniority positions in the state sector, and some of this pattern is still visible after their incomes are controlled for statistically in column 2 of the table. Women who live in extended families and have unemployed females at home perform fewer chores than other wives, while those in families with high living standards, many consumer goods, and frequent household inspections perform more chores than other wives. For women, then, there seems to be a fairly consistent work-home trade-off operating. Almost all wives work in urban China, but those who have the most demanding and absorbing jobs tend to do least around the home, while those who have high consumption standards, concern for public scrutiny of the household, or no other female help do the most. This general pattern fits that found in studies in Western societies, where work demands are the primary factor that may reduce the time spent on household chores by women.[27]

For husbands the patterns are much less clear. Some of the same associations we have discussed for women—income, extended family living, and household consumption standards—show up for men as well, but they are generally much weaker. There is one apparent trade-off between husbands and wives. In large cities, women tend to do fewer chores, and men somewhat more, than is the case in smaller cities and towns. This finding is the only hint of what might be an "enlightenment" effect on the pattern of chore performance. We find, as do many wives, that it is hard to explain what leads some men to help out more than others around the home. Uncertainty is not unusual in studies of this topic. Research in other societies demonstrates clearly that men do not pick up much of

27. See, for example, Joann Vanek, "Time Spent in Housework," *Scientific American* 231 (1974): 116–20; and Lois Hoffman and Ivan Nye, *Working Mothers* (San Francisco: Jossey-Bass, 1974).

any slack when their wives work, and that the degree to which particular husbands help out in the home is not easily predictable from standard sociological factors.[28]

Summarizing the general picture of chore division is not a simple matter. But we stress again that China fits the general pattern of women doing the bulk of the household chores, even though virtually all in their prime ages work in full-time jobs. This is the familiar "double burden" experienced by working women in other societies. Beyond this, situational pressures families face can shift the balance to some extent, and the most important factor is the relative weight of job and family pressures experienced by the women. The absence of clear relationships with political variables, educational attainment, or resource measures combined with the weak or negligible effects of age throws doubt on any idea that the traditional chore division is being broken down as more enlightened younger cohorts enter the ranks of married people and practice more sharing in chore performance.[29]

However, we can still ask whether the double burden of urban Chinese women might be less severe than that found in other societies. That is, do urban Chinese men help out somewhat more than husbands in other societies, even if their wives end up performing the bulk of the chores? There are several problems that prevent us from examining this question in as systematic a way as we have other realms in this chapter. In particular, there are few studies of the household chores division in other societies, and most such studies have been conducted in developed societies. Methods also differ a great deal from study to study, making generalizations hazardous. We will endeavor nonetheless to make a comparison with the societies for which we have appropriate data, but its partial and rough nature must be stressed at the outset.

We selected six different chore areas: the five "feminine" chores we have been examining, plus management of the family purse. For our Chinese data we use as our measure the ratio of the mean score of husbands to the mean score for wives on a particular chore. Thus a score of 0 indicates that husbands do nothing, while a score of 1.0 would mean that husbands do just as much as their wives (with higher scores if husbands bear more

28. See the sources cited in footnote 27, as well as Michael Sacks, *Women's Work in Soviet Russia* (New York: Praeger, 1976), chap. 5; and Joseph Pleck, "Married Men: Work and Family," in NIMH, *Families Today,* vol. 1 (Rockville, Md.: NIMH, 1980).

29. We are not arguing that chores are now divided exactly as they were in urban families in earlier eras. It is plausible to us, and to most of our informants, that men help out a little more now than they did in the late imperial or republican periods. But we are questioning whether there is any trend toward even fuller equality in household chores. A study of changing chore performance over roughly forty years in the Soviet Union found no evidence there of any shift toward men providing any more than minimal help with household chores. See Sacks, *Women's Work in Soviet Russia.*

of the burden). We compare these scores with scores derived from studies using a similar methodology devised by Blood and Wolfe.[30] They asked a sample whether a given chore is always performed by the husband, usually done by him, shared equally, usually done by the wife, or always done by the wife. By assigning values to these alternatives and taking the ratio of the husbands' means to the wives' means, we get a score comparable to our measure.[31] We present the results of our comparison in figure 9, using only data on employed women in other countries where possible.

From figure 9 we can see that for the five "feminine chores" there is nothing remarkable about the helping behavior of Chinese husbands. Furthermore, these data do not show any clear disparity between socialist and capitalist countries in the nature of the "double burden" working women experience. However, for the final item, money management, our Chinese figures do appear more distinctive. It appears that urban Chinese men play less of a role in managing the family purse than do men in the other societies examined. (However, we should caution that part of this difference may be due to variation in question wording; "paying the bills" rather than "managing the family purse" was used in most of the other societies in our comparison.) As we indicated in chapter 6, although there are no systematic data on this point, in urban Chinese families earlier in this century it appears than men more often managed the family budget than is currently the case, and the change may reflect the fact that under socialism families no longer have important property to manage. Even today, when it comes to making a decision about a large purchase, men seem to have a large say in the matter. In sum, with the exception of the item concerning money management, our conclusion must be that in urban China the extent to which men help out with chores usually done by women is minimal in absolute terms and not much different in comparison with other societies, even though the current situation represents a modest improvement over the pre-1949 household division of labor.[32]

30. See Robert Blood and Donald Wolfe, *Husbands and Wives* (New York: Free Press, 1960).

31. To compute the male score we assigned values 4, 3, 2, 1, and 0 to the alternatives listed and computed the average, while for wives we assigned the values 0, 1, 2, 3, and 4 to the same alternatives. In the Soviet, Swedish, and Finnish data three-step, rather than five-step, scales were used: husband, shared, and wife performing the chore. For comparison purposes we assigned values of 3.5, 2, and 0.5 to these alternatives (or 0.5, 2, and 3.5 for wives) in order to compute our mean scores.

32. It may be objected that omission of other developing societies makes the comparison unfair to China. Unfortunately systematic data are simply not available for other developing societies, and the few fragments we have leave the question of what we would find if we could enter them in the comparison ambiguous. One study of working women in the Indian city of Patna suggests that husbands there are generally quite hostile toward helping with

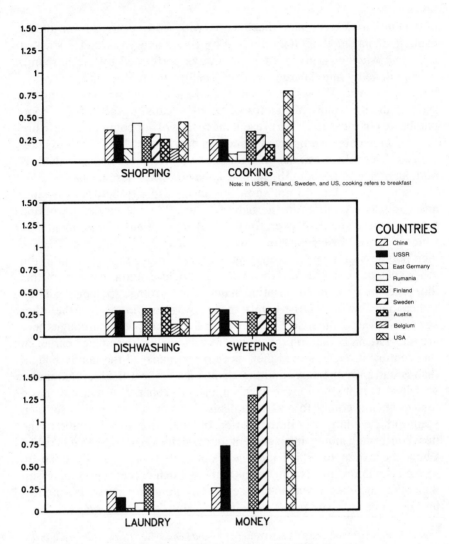

Note: In USSR, Finland, Sweden, and US, cooking refers to breakfast

COUNTRIES
- China
- USSR
- East Germany
- Rumania
- Finland
- Sweden
- Austria
- Belgium
- USA

Figure 9. **Ratio of Mean Husband/Wife Performance Scores by Country**

Sources for Figure 9:

China: Urban neighbor chores sample.

U.S.S.R.: A sample of 430 married women in 1966 (all employed) in the cities of Moscow, Leningrad, and Penza. Gennady Slesarev and Z. A. Yankova, "The Woman in the Industrial Enterprise and in the Family," in *Sotsial'noe Problemy Truda i Proizvodstva,* G. V. Osipov and Jan Sczepanski, eds. (Moscow: Mysl', 1969), p. 430.

Rumania: A subsample of responses of working wives from a larger sample in Bucharest in 1976. Reported in William Moskoff, "Sex Discrimination, Commuting, and the Role of Women in Rumanian Development," *Slavic Review* 37 (1978): 450.

Finland and Sweden: Samples of 271 married women in Helsinki and 442 married women between ages 20 and 45 in Uppsala, both from studies conducted in 1966. (Working wives make up only 65 and 52 percent, respectively, of the samples.) Reported in Elina Haavio-Mánnila, "Convergences between East and West: Tradition and Modernity in Sex Roles in Sweden, Finland, and the Soviet Union," *Acta Sociologica* 14 (1971): 121.

United States: Sample from 1971 Detroit Area Study interviews with over 2,000 residents of that city. Responses of working wives were used here. Beverly Duncan and Otis D. Duncan, *Sex Typing and Social Roles* (New York: Academic Press, 1978), p. 198.

East Germany: An extensive survey (sample characteristics unclear) published in the paper *Der Morgan* on 22 September 1968. Cited in Barbara Jancar, "Women under Communism," in *Women in Politics,* Jane Jaquette, ed. (New York: John Wiley, 1974) p. 225.

Austria: A sample of 1,370 Austrian working women in several cities and towns, all in the 20–30 age range. Maximiliane Szinovacz, "Role Allocation, Family Structure, and Female Employment," *Journal of Marriage and the Family* 39 (1977): 781–91.

Belgium: A sample of 500 representative families in Louvain, Belgium, interviewed in 1961–62. William Silverman and Reuben Hill, "Task Allocation in Marriage in the United States and Belgium," *Journal of Marriage and the Family* 29 (1967): 353–59.

We must stress again, as in earlier chapters, that the situation in regard to household chores in urban China is not strictly comparable to other countries because the double burden is so very heavy. The combination of a low level of economic development with official priorities that devalue consumption needs in relation to production has resulted in a situation in which handling household chores is very tedious. The absence of appliances like refrigerators and washing machines, the difficulties of lighting "beehive coal" fires and carrying out the labor intensive preparations needed for a Chinese meal, the necessity of standing in long lines for many purchases and many other manifestations of China's not being a consumer-oriented society are what make daily living so difficult. Some of these features are shared with other socialist societies, but at least in some of these societies appliances, natural gas, and other amenities are sufficient to lighten the physical burden of chores for women, even if they don't reduce the time spent on such chores appreciably.[33] In urban China the difficulties of coping with the double burden are still felt in full force.

We don't have evidence to prove the point, but we assume that the household burdens imposed on women are one of the important reasons why, in China as elsewhere, women do not play a more active role in politics, advance more rapidly up occupational ladders, or have much time for leisure and self-improvement. If socialist societies differ at all in

---

family chores (See Kala Rani, *Role Conflict in Working Women* [New Delhi: Chetana Publications, 1976], chap. 6.) But another study in a lower working class area of Banaras suggests a pattern of considerable sharing of chores by husbands. (See M. Chatterjee, "Conjugal Roles and Social Networks in an Indian Urban Sweeper Locality," *Journal of Marriage and the Family* 39 [1977]: 193–202.) Time budget data from Lima and Callao, Peru, show women having about the same disparity over men in hours spent on household chores as women in the advanced industrial societies (socialist and capitalist) included in the study. See A. Szalai, *The Use of Time* (The Hague: Mouton, 1973), p. 126. In a replication of Szalai's study in two cities in China, men are said overall to put in three-fourths' as much time as women on chores. This is more than in our study of China or in Szalai's study of any other society. But without more specifics on the Chinese study, we can not say whether this is a true difference or one based on artifacts of method. See Wang Yalin and Li Jinrong, "Research on the Domestic Labor of Urban Employees," *Zhongguo Shehui Kexue*, no. 1 (1982): 177–80.

33. Research in America indicates that increasing availability of household applicances did not make much of a dent in the time spent on chores by housewives, although it did affect the drudgery involved. See Vanek, "Time Spent in Housework." In the Chinese domestic labor study mentioned in the footnote 32, men spend an average of 3.9 hours and women 5.2 hours on domestic chores every day. This is higher than in any capitalist or socialist society described by Szalai, suggesting that everyone in China has less leisure time, less time for cultural enlightenment, more difficulty coping with children, and so forth.

these regards, it is not because in such societies husbands are enlightened and help out more around the house.

Before concluding our survey of women's position in urban China, we need to review those features of familial roles discussed in earlier chapters that are even less given to comparative analysis. In chapter 5, we saw that marked asymmetries still exist in the courting process and criteria used in choosing a mate, with male initiative still dominant, and career prospects primary in picking a husband, but secondary to matters like looks and personality in choosing a wife. The frequency of gift demands from women to their suitors also conveys the continuing asymmetry. In China there is still a tendency to think of marriage as a process by which a man acquires a wife, and this is reflected in the fact that about 40 percent of the newly married couples move in with the husband's parents after the ceremony and very few move in with the bride's parents. Change in this regard is primarily toward separate or neolocal residence for the new couple, not toward women attracting in a husband.

From patterns such as these we might infer that the traditional patrilineal family norms under which women suffer so many disadvantages still obtain in socialist China. Such a conclusion would be incorrect, for familial roles in urban China have in a number of respects become noticeably more bilineal. One of the hallmarks of traditional family life was a preference for sons, a preference which still holds strong in the more developed environment of Taiwan.[34] Clearly some degree of son preference still exists in urban China, but it has substantially weakened. As noted above, in the 1970s most couples seemed quite willing to stop at two children, and some stopped after only one, even if they had not yet borne a son. There were a few isolated cases in our interviews of couples continuing to have one child after another in despair over having a son, but most informants said that now the gender of the children did not make so much difference to most families. In the period since our interviews the government has forcefully implemented a policy of allowing couples only one child, and the success of this campaign obviously depends upon the weakening of the traditional preference for sons. We should note in passing, however, one indicator of a new kind of sex bias—the pressures for controlling fertility fall disproportionately on women, who are the objects of much of the campaign pressure.

34. A Value of Children Survey carried out in Taiwan in 1976 found that 92 percent of an islandwide sample of wives expressed a preference for bearing sons. See Susan De Vos, "The Economic and Old Age Security Value of Children in the Philippines and Taiwan in the Middle 1970s" (Ph. D. dissertation, University of Michigan, 1982), p. 187.

The weakening of the traditional patrilineal emphasis can also be seen in the ways families reacted to the campaign to send urban youths to the countryside. Informants claim that some families worried about sending their teenage daughters to live in minimally supervised conditions in the countryside. When such families had a chance they would try to keep a daughter in the city and send their sons, or try to get their sent-down daughters transferred back to the city first. In our weighted neighbor census sample 61 percent of those who were, or had been, in the countryside were sons. This is not a large disparity, but it does provide one indication that under pressure of a new policy, other considerations overrode concern for reinforcement of patrilineal ties.[35]

There are several other indications in our data of an increasing bilineal emphasis. For one thing, it is now often the case in urban China that daughters as well as sons share the obligation to help support their aging parents. As we saw in chapter 6, this new pattern of sharing can lead to conflicts the traditional patrilineal system avoided. Daughters as well as sons are now generally included in the inheritance of family property, although of course there is less property available to be inherited (mainly consumer durables in larger cities, but some houses in smaller cities). Another shift we noted is that most divorces are now initiated by women, whereas previously this was more of a male prerogative. In 58 percent of our cases women are also favored in obtaining child custody and by a comparable amount in dividing family property. The "tilt" in favor of the female in divorce cases may not seem large, particularly in comparison with the United States. However, it does compare markedly with the bias in favor of the male's interest in property and child custody matters that prevailed in late imperial China and still prevails in rural villages.[36]

These various aspects of changes in familial relations seem to be interrelated and add up, we would argue, to a shift toward more of a bilineal

35. One consequence of this protectiveness toward daughters is that females were by 1980 overrepresented among the urban unemployed. One Chinese source claims that 70 percent of unemployed youths then were female. See *Xinhua* (Peking), 15 September 1980, in *FBIS*, 17 September 1980, p. L17.

36. On the rural comparison, see William Parish and Martin Whyte, *Village and Family in Contemporary China* (Chicago: University of Chicago Press, 1976). We should note one special feature of some divorce cases which qualifies the picture of a shift in favor of the female somewhat. As noted in chapter 6, one of the major causes of divorce is political trouble experienced by the male, and in this sort of case the male is obviously very vulnerable, and the woman is very likely to be favored in any settlement. (If the man is bound for a labor reform camp, he obviously will forfeit rights to child custody and perhaps property as well.) So part of the new advantages women have in divorce settlements may be due to a continuing aspect of inequality—men are in the most prominent positions politically and occupationally, and they are more in danger than women of becoming political targets in campaigns.

emphasis in family life. It seems probable that several structural changes introduced in the 1950s prepared the ground for this shift away from a strong patrilineal focus. The elimination of most private property weakened the resources that could be used to foster patrilineal ties, while the introduction of pensions made people less dependent upon support from grown sons. With the system of housing fostering more separate residence by grown children and more recent changes like the sending-down campaign and campaigns against ancestor worship (particularly during the Cultural Revolution), urban families have reacted by placing less exclusive reliance on father-son ties. The shift is only a partial one, as is shown by the continuing preference for patrilocal residence after marriage and by the statements of some informants that sons still have somewhat larger obligations to support aging parents than daughters. It is also quite compatible with continuing inequalities in familial roles, as we have noted in discussing chore performance. But it is an important movement from patriarchal toward more conjugal family ties, with women clearly primary beneficiaries.

Conclusions

Drawing together the many strands of evidence presented in this chapter is no easy matter, and there are no doubt many aspects of male and female roles too subtle and complex for our interviews to gauge very accurately. In trying to judge how much of the pervasive sexual inequality of pre-1949 China has been eliminated in Chinese cities, we find ourselves faced with a sort of "Is the glass half full or half empty?" dilemma. We present our views here from both angles in order to let the reader consider the issue.

From one perspective, the general picture is a disappointing one. Many aspects of sexual inequality are still clearly visible in our data—women earn less than men, they occupy fewer high status occupations and Party positions, and they end up performing most of the household chores. There is little about the relative position of women in urban China that is remarkable. By a number of indicators urban Chinese women do fairly well in comparative terms, but only in regard to managing the family purse do we have the suggestion of a situation with little counterpart in other societies. (And even here the limited nature of the comparison and problems in comparability prevent us from being conclusive.) The recognition in China that "women hold up half the sky" has not produced a degree of sexual equality that is particularly striking.

Our data can be read as evidence in regard to the more general question with which we began the chapter: "Does socialism liberate women?" Or, to put matters in another way, have Engels's predictions about the pre-conditions for sexual equality been realized? Our response to both ver-sions is a qualified no. Women's lot has clearly improved in socialist societies, but similar improvements have occurred under capitalism. The clearest pattern seems to be that some aspects of sexual inequality are influenced by the level of economic development, and not so much by the nature of the property relations in a society. The disparity in educa-tional levels is the clearest instance of a form of sexual inequality affected by development, but others such as the shift from patriarchal to more conjugal family relations could be cited as well. Engels felt that the elim-ination of private property and the entry in force of women into the workplace would create the conditions for ending sexual inequality. These expectations have not been borne out in other socialist societies, and they are not borne out in urban China either.[37] The achievement of general female labor force participation under socialism seems to be quite com-patible with men's continuing domination of politics and other realms.

It may be objected that China and the other socialist societies do not present a fair test of socialist theory. Some would point out, in particular, that Engels stressed a "third precondition" for sexual equality (besides socialist property relations and full labor force participation by women): public provision of a wide range of service facilities to take the burden of household chores out of the family and to enable women to participate more actively in social life outside the family.[38] In China and in other socialist societies official policies have worked against fulfilling this sort of situation, with some notable exceptions (particularly the provision of nursery schools). As a result the double burden may be even more onerous for working women in socialist societies than for their counterparts in advanced capitalist societies.

Although we discussed this problem earlier, we are not persuaded that the failure to provide such services is the main explanation for the re-maining inequalities. First, it would be possible to try to encourage men to share in the performance of household chores. One other socialist society (Cuba) has made some efforts in this regard, and there seems no reason to rest content with the assumption that family chores remain primarily a female concern. But in China there has been little pressure in this direction—certainly much less than the pressure placed upon women

37. See the evidence in Jancar, *Women under Communism;* L. Wolchik, "Politics, Ide-ology, and Equality: The Status of Women in Eastern Europe" (Ph.D. dissertation, Uni-versity of Michigan, 1978); and H. Scott, *Does Socialism Liberate Women?* (Boston: Beacon Press, 1974).

38. See A. Heitlinger, "Marxism, Feminism and Sex Equality," in *Women in Eastern Europe and the Soviet Union,* T. Yedlin, ed. (New York: Praeger, 1980).

to participate in work outside the home. Second, there is one existing example of a society that tried to socialize all domestic chores, and this case does not bode well for the three preconditions thesis. The Israeli kibbutz practices a form of communism, has general labor force partici- pation by women, and established collective nurseries, laundries, dining halls, and other facilities, much as Engels might have wished. In this instance the result was that the performers of the socialized chores were almost exclusively female, while men continued to dominate the high status jobs and leadership positions.[39] What conditions, if any, might pro- duce fuller sexual equality remains a puzzle, but socialism, even in its Maoist version, does not seem to have found the answer.[40]

From another point of view, however, judging the position of Chinese women against Engels's theory or a standard of total equality may be unfair and unrealistic. Since no society in the contemporary world, so- cialist or capitalist, has come close to full sexual equality, China cannot be severely faulted for similar shortcomings. It is more fair to use as our standard for comparison the position of women in other contemporary societies. In this light, the position of women in urban China looks quite favorable. Many of the traditional restrictions on women are now gone, although of course some of them were weakening even before 1949. The transformation to full labor force participation by women in the course of a generation seems quite remarkable. (In this regard we note that several of the more developed East European socialist societies have lower pro- portions of females in the nonagricultural labor force.) Even though this change has not had the consequences Engels assumed it would, there have clearly been changes in other realms as well. Insofar as there can be said to be a syndrome of socialist womanhood, it would include such traits as very high female labor force participation, relatively equal access by women to education, but underrepresentation in high political and economic positions, and a severe burden of household chores. Our data on urban China fit this pattern much more than they do the patterns of other developing societies. In certain respects our data indicated Chinese urban women may be doing marginally better than some of their socialist

39. See L. Tiger and J. Shepher, *Women in the Kibbutz* (New York: Harcourt Brace Jovanovich, 1975). On efforts to promote chore sharing in Cuba, see Marjorie King, "Cuba's Attack on Women's Second Shift, 1974–1976," in *Women in Latin America*, E. Leacock et. al., eds. (Riverside, Ca: Latin American Perspectives, 1979).

40. One part of the effort to foster sexual equality in the capitalist West is absent from socialist societies, including China: autonomous political organizations formed by women to work for equality. Leninist doctrine has generally been hostile toward feminism as a separate movement, and the Leninist political institutions in ruling socialist societies gen- erally tolerate only women's organizations which are clearly subordinated to the ruling party.

sisters—in higher wages relative to men, somewhat less occupational segregation, and more say in household money management. Given the pervasive male bias of Chinese culture, the fact that by most measures urban Chinese women are doing at least as well as women in more highly developed socialist societies in Eastern European is quite impressive.

These results lead us to take issue with one interpretation of official policy toward women in China. According to this view, the (mostly male) elite in China are mainly interested in exploiting the labor of women and not much in promoting equality in other realms. So measures that are closely related to getting the most value out of female labor (such as equalizing educational opportunity and providing nursery schools) are stressed, while other goals are not. When the requirements of other policy goals make it seem advisable to reduce even the emphasis on women's work participation, the leader's are only too willing to make such adjustments.[41]

In our view such arguments place too much emphasis on the importance of government policies for altering the status of women. Campaigns and propaganda may come and go, and a model women worker heroine may be superceded by a model mother and childrearer.[42] But to focus on such shifts and ignore the implications of the basic institutional changes that have taken place in urban China would be a mistake. The elimination of most family property, the reliance of families on bureaucratic agencies for housing and other resources, the mobilization of women into the work force, the reduction in the educational gap between men and women, and other basic changes in urban social structure have prepared the ground for social forms that are at least closer to sexual equality. The resulting changes go beyond women working in large numbers and include more of a bilineal emphasis in family life, female money management, and a female tilt in divorce cases. Similar structural changes have been occurring

41. See, for example, S. Leader, "The Emancipation of Chinese Women," *World Politics* 26 (1973): 55–79; J. Salaff and J. Merkle, "Women and Revolutions: The Lessons of the Soviet Union and China," in M. Young, *Women in China;* and Ai-li Chin, "Family Relations in Modern Chinese Fiction," in *Family and Kinship in Chinese Society,* M. Freedman, ed. (Stanford: Stanford University Press, 1970).

42. In 1979–83 a more "conservative" atmosphere in regard to women's roles was clearly being promoted in China, symbolized by such things as the disbanding of the Guangdong provincial women's high-electric-wire work group and a new stress on the importance of the mother's role in socializing her children not to be delinquent. Comparable shifts in earlier years, following more radical campaign periods, are described in Chin, "Family Relations in Modern Chinese Fiction." The announcement that the famous women's wire team was being disbanded in 1979 stated the reason was that, "because of the limitations imposed by women's biological characteristics, they are very unsuited to long periods of live-wire work at great heights." See Guangdong Provincial Radio, 13 October 1979, in *FBIS,* 19 October 1979, p. P1.

at varying speeds in other societies, socialist and capitalist, and we would argue that those changes will continue to foster more equal relations between the sexes no matter what the current political winds bring.

In sum, while the current situation still falls considerably short of full sexual equality, Chinese urban women seem to be doing relatively well, perhaps better than one should expect given China's low level of economic development (and patriarchal heritage). Insofar as we accept this positive view of things, we would argue that a primary reason for this favorable picture is that Chinese cities are so highly bureaucratized and the sorts of modern structural changes that make progress toward equality possible are further advanced than one would expect for a country as poor as China.

A similar verdict could stand as a general conclusion to the material presented in this section. Important changes have clearly taken place in family life in urban China. In many respects these changes—later marriage, reduced power of the aged, lower fertility, and so forth—are similar to those occurring in other developing societies and broadly fit the world-wide trend away from the patriarchal family patterns found in agrarian societies to the more "conjugal" forms that predominate in industrialized societies, capitalist and socialist. But some other elements reflect patterns distinctive to socialist societies, such as the high rate of female labor force participation and the importance of political considerations in mate choice and divorce. We have also seen evidence of aspects of family life that seem distinctive to the particular form of socialism constructed in urban China—the unusally rapid decline in fertility, for instance, or the small gap between male and female incomes and the high frequency with which women manage the household purse. In some respects the distinctive political economy of Chinese urbanism, with its tight-knit organizational structure, high distributional equality, and bureaucratic distributional system, can be seen as contributing to such novel family trends. But paradoxically, the effect of this form of urban life has been to reinforce certain aspects of traditional Chinese family life. Because of this, major changes have not produced either family instability nor the form of conjugal family life that is familiar in the West. Instead what has emerged is a modified form of family life which in spite of all the changes is still characterized by a preeminent emphasis on family solidarity and loyalty and enduring marriage bonds, with concern for individual happiness and fulfillment of secondary importance.

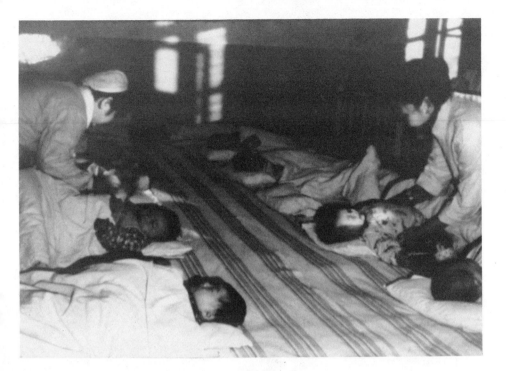

1. Textile mill nursery. Photograph by Martin King Whyte.

2. Kindergarten manual labor session. Photograph by Martin King Whyte.

3. Collective jumprope in a primary school. Photograph by Martin King Whyte.

4. Retired men at ease. Photograph by James Watson.

5. Neighborhood workshop. Photograph by Martin King Whyte.

6. Private bicycle repair. Photograph by William L. Parish.

7. Newly reopened urban free market, 1980.

Photograph by Martin King Whyte.

8. Beehive coal briquets for home cooking.
Photograph by Martin King Whyte.

9. Cooking stove with coal balls. Photograph by James Watson.

10. Street sweeper. Photograph by Martin King Whyte.

11. Criminal sentencing notice with a bill of particulars. The check at the bottom indicates that the sentence was capital punishment. Photograph by Martin King Whyte.

广东省广州市中级人民法院布告

此 布

院长 高崑峯

一 九 七 九 年 十 二 月 十 八 日

12. Bicycle parking lot. Photograph by Martin King Whyte.

13. Older, inner-city lane in Canton. Photograph by James Watson.

14. Older, dilapidated housing in a provincial city. Photograph by James Watson.

15. Newer "workers' village" housing in Shanghai. Photograph by Martin King Whyte.

3 Quality of Life

In the next four chapters we are concerned with the quality of life in contemporary Chinese cities. We want to consider whether various aspects of urban life that may affect the feelings urbanites have about their lives and the city they live in have changed since 1949 and whether they represent distinctive products of the political economy of contemporary Chinese urbanism. Also of concern is what impact the efforts to create a purer form of socialism during the Cultural Revolution decade had on the quality of life in Chinese cities.

8 Crime and Social Control

One important realm that affects how urbanites feel about the places in which they live is crime and disorder. Chinese rulers down through the centuries have always been concerned, and some would even say obsessed, with the problems of social control.[1] This concern was understandable, for one central pillar of the authority of the ruling house was its ability to secure peaceful and orderly conditions throughout the realm. A rise in banditry and crime was often interpreted by the populace as a sign that the current ruling house was about to lose the "mandate of heaven" that legitimated its rule and to be succeeded by a new set of rulers who would be able to restore order. It can be argued that something like this process helped spell the downfall of the Nationalists in 1949. The recurrent lawlessness and personal insecurity that characterized rural and urban areas under the Nationalists helped to undermine Chiang Kai-shek's authority, and once the Chinese Communists were victorious militarily, they felt that an important part of their popular legitimacy depended upon their ability to restore peace and order in people's lives.

In this chapter we will be considering how this effort to secure social order has been pursued in China's cities, and how successful it has been. In order to put the social control drive into perspective, we need to examine the dilemmas of urban social control as they are usually perceived in the West. In general the large cities of the world seem to be disorderly

1. We use the term social control here to mean simply getting people to conform to official rules and laws, even though some other more abstract meanings of the term have been advocated. See Morris Janowitz, "Sociological Theory and Social Control," *American Journal of Sociology* 81 (July 1975): 82–108. For one major study of the traditional social control effort in rural China, see Kung-Ch'uan Hsiao, *Rural China* (Seattle: University of Washington Press, 1960). For the cities, see William Rowe, "Urban Control in Late Imperial China," in *Perspectives on a Changing China*, Joshua Fogel and William Rowe, eds. (Boulder, Colorado: Westview Press, 1979).

and unruly places. Overall crime rates are generally higher there than in small towns and rural areas, and in particular, the rates of vice and crimes against property are higher in cities.[2] Juvenile gangs and adult criminal mobs often arise to terrorize the urban citizenry. In the West we have grown so accustomed to the unruliness of cities that we tend to assume that it is an inevitable feature of urbanism.[3] But is it? The Chinese Communists do not accept this view and feel that it is possible to have large cities that are peaceful and well ordered. In order to judge the obstacles to their goal we need to consider a variety of competing theories in the West that purport to explain why cities are generally such disorderly places. We focus here on three important competing explanations: the solidarity, deterrence, and legitimate opportunity "schools."[4] Each school can best be explained by how it views the differences between cities and small towns.

The solidarity or social integration school assumes that in a small town people tend to know each other and have frequent, face-to-face contacts.[5] From these contacts emerge a sense of solidarity and shared community norms and values. Members of a small town value their social ties with others and internalize the community norms. Because of their belief in those norms and their desire to retain the respect of others, individuals tend to behave themselves and refrain from criminal and other deviant acts. In a large city, in contrast, people cannot know one another or have frequent, face-to-face contacts. Not only the size of the population, but the ecology of the city, with high-rise apartments and offices, keeps social bonds fragmented. Large cities tend to have heterogeneous populations and to attract varied groups in from the outside. Even the people one does come into contact with will often have different jobs, ethnic group memberships, or simply different tastes and interests, so enduring social

2. Evidence on these associations is reviewed in Claude S. Fischer, *The Urban Experience* (New York: Harcourt Brace Jovanovich, 1976), chap. 4.

3. However, there are exceptions, and some recent research discusses cases of cities in developed societies such as Japan and Switzerland that seem quite orderly and safe. See David Bayley, *Forces of Order* (Berkeley: University of California Press, 1976); Marshall B. Clinard, *Cities with Little Crime* (Cambridge: Cambridge University Press, 1978).

4. The three approaches presented here do not exhaust the explanations that have been used to explain crime and juvenile delinquency, but they seem to us the most meaningful ones to use to make sense of our data. For other explanatory typologies, see Fischer, *The Urban Experience;* LaMar T. Empey, "Constructing Crime: Evolution and Implications of Scientific Theory" (Paper presented to the Panel on Research on Rehabilitative Techniques, National Research Council, June 1979); and Ruth Kornhauser, *Social Sources of Delinquency* (Chicago: University of Chicago Press, 1978), chap. 2.

5. This approach is epitomized by the classic, although now much criticized, essay by Louis Wirth, "Urbanism as a Way of Life," *American Journal of Sociology* 44 (1938): 1–24.

bonds are unlikely to develop. Theorists of the solidarity school differ on what the results of this social fragmentation are. In some treatments it is argued that no common set of moral norms emerges and that urbanites live in a state of "anomie," without clear guides for behavior. In other treatments, cities are characterized as having many small groups and subcultures that may have internal cohesion and their own separate sets of moral norms. But these groups are not integrated, and different groups may subscribe to competing norms and engage in conflict with one another, so that no citywide social or moral cohesion can emerge. Some individuals and groups may be hostile to the established authorities and their attitudes may "infect" other people they come in contact with. In either case, the end result is that there is no sense of a general community whose norms individuals have internalized. For this reason, many individuals feel free to flaunt the formal laws that city authorities enact. In the solidarity school, then, crime is the result of the following kind of causal chain:

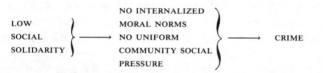

To theorists of this school, large cities may be invariably more crime-prone than small communities, but remedial measures can be taken to control urban crime to some extent. Usually their recommendations involve promotion of social solidarity within a city. For example, urban architecture can be changed to promote more low-rise housing and more common space where neighbors can conveniently come into contact with one another. Neighborhood stability, homogeneity, and associational life can be encouraged, and neighborhood offices of the police and city administration may be opened to foster links between local groupings and higher authorities. These are the kinds of measures that a solidarity approach suggests for reducing the levels of urban crime.[6]

Analysts of the deterrence school tend to see the world quite differently. They doubt that people really internalize moral norms or worry about losing the respect of the community. Instead individual behavior is seen as fundamentally selfish and amoral. What people do respond to is fear of detection and punishment. What makes small communities relatively orderly places is that there is little anonymity and privacy there. The

6. See, for example, Travis Hirschi, *Causes of Delinquency* (Berkeley: University of California Press, 1969); Jane Jacobs, *The Death and Life of Great American Cities* (New York: Random House, 1961).

interpersonal contacts and the gossip and rumors of a small community make it difficult for people to hide their deviant acts. As a result they are likely to fear that they will be detected and sanctioned for deviance. For this reason people tend to behave themselves in small communities. In a large city, in contrast, there is much more anonymity and privacy. The large numbers of strangers, high-rise buildings, and other features of major cities mean that people can more easily contemplate deviance without much fear of being detected, reported, and caught. The specialized social control agencies, largely the police, that bear the main responsibility for detecting crime in large cities cannot be everywhere and see everything, and so there are many opportunities for deviant activities to occur and spread. The chain of causation of crime focused on by the deterrence school is as follows:

$$\left.\begin{array}{c}\text{PRIVACY and}\\\text{ANONYMITY}\end{array}\right\} \longrightarrow \left.\begin{array}{c}\text{LOW FEAR OF}\\\text{APPREHENSION and}\\\text{SANCTIONS}\end{array}\right\} \longrightarrow \text{CRIME}$$

As with the solidarity school, deterrence theorists do have a number of strategies to suggest to help reduce the urban crime rate. Most often they stress beefing up the manpower and resources of the police. But their approach also leads to the view that the certainty (and perhaps also the severity) of punishment should be increased, for example, by having courts reduce the use of plea bargaining, probation, and suspended sentences. This school often provides the rationale for measures like citizen patrols and the use of informers, and for the redesign of urban architecture to make more areas open to constant view by neighbors and others.[7]

Our final school, the legitimate opportunity theorists, sees matters in still a different light. To opportunity theorists, what really matters is whether people have a predictable set of legitimate opportunities in life. If they can see clear chances of getting a solid job, increasing their incomes, building a family, and reaching other goals, then they will exert their efforts to achieve these goals, and they will not engage in deviant acts that might hurt their chances in competition for access to these valued opportunities. If they feel that most legitimate opportunities are blocked off, or cannot be obtained by diligent effort and orderly behavior, then they have little reason to obey society's rules. In fact, they may be led to criminal activities in their efforts to find another way to achieve the rewards that society denies them.

In small communities there may not be a wide range of opportunities for upward mobility, and people are likely to leave in search of a better life. When they leave, they are more likely than not to drift into larger

7. See, for example, Oscar Newman, *Defensible Space* (New York: Macmillan, 1972); James Q. Wilson, *Thinking about Crime* (New York: Basic Books, 1975).

towns and cities, where fame and wealth and other rewards are more abundant. However, cities not only have more opportunities, but also more people competing for those opportunities. In fact the most distinctive feature of large cities in the view of opportunity theorists is that they contain large numbers of marginal individuals, some of them recent migrants, who have very little chance of achieving valued goals through legitimate means. Large slum areas, minority groups, people unemployed and on welfare—these are the characteristics of cities that "breed" crime. The chain of causation of crime, according to this school, is as follows:

BLOCKED OPPORTUNITIES   ⟶   FRUSTRATED ASPIRATIONS   ⟶   CRIME

The legitimate opportunity school also has its partial remedy for the urban crime problem. What will help most are efforts to open up mobility opportunities. Programs to create new employment, to provide job training, and to improve the access of the poor to urban resources are key strategies. Logically, the views of this school might lead to a recommendation that migration into cities be regulated and controlled, but in the American context, at least, this is not considered as a feasible or legitimate measure.[8]

We have oversimplified the views of these three schools and many issues in the rich literature on crime and social control in the West have not been dealt with. Most writers on these topics in fact stress some combination of factors in urban crime, rather than the relatively "pure" explanations presented here. We find it useful to underscore the distinctions between these competing schools as a way of generating insights that can help us understand the effort to secure order in contemporary Chinese cities. As we sketch the Chinese approach to urban social control in the pages that follow, the reader will see all three strategies represented. However, we should state at the outset that the Chinese arrived at their urban social control strategies on their own, without consulting Western research.

Several topics will be taken up in turn. First we present a general descriptive account of the system of urban social control in China. This involves both general features of urban ecology in China that have a

8. In Western Europe, the use of foreign guest workers fits this strategy, since they can be told to leave when depressed economic conditions create employment problems. For discussions of crime reflecting an opportunity perspective, see Richard Cloward and Lloyd Ohlin, *Delinquency and Opportunity: A Theory of Delinquent Gangs* (New York: Free Press, 1960); Daniel P. Moynihan, *Maximum Feasible Misunderstanding: Community Action in the War on Poverty* (New York: Free Press, 1969); and R. W. Gillespie, *Economic Factors in Crime and Delinquency* (Final report to the National Institute of Law Enforcement and Criminal Justice, 1975).

bearing on social control as well as specific organizations and efforts made to combat crime. Then we attempt a general evaluation of the effectiveness of the Chinese system of urban social control, and to account for changes in urban orderliness over time. Finally, we use our interview data to consider whether crime and other forms of deviance are more common in some kinds of neighborhoods and work units than others and to account for the differences that we find.

The Structure of Urban Social Control

Much of the distinctive pattern of urban social organization in China has already been sketched in earlier chapters, but the implications for social control need to be drawn out here. We must emphasize again the importance of China's migration restrictions, and of the household registration and rationing systems that are tied to them. As we noted in chapter 2, these are designed to prevent any but specially selected people from smaller urban places and rural areas from relocating in the city. We also have seen that urbanites have on repeated occasions been subject to dispersal campaigns under which some in their midst are "sent down" to smaller towns and rural areas and, in the process, deprived of their urban household registrations and urban ration privileges. Sometimes these dispersals have been applied to individuals, and sometimes to entire families. The Chinese system of migration controls is not only designed to keep "unwanted" people from migrating into the city, but also to remove "excess" or "undesirable" people from the city.[9]

The Chinese have followed the implications of the legitimate opportunity approach in trying to restrict access to cities so that no large numbers of people reside in urban areas who are unemployed and blocked off from channels of opportunity. With regard to people of rural origins this strategy seems to have been successful, but in recent years the system of restrictions has been quite ineffective in dealing with former urbanites, particularly youths who are sent down to the countryside. This fact will assume importance later when we attempt to explain the deterioration of urban social order that has occurred since the mid-1960s.

A closely related structural basis of urban social control is the predominantly bureaucratic nature of the urban distribution system described in earlier chapters. One of the reasons the migration restrictions are as ef-

9. One special category of undesirables should be noted—those confined to labor camps for political or criminal offenses. In keeping with Soviet practice, some of those who finish their sentences are not allowed to return to their cities of origin, but are kept on at the rural site of the labor camp as "free employees." In this case, people felt to be undesirable may not only be removed from cities but prevented from returning there later.

fective as they are is that, without an urban household registration, it is very difficult to gain access to housing, jobs, food, health care, and other necessities of life. If markets, voluntary associations, and other bases of distribution were more important, it would be much easier to establish oneself in the city even though it is against the rules.

The nature of the distribution system has other implications for social control as well. Since jobs and housing are allocated predominantly bureaucratically, people cannot move around and change their situation at will. People therefore tend to remain fixed in their work and residences for long periods of time. This rootedness gives urban social life in China a distinctive quality. Chinese cities, or rather neighborhoods and work units, are not so impersonal and anonymous as in many other societies. People who live together or work together for a generation have the potential for solidarity and mutual awareness that is lacking in a more transient society. The fact that we could carry out our research in the way that we did is testimony to this high degree of mutual awareness. While it was generally quite easy to get Chinese informants to supply information about their neighborhood and neighbors, even about the schooling, wages, and role in household chores of particular individuals in nearby families, such questions would clearly stump urban informants in the United States or most other societies. This stability and mutual awareness fit the conditions for social control stressed by the solidarity theorists.

Moreover, with no real market in housing, people cannot readily escape a deteriorating neighborhood or move upward to live with a "better class of people." We have argued that the resulting urban neighborhoods tend to be somewhat more heterogeneous in social status than is the case in Western or other Third World cities, and while large areas may be somewhat seedy and run-down, the development of true slums and squatter areas is generally prevented. Since slum areas tend to be seen as "breeding grounds" for crime by both legitimate opportunity and solidarity theorists, we might expect this consequence of bureaucratic control to be important for urban orderliness.

In general, then, Chinese urban areas are characterized by higher levels of stability and solidarity than comparable cities in the West. However, Chinese neighborhoods are not all equally solidary, and we will examine later whether areas that are more solidary have lower levels of crime and other forms of deviance. For this purpose we have classified or coded the neighborhoods described in our interviews according to responses our informants made to our specific questions about neighborhood characteristics. We were able on this basis to distinguish those areas that had particularly low population turnover, residents especially homogeneous in terms of occupations, residents who shared membership in a work unit compound, and housing that was predominantly low-rise. All of these independent traits we take to be indicators of or contributors to neighborhood solidarity, and we will see subsequently whether neighborhoods ranking high on many of these traits tend to be particularly orderly and safe places.

At this point, we should note that neighborhoods also differ in terms of how much access people in them generally have to resources and opportunities that are allocated by the official system described in chapters 3 and 4. If we want to examine the ideas of the legitimate opportunity approach to criminal behavior, we need to also classify urban areas in terms of relative access. This we have done in a parallel fashion. Neighborhoods described in our interviews have been classified in terms of whether most people there live in public, rather than private, housing; whether most people work in state, rather than collective enterprises; whether unemployment is particularly low; and whether there is a predominance of people in white collar jobs in the neighborhood. We also constructed several scales dealing with relative access to rations and supplies. Three measures are used: one summing up informant judgments about how plentiful a broad range of items were locally, another for the actual amounts of various rations that were supplied, and a third tapping how adequately various goods were supplied, with the effects of informant biases partialled out. (Details on all of these measures will be found in appendix 2.) We also investigate whether variations in reported criminal activity are related to neighborhood differences in access to housing, jobs, and supplies. This should enable us to test the ideas suggested by the legitimate opportunity school.

Since so much of people's lives is oriented to their work units, rather than to where they live, we must also be concerned about whether the relative solidarity and access to opportunities that characterize various work units affect crime levels. We have therefore devised a number of parallel measures to classify work units described to us by our informants. Work units are likely to be more solidary if they are particularly small in size, do not employ shifts, have management participating regularly in labor, have frequent contacts off the job by the workers, have many mass organizations active within the unit, and have a great deal of inclusiveness (such things as organizing recreation for staff members, visiting sick employees at the hospital, and arranging jobs for employee children or spouses). Units are likely to have more access to resources and opportunities if they are state enterprises, if they are administered by high levels in the state bureaucracy, if they directly provide many services and facilities for their employees, if they have granted wage raises or employed bonuses or other material incentives and have a short span from lowest to highest wage, and if employees have access to adequate rations and supplies. Again, we will see later whether distinctions of these types are useful in explaining where urban life in China is most orderly or unruly.

There are additional characteristics of urban structure in China which, like those already discussed, seem conducive to a degree of orderliness unknown in Western cities. First, there are few high-rise buildings in Chinese cities. Five story walk-ups are about the tallest structures in most places, and most people live in even lower buildings. Since in American society high-rises and elevators are seen as particularly dangerous places, their virtual absence in China should contribute to order. There are also doormen and gatekeepers in many buildings and organizations who monitor people coming in and going out and may refuse entry. In some cases, work unit and dormitory compounds are surrounded by walls, with a gatekeeper, protecting all inside from the outside world. In the generally low-rise urban landscape, much behavior is open to public observation, a factor stressed as important in the deterrence school of urban social control.

Neighborhoods are also well watched over for other reasons. Work units often have staggered hours and days off, so that adults are often around. Many families consist of three generations, so that old folks can keep an eye on things while younger adults are off at work. Neighborhoods often have a mixed character, with not only housing but also shops, small factories, residents' committee offices, and other facilities. Again, this means that there are generally lots of eyes watching comings and goings in the streets and alleys. In housing, not only are stairways and common spaces shared, but often kitchens, toilets, and water taps. Thus neighbors are often brought into contact with one another. Furthermore, many of the facilities for entertainment and private enjoyment in the West—private automobiles, night clubs, bars, and so forth—are largely lacking in Chinese cities, so that much free time is spent at home or lounging on the stoop or roof with friends and neighbors. Again, both neighborhood surveillance and neighbor mutual awareness are enhanced. In general these various features of Chinese urban ecology should mean that there are fewer "danger spots" where deviant activities can escape detection than is the case in Western cities. So in the views of what we have called the deterrence school, Chinese cities should be pretty orderly places.

Organizing Cities for Social Control

So far we have sketched the "passive" social control structures that operate in Chinese cities, the features built into urban life in that society that are conducive to orderliness, and these are considerable. But we need to consider the other half of the picture as well, the active organizational efforts that are made to control the people who live in Chinese cities. These flow out of the same dual organizational system that was sketched in chapter 2. In both work units and in neighborhoods, efforts are made by authorities to ensure conformity with official standards of behavior. Let's consider work units first.

Again, the reader should keep in mind that belonging to a work unit has much more pervasive consequences than is the case in the West. Work units regularly convene meetings of their employees to deal with a variety of matters that are related to social control. Large meetings are held to transmit new government policy statements to the staff members, and then small group (i.e., work group) meetings are held to discuss the implications of policies for the behavior of group members. In some of these meetings, group criticism and pressure are mobilized against members who are not conforming to the desired standards of behavior.[10] Special meetings may be convened to exert pressure in particular areas of behavior. For example, during the period we are concerned with, staff members with children completing middle school were repeatedly organized for meetings about the campaign to send educated young people to the countryside. In some cases work units organize "dependents' committees" which give some subsidiary work tasks to, and organize the free time of, members of the families of the staff who are not employed elsewhere. Work units also hold meetings to announce cleanliness and sanitation drives and then carry out inspections of dormitories and apartment compounds to see if staff families measure up to the cleanliness standards. Through constant interactions in these meetings and other organized activities, people generally become much more familiar with each other than would be the case in a comparable Western work organization.

Deviance by employees on or off the job is a matter of concern to authorities in their units. Staff members who work poorly, are frequently tardy or absent, or commit other minor infractions of work discipline can expect to receive individual exhortations from their immediate superiors to improve, and perhaps their problems will be discussed in their small groups. If the problem is more serious, such as fighting with other staff members or pilfering small amounts of unit raw materials, it may be dealt with in a large meeting of the plant or office, and the individual may even have to publicly confess and promise to improve. The same range of informal sanctions can be used to deal with what are termed "life style

10. These activities are discussed in detail in Martin King Whyte, *Small Groups and Political Rituals in China* (Berkeley: University of California Press, 1974).

problems"—excessive drinking, gambling, reading forbidden literature, sexual infidelity, and so forth.

At some point that cannot be easily defined, and that is likely to change over time and according to personal characteristics, the individual may become subject to penal or quasi-penal sanctions. Each work unit has a security office which works closely with the police outside in determining how such cases are to be handled. Some offenses may be judged serious enough to merit formal sanctions, but not enough to require incarceration.[11] Examples might be getting a girlfriend pregnant, embezzling a small amount of funds from the work unit, or picking someone's pocket on a bus. In such cases, which can involve acts within the work organization or outside, the matter may be turned over to the unit authorities for handling. There the individual may be let off with simply a public confession, or he may receive a formal warning, a recorded demerit in his dossier, a fine, a demotion, or even be sentenced to a period of supervised labor.[12] In supervised labor the individual continues at work and receives his pay (minus any fines) but is subject to special scrutiny by his superiors and unit security cadres and may have to periodically report on his activities and attitudes. Furthermore, in certain circumstances, work units may exercise much broader quasi-judicial authority over the individual. For instance, during the Cultural Revolution and during some earlier campaign periods, work units established their own mass tribunals and held some employees prisoners in makeshift jails and deprived them of their pay and subjected them to various other kinds of punishment. Even in more "normal" times some unusually large work unit complexes, such as the Anshan Iron and Steel Works in Northeastern China, establish their own courts to deal with the criminal and other violations of their personnel.[13]

Generally, if an offense is serious enough, it is ultimately disposed of by the police, and sometimes by the courts as well. If the employee robs

11. For more detail on the range of sanctions used, criminal and otherwise, see Jerome A. Cohen, *The Criminal Process in the People's Republic of China, 1949–1963* (Cambridge: Harvard University Press, 1968).

12. All adults employed in state work units in urban China have personal dossiers (*dangan*) which follow them from their school days on and are generally kept by the personnel section of their work units. Reports on individual behavior at work and during political campaigns are regularly recorded there, and together with recorded sanctions for misbehavior, they may contribute to the permanent stigmatization of an individual. See A. D. Barnett, *Cadres, Bureaucracy and Political Power in Communist China* (New York: Columbia University Press, 1967), pp. 9–52.

13. Information on Anshan from Michel Oksenberg, personal communication. Since 1978 an effort has been made to institutionalize a revived legal system in China and to require that work units not engage in things like mass trials, but leave the handling of serious cases of deviance to the courts.

or rapes, or embezzles on a major scale, or is labeled as a serious political offender, then he is likely to be processed by these legal agencies outside of the work unit and to be sent to a labor camp or even given the death penalty.[14] In such cases the work unit may not have a major role in deciding how things are to be handled. However, the unit's security officers will almost always be consulted with closely, and there may even be meetings of other staff members to reveal information about the offender or an official condemnation meeting with the offender present before he is sent off to begin serving his term. Furthermore, in those cases in which the person is allowed to return to work in his original unit after his term is served, he is likely to remain subject to the special scrutiny of unit security officers, much as in the case of someone undergoing supervised labor. In other words, not only are work unit authorities much more closely involved in handling the cases of their deviant employees than is the case in American society, but they play the role of parole supervisors as well.

There are other important aspects of the work unit's role in urban social control. Meetings may be convened to discuss general problems of crime and social control in the city, even if the unit itself is not directly threatened. In recent years it has become common to convene meetings of staff members to discuss major crime cases that have occurred elsewhere in the city or the province. These may take a variety of forms. Sometimes they involve cases that have not been solved yet, and staff members will be asked to reveal any information or clues they possess that might help solve the case. More often, discussions are held after an individual has been apprehended for a crime. Sometimes there are "sentencing meetings" in which staff members are asked to discuss the offense and the offender and how severe a penalty should be meted out, even though it is generally understood that the police authorities or people's court will have already made their own decision on the matter. At other times, work units send representatives to attend mass condemnation rallies in a sports stadium or large auditorium at which offenders are led out, their crimes detailed, and sentences announced. After attending such meetings, the representatives are expected to return to their units and lead discussions of the cases. These various kinds of meetings seem primarily designed to

14. The large majority of imprisoned people in China are sent to rural labor camps, rather than to urban prisons. There are two types of labor camps: labor reform camps and labor reeducation camps. The latter incarcerate less serious offenders who have been sentenced simply by administrative authorities and the police, and not by the courts, and the terms there are generally shorter (up to three years). See Cohen, *Criminal Process*, and Whyte, *Small Groups*, chap. 9. On the revised labor reeducation code, see *People's Daily*, 26 February 1980, p. 4.

heighten public vigilance and to warn potential offenders of the penalties they are likely to suffer.

Work units also play a role in organizing personnel for guard and patrol duty. Although this is primarily in the hands of security officers and guards and gatekeepers, at times ordinary staff members get involved as well. Particularly in the period after the Cultural Revolution, when the public security agency (police) was in turmoil and disorder was widespread, a variety of kinds of employee security patrols were formed. Workers' picket corps (*gongren jiucha dui*) were organized and armed with staves and clubs to patrol the immediate neighborhoods of work unit compounds. These corps were sometimes used to patrol other neighborhoods in the city and were called upon to help put down the remnants of factional violence of the Cultural Revolution.[15] In later years, the organizations achieved a semipermanent basis. Workers were released from their regular jobs but continued to receive their normal pay while they trained and served in workers' militia units that patrolled city streets and alleys.[16]

In general, then, we can see that work units have expended a great deal of energy and manpower in the effort to control the lives of their own members and to play a role in social control of the larger urban community. But for all of those who have not lived in self-enclosed work unit compounds, the neighborhood half of the dual organizational structure has been important in social control as well.

Many of the activities of neighborhood authorities parallel those of work units. Residents' committees and small groups convene to discuss government policy statements, and they hold special meetings for matters like enforcing the birth control limits and mobilizing local young people to go down to the countryside. Household cleanliness inspections are a regular occurrence as well. Also similar is the fact that individuals who commit deviant acts may be the target of criticism in neighborhood meetings, and in more serious cases, individuals may be subjected to "supervision" or "control" within the neighborhood. Neighborhoods also organize people to attend sentencing meetings and representatives to at-

15. The role of organized worker groups in putting down student violence in the Cultural Revolution is vividly described in William Hinton, *Hundred Day War* (New York: Monthly Review Press, 1972).

16. In 1976, after the fall of the Gang of Four, it was alleged that the radicals in the leadership had been trying to organize and arm the workers' militias as a rival to the army, to use in seizing power in China's cities after Mao's death. Whatever the facts of the matter, it is clear that much of their activity involved fairly mundane patrol duty to preserve urban social order. After 1979 Chinese press reports noted revival of citizen picket organizations designed to cope with urban disorders. See Shanghai Radio, 9 November 1979, in *FBIS*, 26 November 1979, p. O3.

tend mass condemnation rallies, and they regularly warn residents to be vigilant against disorder.

Since neighborhoods are inherently more "open" to outsiders than are work unit compounds, their problems of security are generally more complicated.[17] Residents' committee officers and security officers or committees play the key role in trying to supervise things, but they operate under dual leadership. They are subject to both the ward office and the ward police station. In matters of social control the role of the police station is clearly predominant, and as noted earlier, it is very common to have an individual police officer assigned to work with one or a few residents' committees on a day-to-day basis, supervising the effort to keep the area under control. Residents' committees and small groups try to cultivate a group of "activists" within the neighborhood to assist them with their onerous tasks. Much of the effort is aimed mainly at keeping track of people and their movements. Activists and residents' committee personnel are expected to report suspicious people or activity in the neighborhood to the police. For example, they are supposed to be on the lookout for illegal peddling, black marketeering, and people staying in the neighborhood without proper registration. If a family has a visitor they don't report to the police, they are likely to receive a friendly visit from the residents' small group head or a residents' committee officer, who will inquire who the visitor is, what the purpose of the visit is, and warn the family to report the visitor to the police station without further delay. If there is suspicion that a particular family is harboring an illegal resident or engaging in other suspicious activity, the neighborhood officer may notify the ward police and lead them in a surprise, nighttime search of the family's apartment. Individuals discovered in this way can be carted off to the local police detention station if they are not able to provide a satisfactory justification for their presence.

The residents' committee officers, and the security officer in particular, devote a great deal of attention to keeping track of various kinds of suspect individuals and families in the neighborhood—individuals under "mass supervision," released convicts, people with bad class backgrounds or political histories, or simply those suspected of engaging in illicit activities. At times, some of these "negative elements" have had to regularly report on their activities and attitudes and even to perform menial labor around the neighborhood (e.g., sweeping public places, cleaning out public la-

17. In traditional times, not only did many cities have surrounding walls, but individual streets and lanes within them sometimes had gates that were closed at night for protection. After 1949 these were generally dismantled to facilitate the free flow of traffic, but in the violent stages of the Cultural Revolution some neighborhoods erected new gates at the ends of lanes and had guards manning them. Most of these are gone again now.

trines). Neighborhoods may also organize people for guard and patrol duty. In the early 1970s there were "residents' picket corps" (*jumin jiucha dui*) as well as workers' pickets, which patrolled the neighborhood to keep an eye on things. Generally during times of disorder or on national holidays or during the visits of important foreign dignitaries, it is common to have residents organized to stand guard and patrol and to order certain suspect individuals in the neighborhoods to stay at home.

In general, then, neighborhoods have many of the same social control activities that work units do. Many individuals, who work in one place but live in another, may be subject in various ways to the supervision of both kinds of social control systems. But the effort to exert social control in neighborhoods seems generally more problematic, for a number of reasons. First, as we have already noted, neighborhoods are often more heterogeneous places, and the people living there may have little basis for a sense of community outside of their prolonged residence together. Second, the social control personnel are in many cases middle-aged women or retired people, many of whom are illiterate, and although in some cases there is the form of an election, in actual fact these officers have been appointed by the ward office, in coordination with the police station, and can only be removed at their pleasure. These officers may not be people who have much status within the neighborhood, and they may even be seen as meddling busybodies (relations with these local leaders will be discussed further in chapter 9). Third, many people in the neighborhood see themselves as primarily involved in their work unit lives, and only peripherally as members of the neighborhood, and they may resist attempts to organize and supervise them where they live. Finally, neighborhood officers do not have many positive resources they can use to induce compliance in those who live there. They are of minimal help in getting people access to things like jobs and new housing, and they only control the livelihood of people who work in neighborhood enterprises. However, if you get on the wrong side of them they can make a fair amount of trouble for you. These features seem structured to produce a minimal degree of cooperation rather than the active involvement that is desired, and this is likely to make neighborhood social control tasks more difficult than is the case for work unit authorities.[18]

In general the Chinese urban system has developed control and sanctioning mechanisms to a much fuller extent than in cities in the West. However, as we have suggested, urban areas can be expected to differ in

18. The perennial difficulties of residents' committees in eliciting compliance are discussed in Janet Salaff, "Urban Residential Committees in the Wake of the Cultural Revolution," in John W. Lewis, ed., *The City in Communist China* (Stanford: Stanford University Press, 1971).

how well developed a system of sanctioning deviance exists. To examine the importance of deterrence mechanisms in controlling crime, we categorized our work units and neighborhoods in these terms, just as we earlier classified them in terms of their degree of solidarity and relative access to opportunities. For work units the following variables were constructed: a unit sanctions scale (composed of nine items; for example, the role of the unit in approving marriages, in sending employee children to the countryside, in holding sentencing meetings, and in firing employees); a measure of whether criticism and self-criticism sessions were frequently held, of how often political study sessions were held, of how often model worker competitions were held; and a measure of how vigorous the steps were that were taken to restrict employee fertility. For neighborhoods we also devised a variety of measures of the sanctioning system: a scale of neighborhood infrastructure (with nine items, for example, whether reading rooms and enterprises were set up to organize the activities of residents and the role of the neighborhood in enforcing the campaigns for birth control and sending youth to the countryside); a household control scale (with five items, such as the frequency of residents' patrols and militia patrols and of inspection of households for unregistered individuals); a measure of the frequency of political study meetings, and of the control and deportation of youths returning illegally from the countryside. If effective sanctions are the major mechanism for securing urban social order, we would expect work units and neighborhoods that rank high on the various traits discussed here to be the most orderly places, and we will test this prediction later on in the chapter. (Details on these measures and their interrelations will be found in appendix 2.)

The Effectiveness of Urban Social Control

The combination of restricted access to urban residence and a highly penetrating organizational system is designed to promote tight social control and orderly behavior in Chinese cities. It is important to stress that the great efforts expended to construct this social control system indicate that Chinese authorities do not assume that the transformation to socialism and other "progressive" reforms automatically make cities safe and peaceful places. Rather, cities are seen as potentially dangerous places where vigorous efforts must be made constantly to preserve public order. The control system is designed to ensure, as much as possible, that cities have no "dead corners," areas not effectively supervised where deviant activities can develop. One rather emotional plea broadcast recently over Shanghai radio makes the spirit clear: "We should create an atmosphere in which the black sheep find themselves like rats scurrying across the street with everyone yelling, 'Kill them!' 'Kill them!' so that they can find no market and no hiding place.''[19] However, we still have to consider how well this social control network works in practice, and how orderly Chinese cities actually are.

Unfortunately, there are no detailed statistics published in China on matters like crime trends and vice, and in many periods no articles at all that touch on these matters. At best, we can piece together a picture, relying upon our interviews and on scattered other pieces of information. First, it seems clear that Chinese cities are much more orderly than they were before 1949 and that they are probably more orderly than comparable cities in the West. We should keep in mind that earlier in the twentieth century, Chinese cities were riddled with crime and vice. Even then Shanghai was not a typical Chinese city, given its large areas of foreign control and influence as well as its huge size, but it was not completely atypical. This was the city that contributed the phrase, "being Shanghaied" to our vocabulary, that reportedly had a higher ratio of prostitutes to population than London, Berlin, Paris, Chicago, or Tokyo, and that was typically described as a "sink of iniquity."[20]

Shanghai today does not fit this picture, nor do other Chinese cities. Secret societies and organized crime gangs are gone, as are brothels, opium dens, and other forms of organized vice. Furthermore, during most periods, crime has been seen as a relatively minor problem. For long periods in the 1950s and 1960s people felt they could walk alone at night in Chinese cities with no real danger, and in general they had little fear of crime victimization. People we talked to who remembered the lawlessness of urban areas before 1949 took pride in the degree of security and safety that was achieved gradually in the 1950s and felt it was a major accomplishment of the Chinese Communists. Our informants also generally contrasted the cities they lived in favorably with Hong Kong, where they saw much more crime and danger of being victimized (and Hong Kong, it might be noted, is a fairly "safe" city in comparison with many American cities). Of course, perceptions of crime and actual crime rates are not the same thing, and in a country where the media rarely report crime, perhaps people remain ignorant of its true extent. Nevertheless, our general conclusion, admittedly impressionistic, is that Chinese cities after 1949 became remarkably orderly.

19. Shanghai Radio, 6 April 1979, in *FBIS*, 10 April 1979, p. O4. The verbiage seems to be catching, since later media accounts have used the same phrases: Peking Radio, 25 July 1980, in *FBIS*, 5 August 1980, p. R2.

20. See Rhoads Murphey, *Shanghai: Key to Modern China* (Cambridge: Harvard University Press, 1955), p. 7.

This conclusion is based partly on the fact that the Chinese authorities have pursued almost all of the strategies that Western experts on these matters say are likely to contribute to urban social order. The discussion in our preceding sections should have made this fairly clear. The usual strategies involve things like limiting unemployment and slum development, promoting neighborhood roots and solidarity, eliminating criminal gangs, avoiding severe ethnic and racial conflicts, fostering low-rise, heterogeneous neighborhoods, limiting areas that are not under regular public view, and providing secure employment channels. Particularly important, and difficult to achieve, are the devices to promote high levels of citizen involvement in social control, rather than leaving the major burden in the hands of the police. All of these things seem to be built into the Chinese approach to urban social control. And other facets of Chinese urban life we have not mentioned also fit the pattern described in the West as "healthy": for example, the general absence of handguns, very low marital instability, strongly developed intergenerational ties in the family, and limited development of an autonomous youth subculture. We have seen that aspects of all three of our approaches to social control—solidarity, deterrence, and legitimate opportunity—are stressed in Chinese cities. So on balance it should not be surprising that the Chinese are able to achieve more orderliness in their cities than is the case in America or most developing societies.

However, our second major conclusion is that there have been important fluctuations over time in the orderliness of Chinese cities. In particular, after an interlude of high security in the late 1950s there was a more disorderly period in the early sixties, after the collapse of the Great Leap Forward. After this, more orderliness returned, but a severe and prolonged deterioration of urban social control occurred following the Cultural Revolution, which Chinese authorities are still struggling to combat. This recent "crime wave" does raise questions about how orderly Chinese cities "generally" are, and explaining it will be our focus in much of the rest of this chapter. We are particularly interested in exploring how such an upsurge of urban unruliness could have occurred given the impressive social control system we have described.

We must first justify our conclusion that there have been such fluctuations, that in recent years there has been an upsurge of urban social control problems. The Chinese media are openly discussing crime cases and trends now, and these articles do claim a recent, serious increase in urban crime. Witness the following statement about the city of Tientsin, for example:

> Before June 1966 . . . although there were various types of criminal phenomena and crimes committed by some hooligans in soci-

ety, the scope of their activities was limited and their activities had very few supporters. In those days, if individual scoundrels moved an inch out of place, they would immediately be castigated. In those days, this miraculous situation existed in many areas and units: There was no need to close the doors at night; no one picked up and pocketed anything lost on the road. The new socialist morality . . . had become common practice in the whole municipality. [Then came the Cultural Revolution and the reign of the Gang of Four] thus seriously disrupting the socialist legal system and order in society, daily life, production, and work, making people live in an abyss of misery. Many of the present young criminals are influenced by the anarchism [the Gang of Four] instigated. Some of these young criminals have taken them as the models, regarded it very clever to do all kinds of evil and ride roughshod over good people, taken "pride" in lawless behavior and running amuck and even show no fear for violating the criminal law and falling into the net of justice.[21]

Recently, the Chinese government began releasing nationwide figures on crime trends for the first time, although the statistics involved are still fragmentary and give no hint of what they include and how they were collected. According to these official claims, China had a rate of crimes per 10,000 population of 9.3 in 1950, one year after the Chinese Communists came to power. By 1952 this had been reduced to about 4.2 per 10,000. From 1950 to 1965 the rate is said to have fluctuated, but to have averaged 4.5 per 10,000. No figures are given for the period 1966–76, but in the years 1977–79 the rate is said to have jumped up to 6.5 per 10,000.[22] We cannot make too much of these figures without knowing anything about how they were arrived at, and they are said to refer to the whole country, not just to urban areas, but they do reinforce the picture of a noticeable increase in crime in recent years from what had been a quite low level.

21. *Tientsin Daily*, 14 November 1979, p. 1, in *FBIS*, 30 November 1979, p. R5.

22. *Xinhua*, Peking, 27 August 1980, in *FBIS*, 4 September 1980, p. A1. These figures suggest that serious crimes in China are about 15 times less common than in the United States. However, we have no information on how the Chinese figures are collected and how inclusive they are, and we doubt that the disparity is quite that large. Our own crude effort to compare perceptions of the crime danger (as distinct from the actual crime rate) in Canton and one American city of comparable size, Detroit, leads us to conclude that Canton is safer, but not by quite this wide margin. For example, 8 percent of our Canton informants reported crimes committed against members of their families within the previous year, as compared with 22 percent in a Detroit sample, and 18 percent of those from Canton as compared with 49 percent in Detroit report crimes in their neighborhoods within the past year. The Detroit figures are from Michigan Commission on Criminal Justice, *Crime in Michigan* (Detroit, 1978), pp. 7, 9.

How did this decay of social control manifest itself to urbanites? Informants testified to a variety of activities being more widespread in the 1970s than earlier: black marketeering, speculation in ration coupons, gambling. In some cities, consulting fortune-tellers and other "superstitious specialists" was also described as increasing, and the Chinese press now carries surprising stories about urban witchcraft. Most families were not too concerned or threatened by these kinds of "victimless crimes," but they were much more alarmed by the rising threat of crimes against persons and against property. Thefts of drying laundry and bicycles from outside the home increased, breaking and entering became more common, and families took increasing precautions to avoid having their possessions stolen. Bus and trolley lines were increasingly plagued by pickpockets and mashers, and people walking late at night were in more danger of being assaulted and raped than in the past. Lurid cases of robbery and murder frightened the populace. In some cities gangs that engaged in the systematic theft of particular items like bicycles were reported. Families began to see youth gangs, or "black societies," emerging and to feel that their children had to be guarded against being influenced by such groups and getting involved in gambling, theft, illicit sex, and other deviant activities. These youth gangs reportedly laid claim to particular urban "turfs" and developed their own organizational structure, with a leader, warrior-lieutenants, pickpockets, molls, and child auxiliaries. Some of the gangs periodically engaged in battles with rival gangs in a fashion familiar elsewhere on the globe, determined to protect their territory and their honor. People learned to avoid particular areas known to be gang stomping grounds. In at least some cities, fighting with knives and handmade zipguns occurred, and the police felt compelled to order new measures for gun confiscation and control.[23] In general, then, in both their homes and on the street people did not feel as safe as they had in earlier years. Several examples of recent crime cases known to our informants illustrate the changed atmosphere:

> In our neighborhood [in a Guangdong district town] there was the case of two social youths who were both around 20 years old. They engaged in a lot of petty theft around the town during the

23. On trips to Canton in 1978, we observed official notices dealing with control over firearms. For media notices on the gun problem, see Heilongjiang Radio, 30 June 1980, in *FBIS*, 6 June 1980, p. S2; Shanghai Radio, 21 July 1981, in *FBIS*, 22 July 1981, pp. O3–4. For a sampling of general crime reports, see Shanghai Radio, 21 March 1979, in *FBIS*, 21 March 1979, pp. O5–6; Jiangsu Radio, 31 March 1979, in *FBIS*, 3 April 1979, pp. O5–6; *Ningxia Daily*, 22 July 1981, in *FBIS*, 24 August 1981, p. T1. For a more detailed picture of current gang organization and activity, see Gan Weimin, "Underground Gangs among Mainland Youths," *Huang He*, no. 5 (1979): 28–31.

Cultural Revolution. They would shoplift from stores and swipe things from workshops and factories and then sell what they had stolen. They had been under suspicion for some time because they would be seen eating rich restaurant meals they shouldn't have been able to afford, but only in 1969 when they were caught in the act of stealing something was there enough evidence to arrest them. The case was investigated and, because they had not been arrested before and had good class backgrounds, the penalty was fairly light—six months detention. After their release, one of them agreed to go down to the countryside, but the other remained in the town, still unemployed. A couple of years later this youth got into a fight in the town and knifed his opponent. He was again arrested, his family had to pay a fee to cover the medical expenses caused, and this time he was sentenced to a five-year labor camp term.

In 1976 there was a notorious case in Canton. There was a group of young males led by the son of an officer in the local military district. One night they put on arm bands to disguise themselves as members of a local picket corps and managed to commandeer a truck. They drove along the streets of the city until they spotted an appropriate female walking alone. They jumped off, grabbed her, and pulled her into the back of the truck. They then drove off to the suburbs where she was gang raped. Police investigation subsequently led to their capture, and the leading figures in the group were all executed.

In our apartment building in Shanghai there was a rash of theft cases in 1971–72. In one case there was an elderly maternal grandmother at home tending her granddaughter, but the old lady was hard of hearing and the apartment was fairly large, and the culprits climbed up over the garden wall from below, broke into a desk, and stole some cash, a watch, a ring, and some other items. Another case occurred at around the same time in an apartment on the fifth floor. Again they had to climb up from below and they stole a watch, money, a radio, and other valuable items—all without disturbing a grandmother who was sleeping in another room. The police came around and interviewed everyone about these cases, and they suspected that they involved an unsavory young woman who lived in the building whose husband, an overseas Chinese, had left to return to Indonesia in 1961, and she had since been seen in the company of various boyfriends. They assumed that someone who knew the building well and the schedules of its residents had to be involved in order to escape detection in these daytime thefts, but they never got enough evidence, and nobody was ever caught in these cases.

In my Canton middle school, right after the Cultural Revolution there was a special "study class" set up to discipline students who were causing problems. Two former Red Guard activists from the Cultural Revolution were put in charge of this disciplinary group, and they were super-activists who made the lives of these problem students miserable. For a long time during 1969–70 they had to engage in round-the-clock study and self-criticism, they could not go home, and even when they had to go to the bathroom someone was supposed to accompany them. After the study class had been disbanded some of its members came upon the two activists late one night in a Canton alley and beat them up. The incident was investigated for a long time, but the two victims could not identify the individual attackers due to the darkness and nobody ever confessed, and so the case was never resolved.[24]

We have been discussing different kinds of deviance as if they were objectively specifiable and constant. But we should clarify that deviance is not simply something that is "out there," but is to a significant extent something in the eyes of the authorities. In China, as in other societies, how much deviance there is, and who the deviants are, is to a large degree affected by the attitudes and enforcement procedures of the authorities, and these change over time.[25] Having a third child and engaging in domestic worship were not regarded as deviant in the 1950s, but they were in the 1970s. Listening to foreign broadcasts could get you in trouble during the mid-1970s, but now it is allowed and even encouraged. Similarly, peasants coming in to peddle produce in the city were subject to arrest in the mid-1970s, but now the authorities have set up special free market sites throughout urban areas for such activity, as had been the policy in earlier years. Furthermore, activities engaged in by ordinary people with impunity could give rise to official wrath and sanctions when engaged in by various suspect groups, such as those with bad class labels and political histories, even though since 1979 the stigmatization of people based upon class background is supposed to be discouraged. With this

24. In succession from interviews FSP2:7; KSP9:12; KSP1:18; KSP1:4.

25. "Labeling theory," which explains much variation in crime rates in terms of the actions of authorities rather than the behavior of deviants, is a major school of interpretation within American studies of crime and juvenile delinquency. See Frank Tannenbaum, *Crime and the Community* (New York: Columbia University Press, 1938); Howard Becker, *The Outsiders* (New York: Free Press, 1963); Edwin Lemert, *Human Deviance, Social Problems, and Social Control*, 2d ed. (Englewood Cliffs: Prentice-Hall, 1972). For an application of this perspective to contemporary China, see Sidney Greenblatt, "Campaigns and the Manufacture of Deviance in Chinese Society," in *Deviance and Social Control in Chinese Society*, Amy Wilson et al., eds. (New York: Praeger, 1977).

"labeling" perspective in mind, we should recognize that at least part of the apparent increase in deviance after the Cultural Revolution may reflect the fact that the authorities tried to enforce much stricter controls over various activities at that time than they had previously—limiting fertility, preventing unemployed young people from staying in the city, eliminating religious worship, terminating free market activity, and so forth. This more ambitious control effort flowed from the desire of the radicals to eliminate all kinds of behavior and customs that did not fit their conception of socialism.

. In order to take this factor of fluctuations in social control demands into account, when we examine variations in crime problems we will check how the reported frequency of crime relates to whether the report is for a "high tide" of a campaign or not. We do this by defining a "radical year" variable to distinguish high tide periods dealt with in our interviews (1966–71 and 1974–76) from other years.[26]

We doubt that the variation in perceptions of crime can be explained simply in terms of this kind of labeling effect. In general, the rising tide of deviance, and particularly of crime, had its roots in the changes that the Cultural Revolution ushered in. These changes especially had an impact on the lives and future prospects of young people, and most of the deviance problems are attributable to the actions of people below the age of thirty.[27] However, these problems can be seen emerging even earlier than the Cultural Revolution.

It can be argued that in the years after 1949 the influences not only of neighborhoods, but also of the family and the school, were generally conducive to orderly conformity and high aspirations and efforts among school-age children.[28] As we have seen, during the 1950s those efforts were generally rewarded. China's shortage of skilled personnel to staff

26. We make this "radical year" distinction in response to the ideas of Skinner and Winckler, who argue that there are regular cyclical phases in Chinese political life, with predictable differences between radical high tide periods and more moderate phases. See G. W. Skinner and Edwin Winckler, "Cyclical Compliance and Rural Social Change in Communist China," in *A Sociological Reader in Complex Organizations,* 2d ed., Amitai Etzioni, ed. (New York: Holt, Rinehart and Winston, 1969).

27. Our informants saw crimes as primarily being committed by young people. Fox Butterfield (*New York Times,* 11 March 1979) was told by a professor of law at Peking University that about 60 percent of China's crime is caused by young people. This appears comparable to the situation in the United States, where people under twenty-five accounted for about 56 percent of all arrests in 1977. Moreover, a Peking official more recently stated that 80 percent of the criminals arrested between 1977 and 1980 were people below the age of 25, and that this contrasted with youth being only 20 percent of those arrested before the Cultural Revolution. See Wei Min "Reforming Criminals," *Beijing Review,* no. 8 (1981): 22–24.

28. This argument is developed in detail in Martin K. Whyte, "Child Socialization in the Soviet Union and China," *Studies in Comparative Communism* 10 (1977): 235–59.

the expanding bureaucracy and fill the needs of the growing economy (as well as the depressed state of the rural economy and educational system) meant that pretty much all of those urban youths who completed middle school who wanted to enter the university could do so. There were secure urban jobs even for those young people who dropped out of school earlier or didn't want to continue their schooling past middle school graduation. But the collapse of the Great Leap Forward combined with the urban baby boom, the large-scale migrations into the city still possible during the 1950s, and the emphasis on capital intensive, low employment heavy industry meant that, by the early 1960s, China began to experience a situation familiar in other developing societies, in which there were more educated young people being produced than the urban economy could absorb. So prior to the Cultural Revolution China's cities began to have a problem of how to deal with the educated unemployed, and these young people were seen as a growing threat to social order.

The Cultural Revolution began in 1966 and introduced a number of changes which, while conceived as promoting social cohesion and compliance, ultimately aggravated the social control situation very seriously. First, there were the activities young people were allowed and encouraged to engage in during the Cultural Revolution itself. Youthful Red Guard groups formed that travelled all over the country, seized control of their schools and then of major urban institutions, carried out searches of people's homes looking for forbidden objects, and in general experienced a degree of freedom and power that had never been theirs before. As the Cultural Revolution wore on, the Red Guard activities descended into factional warfare, and some young people gained increasing skills in fighting, handling weapons (seized from armories and other sources), deception, and simply in group organization. Many also experienced keen disappointment as they saw the leadership in Peking, in whose name they were manning the barricades, willing to sacrifice them and support their factional enemies, or to suppress them with troops. The Cultural Revolution was also an eye-opening experience for those youths who withdrew from factional battles. They had been brought up to respect figures in authority and the Communist Party, but the revelations of corruption, abuse of power, and illicit activities by those in authority that came out during that period contributed to a growing feeling of cynicism about the authorities. The last straw came in 1968, when Mao declared that the Red Guards should atone for their errors and excesses by going down to the countryside to become lifelong peasants. Young people who had been eager idealists and then powerful operators found themselves bundled off into apparently permanent rural exile. Moreover, those who had been in the midst of their middle school education when the Cultural Revolution started were simply declared graduated and forced to join the rustication campaign. Many of them, particularly the younger ones, ended up poorly educated or even barely literate.

If the Red Guards and their age cohorts had been the extent of China's "lost generation" it would have been serious enough, but they were not. The Cultural Revolution brought in its wake a series of reforms in how urban institutions worked that had fundamental effects on the lives of young people who came up through the urban schools in subsequent years. These reforms were designed to make schools more egalitarian and less divorced from society, as noted in earlier chapters. Schools were no longer to play a major role in selecting which urban youths would be able to attend the best schools and be assigned to the most desirable jobs. Instead, all were supposed to progress through neighborhood schools without the compulsion of grades and examinations and, when they had completed middle schooling, to be willing to serve the state as needed. During the radical period, the state mainly needed them to leave the cities and settle permanently in the countryside. Those fortunate enough later to be selected to attend college (after universities began to reopen in 1970) or to be allocated to a job back in the city would find that labor performance, political record, or simply personal connections, rather than how they had performed in school, would be the decisive factors.

We noted in chapter 3 that these reforms had their intended effect. But the changes in the school system also meant that the connection between how children performed and behaved in school and their future prospects was almost totally severed. No matter whether they learned their lessons or even attended school regularly, they could count on being promoted year after year. On the other hand, no matter how hard students studied or performed their other school tasks, there was not much chance of it making a difference in whether they were assigned to an urban job, and they couldn't be selected for a higher quality upper-middle school or enrolled in a university by performing well. Students increasingly felt they had no control over their own fates, and that nothing they could do would make much difference. Parents were increasingly concerned about the deteriorating motivational levels of their school-age children, but they also began to perceive that it did little good to place high demands for school performance on their offspring, and they were more and more at a loss as to how to help their children prepare for the future.

Given this situation, pupil unruliness in school increased, as did truancy, vandalism, and other unsavory behavior. But while school-age youths contributed to urban disorders, more serious problems were presented by those who had already finished their schooling. These were the waves of urban youths, one to two million a year, who followed the first Red Guard generation into rural exile.

Authorities tried to portray the program of sending urban "intellectual youths" down to the countryside as a glorious campaign, and they organized joyous send-offs at railway stations and posted honorary signboards outside the doors of families that had sent sons or daughters. But there is little doubt that parents, who both before and after the revolution saw the culture around them emphasizing the pride one could take in the occupational success of one's children, and the pleasure that grown children near at hand could give in one's declining years, found this program a bitter pill to swallow. This was as much or more true for young people, as young as 15 and 16, who found themselves plunked down in a distant village, sometimes one inhabited by a minority group or speakers of a different dialect, and were told they must adapt to heavy work burdens, harsh living conditions, strange customs and cuisine, and the absence of their loved ones. Some nonetheless made the best of their lives and were eventually able to earn their keep and the respect of local peasants, even getting selected to local Party and village leadership positions.

However, as we have seen, within a short time it became common for large numbers of sent-down youths to return illegally to the cities they came from. Many of them spent their time in relatively harmless ways— reading and studying at home, relaxing with friends, engaging in sports, and so forth. But the social control system worked to ensure that at least some of them would create serious problems. Because they were not registered and did not belong to a unit, they were in a certain sense "invisible" to the authorities, and therefore their activities could not be organized and supervised (this is the meaning of the term "black person-black household" for unregistered people). Furthermore, it was against regulations for any work unit to employ illegal returnees. As a result, these young people had plenty of free time on their hands and no way to legally earn an income and ease the burden they constituted to their families. The combination of leisure time, boredom, economic insecurity, and frustration about their future led some returned youths into a variety of illegal activities—private furniture making, picking pockets, gambling, and black marketeering, to mention a few of the most prominent pursuits. Some of them consulted fortune-tellers to try to find clues to their fate that would allow them to gain some control over their lives. Others more boldly tested their wits against the social control system, using forged passes and other documents to engage in intercity trade of cigarettes, medicines, and other scarce items for their own private profit. Even if some of them were caught in the act and sent away to labor reform camps, the fact that each year urban middle schools were producing new graduates to be assigned to the countryside guaranteed that the flow of illegal returnees would continue to expand, and with it the tide of juvenile delinquency.

Our informants generally agree that illegal returnees posed the most serious threat to the urban social control system, since they had no real stake or responsibilities in the city, and could not hope by behaving to earn a job and an urban registration. They saw themselves as living by their wits, outside of the system, and they were not easy to shame into repentance and good behavior. However, there were others contributing to urban disorders, again generally young people. We have referred to unruly schoolchildren, but there are other categories of young people to consider. One is a rather select group of urban middle school graduates who were allowed to stay in the city even though they were not assigned to jobs. Young people exempted from the rustication campaign were supposed to live at home and participate in neighborhood activities and there await some possible future urban job opportunities. These young people retained their urban registrations, but at least initially they had no jobs. Even later they might only get temporary and menial jobs, hauling or construction work. They also had a relatively small stake in the urban system, then, although they were not generally as alienated from it as the sent-down youths.

Finally, some young people did manage to get assigned directly to jobs after middle school graduation. However, in many cases these also were relatively menial jobs. In fact, in many cases parents were glad to see their children assigned to jobs as janitors or as cooks' helpers in their work units or elsewhere, if only to safeguard them against being sent to the countryside. Youths welcomed these jobs as an urban refuge, but still saw the stigma of menial, service jobs held in low esteem by the population. Furthermore, in the mid-1970s wages were frozen and there was little chance for job mobility, or for increasing one's income through bonuses and piece rates, which were forbidden at the time. The official late marriage policy (see chapter 5) prevented these youths from marrying and assuming other adult responsibilities until their late twenties at the earliest. Moreover, they had substantial job security. Absenteeism, pilfering, or simply shoddy work might cause them to be lectured by a unit cadre, but would not affect their income or get them fired. In other words, the same disengaging of present behavior from future rewards that we saw operating in the schools in this period was also typical in work organizations. The result was not only poor morale and productivity at work, but alienation and deviance by young workers off the job.

At the time of our interviews, then, young people of all types were contributing to urban social control problems—not only illegally returned sent-down youths, but also middle school students, unemployed neighborhood youths, and young workers. The levels of crime and gang behavior remained modest in comparison with American society; nevertheless, they were seen as representing a serious deterioration in what was once an orderly and safe urban scene.[29] What does this deterioration tell us about the mechanisms of urban social control?

When we examine the Chinese urban scene in the 1970s in terms of the three approaches to social control with which we began this chapter, it becomes apparent that little changed in regard to the first two. Indeed, it could be argued that measures taken during these years reinforced both solidarity and deterrence mechanisms. The shift to neighborhood schools reinforced the links between neighborhoods and schools, while the system of inheritance of parental jobs fostered more work unit solidarity. And a variety of reinforced citizen patrol and inspection procedures were designed to supervise citizen behavior more closely, facilitating deterrence. But in regard to the third, legitimate opportunity, approach to social control, a major deterioration occurred. Urban youths no longer could see clear strategies for planning their futures, and had neither predictable rewards for good behavior presented to them, nor certain penalties for getting in trouble. We argue, then, that this disruption (or, more precisely, dismantling) of the urban opportunity structure was sufficient to offset the solidarity and sanctions mechanisms fostering urban orderliness and is the primary factor responsible for the rising levels of crime and other deviant behavior in China's cities in the 1970s.

The trends in Chinese urban disorders present a clearer case for the legitimate opportunity approach to social control than is generally seen in the study of crime and juvenile delinquency in the West. In American cities, a partial listing of the urban features conducive to high crime rates would include poverty and high unemployment, ethnic conflict, high marital instability, high mobility and anonymity, a dangerous urban ecology (high-rise apartments, unsupervised elevator shafts, etc.), easily available handguns, and drug addiction. With so many possible causes operating, it is little wonder that American criminologists have not been able to agree on what the main causes of urban crime are. From this perspective, the Chinese urban scene looks quite different. Most features seen as conducive to crime in American cities are absent or of minor importance in Chinese cities. But in the years since 1966 unemployment and a disrupted opportunity structure did come to characterize Chinese cities, and this

29. Our analysis of the rising crime rate agrees with official press reports in general terms but differs in regard to timing. While official reports imply that the crime rise dated from the mid- to late 1970s, our informants saw the deterioration beginning about 1970.

one important change was primarily responsible for the increase in urban crime and delinquency that authorities are now trying to cope with.[30]

Before examining in detail how social control varies with the urban landscape, we still need to explain how it has been possible for deviant individuals to evade the control systems so elaborately constructed to deter them. Although illegally returned sent-down youths no longer had urban household registrations and ration privileges, they could still live with their families and rely on family belt-tightening for food, perhaps supplemented by purchases from rural free markets or the urban black market. Their parents were often sympathetic to their desire to come back to the city or were simply unable to force them to return to the villages. Some residents' committee and residents' small group leaders were also sympathetic to the plight of the youths and their families—some had children of their own in the same boat. Others were unwilling to alienate large numbers of local families by being too vigorous in alerting the police to these long-term "visitors." What's more, young people "steeled" in the battles of the Cultural Revolution and by the hardships of life in the countryside could often outwit or intimidate the mostly middle-aged, female personnel who staffed neighborhood organs. It was thus much more difficult to deal with the large numbers of returned youths than had been the case with a small number of "bad elements" or strangers in the neighborhood. It seems to have become common for residents' committees to adopt a strategy of looking the other way and leaving these young people alone as long as they were thought to be staying out of trouble. If the police and neighborhood officers did get tough, however, it was an easy matter for youths to spend a few days with friends elsewhere in the city and to return once the "heat" was off. Even if caught and returned to their rural villages, they might simply wait a few weeks and then head back to the city again, perhaps with grain earned for agricultural labor and choice food delicacies to use to curry favor with neighborhood authorities. Youths might repeat this pattern over and over again, and generally they received no sanction other than forced return to the village as long as they were not caught in other kinds of deviant behavior.

Students, young workers, and unemployed youths allowed to remain in the city did have urban registration and ration privileges, but their

30. One aspect of the crime problem that seems to contradict this explanation is the flagrant criminal behavior by the offspring of high-ranking cadres. The Chinese media suggest that the operating factor in such cases is what we have termed the sanctions approach— since these youth do not have major worries about jobs and careers and may feel that having powerful parents enables them to literally get away with murder. Perhaps this is true, but we suspect that despite widespread publicity, these cases are quite few in number and quite unrepresentative of the overall crime problem.

behavior also became increasingly hard to control. Even if they committed deviant acts, their families found it difficult to shame them into behaving properly, given the absence of predictable opportunities and costs in the urban environment. Indeed, in some cases youths engaging in gang behavior were the offspring of powerful local leaders, and their parents' positions gave them essential immunity from the control efforts of neighborhood and work unit authorities, since nobody wants to offend the powerful.[31] Not only neighborhood and family influences, but also general urban public opinion became less effective in controlling crime. The urban population, with vivid memories of the violence done by Red Guards a few years before, became increasingly intimidated. It is one thing for alert residents' committee activists or shop personnel to notice and catch a lone thief and turn him over to the police. It is another if you think that the person running off with your bicycle may turn on you with a knife if you give chase, or may have buddies who will come back and beat you up or throw rocks through your window if you get him apprehended. So the boldness and willingness to resort to violence of some youths made it increasingly likely that urbanites would act as passive bystanders, rather than as vigorous fighters in the battle for urban social order.[32]

Perhaps the major reason some juvenile delinquency escaped the urban social control system is simply that Chinese cities are, after all, cities. The urban social control system is based on a conception of tightly organized, multiple and overlapping cells, the work units and neighborhoods. Each cell has its social control mechanisms and looks after its own membership. The real geography of Chinese cities, however, is not that simple. There are not only self-enclosed work units and neighborhoods, but bus lines, large stores, parks, back alleys, waterfronts, and many other kinds of terrain. These are generally public territory, through which all kinds of people can go without standing out as "suspicious strangers." There are large parts of each city that, if not "dead corners" totally free of any supervision, are at least outside of the boundaries of the individual neighborhood and work unit cells of the social control system. In these areas social control becomes primarily a matter for the police, rather than local activists, and anonymity and lack of community solidarity are the general pattern. Therefore, for Chinese juvenile delinquents there are lots of areas in Chinese cities where social control is weak and where the chances of detection and apprehension for deviance are relatively low.

31. See, for example, *Xinhua* (Peking), 8 November 1979, in *FBIS,* 16 November 1979, pp. O14–15, *Peking Daily,* 9 August 1980, in *FBIS,* 11 August 1980, pp. R1–2, *People's Daily,* 4 October 1980, p. 3, in *FBIS,* 9 October 1980, p. L9.

32. See Zhang Yuwen, "The Master's Duty," *People's Daily,* 29 December 1979, p. 6, in *FBIS,* 10 January 1980, p. L13; *Beijing Review,* no. 16 (1980): 8.

Some informants claimed that young people self-consciously tried to behave themselves and stay on the good side of local neighborhood and work unit authorities while engaging in their deviant activities in other, less tightly controlled parts of the city. And of course a good proportion of those causing trouble, the illegally returned youths, are not even considered members of either neighborhood or work unit social control "cells." In short, the Chinese urban social control system is far from perfect, and the bold juvenile delinquents of recent years have shown considerable ingenuity in learning how to avoid and outwit the control mechanisms.

Variations in Urban Social Control

Up to this point we have been concerned mainly with explaining the general deterioration in urban orderliness that occurred in China in the post-Cultural Revolution years. We can also consider how orderliness varied within China's urban landscape during this period. Earlier in the chapter we noted that some neighborhoods and work units have more features promoting solidarity, facilitating deterrence, and providing legitimate opportunities than do others, and we also have judgments from our informants about the prevalence of a variety of specific kinds of criminal and other deviant activity in the neighborhoods and work units they lived and worked in. We can use these two kinds of information to explore the relationship between urban social structure and social control in further detail. In the pages that follow, we will be examining whether the neighborhoods and work units that were judged relatively orderly were ones that had high solidarity, effective sanctioning mechanisms, more opportunities, or perhaps all of these social control mechanisms in combination. This ecological comparison of our social control mechanisms supplements the chronological comparison already presented.

The reader should bear in mind that our findings are intended to be preliminary and suggestive. There are several problems with the data we are using that prevent us from being more certain of our conclusions. Most important is the fact that our informants are presenting cases of crimes and other kinds of deviance they were aware of, and that we don't have actual rates of various kinds of deviance reported for either neighborhoods or work units. So variations in our dependent variable scales, measures of deviance, may reflect not only differences in the rate of occurrence of various acts, but also differential awareness and concern. We may be dealing here as much with perceptions of crime as with its actual rate of occurrence.

We constructed three separate scales to assess the degree of control over crime and related urban deviance. One scale involves neighborhood codes for the prevalence of crimes against persons and property. It is composed of the following items: reported recent crimes against one's family, recent crimes to nearby neighbors, recent crimes committed by neighbors, danger in walking nearby streets at night, regularity of locking up when going out, gang fight problems nearby, and a perceived overall high crime level in the area. From these items we composed a mean scale which was then reversed, so that a high score means a low level of crimes against persons and property reported in the neighborhood. Deviance is not restricted to these kinds of crimes, however, so we also constructed a measure of the prevalence of victimless economic offenses and other urban regulation violations. The items used here were the extent of private peddling in the neighborhood, extent of moonlighting nearby, cases of refusal to accept assigned jobs, number of local "black persons and black households," amount of neighborhood littering, the sale of grain ration coupons, black market sales of food, "going by the back door" to gain access to goods and services, violations of housing regulations locally, refusal of local youths to go down to the countryside, and the number of youths who refuse to go to the countryside managing to find work. Again these items were used to compute a mean scale, and then reversed, so that a high score means reported low levels of these kinds of deviance. Finally, we composed a scale of crime in reference to work units. This utilized four codes used in regard to informant descriptions of the units in which they worked: extent of theft of unit materials by employees, extent of corruption by employees, crimes occurring in unit or unit dormitory, and crimes committed by work unit personnel. As with our other two scales, a high score indicates low levels of reported crime problems in work units. (For details on the items in these scales, see appendix 2.)

In table 29 we examine the correlations between our neighborhood crime scale and a variety of indicators of urban social structure introduced earlier in this chapter. This and the following tables follow the same general format. The column on the left lists the simple correlations between our scale of low crime prevalence and a variety of neighborhood (and city and interview) characteristics. A positive sign means that the variable in question is associated with low reported crime levels. The remaining columns present partial correlations, which are used to control for spurious associations. For this and subsequent tables we picked several variables that are strongly correlated with our dependent variable scale, and by controlling for each of them individually, and then for several at the same time, we can determine whether the remaining associations in the table are spurious or hold up even when the other variables are partialled out. This procedure is necessary because our neighborhood

Table 29   Crime by Neighborhood Characteristics
                                                (+ = Low Reported Crime Level)

	Bivariate Correlations	Partial Correlations Controlled for	
		Informant Optimism	Five Variables[a]
Neighborhood Solidarity			
Stability of residents	-.18*	-.13	-.09
Homogeneity of resident	.00	.02	-.01
Low-rise housing	.13	.15	.09
Work unit compound	.19*	.12	-.07
Deterrence Efforts			
Service infrastructure	-.28*	-.22*	.07
Household control scale	-.50*	-.46*	--
Political study	-.19*	-.22*	-.07
Controls on sent-down youth	-.02	-.09	-.02
Radical year	-.26*	-.22*	--
Opportunity and Access			
Ration-supply scale	.28*	.23*	--
Ration amounts	.13	.13*	.14
Private housing rare	-.01	-.06	-.00
State employment common	-.15*	-.21*	-.07
Low unemployment	.15*	.10	.05
White collar neighborhood	.16*	.17*	.19*
City Characteristics			
Administrative level	-.33*	-.35*	-.22*
City population	-.38*	-.38*	--
Lingnan Region	.02	-.02	.15
Median N	(85)	(51)	(47)

Source: Sample of neighborhoods, total N of 133.

[a]The five controlled variables are city population, ration-supply scale, household control scale, radical year, and informant optimism.

-- = not relevant because of statistical controls.

*$p \leq .10$

variables are in many cases intercorrelated, so it is hard to tell which have effects on our crime scale in their own right.

What does table 29 tell us, then? First, if we look in the city variables panel of the table, we see that crimes are reportedly more common in high level, populous cities. China thus does not appear to escape the widespread pattern of crime being more common in large urban places than in small ones. The low correlations in the Lingnan Region indicate that we can discount the idea that cities like Canton and nearby areas have unusually high reported crime rates in comparison with cities elsewhere.

The crux of our analysis concerns relations in the top three panels in table 29 where we distinguish neighborhoods within cities in terms of their structural characteristics. The variables introduced above are listed in three categories which correspond roughly to our three approaches to social control: solidarity, deterrence, and legitimate opportunity. One pattern stands out quite clearly in these correlations: neighborhoods with more vigorous sanctioning mechanisms (and radical time periods when sanctioning efforts were increased) are associated generally with higher, not lower, reported crime problems. The two variables that tap this dimension most directly—our household control scale and our radical year measure—both have an independent effect on the reported crime measure, and when their effects are partialled out (in column 3 and in statistics not shown here), the influence of the remaining sanctions variables is pretty much eliminated. There are ambiguities in how this finding should be interpreted, however. One interpretation is that harsher deterrence efforts result in more behavior being considered deviant and criminal than would be the case in a less sanction-prone environment. This is precisely the sort of mechanism that Western "labeling" theories of deviance focus upon. But another interpretation might be that the causation is working in the other direction, and that in situations where more serious crime problems exist, more vigorous deterrence efforts will be made to combat them, producing the sort of association reflected in the table. Still a third view would be that when deterrence mechanisms are more vigorously developed, people may become aware of, and concerned about, crime, even if the rate of criminal activity has not changed. We have no clear way to "prove" that one or another of these interpretations is the correct one. But the figures in the table do at least allow us to conclude that there is no evidence here that neighborhoods (or time periods) with more vigorous deterrence efforts are characterized by lower crime rates.

The patterns for our other two panels in the table, concerning solidarity and opportunities, are less clear-cut, since there are both positive and negative correlations visible. When other variables are partialled out, the correlations holding up best are those in the opportunity set, in particular, our ration and supply scale and our indicator of a white collar neighborhood, and these support our hypothesis that more opportunities produce less crime. To sum up, our examination of our neighborhood crime scale shows that the clearest patterns are for large cities to have more reported crime, for neighborhoods with more access to opportunities to report less crime, and for crime to appear more common when vigorous sanctioning efforts are supplied.[33] The evidence is complex and not devoid of prob-

33. The generalizations above are further supported in regression results for the most highly correlated items. With seven items in the equation, the standardized regression coefficients are as follows: household control scale $-.33$, radical year $-.20$, ration-supply scale $.23$, white collar neighborhood $.12$, administrative level $-.42$, city population $.21$, and informant optimism $.09$. Thus, with other items controlled, deterrence efforts fail to prevent

lems, but it points to the same primacy of opportunity factors that we stressed in our earlier discussion of the deterioration of urban orderliness over time.

In table 30 we examine neighborhood and city variations in reported rates of economic offenses and regulation violations (which we will refer to as "economic deviance"). The items in this scale, unlike those in our neighborhood crime scale, concern "victimless" offenses such as illegal peddling and black marketeering that can be expected to be of more concern to urban authorities than to ordinary citizens. In table 30 the correlations of our city variables all appear to be spurious; when controlled for our ration and supply scale, these associations are all greatly reduced. Apparently it is more the level of supplies in a city than the city size or location that influences the prevalence of economic deviance.

In table 30, two of our interview quality variables—whether the informant was female and relative optimism about supplies—are correlated with reported economic deviance, but when we control for these variables (in columns 2 and 3), the other correlations in the table are not appreciably reduced. So informant biases do not explain away the other associations.

In the first two panels of the table, most of our solidarity and sanctioning variables either have no strong relations with reported low economic deviance or, in a few cases, negative associations, with such deviance reported more common in work unit compounds and during radical years once our control variables are partialled out. The strongest correlations appear in our set of opportunity-related variables, and these are generally even stronger than the comparable correlations in table 29. All of the variables listed have significant bivariate correlations with low reported economic deviance, but most of this effect is picked up by two variables, ration and supplies and low unemployment. In sum, if we consider not crimes against persons and property, but victimless economic offenses and regulation violations, the importance of access to opportunities is even more clear.[34] Areas where black marketeering, sales of ration coupons, and similar activities are widespread seem to be areas where un-

---

crime and may even increase it, opportunity and access inhibits crime, higher level cities have more crime, and informant optimism does little to distort the results. (We suspect that the positive coefficient for city population is an artifact of including population and administrative level—two highly correlated items—in the same equation.)

34. In a regression equation with five items, the standardized coefficients are as follows: work unit compound $-.27$, radical year $-.23$, ration-supply scale $.47$, low unemployment $.38$, informant optimism $.25$, informant quality $-.18$, and female informant $.12$. Thus, as in the text, opportunity and access items have the dominant influence on economic deviance. Situations high in control potential, such as work unit compounds and radical years, fail to control deviance. Quality control items have somewhat more influence on these results but fail to wash away the dominant findings.

Table 30   **Economic Deviance by Neighborhood Characteristics** (+ = Low Level of Reported Economic Deviance)

	Bivariate Correlations	Partial Correlations Controlled for		
		Female Informant	Informant Optimism	Five Variables[a]
Neighborhood Solidarity				
Stability of residents	-.22*	-.20*	-.15	.10
Homogeneity of resident	-.05	-.04	-.04	.04
Low-rise housing	.10	.10	.13	.12
Work unit compound	.03	.01	-.11	-.38*
Deterrence Efforts				
Service infrastructure	-.09	-.10	.02	.16
Household control scale	-.07	-.09	.02	.09
Political study	-.08	-.14	-.13	-.19
Sent-down youth controls	.07	.09	-.02	.02
Radical year	-.19*	-.20*	-.12	--
Opportunity and Access				
Ration-supply scale	.46*	.44*	.40*	--
Ration amounts	.24*	.21*	.24	.02
Private housing rare	.21*	.19*	.16	.05
State employment common	.22*	.21*	.17	-.01
Low unemployment	.55*	.54*	.52*	--
White collar neighborhood	.21*	.17*	.25*	.17
City Characteristics				
Administrative level	.15*	.11	.15	.03
Lingnan Region	-.22*	-.18*	-.17	-.00
Median N	(81)	(78)	(54)	(49)

Source: Sample of neighborhoods, total N of 133.

[a]The five controlled variables are unemployment, ration-supply scale, radical year, sex of informant, and informant optimism.

-- = not relevant because of statistical controls.

*$p \leq .10$

employment is a problem and where rations and supplies are not sufficient to meet popular needs, and in this sort of setting it is perhaps not surprising that people do not all play by the rules, but resort to their own devices in an effort to meet their needs.[35]

Our final analysis, in table 31, concerns the factors conducive to low reported crime levels within work units, rather than within neighborhoods. The format of table 31 is much the same as before, although now work unit-specific variables are used in place of neighborhood-specific ones. In table 31 we also separate out a panel labeled "Unit Resources" from the

35. We find no evidence for the curvilinear relationship between supplies and deviance hypothesized by Lynn White, *Careers in Shanghai* (Berkeley: University of California Press, 1978).

rest because it is ambiguous how these variables should be characterized in terms of our three approaches to social control. Having resources can be seen as an ability to provide opportunities as well as a capacity to apply sanctions, so we place these variables in a separate, intermediate position.

In table 31, city characteristics are not strongly associated with reported work unit crime levels, although there is a weak indication that there is

Table 31   Work Unit Crime Scale by Unit Characteristics (+ = Low Reported Crime)

	Bivariate Correlations	Partial Correlations Controlled for		
		Female Informant	Informant Optimism	Five Variables[a]
Work Unit Solidarity				
Small size	.22*	.27*	.20*	--
No shift work	.15	.14	.19	.01
Unit inclusiveness	-.45*	-.47*	-.50*	-.36*
Contacts off job	-.01	-.07	-.05	.02
Mass organs in units	-.42*	-.38*	-.41*	-.28*
Management does labor	-.04	-.03	-.07	-.06
Unit Deterrence Efforts				
Unit sanctions	-.43*	-.45*	-.42*	-.26
Criticism/self-criticism	-.09	-.08	-.24	-.16
Political study	.01	.01	.02	.11
Birth control activities	-.26*	-.35*	-.33*	-.30*
Model worker selections	-.23*	-.22	-.26	-.10
Radical year	-.02	-.03	.07	.01
Unit Resources				
State enterprise	-.24*	-.28*	-.26*	-.11
Resources scale	-.13	-.19	-.24*	.04
Unit "heft"	-.35*	-.36*	-.36*	--
Level of administration	-.06	-.11	-.08	.06
Unit Opportunities				
Wage raises received	.26*	.24*	.20	--
Low wage span	.45*	.40*	.55*	.44*
Ration-supply scale	.20	.16	.10	.15
Ration amounts	-.14	-.09	-.02	-.06
Material incentives used	-.10	.02	-.01	.09
City Characteristics				
Administration level	-.08	-.16	-.09	-.08
Lingnan Region	.10	.20*	.19*	.20
Median N	(45)	(43)	(31)	(22)

Source: Work unit sample, total N of 91.

[a]The five controlled variables are unit size, unit "heft," wage raises, sex of informant, and informant optimism.

-- = not relevant because of statistical controls.

*p ≤ .10

less of reported crime in the Lingnan Region, once other variables are controlled for. In this table, as in table 30, we see that female informants and informants relatively optimistic about the local supply situation were more likely to report low levels of work unit crime problems, but that controlling for these variables does not appreciably reduce the other correlations in the table. Thus neither city effects nor informant characteristics can account for the correlations shown elsewhere in the table.

In the top panel of the table, while small size is correlated with low levels of reported crime problems in work units, the other solidarity measures either have no strong relationship or show strong negative relationships. In the panels dealing with sanctioning efforts and resources much the same pattern emerges. The only strong relationships are negative ones, with units with more resources and sanctioning mechanisms characterized, if anything, by higher reported crime levels. We argue that there is a common syndrome underlying many of the correlations in the first three panels of the table. Work units in China tend to vary consistently along a number of dimensions. Large state enterprises tend to have more resources, more sanctioning mechanisms, more mass organizations functioning, and more activities to involve the lives of their employees and their families. The correlations among these aspects of organizational structure were high enough that we were able to combine several of the work unit scales into a single "scale of scales" which is called simply unit "heft" in table 31. Unit heft thus represents the core dimension of these several work unit scales. Units ranking high on heft will have high resources and sanctioning power, but their implications for solidarity are mixed; their organizational life and inclusive activities promote solidarity, but their large size and internal differentiation reduce solidarity.

The most important point, however, is that these "hefty" units are characterized by significantly higher rates of reported crimes. This finding parallels the pattern seen in table 29, where neighborhoods with well-developed infrastructures and sanctioning mechanisms exhibited higher reported crime rates. Once again we cannot give an unambiguous interpretation of this finding. Perhaps large and resourceful work units have more crime problems; but it is also possible that their vigorous sanctioning procedures make people employed there more concerned about "crime."[36] Only a conservative conclusion seems warranted: that high development of resources, sanctions, and solidarity mechanisms in a work unit does not produce low levels of crime problems.

36. Larger size units might also have more reported crime because there is simply a broader field of view within which crime problems could come to an informant's attention. But when we control for unit size, in separate calculations, unit "heft" is still significantly related to crime.

We are left, finally, in panel four of table 31, with some indications that the availability of opportunities does contribute to lower reported crime levels. Here the level of rations and perceptions about them do not appear quite so important as in earlier tables, and the use of piece rates or bonuses ("material incentives used") does not seem to be strongly associated with our unit crime scale. But units that have a low wage spread and in which people have been able to move up in the wage scale during the post-Cultural Revolution period do seem to be characterized by lower reported crime problems.[37]

Again summaries are not easily arrived at, but we argue that table 31 can be interpreted in a manner not too different from our earlier tables. Measures of solidarity and deterrence efforts give a mixed picture, and if anything they indicate more crime problems when such structural features are well developed. Access to opportunities, on the other hand, seems to be associated with lower reported crime rates, a pattern we saw even more clearly in tables 29–30.[38]

Conclusions

The general patterns found in our comparison within China's urban landscape reinforce the conclusions we drew in considering why social order deteriorated in Chinese cities in the post-Cultural Revolution period. Our data are imperfect in many ways, but from all the evidence available a consistent picture emerges. Chinese cities are distinctive in comparison with our own in having structural mechanisms that reinforce social solidarity and provide a highly penetrating deterrence network. Yet these solidarity and sanctioning mechanisms do not appear to be the major factors in the level of orderliness of Chinese cities. For example, we had anticipated that the most tightly organized work unit compounds would be perceived as safer environments than the less easy to organize mixed neighborhoods, but our data provided little evidence for this view. In fact, there are some indications that crime is perceived as more prevalent in the most solidary and sanction-prone urban settings. The variation that appears most important for securing urban orderliness concerns access

37. Large units and units that are "hefty" tend to have wider wage disparities than smaller units. However, the low wage span variable holds up even when controlled for unit size and "heft."

38. In a regression equation with six variables, the standardized regression coefficients are small unit size $-.07$, birth control activities $-.27$, unit "heft" $-.24$, wage raises .08, informant optimism .35, and female informant .34. This equation is dominated by the last two quality control items of optimism and sex of informant, but the equation still suggests that deterrence efforts (such as birth control activities) fail to deter crime.

to opportunities. When the opportunity structure was dismantled, crime problems increased in Chinese cities, in spite of efforts to promote social solidarity and invigorate deterrence mechanisms. And within this more disorderly urban scene, neighborhoods and work units in which people had more access to opportunities to purchase needed commodities and acquire secure employment and promotion opportunities seem to have remained more orderly than other areas. The implication of these findings for Chinese urban authorities seems clear: what is needed to restore and maintain the high levels of urban social control that existed in earlier years is not so much to improve the devices for detecting and sanctioning offenders or for promoting social solidarity, but to repair the disrupted opportunity structure, so that urbanites will feel that they have predictable chances for improving their lives and will be motivated to exert themselves and obey the official rules.[39]

Since the mid-1970s, Chinese authorities have recognized the critical importance of restoring the opportunity structure in cities, and of providing incentives that link present behavior with future rewards.[40] While they have also done such things as beef up juvenile reformatories and intensify neighborhood patrols, a key element in their effort to combat juvenile delinquency has been the attempt to restore competition for desirable futures. Several kinds of changes have occurred, as noted in part 1. Beginning in about 1974, the program of sending urban youths to the countryside began to be modified and curtailed. At first young people were simply promised that they could go to special youth farms near their own cities, rather than to distant communes and state farms, and that after a few years they could expect to be reassigned to an urban job. In

39. It should be noted that a number of efforts to test the legitimate opportunity approach to crime control in the United States have produced ambiguous and conflicting results. We hypothesize that part of the problem is that most such efforts involve modest efforts to increase the opportunities for arrested individuals or released convicts (through work release, job training programs, and so forth) rather than to provide a predictable structure of long-term opportunities for young people who have not yet gotten into trouble. See P. J. Cook, "The Correctional Carrot: Better Jobs for Parolees," *Policy Analysis* 1 (1975): 11–51; E. S. Friedman, "An Interim Evaluation of the Supported Work Experiment," *Policy Analysis* 3 (1977): 147–70; P. H. Rossi, R. A. Berk, K. Lenihan, *Money, Work and Crime* (New York: Academic Press, 1980). Also, we have noted that in the American setting other features of the social structure are more conducive to crime than is the case in Chinese cities.

40. The problem of crime has been taken to be so important that since the fall of 1979, Party units all the way down to the lowest levels have been instructed to undertake a program of "comprehensive treatment" (*zonghe zhili*) against crime involving all aspects of political, economic, educational, and legal work in each local administrative region. For recent examples of this comprehensive effort, see *People's Daily,* 11 August 1982; 13 August 1982, p. 4; 14 August 1982.

other words, initially there was an effort to change this campaign from one involving permanent and often distant rural exile to a nearby rotation system. Then in 1977 the entrance examinations for universities were restored, and it became possible once again to go directly from middle school to college, without having to put in a period of rural labor at all. Shortly after that, authorities began an effort to expand the number of new urban jobs, particularly in collective enterprises engaged in various kinds of urban services, and to use these to soak up some urban middle school graduates not accepted into college, as well as some young people returning from rural labor stints. The Chinese press reports that in 1979 about nine million young people were newly assigned to jobs in this manner. These changes mean that only a few urban youth will still have to temporarily go down to the countryside, and that most who perform reasonably well on tests in school will be able to avoid this and will get into an urban job or college.

At the same time, the changes in the educational system noted in chapter 4 have been significant, with tests, homework, failures, and other accoutrements of highly competitive academics back in style in a big way. Strict classroom discipline and respect for teachers are also mandated now, and stints working in factories and communes have been reduced to nominal periods. As a rule, students no longer attend neighborhood schools, but sit for entrance exams at lower levels, and these are used to sort out the best students to attend "keypoint" schools that are favored in terms of resources, teacher quality, and curriculum richness. Within schools, tracking into slow, average, and fast classes has even been adopted in many places, so that students who want to do well eventually on the university entrance exams have to first worry about succeeding on lower level exams that allocate them to better schools, and then getting placed in more demanding classes within those schools. In general these changes are surrounded by new propaganda that suggests that lives as intellectuals and experts are among the highest things that young people can aspire to and involve more prestige than common manual labor.

Work units have also implemented changes, as we saw in chapter 3. Since 1977, systems of piece rates and production bonuses have been restored in various kinds of work units, as have related material incentive devices, such as royalties for writers and journalists. Employed people have been given to understand that they can expect periodic promotions in the future, and two general wage raises have been carried out, in 1977 and in 1979–80. In the latter of these, it was clearly indicated that those who make the most contributions to the work of the unit, rather than those who are most poorly paid or politically worthy, would be favored in receiving raises. The other side of the coin is that campaigns have been launched to deal with severe work discipline problems, and some authorities are even advocating that demotions and firings be used more liberally, so that employees can't think of their jobs as "iron rice bowls."

Authorities in China are thus moving on several fronts to restore systems of incentives and career opportunities that were discarded during the Cultural Revolution, in the hope that these changes will solve the current juvenile delinquency problems. We have suggested that the absence of such structured opportunities was the main reason why the urban social control system was unable to cope with the problems caused by young people. The effort appears to have begun to have some effect. In China's eighteen largest cities with over a million population each, the crime rate during the first half of 1982 reportedly declined by a fourth over what it had been during the same period just a year before.[41]

Nevertheless, the crime rate may still remain difficult to press back down to earlier low levels. Many youth continue to feel that their aspirations are being frustrated. These frustrated youth include some who still remain stuck in the countryside. At the time of the Spring Festival in 1979 there were major demonstrations in Shanghai and other cities, staged by youths who were demanding to be brought back from rural exile.[42] There is also likely to be frustration among graduates who continue to pour out of middle schools in large numbers only to find that the further education and job opportunities that they expected are not available. Even if university enrollments continue to expand, they cannot absorb more than a tiny fraction of those turned out by urban middle schools each year. Furthermore, it is now clear that most of the people assigned to new urban jobs are being placed in collective enterprises in the service sector, in jobs that are generally held in low esteem and that in most cases provide low pay and fewer fringe benefits than jobs in the state sector. In other words, there is a danger that young people will see these as "dead-end jobs" that do not match their abilities and aspirations, and the propaganda in the media about the glories of intellectual work are likely to heighten this perception. There will still be many disappointed and frustrated young people, and now they will be legal residents of the city, rather than out of harm's way in the countryside. Finally, over the last decade a juvenile gang subculture, as well as groups of cultural and po-

41. *Beijing Review,* no. 33 (1982): 6.

42. The exact rules remain unclear, but it would appear that most of the youths sent to the countryside after 1966 are now eligible to return to the city. However, those sent before this date are obliged to remain in the countryside as are post-1966 youths who got state sector jobs in small towns, however remote. Also, some post-1966 youths on state farms (as opposed to communes) have been urged to remain on these farms. It was the latter group that seems to have fueled the 1979 demonstrations.

litical dissidents, has grown up in China's large cities, and so there are sources of deviant socialization and deviant association that did not exist in earlier years. Young people disenchanted with their lives will find reinforcement in such deviant collectivities, and the official social control system will continue to be undermined. In short, it is not likely to be an easy matter to restore the degree of urban security of earlier years.

Our inquiries in this chapter have led us to the conclusions that Chinese cities have been generally more orderly places than American cities and that the primary reason for this orderliness is not so much the distinctive social arrangements and sanctioning systems of Chinese cities as the capacity to provide predictable and rewarding opportunities for urban residents, and particularly for urban youths. Over time and within cities, as this capacity has been weakened, social order problems have multiplied. Although Chinese authorities appear to grasp the importance of opportunities in securing social order, providing them remains a problem. Chinese socialism has not produced a mechanism to avoid or solve what is a worldwide problem, the overproduction of educated youths. China appeared to have found a solution in the massive program of sending urban educated youths to settle in the countryside, but it is now clear that this was a costly and unpopular policy which aggravated urban social control problems. As a result, the program of sending youths to the countryside has been curtailed, while efforts are being taken to expand urban employment. But the imbalance between the number of ambitious and talented young people annually graduating from schools and the number of jobs suitable for their talents (or enrollment slots in China's universities) will continue to create problems in China for some time to come. Urban social order can be expected to improve, but it may never be possible to regain the degree of safety and security that informants and the Chinese press say characterized the late 1950s or mid-1960s.

9   Political Control

The quality of life for Chinese urban residents is shaped not only by whether there is crime in the streets, but also by whether they feel they are in control of their environment, not victims of it. In Marxist writings, one of the promises of socialism is to eliminate the powerlessness which is a part of the alienation that afflicts people in modern capitalist societies. The task of this chapter is to examine whether this form of alienation has been successfully attacked in China, or whether as in many other socialist states, the loss of control to a large bureaucracy led by ideologues has deprived average citizens of any sense of control over their lives.

In earlier chapters, we noted the extension of bureaucratic structures into many aspects of Chinese urban life, not only planning production, allocating jobs, setting prices, distributing health care, assigning housing, and rationing many other services, but also controlling marriages, divorces, births, and many other aspects of personal life. Friedrich Hayek and Milton Friedman, among others, suggest that much of this kind of bureaucratic intervention is inevitable in a society that abandons market distribution of social goods and services. Once this kind of bureaucratic intervention is widespread, any hope of individual control over one's life is doomed.[1]

With the state as the only employer, few will dare speak out against the government. Without independent sources of income, there will be no free press nor the possibility of organizing groups and campaigns against official policy. Government bureaucrats cannot resist using the tremendous concentration of power in their hands. Bureaucrats will pursue their interests in staying in power and none will be able to prevent them. Mistakes in planning and the improper signals given out by administered

1. Friedrich Hayek, *The Road to Serfdom* (Chicago: University of Chicago Press, 1948); and Milton Friedman, *Capitalism and Freedom* (Chicago: University of Chicago Press, 1962).

as opposed to market prices and wages cause discontent, and that discontent can be quelled only by the imposition of firmer government controls. The hope that socialist states would be able to reform themselves from within, providing self-imposed restraints on the power of central bureaucrats, is a vain one. Hayek and Friedman do not stand alone in this critique. They have been joined by a number of Eastern European reformers, such as Djilas, Bahro, Hegedus, and Vajda, who also point to the dangers of large bureaucracies that serve the interests of the bureaucrats while suppressing the interests of the larger society. These East European reformers, writing within socialist states, are not quite so pessimistic about the possibilities of reform as Hayek and Friedman, but their description of existing problems is rather similar.[2]

As we have noted in earlier chapters, China has not ignored these kinds of criticisms. Led by Mao Zedong, radical reformers in China made a concerted attempt to root out what were seen as the evils of bureaucracy. They wanted to avoid the bureaucratic stultification that they thought they saw in the Soviet Union and that increasingly threatened the socialist revolution in China as well. Their answer was to force all levels of the bureaucratic apparatus through a series of periodic political campaigns and weekly study and criticism sessions that would keep them attuned to service of society ("the people") rather than to pursuit of their own interests. And when these measures proved insufficient to satisfy the radicals, errant bureaucrats were harshly attacked in the Cultural Revolution. Earlier campaigns were clearly controlled from above and had certain limits placed around them. But in the Cultural Revolution, students, workers, and other rebels were urged to attack the leaders of the bureaucracy with no holds barred. In the aftermath, the bureaucratic apparatus was simplified, rules and regulations abandoned, and political study and ideological commitment put in their place. By eliminating or drastically reducing the bureaucracy and its rules and regulations that stood between correct-thinking Party leaders and the masses, it was hoped that a new national unity could be produced. It was only necessary to make sure that right-thinking bureaucrats were selected and wrong-thinking bureaucrats and other individuals kept under control in a newly revitalized "proletarian dictatorship." With a proper militance against class enemies, moral virtue and a new unity with the proletarian masses could overcome the obstacles to national growth and social transformation.

2. Milovan Djilas, *The New Class: An Analysis of the Communist System* (London: Unwin Books, 1957); Andras Hegedus, *Socialism and Bureaucracy* (London: Allison and Busby, 1976); Mihaly Vajda, *The State and Socialism* (London: Allison and Busby, 1981); and Rudolf Bahro, *The Alternative in Eastern Europe* (1977; 2d ed. London: NLB, 1978).

Unfortunately, this approach to bureaucratic problems has potential problems of its own. Lyford Edwards and Crane Brinton have pointed out that this "moral virtue solution" to the problems of governing a complex society is common to many revolutionary regimes.[3] In the typical revolutionary regime, a broad coalition of political groups follows a moderate course in the initial years of the new government. But then as the government is unable to handle all the complexities of running the society, radicals who had been at the core of the revolution take over and try to force their ideals on everyone. In this reign of virtue (often accompanied by terror, because of the radicals' insistence on making everyone conform) "politics becomes as real, as pressing, as unavoidable for [the ordinary man] as food and drink, wife or mistress, his job and the weather. Political indifference . . . becomes impossible."[4] Radical asceticism is forced on everyone. There is a mania for destroying cultural artifacts of the previous regime and streets and other objects must be renamed with more appropriate revolutionary labels, "the conventional backbiting, gossip and hatred of ordinary social life are intensified" and acquire political significance. "Even the humblest person, the person most indifferent to politics, can never tell when the lightning is going to strike him or his household, when he may be hauled into court as a class enemy or a counterrevolutionary." But these attempts to realize revolutionary ideals in the immediate here and now generate their own counterrevolution as people tire of the heat of political enthusiasm and the threat that they will be attacked for errors real and imagined at any time. What follows is a "thermidor" period with many of the moderate elements of the initial years of the revolutionary regime returning to power. Emotionally exhausted, people no longer have stomach for the rigors of revolutionary fervor, and the government begins to rest more lightly on its people.

Another danger in the radical, moral fervor solution to bureaucratic problems is the possibility that simplifying bureaucratic institutions and eliminating rules and regulations will destroy all meaningful social groups that might stand between the central government and individuals. Following Hannah Arendt, William Kornhauser identifies these intermediate social groups as vital to the health of modern societies. Without them, modern governments with new communication and transportation facilities will have the means to impose direct control over all individuals.

3. Lyford P. Edwards, *The Natural History of Revolution* (Chicago: University of Chicago Press, 1927); and Crane Brinton, *The Anatomy of Revolution* (Englewood Cliffs: Prentice-Hall, 1938).

4. Here and below, the quotes are from Brinton, *Anatomy of Revolution*, pp. 186–92.

There will be no social buffers between the state and the individual and the society will descend into totalitarianism.[5]

Alvin Gouldner suggests that an inattention to this need for social buffers is one of the great remaining problems in Marxism. Focusing on the transformative power of the socialist revolution and wanting to rid society of flawed bourgeois social institutions, Marx said almost nothing about the new family, neighborhood, and other communal institutions that would come to replace them.[6] In China the new socialist government has not been completely insensitive to the need to build on intermediate institutions. As we have seen, neighborhoods and work units are much more elaborated and have much more of a potential communal function in China than in any European socialist states. The residential stability of neighborhoods and work units leads one to wonder whether these intermediary institutions fill the buffer role that Kornhauser sees as so necessary or whether they are just one more instrument of a more thorough bureaucratic control.

Political Criticism

By now many of the characteristics of China's reign of virtue are well known. With an emphasis on class struggle conducted in mass campaigns and no institutional guarantees of individual rights or legal bases for appeal, excesses were rampant. Chinese society took on many of the characteristics of other radical societies. Our interview transcripts as well as the current Chinese media are full of tales of atrocities from this period.

The reign of virtue, though realized most completely during the Cultural Revolution, actually began to emerge in the political rectification movements of the 1940s. Intellectuals suffered in a number of separate campaigns in the 1940s and 1950s and particularly in the 1957 antirightist campaign that squelched those who dared criticize government policy after being invited to do so in Mao's "Let a Hundred Flowers Bloom" campaign. These campaigns continued in the 1960s, culminating in the Cultural Revolution.[7] In the Cultural Revolution, students and others who were powerless but highly idealistic were urged to attack leaders who

5. William Kornhauser, *The Politics of Mass Society* (Glencoe: Free Press, 1959).

6. Alvin W. Gouldner, *The Two Marxisms* (New York: Seabury, 1980).

7. On this succession of campaigns, see Frederick C. Teiwes, *Politics and Purges in China* (White Plains, N.Y.: Sharpe, 1979); Gordon Bennett, *Yundong: Mass Campaigns in Chinese Communist Leadership* (Berkeley: University of California, Center for Chinese Studies, 1976); Charles P. Cell, *Revolution at Work: Mobilization Campaigns in China* (New York: Academic Press, 1977). Charles Cell tries to present a more positive image of the success of campaigns, but to us his data suggest that as campaigns became more harsh they became more counterproductive.

followed old bourgeois or new Soviet revisionist ways leading away from Mao's line of simple thought and radical equality. Hundreds of thousands, and probably even millions, of those criticized were removed from office, deprived of their household furnishings, spat upon, slapped around, verbally abused, denied medical care, killed, or forced to commit suicide to escape further abuse.

Even if imperfect, the data from our sample of neighbors provide some indication of the full impact of the Cultural Revolution and of other campaigns that preceded and followed it. Among adults age sixteen and over, both male and female, from small as well as large towns, a total of six percent were known by neighbors to have been publicly criticized for political errors of various sorts.[8] Some of these errors dated from the 1950s, when people were attacked not only for "rightist" criticism but also for many other kinds of activities that might be labeled as counterrevolutionary. About one percent of all neighbors were known to have been criticized in early political campaigns. In these campaigns, procedures were established for determining who would be called upon to confess their political errors before their peers in a small group or in a mass work unit meeting and who would receive harsher sentences, such as having their civil rights removed, being sent to a labor camp, or other kinds of punishment.

At the start of the Cultural Revolution, these established methods were abandoned as student, worker, and army rebels were encouraged to mete out mass justice. Another two percent or so of the nonagricultural population fell before the onslaught of these rebels. Then, as the Cultural Revolution wound down and radicals were attempting to consolidate their power, there was a succession of other campaigns through the late 1960s and early 1970s. The 1969 "Clean the Class Ranks" campaign tried to further purge urban work units of those felt to be of the wrong ideology or class background. Some people without any record of previous difficulty were labeled "slipped-through-the-net-landlords or -capitalists" because of their fathers or grandfathers' occupations, and they along with their families were sometimes shipped to rural villages.[9] Others were caught in the 1971 "Hit One, Oppose Three" campaign. To the extent that our statistics are representative, these two campaigns and some other small post-1968 campaigns criticized an additional one percent or so of the nonagricultural population, subjecting them to group criticism as well

8. These are criticisms that were harsh enough to become known by neighbors. Were milder criticisms that remained restricted to one's work group included, the percentages would be even higher.

9. Ninety percent of our informants knew of examples of families shipped to the countryside in this way in their neighborhoods.

as occasional harassment before mass meetings and sometimes to further physical punishment as well.

Besides these new victims, there were many old targets who were subject to additional criticism in each of the new campaigns. A black mark in a dossier at work or in a household register at the neighborhood police station made one a ready target for additional harassment in subsequent political campaigns.[10] Some became practiced craftsmen in the art of writing confessions and in standing bowed at the waist while being harangued by an assembled crowd. Thus, the total attacked in any new campaign in the 1960s and 1970s would have been somewhat larger than our figures on new targets indicate.

One of Mao Zedong's supposed innovations in the history of socialism was to emphasize the possibility of rehabilitating individuals through criticism and self-criticism among a group of peers. When held up for special criticism in political campaigns, some did express sufficient contrition and willingness to reform, or had errors judged sufficiently mild, that their offences would be largely forgotten once an episode had passed. However, for about two-thirds of those publicly criticized, or about four percent of our sample, the consequences were more lasting (table 32).

Beyond writing confessions and public harassment, there were several additional degrees of punishment, all graded to suit the seriousness of the offense and the contriteness of the offender. Table 32 arranges these punishments in approximate order of increasing severity.[11] During the Cultural Revolution, rebels often detained fallen leaders at their place of work, imprisoning them in a back room or basement or makeshift shed (often called a "cowpen") and demanding successive written confessions, subjecting prisoners to repeated public abuse, and engaging in further investigation. In our interviews, we were told that a number of such people committed suicide while under detention.[12]

In a more regular procedure predating the Cultural Revolution, people continued working in their usual jobs but reported more regularly to their supervisors and security personnel about their movements and the gradual

10. For accounts of how dossiers and household registers were used to pinpoint people with bad class labels and past political difficulties for attack by rebel groups at the start of the Cultural Revolution, see Gordon A. Bennett and Ronald N. Montaperto, *Red Guard* (Garden City, N.Y.: Doubleday, 1971), p. 78; and Ruth Earnshaw Lo, *In the Eye of the Typhoon* (New York: Harcourt Brace, 1980).

11. For more systematic treatment of the different grades of punishment, see Jerome Cohen, *The Criminal Process in the People's Republic of China, 1949–1963* (Cambridge: Harvard University Press, 1968); and Victor Li, *Law without Lawyers* (Boulder: Westview Press, 1978).

12. For a literary account of this kind of suicide, see the story of Jen Hsiu-lan in Jo-hsi Chen's, *The Execution of Mayor Yin* (Bloomington: Indiana University Press, 1978).

Table 32   Adults Punished or Criticized for
                                              Political Error

---

Type of Punishment by Increasing Severity
   Detained at place of work   0.1%
   Supervised labor at place of work   0.5
   Supervised in neighborhood   0.5
   Demoted   0.3
   Fired   0.3
   Sent to countryside   0.2
   Sentenced to labor camp   2.1
   Unknown   0.2

   Total Punished   4.2%

Only Criticized   1.8

Never Punished or Criticized   94.0

Total   100.0%

Number of Adults   (1,405)

Source: Weighted sample of neighbors age 16 and above.

evolution of their thought. Those who were unemployed or who had returned from labor camp without a regular state job could be supervised by neighborhood leaders. Called "controlled elements," these people were excluded from normal neighborhood political meetings and periodically (sometimes weekly) had to give reports on their activities, write self-examinations, and perform compulsory labor such as sweeping neighborhood lanes. With more serious offenses, people could be demoted, fired, sent to the countryside (as in the Clean the Class Ranks campaign), or sentenced to a labor camp. A total of about two percent of the adult members of families in our sample of neighbors was either currently in a labor camp or had been there sometime earlier in their careers.[13]

Some groups were more vulnerable than others to these kinds of punishment. This was particularly true of intellectuals. By the mid-1970s as many as a third of all college graduates had been publicly criticized, and over ten percent had received even more severe punishments (see figure 10). In contrast, only one or two percent of those with minimal education encountered political difficulty. Similar patterns were repeated in the occupational world, with those in higher status positions receiving the most criticism. One was also very vulnerable if from the wrong class background, especially if from a former capitalist or landlord family. Communist Party membership provided no exemption from criticism, though it may have provided some relief from extreme punishments. Older people in more responsible positions were more likely than the young to en-

13. The figure of two percent strikes us as a bit high and unlikely to represent the situation in the general population, but we have no way of checking this figure with published reports.

counter difficulty and males were more vulnerable than females (again, see figure 10).[14]

In some social circles, then, the proportion of the population affected was quite large, and one was very likely to have had a family member or close neighbor attacked. In our sample of neighbors, among heads of households alone, twelve percent were at least criticized and eight percent received further punishment. Thus, if our statistics are representative, at least one urban family in ten had been directly struck by political campaigns in the first three decades of socialist rule. And in our sample of neighborhoods, fully three-fourths were said to have a resident who remained under neighborhood political supervision because of past errors, political or otherwise.

The experience of being victims rather than masters of the system was quite widespread by the 1970s, and once a victim, always a potential victim. Old errors were not forgotten but were permanently recorded in work unit dossiers and neighborhood police registers for possible use in subsequent political campaigns. In earlier years, many people in the population could believe that these black marks were reserved for only a very small minority of really bad people in the society. Mao Zedong sometimes used to say that only 5 percent of the population consisted of class enemies that had to be controlled and that the other 95 percent were good, and therefore most people should join behind him in pushing through new political campaigns. But with the mounting frequency and intensity of campaigns in the 1960s and early 1970s, and the stacking of new errors on top of old errors, the number of individuals and families under a political cloud soon exceeded this mythical 5 percent. It became very hard to believe that the politically suspect were just a small minority of class enemies or that one would be safe just so long as one went along with the newest campaign.

Community Control

Even though political outrages were rampant in the larger world, neighborhood life need not have been quite so oppressive. Neighborhoods might

14. In Peking, over 60,000 municipal cadres, or one-fifth of the total in the city, are said to have been criticized and investigated in the Cultural Revolution (*Xinhua* [Peking], 6 October 1979, in *FBIS*, 11 October 1979, sec. R, p. 1). Nationwide, 2.9 million out of 18 million cadres, or sixteen percent of all cadres, were rehabilitated after the Cultural Revolution, implying that at least this many were seriously attacked in prior years ("Deng Xiaoping's Report on the Present Situation and Task," *Zhengming* [Hong Kong] 29 [1980]: 11–23, and *People's Daily*, 6 December 1980). Both the Peking and the nationwide figures suggest that the proportion reported criticized in our figure 10, panel 2, is close to the correct figure.

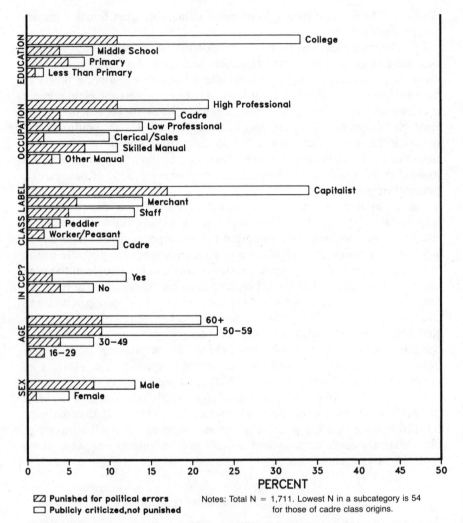

Figure 10. **Percentage of Adults in Political Difficulty by Selected Background Characteristics**
Source: 1972–78 Chinese urban sample, adults only (age 16 and above).

even have served as somewhat of a buffer between the individual and the government campaigns. For example, our earlier research on Chinese villages showed that the solidarity of small village communities has helped shield peasants from the political whirlwinds of the outside world. In matters other than economic policy, villagers have often remained masters of their own destiny, selecting their own leaders and deciding through local community opinion what central government social policies they would follow or reject.[15]

The question is whether urban neighborhoods have been able to respond in the same way. Urban neighborhoods contain residents from more diverse backgrounds than do villages, and except for some collective industries and services run by the ward, they have few economic interests in common. Yet, their exceptionally low rates of residential mobility, relative income and consumption equality, as well as the frequent sharing of kitchens and toilets suggest bases for community solidarity potentially approximating that found in villages.

The nature of the local administrative units and their leaders indicates some additional similarities between city and countryside. The urban ward, residents' committee, and small group more or less parallel the rural commune, brigade, and team structure—the last unit containing 20 to 40 households in both places. As in the countryside, the power, education, and pay of leaders declines regularly as one descends the administrative hierarchy. Small group leaders tend to be unpaid or only nominally paid females in their early fifties who received little education and typically never had a regular job (table 33). The status of residents' committee officers is only slightly more powerful and regular than that of the small group leaders. Over half serve voluntarily without pay, very few have jobs other than their neighborhood work, and they average slightly less education than other adults. It is only at the ward level that all officials become regular state employees with better than average education, adequate pay, and, frequently, Party membership. It is also at this highest level that females are in the minority. Except for the small role of rural females at any level, all these trends duplicate those found in the Chinese countryside. From this analogy, one might expect considerable community control over at least its lowest level officers.

However, on other dimensions there are very great differences between lower level urban and rural administrative units that distinctly reduce the power of urban dwellers over their local leaders. One is that for the majority of workers who work outside the neighborhood (in contrast to peasants who virtually all work in their village under local leaders), there is simply not much interest in neighborhood work. Not being required to participate in neighborhood political study, state workers seldom go to neighborhood meetings or participate in local elections when, and if, these are held. Nor do they participate much in neighborhood gossip networks of the sort that in rural China help control the behavior of village leaders.

15. See William L. Parish and Martin K. Whyte, *Village and Family in Contemporary China* (Chicago: University of Chicago Press, 1978).

Table 33   Neighborhood Officer Personal
                                            Characteristics and Pay

	Small Group Head	Residents' Committee		Ward		Adult Population[a]
		Executives	Security Officers	Executives	Security Officers	
Female	90%	70%	50%	37%	15%	51%
Years of Schooling[b]	2.8	5.3	4.1	7.6	8.4	6.9
Age[b]	54	48	49	47	38	46
Median N[c]	(66)	(71)	(12)	(19)	(13)	(733)

Source: Officer and weighted neighbor samples.

[a]Total adult population age 30 and over.

[b]Average (mean) years.

[c]Average (median) number of leaders with information for above statistics.

Residents, particularly unemployed youth and others who look to the neighborhood for possible jobs and economic support, are more concerned about the neighborhood and its leaders. In the 1970s, some residents came to have very strong feelings against their local leaders, especially against leaders who were sticklers for going by the book and constantly reporting suspicious activity to the police. The household registration system, political campaigns, and other devices provided ample opportunities for willful leaders to harass residents. A sixty-year-old residents' committee chair in Shanghai was said to be feared by the residents. "If one crossed him, he would send officers to check one's household registration almost nightly and require that one follow the letter of the law in reporting any visitors." A Canton ward leader in his thirties was disliked because he "took an activist position, was severe, and didn't listen to any excuses." A county residential committee leader in his sixties was said to "always be putting people down." A residents' committee security person "stepped on others to get ahead herself. She accused residents of things they hadn't done, including not paying for water they had taken from a public tap." And, she "used her authority to serve the interests of her own family," including cutting other family's cotton cloth rations to increase her own while reserving special cinema and cultural performance tickets distributed through the neighborhood apparatus for her own use. In another Canton neighborhood, the thirty-six-year-old female small group head earned the nickname "Severe Lane Hen," for the way she cursed youth in trying to get them to go to the countryside even while her own children remained in the city. Similarly, a sixty-year-old residents' committee leader in Swatow got the name "Old Tiger Lady" because of her fierce nature.[16]

Other leaders were perceived more favorably, particularly when they were not so active in pursuing small violations of the law. Everyone thought well of one Canton small group head because, "she didn't make small reports (*xiao baogao*)" to the authorities like some other small group heads. "She was more of a service person than a leader type." Assuming more of a service than an enforcer role is one of the characteristics of popular local leaders. They sometimes help get bills paid when residents are away at work, tend to small children who come home from school before their parents come home from work, or see that needed housing repairs and other matters get reported to the proper offices. Some are like the sixty-year-old spinster in Canton who had always been active in neighborhood work. "She often helped others. For example, if she saw another family's child had gotten dirty at play, she loved to call the dirty child to her and clean him up." Or, there was the sixty-year-old school teacher who became a Canton small group leader on retirement. "Since she helped residents write letters and fill out forms, everyone had a good impression of her. She had two children who had been sent to the countryside, so we listened to her when she came mobilizing us to go to the countryside." A sixty-five-year-old retired construction worker in Canton became ward leader because he didn't like sitting around home. "He got along well with the masses. They respected him and would often go directly to him with their problems. He didn't just sit in his office but got out to see people and often joined the rotating evening street patrol, which also gave people a good impression."[17] In our interviews, about a quarter of our informants saw their residents' committee chiefs as helpful and friendly, another quarter saw them neutrally, and about half saw them as nasty and meddling. Residents' small group heads were not seen in quite as negative a light.

Whether admired or despised, neighborhood leaders were only minimally controlled by public opinion in the 1970s. Ward and small group leaders were all appointed from above. It was only the residents' committee officer that could be elected, and these elections were not always held. If held, the election of residents' committee officers tended to be pro forma with participants (typically supposed to be one from each household) simply raising their hands to approve a single list of nominees. Or,

16. In succession, from interviews SSM2:1; KSM12:4; CSH5:1; KSM19:1; KSM21:1; SWP1:2.

17. In succession, from interviews KSM25:27; KSP1:1; KSM21:1; KSM12:4. Also see the story "My Neighborhood," in Bernard Frolic, *Mao's People* (Cambridge: Harvard University Press, 1980).

if there was secret ballot, with blanks for writing in additional names below the prepared slate, most people felt it was pointless to do so. To be more precise, only 30 percent of our informants said that any election meetings were held to select residents' committee officers, and even in these cases the neighborhood authorities simply nominated the people they wanted chosen, so that only 5 percent felt they had any real influence on who these local leaders were.

As a result of the lack of popular control, most neighborhood officers remained in office until they moved away, died, or simply got too sick and decrepit to continue. The Cultural Revolution provided only a slight break in this pattern. During the late 1960s, when people were urged to speak out against the bureaucracy, some of the more unpopular local leaders were publicly criticized.[18] But even with this short interregnum, most mid-1970s leaders had served at least seven years in their present position (table 34). This is particularly striking at the small group level, where 84 percent had served at least seven years. In a comparable position, only 45 percent of team leaders in our earlier rural research had served so long, while a third had come to office during the previous two years.[19] Because it was so immune from adverse public opinion or control, urban leadership was far more stable.

In the countryside there have been more informal as well as formal ways of controlling and ridding oneself of unpopular leaders. The informal means have included refusing to obey a leader's commands and socially ostracizing his family. There are a few instances that come close to this in our urban interviews. One group of neighborhood youths laid plans to beat up the children of a particularly unpopular small group leader. She reputedly got wind of the plot and fled the neighborhood. Another fled after youths threw rocks on top of her house in the middle of the night, causing part of her tile roof to cave in.[20] But these are very isolated instances and quite atypical of the situation in most neighborhoods.

More normally, residents have been afraid to criticize local leaders for fear of retaliation. An emigré from a county seat suggests,

> The masses wouldn't dare mention any dissatisfaction with them,
> for to do so would lead to one's being suspected of attacking a
> cadre and being criticized in meetings. So we all dare to hate but
> not to speak (*gan nu bu gan yan*).[21]

18. In our sample of local leaders, popularity and public criticism are inversely correlated at − .39

19. Parish and Whyte, *Village and Family,* p. 108.

20. KSM21:1; KSS2:3.

21. CSH5:1.

Table 34   Neighborhood Officer Public Relations

	Small Group Head	Residents' Committee		Ward	
		Executive Officer	Security Officer	Security Officer	Executive Officer
1. Resident in neighborhood	100%	91%	88%	80%	92%
2. Years in current office:					
seven or more	84%	75%	60%	89%	75%
two to six	14	20	40	11	25
less than two	3	5	0	0	0
total	101%	100%	100%	100%	100%
Average (mean)	10	9	8	10	9
3. Relations with neighbors/workers:					
good	26%	27%		30%	40%
average	40	35		10	40
poor	33	38		60	20
total	99%	100%		100%	100%
4. Communist Party membership	50%	92%	20%	100%	100%
5. Gainfully employed	23%	63%	50%	100%	100%
6. Paid for administrative work	15%	46%	40%	100%	100%
7. Average pay for administrative work (yuan)[a]	18	33	--	46	61
Median N[b]	(40)	(42)	(7)	(8)	(11)

Sources and notes: See table 33.

[a]Median pay to those paid for administrative work.

[b]Figures based on less than five cases are omitted.

After cataloguing the rationing, housing assignments, job assignments, political study, and myriad other aspects of personal life in which the neighborhood is involved, a Shanghai legal emigrant suggests,

> From all this, you can see that although lane [residents' committee] and ward authority looks piddling at first, in reality they have a great deal of authority. If you get crossed up with a lane cadre, you've had it, for in the lane they are the law. There is no other law under which they must operate.[22]

This is an extreme view to be sure, but one which appears to have been shared by a number of residents.

22. SSM1:4.

A final way in which urban neighborhoods differ from villages is the much greater penetration of neighborhoods by the state security apparatus. Most rural counties have but a few police posts and most villages seldom see a policeman. In contrast, every urban ward is run by a police station that parallels the civilian ward office, and beat policemen are in regular contact with residents' committee security officers and small group heads. In the 1970s these policemen and the local security officers could become unpopular because of overzealousness in late night household registration checks, pressure to get youth back into the villages, harassment of controlled elements, and also because of potential corruption. Some policemen were besieged by gifts of food and other rural goodies from youth returning from the countryside, in the hope that they would look the other way when visiting permits were overstayed. Similarly, overseas Chinese trying to get application forms for exit visas had to go through their local policemen.[23] They and others trying to get various sorts of forms would sometimes offer gifts in order to get prompt attention. There are a number of examples in our interviews of local policemen being publicly accused of corruption and removed from office as a result of these temptations, as well as of accusations of corruption not yet brought to official attention. For all these reasons, policemen and security officers in our sample were more likely to be unpopular than the average neighborhood leader (see table 34). As with other neighborhood leaders, in the 1970s there was little chance of residents being able to do anything about their like or dislike of security personnel.

Variation among different kinds of neighborhoods also shows the difficulty urbanites have had in controlling their neighborhood leaders. From the village analogy, one would expect neighbors to have the most control over their leaders when there was considerable neighborhood solidarity resulting from low rates of residential mobility, considerable status homogeneity, and mostly old and private housing. However, these are the very urban neighborhoods that have the most highly developed means of bureaucratic control. Neighborhoods high in the characteristics that could promote social solidarity also have a more elaborate infrastructure of neighborhood services, including nurseries, health stations, welfare, street sweeping, and bicycle repair. And they have a more bureaucratic supervision of households in the form of late night household registration checks, cleanliness inspections, political study, criminal sentencing meetings, and family disputes mediation, as well as more reported power by the residential committee head.[24] The net result is that the conditions which might

23. As in the Soviet Union, only those who grew up abroad or who have close kinsmen abroad have been able to apply for an exit visa.
24. For details on these intercorrelations, see appendix 2.

otherwise promote social solidarity and control of local leaders fail to do so. Residents' committee officers have less power in neighborhoods with mostly private housing. Otherwise, there is no relationship between stability, homogeneity, low-rise housing, and either leadership power or the character of relations with leaders of the residents' committee (table 35).

A similar story is repeated in residents' committee elections and in relations with the small group head. In statistics not reproduced here, there is no relation between the reported openness of residents' committee elections and the solidarity or any other characteristic of a neighborhood. The nature of small group leadership depends much more on the personality of the individual small group head than it does on the nature of the neighborhood. Neither the reported power of the small group head nor how agreeable her relations are with other neighborhood residents is related statistically to the background characteristics of neighborhoods.

Neighborhoods, then, have not acted as buffers between the individual and the larger political system. They have typically not been as threatening to individuals as work units, for it is in work units that one's career is determined, where one's personal dossier is stored, and where one experiences political study, criticism, and self-criticism among a small group of workmates. But neighborhoods also posed a danger if your household

Table 35   Characteristics of Residents'
                                        Committee Head by Neighborhood
                                        Characteristics (Correlations)[a]

	Power	Agreeable Relations
Neighborhood Characteristics		
Stability of residents	.01	-.03
Homogeneity of residents	.04	-.05
Low-rise housing	-.08	-.07
Private housing	-.36*	-.06
Work unit compound	-.15	.06
Deterence Efforts		
Service infrastructure	.16	-.24
Household control	.26*	-.23
Radical year	.08	.14
Resident head's power	--	-.20
City Characteristics		
Administrative level	.18	-.06
Number of neighborhoods	(46)	(23)

Source: Sample of neighborhoods.

[a]In column two, these are partial correlations with informant optimism controlled.
*p $\leq$ .05

register at the ward police station was checked for negative class label and past political problems or if local neighborhood leaders turned against you. There was no way that neighborhood residents could control this aspect of their environment. Instead, the government had been able to thoroughly bureaucratize the neighborhood apparatus, coopting this potential informal resistance group for its own purposes. Even when the neighborhood was essentially neutral, or when neighborhood leaders were helpful individuals, neighborhoods did not represent one's interests or play a buffer role in the larger political arena. Neighborhoods were at best transparent entities between the individual and the state above, and it is perhaps not too surprising as a result that neighborhood structures seemed to generate little enthusiasm, interest, or loyalty among the people in our interviews.

Access to Information

Any attempt by urban residents to control their environment was also inhibited by their very limited access to information on policies and events that shaped their daily lives. This drought of information in the official news media did not occur immediately with the onset of the new socialist regime. The early and particularly the mid-1950s were times of relative openness. But after the antirightist campaign and then the Great Leap Forward of 1958, many publications were closed or highly restricted in the kinds of information that they could publish. The Cultural Revolution completed the process of restricting news by closing all but a few non-Party newspapers and forcing Party newspapers to hew to a narrow political line.[25] The media endlessly repeated upbeat news on the successes of model farms, factories, and schools with seldom a word on problems that were not being overcome. The flow of books, magazines, and other publications also slowed to a small trickle.

Only a few channels remained open. High level officials were exempt, with access to special translations of foreign press materials and many other special publications as well. By 1971, citizens down to the levels of high school teachers and shop foremen could subscribe to the *Reference News*. A four-page daily tabloid that translates Reuters, Agence France Presse, United Press International, and other foreign wire services without comment, this source provided a ready and not all that biased window on the outside world. For most people and most news, however, the ordinary urban resident had to depend on other sources.

25. Even "non-Party" newspapers fall under the control and censorship of the Party's propaganda department, but their mandate has been to publish a broader range of articles than appears in official Party organs such as *People's Daily*.

Much of the news about domestic events came through oral channels. Typically new policies and news about major political events were disseminated through public meetings starting first at the top of the bureaucracy and then sifting through special report meetings (*quanda huiyi*) down to the level of the neighborhood and work group. This type of flow might be strictly limited to certain levels in the bureaucracy, and much information so disseminated was never published or appeared only much later in the printed media. Savvy officials who had access to these higher level meetings often paid little attention to newspapers, even the *People's Daily*. Even before the Cultural Revolution, a former provincial cadre reported,

> On getting the *People's Daily* for the day, I would first turn to see if there was an editorial, usually on the second page. This would tell me whether there was any impending shift in the political wind. Only when I had finished the editorial would I turn to glance briefly over the headlines on page one to confirm for myself that the policies which I had heard announced earlier in verbal report meetings were in fact being implemented.[26]

Even for ordinary citizens, all startling news tended to come first by word of mouth. For example, this is how people first learned about Lin Biao's fall in 1971. According to one informant from the city of Kunming in Southwest China,

> I first heard about the Lin Biao affair through leaks in the report meeting process some fifteen to twenty days after the event occurred. . . . Then a short time later, I heard about it through formal documents sent down through official channels. Then, maybe another half month later, I read about it in the newspaper. Only after the complete report meeting process, starting at the top of the bureaucracy and then gradually moving down and across the whole country, are startling events announced on the radio. That way people don't feel shocked or get the sense that things are out of order (*shiqing da luan*).[27]

Richard Nixon's first visit in 1972 was announced in a similar manner. Even while the foreign press marveled at the absence of any news of the impending visit in the Chinese press, the average citizen was well aware of the upcoming visit through the oral report meeting process.

26. Interview LY1. Being unsigned, the editorial is often translated as "commentary." Those who have read Solzhenitsyn's *Cancer Ward* will recognize this way of approaching the Party press as a common one in socialist societies.

27. KUD1:4.

The result of this process was that news was often stale before it reached the papers. Our informant from Kunming commented on the difference between news in Hong Kong and back in China,

> Here news is news—it is fresh and up to date. What happens in Tokyo today we will hear about here [in Hong Kong] today. But there the news is much staler, less interesting. It can be a long time after an event before you hear about it. The newspaper, for example, prints only those articles that were read on yesterday's evening news. And the evening news often reports events after they have been disseminated through oral channels.[28]

The news was also less interesting because it had few of the human interest stories that are the staple of the Western media. In the 1970s, the *People's Daily,* with ten million copies every day, was one of the few sources available. Even as late as 13 February 1981, when things had loosened up considerably, the contents made for pretty dry reading. On that day, the top middle insert just to the right of the paper title did stoop to such mundane lows as giving the day's weather around Peking. But the top right corner, once reserved for Mao's quotes, gave the new State Council regulations for savings banks. The same theme was repeated in an article in the bottom left corner and at the top of the second page. The first page also had articles on a number of official visiting delegations, including one by the French Socialist Party, articles on conserving gasoline, the work of the Youth League, and dredging the Yangtze River. Later pages continued with articles criticizing kickbacks, praising a model female ward Party secretary, describing how a youth was saved from a life of crime, praising an older worker for saving a second grader from drowning, and noting how Tientsin City's struggle against crime had diverted 81 percent of all youthful offenders from further criminal activity. Half of the center four pages were for foreign news and half for lengthy stories of exploits during the pre-1949 revolution and a few short literary essays. Advertisements for industrial machinery as well as the tables of contents of newly published journals such as *China's Youth,* features restored only in recent years, occupied less than a full page in this center section.

In the 1970s, then, Chinese official news was characterized by a virtual absence of human interest stories, by the stale character of news in the printed and electronic media, by stratified news dissemination with those at the top of the state bureaucracy getting far more news than those down below, and, of course, by a strict political straitjacket on materials for the

28. KUDI:3.

ordinary citizen. There were several responses to these characteristics.[29] One was to turn to private channels, including to rumor mills that began in high places. Information from report meetings that were supposed to be restricted to bureaucrats above a certain administrative level were leaked in what were sometimes called "small broadcasts" (*xiao guangbo*). Or there was the more general form of rumor frequently referred to as the "alley news" (*xiaodao xiaoxi*), which could contain more than one type of information. In Peking, where the alley news was rampant,

> It is of two types. One type is about major central events. The Lin Biao affair provides one example. His affair seems to have started at the central level on September 15, but we heard about it first not through report meetings but rather through the alley news starting September 21. At first we dared not comment on the news, but then in the next few days since there was so much of it we began to comment openly on it in study groups. For us, report meetings on the affair did not begin until October 1, National Day. According to the alley news, when General Chen Yi was in his hospital bed and was taken the news of Lin Biao's fall, his first comment was "Bring me some mao-tai, I want to drink to this!" This sort of alley news is always reliable.
>
> The second kind has to do with events of lesser importance, like what free market prices are today, where there has been a crime, and so on. This news too is usually reliable, but not always.[30]

The first type was particularly rampant in Peking in the early 1970s when factional fights were common. The alley news spread the information that the anti-Confucius campaign, which many Westerners took initially at face value, was really an attack by radicals against Premier Zhou Enlai. Confucius was just a historical allegory for Zhou.

Because of the hierarchical distribution of information, the sons and daughters of higher officials were particularly useful for this and all other kinds of information. Thus a factory worker from Peking reports, "Normally we didn't want to have anything to do with the sons and daughters of cadres . . . But they were such valuable sources of information that we sometimes catered to them anyway."[31] This kind of linkage has also

---

29. There are many similarities between the Chinese information system and that of the parent Soviet system, including highly stratified access to both oral and printed information and an emphasis on matters of state instead of stories of human interest. The responses by the public to this situation are also similar. See Hedrick Smith, *The Russians* (New York: Quadrangle, 1976), chap. 14.

30. PED3:9.

31. PKD1:31.

been reported in the official media. For example, in 1980 Peking Radio suggested that,

> because of age and infirmity, certain leading cadres spend much time at home reading documents and chatting about their work. And some comrades forget the Party regulations on guarding secrets because they are in their own homes and arbitrarily allow family members and children to come into contact with important Party and state secrets.
>
> As soon as Party and state secrets are conveyed to the sons and daughters of cadres, they are very prone to spread around in society. The associations and contacts of these people are much more complex and extensive than those of their parents. They have fellow students, colleagues and friends in all sectors and trades. Of course, the great majority of cadres' children pay attention to avoiding the spread of inner-Party secrets. However, some of them have feelings of blind superiority, capitalize on their privileged position, neglect the Party's security discipline, and talk everywhere about inner-Party secrets which other people did not know about to demonstrate that they are different from the crowd.[32]

Outside Peking, more mundane affairs often become the main content of the alley news. Items that fill the typical American newspaper spread via the Chinese alley news instead. In the capital of Henan Province in Central China, "the alley news includes some high politics but more cases of theft and rapes as well as which types of schools are giving what kinds of exams and other kinds of useful information not found in newspapers." In a Central China county seat it included, "stories about an explosion in Peking's main shopping street, a fire in Shanghai's grain warehouse, and a train collision in Henan Province." In Shanghai, it included stories about fires, robberies, and, a particular favorite it seems, from the number of times they were repeated to us, hatchet murders—with full details as to where various parts of the bodies were finally located. In Canton, the alley news included "details of cadres' personal lives (such as Mao Zedong's three wives, Lui Shaoqi's five wives, Jiang Qing's four husbands) or news about how to escape to Hong Kong (such as which communes had organized antiescape patrols)."[33]

In some places there was also an oral tradition of short stories that made sly jest of current living conditions in cities. One would hear these stories one month and then again a couple of months later when they had become even more embellished.

32. Peking Radio, 23 April 1980, in *FBIS*, 7 May 1980, p. L23.
33. In succession, from interviews ChD1:49; AnH1:12; KSM21:6.

Besides turning to informal gossip, either highbrow from the cadres above or lowbrow from the masses below, people could also turn to foreign shortwave radio broadcasts. This was technically illegal during the Cultural Revolution decade and if detected could earn one criticism from neighborhood officials and workmates. Also, certain foreign "freedom stations" were jammed in the major cities. However, many radios had a shortwave band and some people were sufficiently brave to tune in. Among the brave, the BBC's news was particularly prized for its comprehensiveness and objectivity. In the South, a Christian radio station out of the Philippines also got high marks and the Voice of America came in a poor third. However, Voice of America's English lessons were appreciated, and even before the fall of the radicals, some English students and teachers became regular listeners—even subscribing to the booklet which accompanied the lessons.

These informal and foreign sources of information proved poor substitutes for reliable public sources of news. Most residents simply remained in the dark about what was really going on in their country. Many people knew that they had to discount glowing claims in the official media, but few knew how much to discount. There was little that the average citizen could do except to remain passive in the absence of reliable information.

Current Developments

The result of all these developments was that Chinese urban residents remained victims rather than masters of their own fate. They had little reliable information on which to base potential political action and no intermediary communities to help organize their action even if they had wanted to act. The number of people under political fire continued to mushroom and more and more citizens began to fear that they might be next in line. Those who had already been attacked held out little hope of ever being restored to their rightful place in society. China became an extreme example of the sorts of problems William Kornhauser and Alvin Gouldner suggest can occur when there are no intermediate buffers between the individual and political rulers, and of the sorts of problems Crane Brinton and Lyford Edwards suggest can occur during a reign of virtue when extreme revolutionary ideals are forced upon everyone in all aspects of life.

Since the rise of the new reformist elite in 1976, alleviation of many of these problems has been of great concern. Millions of people have been restored to their former positions and many new measures to prevent future purges have been introduced. The immediate effects have been to move China from an extreme radicalism toward more simple authoritarianism that rests more lightly on the everyday lives of ordinary citizens. Whether these reforms will progress even further to allow levels of democracy and guarantees of individual political rights rare in most socialist states is a matter of current debate.

In the legal sphere, a new criminal and other sorts of codes have been introduced so as to give the individual citizen more of a basis for legal redress. More lawyers are being trained, and the courts are ostensibly being given more autonomy. It has been declared that large-scale political campaigns are at an end, and class labels are to be ignored in judging a person's guilt or innocence. These are all rudimentary changes so far, and whether even these can be fully institutionalized free of arbitrary Party intervention remains to be seen. Nevertheless, the current situation is a sharp break with the immediate past.[34]

At the level of community control, there has been an attempt to restore a somewhat more direct voice in government for ordinary citizens. Most neighborhood officers continue to be appointed from above, but residents' committee elections are supposed to be restored. And at the district (qu) level, above the ward and residents' committee officers that we have discussed so far, people's congress representatives are elected directly through mass secret balloting as was done in the 1950s. As was not done earlier, the public helps in preparing a list of nominees (still requiring approval from higher level officials) that is longer than the number of seats to be filled.[35] And, most impressive of all, in a few elections, nominees have been able to run on platforms that supported the concerns of special interest groups. For example, in one Peking district election, in late 1979, Yu Yiwen, 61, a kindergarten teacher for 40 years and just elected to the district people's congress, "said that she would urge the government to run more kindergartens and nurseries and train more staff for these establishments to meet the growing needs of the district."[36] Imam Chen Guangyuan of the Dongsi Mosque "said he would ask the government to set up more public baths for Muslims in the district since Muslims have the habit of taking a bath before religious services." He, along with 18 other Muslim deputies, represented the 16,000 people of Hui nationality in a total congress of 350 representatives. With such large congresses, consisting of part-time representatives, it is unlikely that there could be

34. See Shao-chuan Leng, "Criminal Justice in Post-Mao China," *China Quarterly* 87 (1981): 440–69.

35. On earlier practices, see James R. Townsend, *Political Participation in Communist China* (Berkeley: University of California Press, 1968), pp. 115–37. On recent practice in the rural unit analogous to the urban district, see Brantly Womack, "The 1980 County-Level Elections in China," *Asian Survey* 22 (1982): 261–77.

36. *Xinhua* (Peking), 21 November 1979, in *FBIS*, 23 November 1979, p. R1.

much public supervision of the day-to-day work of formally appointed neighborhood officers. But the steps taken so far suggest the potential for much more far-reaching reforms in the future, with popular representatives being able to stand up for the interests of their constituents.

Similar trends are occurring in work units, with some groups electing workers' councils and other representative bodies to see to their interests. Widespread reform in this area, in which Party organs step back to allow full representation of worker interests, would have an even more profound effect than similar reforms in neighborhoods. For it is in work units that adults spend most of their waking hours, and through work units that most adults engage in political study, get permission to marry and divorce, get purchase certificates for things such as bicycles and better brands of watches, get group sponsored trips and other forms of recreation, get hardship allowances, and often housing as well. With employee input on decisions regarding the distribution of these goods and services as well as pay and promotion possibilities, the nature of city life might change considerably, or so one suspects. Whether such far-reaching reforms can be fully implemented, however, remains to be seen.

Important changes have also taken place in the flow of information. Non-Party newspapers such as the *Peking Evening News* and Canton's *Yangcheng Evening News* have resumed publication. They are more open in their reporting, and more likely to print human interest stories. Many old magazines and journals have also resumed publication, and hundreds of new ones have sprung up over the last few years. The publication of books has increased tremendously compared with previous years.

Even within Party newspapers, the content is much freer than in years past. An author will publish an interpretation of the meaning of socialist democracy one week only to have another author publish a rebuttal a week later. The Letters to the Editor column has also become quite important in both Party and non-Party newspapers. Ranging from consumer problems with a particular brand of radio that doesn't work to complaints about bureaucratic corruption, the Letters to the Editor staff goes out to investigate complaints and seek redress, thereby serving a major ombudsmen service in Chinese society. The flow of letters is tremendous, with *People's Daily* alone receiving 2,000 letters a day in 1980 and the *Peking Evening News* receiving 300 letters a day at the same time. Other newspapers and magazines have had a similar flow.[37]

37. *Beijing Review*, no. 1 (1980): 6; *Xinhua* (Peking), 29 April 1980, in *FBIS,* 30 April 1980, p. R1. For a convenient collection see Hugh Thomas, *Comrade Editor: Letters to the People's Daily* (Hong Kong: Joint Publishing Co., 1980). The letters to the editor tradition is not special to China but appears in other socialist states as well, allowing, some argue,

The flow of foreign news increased as well. After 1977 it became legal to listen to foreign broadcasts. The occasional jamming of foreign stations that had occurred in some cities ceased, and the BBC, the Voice of America, Radio Japan and other stations began to provide a regular diet of news about events both within and outside China to those who cared to listen. In domestic sources as well, the flow of news about foreign events began to increase. With new satellite reception stations, American television film clips became a regular staple on China's evening news broadcasts, and televisions became much more widely available than before. And, in the eyes of some emigrés, the *Reference News* began to print material more critical of China.

All these changes have produced dramatic consequences. Foreign visitors frequently comment on the much greater openness among the Chinese people today than a decade ago. Visitors who have been both to the Soviet Union and China sometimes comment favorably on how much more open things seem in China than in the Soviet Union, particularly when it comes to criticism of their own society.

These sharp changes suggest that many of the problems of earlier years had little to do with the bureaucracy per se. Contrary to many of the assertions by Hayek and Friedman, the Eastern European reformers, and Maoist radicals, it was not a large bureaucracy out to protect its privileges that caused so many difficulties for the ordinary citizen. Indeed, during the Cultural Revolution years the bureaucrats did not spur the attacks on the ordinary citizenry but were themselves the victims of attacks. The Cultural Revolution was the attempt by the radicals to rid the country of bureaucratism and the pursuit of special privilege. Unfortunately, the cure was worse than the disease. Once the radicals took over without any intervening rules, regulations, or other institutions to impede their effort at social and psychological transformation, the numbers of people who became victims of political control rose sharply. The experience of these years would seem to be more properly interpreted as a classical reign of virtue, as outlined by Edwards and Brinton, rather than as the result of a new class of bureaucrats out to protect their power and privilege, as outlined by Hayek and others.

The characterization of the following years as a "thermidor" period in which many moderates return to power and in which most of the people no longer can stomach the revolutionary fervor would also seem to apply.

---

the populace to let off steam against lower level officials rather than against the system as a whole. For comparison, the Soviet Union's *Tass* was getting 40,000 letters a month in the early 1970s, which is not all that much less than *People's Daily*. See Smith, *The Russians*, p. 495.

All this suggests that the government will rest more lightly on the people in the years to come.

Nevertheless, much of the political system that once oppressed so many people is still in place. The efforts to institutionalize reform are still in flux, and some recent developments may well make urban residents concerned about how much security and freedom from control they will have in future years. Despite an ostensible commitment to legal procedures, the trial of the Gang of Four took on many characteristics of the traditional purge. And the 1982 reform and paring down of the bureaucracy appeared to fall disproportionately on those who disagreed with present policies. Much of the apparatus of dossiers in work units remains in place and could be used by any subsequent regime that wanted to eliminate people who stood in the way of its program. The cadre of lawyers and the body of law which might protect individuals against such a turn of events remain small and weak.

At the local level, there continue to be few buffers between the individual and the central state apparatus. The Party remains the dominant organization in the work units and neighborhoods, and the general public has gained electoral control over only minor people's congress positions and over very few direct administrative posts. Without greater control over their neighborhoods and work units, people in China remain potentially subject to the whim of local officials and immediate supervisors. This subjection alone can be a powerful constraint on individual speech and action, depriving urbanites of a sense of control over their lives.[38]

Despite the changes described above, the flow of information also continued to be restricted in certain ways. One is that only approved newspapers, magazines, and books are permitted. For a time in 1978–79, it appeared that more would be allowed. Democracy walls and independent tabloids blossomed in major cities such as Peking and Shanghai, and budding reformers had a new outlet for their views on how to build a new China. But by the end of 1979, the walls were scratched clean, most of the journals shut down, and several of their editors arrested and imprisoned. Much of the emphasis in 1980 and 1981 was on making sure that no unauthorized publications slipped out, with punishment for officials and workers who lent mimeograph and other machines for the publishing of unauthorized works.

38. Perhaps exaggerating a bit, Fox Butterfield emphasizes how these local units continue to hem one in on every side. See *China: Alive in the Bitter Sea* (New York: Times Books, 1982), chap. 15. Paul Hollander suggests that in all Marxist socialist states we are likely not to appreciate the full extent of control because we pay insufficient attention to the informal means of control in work places and elsewhere ("Research on Marxist Societies," *Annual Review of Sociology* 8 [1982], p. 329).

A second issue is whether the official media will remain open to op-posing views. There was active debate over this issue in the early 1980s. For example, in its criticism of the film, *Bitter Love,* the *Liberation Army Daily* argued that the author, Bai Hua, had gone too far in criticizing Mao Zedong and in propounding the bourgeois value of humanitarianism. Other newspapers provided a mild rebuttal, but in the end an uneasy compromise was reached which left the issue of future freedom to publish and perform still in doubt.

A third potential problem is that even while the total flow of information is much greater than in the past, access is still highly stratified. An elab-orate system of reference materials prohibited to the ordinary reader remains in place, and as before, oral channels often remain rich sources of information about what is occurring in central politics.

All this suggests that the interpretations of political control as a problem of bureaucratic intervention cannot be completely dismissed. In the earlier totalitarian phase there was a negative interaction between bureaucratic control and the reign of virtue. The consequences of a reign of virtue are particularly severe when the population's overwhelming dependence upon bureaucratically controlled resources leaves them with no way to resist the demands of such a reign or prevent a new one from arising in the future. And in the current authoritarian phase there are many tendencies that are analogous to the experience of the Soviet Union since the 1950s. Much as in China, the Soviet Union went through a heady liberalization in the two years following Khrushchev's initial attacks on Stalin in 1956. But this was followed by a reimposition of authoritarian limits that persist to the present. The later authoritarian period clearly allowed greater free-dom of action than the earlier totalitarian period, but the state bureaucracy remained reluctant to relinquish control of many aspects of social and intellectual life. There was a pressure for some continued liberalization, as Barrington Moore argues, because of the need to secure the cooperation of intellectuals for the process of economic modernization—a process that is occurring in China as well.[39] But the one-party state was still legitimated by a Marxist ideology, and challenges to this ideology were seen as chal-lenges to the state.[40] The continuing attempt to provide equality and se-curity for the average urban resident still required a large bureaucracy to dispense the myriad services that no longer flowed through the market.

39. *Terror and Progress: USSR* (Cambridge: Harvard University Press, 1954).

40. Hollander, "Research on Marxist Societies," pp. 323–27. Our use of the term au-thoritarian here is meant to emphasize the contrast with the Cultural Revolution decade. We can't deny that in some respects governmental controls over society in China, as in other socialist societies, remain much more pervasive than in military dictatorships and other authoritarian regimes elsewhere in the world.

And this pervasive bureaucracy, with control over so much that is essential to everyday life, could effectively block challenges to its authority.

Some Chinese leaders are trying to break free of these problems. The reform efforts include the new formulation that many of society's problems can be solved not by a single correct ideology found in Marxist texts, but rather by free and open scientific inquiry that concentrates on the problems of today. Other efforts included an attempt to simplify and reduce the size of the bureaucracy, plus all the other reforms we have listed above. However, the continuing need for a large bureaucracy to supply social services and run the economy and the experience of the Soviet Union suggest that definite limits on the freedom of individual action will still remain, and that feelings of powerlessness and alienation will still be generated.

10 Religion and Social Values

In his 1959 discussion, Melvin Seeman suggests that after "powerlessness," the second major interpretation of the term alienation is "meaninglessness."[1] The question of meaninglessness, or more precisely, the conflict between different sources of meaning and its presence or absence, is the topic of this chapter. As with powerlessness, the promise of socialism has been to provide a new basis for meaningful activity in everyday life. With a new-found security and sense of purpose, people would no longer turn to religion as an "opiate," but would turn to service of the whole people as a goal in itself. Indeed, in many socialist states, including China, service to the state, the revolution, and the revolutionary leader has often taken on a religious quality all its own. Our question, then, is the degree to which people have turned away from old religions and rituals, and in turn, embraced new socialist forms of belief to provide meaning and structure in their lives.

In China, the tension between old and new belief systems has frequently been intense. This tension has had three major sources. First, the old belief system emphasized how a horde of other-worldly beings impinged on one's daily life. The gods, ghosts, and departed ancestors that surrounded one might be cajoled or warded off by proper worship and sacrifice. The intent of the other world and the proper means of worship and sacrifice could be intuited by a variety of devices, including divining blocks at temples that one used by oneself and trances that religious shamans used. Other divining devices, such as palm and facial readings or calculations based on date of birth, might give some premonition of the future and thus make one better prepared to meet fate. This partially manipu-

1. "On the Meaning of Alienation," *American Sociological Review* 24 (1959): 783–91. Though Chinese Marxists are curiously silent about alienation, we still feel it is an appropriate construct for organizing our discussion in this part.

lative, partially fatalistic way of contending with life characterized much of Chinese popular religion.[2]

To this way of dealing with uncertainties in life, the new socialist government posed a rationalistic alternative. Uncertainties were knowable and usually created by ignorance and the oppression of exploiting classes. Once oppression was removed and the population provided with economic and social security as well as given proper education, much of the old feudal superstitions about gods, ghosts, ancestors and the need for divination would pass away.[3]

Second, traditional religious beliefs were inconsistent with the new socialist order because they tended to celebrate narrow community and family interests rather than the interests of the larger society. Typically, every neighborhood, every occupational guild, and just about any other significant social group had its own special god. These gods looked after the well-being of the group. The carpenters had a god of carpentry, fishermen had a god that looked after boats, and so forth. Neighborhoods often had their own territorial god as well. Thus, neighborhoods, guilds, and other social groups came to have a religious as well as a utilitarian significance in traditional Chinese cities.[4]

This mix of religious and utilitarian significance was also true of families, and it was perhaps the religious significance of the family that was the core of traditional Chinese society. Sons were obligated to support their parents not just while they were alive but also in the afterlife, with periodic offerings of imitation bullion, incense, and food. This obligation stopped not with a single generation but extended to grandparents, to great-grandparents, and potentially to even earlier generations. And this obligation stretched into the future with the duty to provide sons, grandsons, and great-grandsons who would continue to provide proper ancestor worship and maintain, if not expand, the family fortune and good name. Without this worship the ancestors would languish in the other world, perhaps becoming hungry ghosts who wandered about lonely and disturbed the

2. For summary statements of the role of religion in Chinese cities, see John Shryock, *The Temples of Anking and Their Cults* (Paris: Lib. Geunther, 1931); and C. K. Yang, *Religion in Chinese Society* (Berkeley: University of California Press, 1961).

3. For convenient summaries of post-1949 official religious policy, see Donald E. MacInnis, *Religious Policy and Practice in Communist China: A Documentary History* (New York: Macmillan, 1972); and Holmes Welch, *Buddhism under Mao* (Cambridge: Harvard University Press, 1972). For a recent restatement of long-standing policies toward religion, see Xiao Wen, "Policy on Religion," *Beijing Review*, no. 51 (1979): 14–22.

4. John Stewart Burgess, *The Guilds of Peking* (New York: Columbia University Press, 1928), chap. 11; and Kristofer M. Schipper, "Neighborhood Cult Associations in Traditional Tainan," in *The City in Late Imperial China*, G. William Skinner, ed. (Stanford University Press, 1977); and chapter 2 of this volume.

living. But with proper worship, the ancestors would look benevolently on one's family and improve one's fate. These sorts of beliefs helped inspire hard work among filial sons who had several generations of family tradition past, present and future to live up to.[5]

Some of these loyalties had already begun to give way in the first half of this century as labor unions began to replace guilds, as rapid rates of migration weakened old neighborhood structures, and as intellectual currents from the West stressing rationality and science began to weaken the hold of religion, particularly among intellectuals.[6] But many loyalties to occupation group, neighborhood, and family still remained, particularly in medium and small cities less exposed to Western influence. These types of loyalties were too narrow for a government that wanted to emphasize a new loyalty to the nation and the socialist revolution. To help bring about a shift in loyalties, a whole series of new symbols, holidays, rituals, and sacred texts were created. These ranged from a new square at Tiananmen in Peking for periodic national parades and mass demonstrations, to new national holidays, to the very persona of Mao Zedong and his writings. A new kind of civil religion was in the making and, if successful, would supplant the narrower loyalties of the old religion.

Finally, the old religions and their rituals were opposed because they were seen as wasteful of precious financial and human resources that had to be mobilized for the new campaign of national growth. The traditional family and community rituals could require massive expenditures of money. A properly filial son would use many years' savings and would borrow many years' future earnings to provide his father and mother a proper funeral with an expensive wooden casket, priests for a proper ceremony, geomancers to pick an auspicious grave site, jugglers to entertain guests, cooks for a proper postfuneral feast, and many other expenses. In the eyes of the new regime, this money and the time spent in funeral preparations and mourning might be better turned to the building of a strong nation. The considerable wood used for elaborate caskets (often the better part of a large tree) as well as the precious agricultural land sometimes used for grave sites could also be better used. Traditional religious festivals scattered throughout the year were also seen as wasteful, with large sums of money spent on clothes and gifts. Many of the traditional ritual activities had to be discouraged or to be drastically secularized and simplified so as to not compete with the new values of national loyalty and national growth.

5. See Maurice Freedman, *Chinese Lineage and Society* (London: Athlone, 1966); and Emily Ahern, *The Cult of the Dead* (Stanford: Stanford University Press, 1973).
6. See Yang, *Religion in Chinese Society*, chap. 13.

In this competition between old and new values several different forces were at play. In part, the new regime promised, much as in other socialist regimes, that the increase in security, equality, and the other improved conditions of social life that we have described in earlier chapters would make religion unnecessary. Religion would no longer be needed to explain away intolerable conditions brought on by exploitation, and in time it would wither away. But that withering would not be an entirely spontaneous process, for China, to a greater degree than any of the European socialist states, created small study groups and other structures for re-socializing the population in the values of the new regime. With these newly internalized values emphasizing service to the whole people and the socialist revolution, people would turn from the narrower "superstitions" of the past. And, finally, as in other socialist societies, the state was prepared to intervene with administrative measures against old religious organizations that were seen as a threat to the new regime.

Our task is to assess the degree of conflict between the old and new value systems, to assess the degree to which change in these systems was brought about by increased rationality, security, conversion, and force, and finally to discuss the probable trends in these values and religious practices in the future.

Public Religion

In the European socialist states, the fate of organized religion has varied tremendously. In the Soviet Union, where the Russian Orthodox church opposed the new regime, the church was severely repressed and today remains rather weak. In Poland, where the Roman Catholic church was highly organized prior to the socialist takeover and where that takeover was not opposed by the church, the church remains a powerful body that has many believers and must be reckoned with in political affairs. Thus, the fate of religion depends heavily on the presocialist position of organized religion and on the degree of overt political conflict between organized religion and the state. The degree of earlier organization and later conflict has also shaped the fate of religion in China.

Despite the pervasive presence of gods, ghosts, and ancestors in all aspects of life, organized religion in traditional China was quite weak. This was so partly because the attempts to control religion began, not with the new socialist state, but much earlier. In earlier centuries, the Chinese imperial government made clear distinctions between established, popular, and family ancestral cults. They promoted the ancestral cult because of its harmony with the dominant Confucian values of the state. They tolerated popular religion because it gave the masses solace.

But except for a rarified official cult of Confucius and a flirtation with Buddhism in earlier centuries, they remained wary of established religion that might threaten imperial domination. Established religions as well as popular cults were carefully watched for signs of any growing hierarchies or mass movements that might threaten the state. Strict limits were placed on the number of Buddhist and Taoist priests that could be trained and on their organization. As a result, though heterodox cults sometimes fueled local rebellions, established religious bodies were never very powerful. There was no equivalent of the Catholic hierarchy centered on Rome that could challenge the authority of the imperial state. By and large, individual temples had no priest of their own nor any established congregation committed to a single religious orthodoxy. Believers tended to shift from one god and temple to another as the reputation of gods waxed and waned or as they had need for special appeals concerning drought, infertility, disease, a son's impending exam, and so forth.

Imported religions, such as Buddhism, tended to meld into the larger Chinese belief system that accepted many different gods serving different specific needs. Those committed to more exclusive belief systems remained but a small minority throughout China. Except in Tibet, orthodox Buddhists remained small in number. Chinese Muslims, including many ethnic minorities of the Northwest as well as small pockets of believers in major cities, constituted less than ten million of the total population in 1949. Christianity, which arrived in force only in the last century, had less than four million converts by 1949.[7] Organized religion, then, was in a very weak position vis-à-vis the central government at the beginning of socialist rule and was ill prepared to press its interests.

Nevertheless, in the initial years, there were some allowances for these religions, with the new constitution guaranteeing freedom of belief for orthodox Buddhism, Islam, and Christianity. The interests of some Buddhist and Muslim ethnic minorities, as well as the interests of some Westernized intellectuals who had turned to Christianity, were thereby protected. But while accepting orthodox beliefs, the government and the new constitution also guaranteed the freedom to proselytize against religion and both were unalterably opposed to "superstition"—a broad term that included fortune-telling, seances, geomancy, shamanism, and other unorthodox ways of divining the purposes of the other world or curing disease and mending ill fortune. Hordes of practitioners of these various occult practices were forced to abandon their professions.

7. One source reports that in 1980 Muslims totaled 10 million, but in 1949 Catholics totaled 3 million and Protestants 700,000. See *Zhongguo Baike Nianjian, 1980* (Chinese encyclopedia yearbook, 1980) (Peking: Chinese Encyclopedia Press, 1980), p. 41.

Community and other temples were also suspect on several grounds. Many had divining blocks and slips of paper and bamboo for predicting fortunes and prescribing cures for illness and misfortune, which suggested that they did little but promote superstition. Many had management committees composed of former capitalists, merchants, and other local notables who were suspect under the new regime. And many simply lost their financial base when rental property that endowed the activities of temples was taken taken over in the 1950s. By the 1960s many of the temples had already been converted into warehouses, factories, government offices, schools, and multifamily residences.

Christian churches soon ran into problems as well. With the outbreak of the Korean War in 1950, the foreign ties of Christianity came into more obvious conflict with the new values of national loyalty. The demand that Catholics, who constituted perhaps three-fourths of all Christians, renounce their loyalty to Rome in favor of loyalty to Peking caused bitter dissension in the Church. Protestant churches had similar problems as they tried to become sinicized and to renounce the past history that made them appear to be the religious arm of economic and political imperialism. Priests and ministers were accused of being foreign spies or counter-revolutionaries, and many were marched off to prison. Several of the people we interviewed recalled local priests or ministers subject to these kinds of charges in the 1950s and 1960s. Other difficulties, including the loss of income-earning property, the closing of seminaries, restrictions on public preaching, and discrimination against church members, made the life of Christians increasingly difficult. The opposition by dissident groups who wanted to maintain their ties to Rome and other foreign religious bodies only exacerbated the situation.

Despite these difficulties, a small number of urban churches, temples, and mosques remained open through the early 1960s. A few of the people we interviewed mention attending church service themselves or having had secondary school teachers who attended. A few temples of special architectural value such as the Zu Temple in Foshan outside Canton were maintained by the Historical Relics Commission and continued to draw a steady stream of petitioners burning incense and imitation paper money. In major cities with sizable Muslim minorities, such as Peking and Canton, mosques remained open and held regular services.

This was all brought to an end with the Cultural Revolution. Some new criticism came as early as the "Four Cleans" movement in 1964, but the full intensity of criticism came with the "Destroy Four Olds" movement of 1966 in which student rebels set out to destroy all remnants of "feudal" practices. This led to a ransacking not only of homes in search of old books, ancestral plaques, bibles, and other "feudal" paraphernalia, but also of temples and churches.[8] Accused of preaching superstition and counterrevolution and of being foreign spies, the remaining priests and ministers were sent to work in factories, farms, and labor camps. Virtually all the surviving churches and temples were converted to factories, warehouses, and other uses. Being a significant minority group, Muslims received some concessions, particularly, special beef coupons and other dietary allowances. A few show temples, mosques, and churches remained open for foreigners or were occasionally opened for visiting dignitaries from Muslim and Buddhist states. And there were regional pockets such as around Swatow in Guangdong where Christians continued to worship in small groups in each others' homes. But for both Muslims and Christians, the normal channels of worship in open mosques and churches were closed. Thus, by the 1970s, very little of the very rich religious life that had permeated Chinese urban communities in earlier centuries was left.

Some of this religious activity would have disappeared anyway. Much of it was so closely linked to specific needs and specific groups that it would have passed away as a matter of course. As we have seen, some was already disappearing by the first half of this century. Even when specific needs persisted, such as doing well in exams or coping with medically uncurable disease and sudden death, the absence of a consistent, overarching belief system for most people would have made old religious practices vulnerable to increasing education and an emphasis on rationality over blind faith. Nevertheless, in other Chinese settings such as Hong Kong and Taiwan that are even more economically developed and educated, many of the popular religions still persist, as do the more organized faiths. What is most striking, then, in an initial survey of events since 1949 is the heavy hand of administrative intervention in religious affairs. Religion did not just wither away because people had found new sources of security and new sets of beliefs to embrace. Rather it was coercion that caused the great decline of public religion. Traditionally, with so little organized power of their own, religious institutions could easily be disbanded, their professionals forced out of work, and believers harassed for their beliefs. Under these sorts of conditions, organized public religion faded more rapidly in China than in many other socialist states.

8. One colorful document from this period includes religion among 100 demands for changed behavior. Other demands include no manufacture of perfume or playing cards, no drinking or smoking, and no raising of crickets, fish, and other "bourgeois" pets. See Maoism School of Peking, "The One Hundred Items for Destroying the Old and Establishing the New," translated in *Chinese Society and Anthropology* (Spring-Summer 1970): 215–27 (original document dated September 1966).

Family Religion

Given the pre-1949 weaknesses, it is perhaps not too surprising that public religion should fade so rapidly. Family religion, centered on worship of the ancestors and selected domestic gods, is another matter. The worship of ancestors touches deeply on what it has meant to be Chinese, and virtually everyone has believed in this cult. To bring about a dramatic change in these religious practices and beliefs would mean a sharp change in how people think about the meaning of their lives. Derk Bodde notes, in commenting on the campaign to promote cremation and eliminate graves in 1949, "If this movement really gains headway, it will mark one of the sharpest breaks with tradition since the philosopher Mo Tzu vainly fulminated against the Confucianists for encouraging lavish funerals [in the fifth century B.C.]."[9] A thorough change would involve a break in how one worshipped both at the family grave and at the family altar inside the home.

Traditionally, the worship of ancestors at the grave began with an elaborate funeral surrounded by multiple rituals and continued with periodic offerings before the grave itself in subsequent years. At the time of death, which ideally occurred at home, the body had to be cleaned and placed in a coffin in the main hall next to the ancestral plaques. At the encoffining, led by professionals knowledgeable in the prayer rituals, the various kinsmen who gathered around had precise roles to perform. The coffin itself was constructed of special wood and heavily lacquered. Once an auspicious day and time for the burial was selected, the funeral party set out with the kinsmen walking along behind wearing hempen garments and other special grades of mourning dress, defined by closeness of kinship. Firecrackers were thrown to frighten away ghosts who might threaten the procession, and in some places women had to turn back half way to the grave lest they bring bad luck as well. After the burial, the family and guests might return home for an elaborate feast attended by jugglers and actors to provide entertainment. This feast and entertainment helped add to the great expense of funerals that was so necessary if a family was to maintain its reputation and proper social position. The funeral feast might be followed with feasts on selected dates while lengthy mourning rituals were still being observed. After the mourning period, the immediate family returned to the grave at least annually at the spring Qingming festival to clean the grave and offer cold food offerings as well as burn paper money and incense. Among the well-to-do in some parts of China, the bones might be dug up after time, cleaned, placed in a jar and surrounded by

9. Derk Bodde, *Peking Diary* (1950; reprint ed. New York: Fawcett, 1967), p. 196.

an elaborate tomb that was sited by geomantic principles so as to bring good fortune to the family.

Some practices, always difficult for the poor, became increasingly difficult for everyone in large cities after 1949. The new cremation policies that Derk Bodde had observed in their initial stages became quite general in later years. Graveyards in and around the major cities were closed. Except for those who lived in small towns with no crematorium or who had cooperative kinsmen in a village where the deceased might be buried, cremation was the only way out, and the government's goal of saving wood, land, and money was achieved. Not only could new ancestors not find resting places but also many old ancestors had to be disturbed. In an effort to expand urban construction sites and agricultural land from the 1950s on, many graveyards in and around cities were dug up. Several of the people we interviewed reported having to go to the cemetery to take away the bones of some ancestor. One informant reported how her grandmother "cursed the Communist Party . . . for interfering with the ancestors when grandfather was exhumed and his remains cremated in 1958."[10]

With the increase in cremation, funeral rituals were greatly simplified over those of the past. There were no ritual specialists to officiate. Most deaths in large cities began to occur in hospitals, despite the traditional preference for death at home. And with death away from home, there is no traditional service in the home. Rather, in a day or two, the family and friends gather for a brief funeral in the memorial room at the crematorium. The coffin and a wreath or two are rented. There is a simple service, with a little recorded music sometimes being played and family members saying a few words about the deceased. After everyone gathers about the body for a few minutes of silence, it is taken off to be cremated. Occasionally, the work unit of the deceased participates in the ceremony, particularly if the deceased was from a state work unit and if he or she was in a managerial or professional position. Then the service may be a bit more elaborate, with official representatives from the unit giving a short statement about the contributions of the deceased and trying to comfort the survivors.

After cremation, the ashes may be taken home on the same day or left for storage at the crematorium. The family may select a box for the ashes ranging in cost from about five to perhaps sixty or more yuan. If the box is left at the crematorium for a period sometimes limited to several years because of a shortage of space, the family then pays several yuan rent a year. Assuming that a more modest box is selected, the total cost of the

10. Interview KSM1:8.

funeral including cremation and memorial room will typically be within fifty yuan. With state work units picking up many of these expenses, costs to the family are further reduced.[11] When the unit does not assume these expenses and the family is poor, there are examples in our interviews of fellow workers simply passing the hat in order to help the family with the funeral. The financial burden of funerals is thus greatly reduced over what it was in the past, and over what it can be in the countryside even today.[12]

Other marks of the new simplicity include dress and feasting at the time of the funeral as well as subsequent mourning rituals. Instead of special hemp and other garments, family members typically wear only street clothes, frequently with a black patch or armband or occasionally with a white flower attached. A few families invite those who attended the memorial service back home for a meal, but the number invited is typically small and the fare simple. The elaborate entertainment that might have gone with this meal in the past is gone. Guests only occasionally bring small packets of money. And gifts from the deceased's family to those who attended the memorial service are restricted to a small towel and sometimes a piece of candy, signifying that one should think of sweet things.

The mourning period is abbreviated, with families at most observing the seven- and twenty-one-day memorials of the death. On these occasions a few close kin may be invited to participate in a meal including dishes that the deceased enjoyed, with the meal being offered before a picture of the deceased along with the occasional burning of incense—often insect repelling incense in the 1970s because ceremonial incense was unavailable on the state market.

Things are not quite so simple in small towns, where burial is still possible and often mandatory since there is no local crematorium. Along with burial, many more traditional practices persist. One example is the 1972 burial of a sixty-eight-year-old neighbor who died of tuberculosis in a Guangdong county town.

> He died at home. The body, still in bed, was placed in the main
> sitting room where it stayed for three days while all the kin gath-
> ered to pay their respect. On the burial day, the descendants of
> the old man wore a white cloth band around their heads. One of

11. Labor insurance regulations stipulate that the family of the deceased is to receive funeral fees equivalent to three months' salary if the death is work related and two months' salary otherwise. See Fujian Province, Revolutionary Committee Planning Commission, *Laodong Gongzi Wenjian Xuanbian* (Fujian, 1973), pp. 310, 315.

12. For comparative data on the countryside and earlier periods, see William L. Parish and Martin King Whyte, *Village and Family in Contemporary China* (Chicago: University of Chicago Press, 1978), chap. 13.

the sons, holding aloft a paper flag, and another son, carrying a basin, went to fetch water. When they arrived at the bank of the river, they cast in some coins and then fetched a basin of water to bring home. While waiting for the water, all the relatives stood in line, crying and singing funeral songs. When the water arrived, the person in charge of the funeral ceremony washed the body and dressed it in new clothes. The coffin was then brought in, carried by four people. The body was placed in the coffin. The family and relatives went to the front of the coffin to give their final respects. The coffin was then covered and nailed shut. They waited until what had been determined to be the auspicious hour, and then set out to bury the body. In the procession, people wept and sang funeral songs all the way to the grave.

As the mourners dispersed from the grave, they were given a white towel and two cents of lucky money. In the evening, a mourning party was held, with people showing a good appetite and drinking liquor.[13]

There is much in this account that is similar to funeral practices in earlier times and to practices in the countryside today. This type of funeral, with the casket alone costing as much as 100 yuan, is also considerably more expensive than those held in big cities. And in some places, traditional practices such as making women leave the funeral procession half the way to the grave and having men complete the final burial are still seen.

Nevertheless, people we met from small towns noted that during the 1970s funerals were not so elaborate as in the past. At the funeral, people did not wear elaborately differentiated mourning dress but simply more subdued clothing, often a white shirt or blouse with the black mourning patch. It was extremely rare that religious professionals helped with the ceremony, and the feast after the burial was typically only for close friends and kin. Mourning ceremonies on the seventh and successive seventh days after the burial were of minor importance or absent altogether. Thus, even while ceremonies in small towns remained more elaborate than those in big cities, they were considerably simplified.

The cremation and simple ceremonies in big cities have not been to everyone's liking, particularly not older people's. For example, the seventy-five-year-old mother of one of our informants didn't want to stay in the city for fear of dying there and being cremated. Each winter as her physical condition worsened with the weather, she would make a fuss about going back to her village to be buried. This very traditional desire for a proper burial in one's native place was finally realized in her case,

13. PYH1:24–25.

but not for many others.[14] In spite of these kinds of desires among older people reared in earlier times, among most people under age sixty the idea of cremation appears to have been accepted. A desire for perpetual worship at the grave site is dying out.

Traditionally, after burial, descendants would gather at the grave at the spring Qingming festival and in some locales at the autumn Chongyang festival as well. Now, with no holidays from work on either of these occasions, any worship at a grave or crematorium must be on the family member's one day off each week. In the 1970s, a family visiting the family grave continued to sweep the grave, burn whatever kind of incense or imitation paper money that could be found and provide simple food offerings. At crematoriums, the worship was more restrained, with the ash jar being taken down from its niche for dusting and a few flowers being presented in memorial. Thus, the frequency and ceremony of worship at the grave or crematorium was but a pale image of past forms. Elaborate funerals and worship at the grave have been in jeopardy in part because these practices depend so much on publicly controlled goods and facilities. The government has been able to exert control simply by cutting off the supply of wood for caskets, closing cemeteries, and providing the cheap alternative of crematoriums.

Worship of ancestors in the home has not been quite so vulnerable. Traditionally, worship before the family altar, a raised table in the main sitting room of the home, was more frequent than worship at the grave. The altar would contain one or more wooden plaques, each bearing the name of a deceased parent, grandparent, or more distant senior kinsman of the male line. And in recent decades there might also be a picture of the deceased on the wall behind the altar. The altar might also have the image of a favorite family god. A devout family would burn incense on a low table before the altar daily. Others would be certain to burn incense at the first and fifteenth day of each lunar month. Periodically, at major festivals and at the anniversary of the ancestor's birth and death, cooked food would be offered and imitation paper money or bullion burned, thereby taking care of the ancestor's needs in the afterlife.

Cremation in place of burial was not an absolute threat to this worship at home. Instead of leaving ashes at the crematorium or scattering them outside the city, a family could bring the ash box or jar home and place it on the family altar. The box or jar itself could thus become an object of worship. However, several other government and radical student activities had a more negative impact. As Derk Bodde noted in North China in 1949, the government was increasingly forcing factories that made

14. CHD1:58.

incense and paper money or bullion out of business. The Red Guards completed the process, and in the 1970s proper incense and paper money were very difficult to find. Insect repellent incense could be used but was a poor substitute. Worship was also inhibited in those areas where radical Red Guards had ransacked houses in search of feudal objects at the start of the Cultural Revolution. Ancestral plaques were one of the favorite targets of this search and many a bonfire was fueled by old plaques, leaving many houses stripped of their former worship objects. Afterwards people understood that worship in the home was not appropriate under the radical ethos of those times.

Some old people continued to worship even in the absence of proper plaques or ashes, putting up red slips of paper with the name of the ancestor or photographs instead. But this worship tended to be performed at infrequent intervals, and with the door closed to outsiders. The young remained largely uninterested. In one Canton neighborhood,

> A few Buddhists still have images of Guan-yin or other gods in their home. Some worship every morning with sanitary [insect repellant] incense, but most worship with incense just once or twice a month. In my home, it was only grandma. It is generally true that only middle-aged and older women worshipped.[15]

Similarly, in another Canton neighborhood,

> Older people sometimes worship. . . . They burn incense but not paper money. They put out food only at the lunar new year and on the first and fifteenth of the lunar month. . . . There are no ancestral plaques but there are occasional ancestral ashes and pictures of the deceased.[16]

But in a working class neighborhood of Canton,

> Generally, in our neighborhood, ancestral plaques were not destroyed in the Cultural Revolution. In our lane, even Party members have plaques. Because we had no capitalists in our lane to attract them, no students came to rip out ancestral plaques or other old things from houses. . . . True, being outside and highly visible, the lane's earth god disappeared forever in the Cultural Revolution. But after being put away for a time, images of other gods were soon brought out again. The most common is Guandi. . . . For some reason, my family had Qitian Dashen, the monkey in the novel *Journey to the West*. But these gods are not worshipped anymore. It is just the ancestors who are worshipped on

15. KSM21:8.
16. KSM28:3.

their birth and death anniversaries with food, wine, goods, paper ingots, incense, and candles. Yes, people still worship the stove god at lunar new years and also at new years some people put up a piece of paper signifying the god of heaven.[17]

Thus there was some variation even within a major city such as Canton, with educated higher status groups abandoning traditional practices faster than others.

In smaller places, practices remained more liberal. In a county seat on lunar new year's eve,

We were not allowed to worship gods. But every family still kept its altar in the main sitting room opposite the front door. A piece of red paper with the characters "remember our family" was pasted above the altar, and before starting the meal all the dishes were placed on the altar below this paper. This expressed remembrance of those who had passed away, allowing the deceased to partake of the meal before the rest of the family. Also before beginning to eat, they would place their palms together before their chests and bow towards the table. . . . Some families also set off firecrackers before the meal.[18]

But even in small towns, the youth often failed to participate in regular worship at home. According to an informant in a commune seat, "Some young couples in town simply never worship ancestors—rather at new year when there is a better meal we say that they worship their stomachs."[19]

Besides gods and ancestors, there was traditionally a third kind of otherworldly being that had to be dealt with in everyday life—ghosts.[20] Ghosts were not to be worshipped but to be placated and warded off. Offerings, often cold food placed by the back door, helped to satisfy the ghosts and kept them from bothering one's family. The ghost festival in the middle of the seventh lunar month was a particularly important time to put out food offerings in order that the ghosts not be hungry and troublesome. Sometimes ghosts required stronger medicine and divination to decide what would be a proper cure. Shamans and other kinds of spirit mediums might be used to discern what was troubling a ghost, and if it was found that the ghost was a young person who had died without marrying, then a wedding with paper dolls representing the deceased and partner might be arranged. All these practices seem to have disappeared in cities both

17. KSM24:6.
18. PYH1:21.
19. STC2:11.
20. See Arthur Wolf, "Gods, Ghosts, and Ancestors," in *Religion and Ritual in Chinese Society*, Arthur P. Wolf, ed. (Stanford: Stanford University Press, 1974).

large and small. There is no mention of offerings at the time of the old seventh-month ghost festival, spirit mediums no longer ply their trade, and there is no mention of people being pestered by ghosts. There are a few fortune-tellers in small towns and villages, but their functions have little to do with manipulating ghosts. The belief in ghosts, then, has lost much of its former importance.

Overall, then, family religion has experienced a distinct break with the past. In covert practice, that break is not quite so dramatic as it is with organized public religion. In smaller towns and in some working class neighborhoods among older people, worship at the family altar continues in an attenuated form. And in smaller places without cremation facilities, funerals and later worship at the grave retain some of their former flavor. But for the majority of people in major cities, and especially for youth, the break with three thousand years of tradition is dramatic. The most pervasive beliefs about what a person should live for seem to have been profoundly altered, and this in many ways makes the changes in family religion even more significant than the changes in organized public religion. Among the majority of urbanites in major cities, the meaning of life is no longer intimately tied to providing worship, sustenance, and glory to departed ancestors. One still lives very much for one's immediate living family, but many of the ties to ancestors and descendents, which would have been characteristic of most traditional families, seem no longer to hold for many urban residents.[21]

Again, this is not a change that would have occurred with increasing education and modernization of the labor force alone. Though weakened compared to past practice, family rituals both within the home and at the grave still remain very strong in the urban centers of Hong Kong and Taiwan where education and economic change are much more advanced. However, the certainty of one's economic condition must have had some impact in mainland China. Through these years one could do little to improve one's economic condition and the state provided a safety net below. There was little chance for extreme movement toward either end of the economic spectrum. The uselessness of striving to benefit oneself in opposition to the entire collectivity would seem both to reduce anxiety (the fear of ghosts) and overweening ambition (the reverence of ancestors). Then, too, coercive or administrative measures such as prohibiting religious professionals, prohibiting cremation and stopping the production of religious paraphernalia have all had an impact. Whether the propagation

21. This loss of ritual obligation to ancestors may be one of the factors that helps explain the success of the birth control effort in cities. Without such obligations, the motivation to provide a male heir is greatly weakened over what it would have been in the past. People can be satisfied with having only a daughter and no male heir to continue the family line.

of alternative beliefs and ideals has also had an impact is a subject we will turn to once we have considered the role of annual festivals in contemporary life.

Festivals

The texture of life in Chinese cities was once shaped not only by community religion and family ritual but also by a number of traditional holidays scattered throughout the year. Though these holidays provided periodic respite from the humdrum of everyday life, the new government considered many of them wasteful and loaded with feudal content inappropriate to the goals of the new society. To cope with these problems, the new government began in the 1950s to simplify and eliminate traditional holidays while adding new national holidays in their place as well as providing new recreational activities throughout the year.

The most important traditional holiday was the lunar new year, falling in the interval between late January and mid-February on the solar calendar. Reaffirming family and social ties, this holiday formerly required many days and even weeks for preparations and subsequent activities.[22] The major effort of the new government, starting in the 1950s, was not so much to eliminate this holiday as to simplify and secularize it. People working in state units were limited to three days off starting on the first day of the new year. The name was changed from "New Year" (*xinnian* or *guonian*) to "Spring Festival" (*qunjie*)—people now use both names interchangeably. Fewer extra foods were made available. Additional activities in parks and cultural halls were provided to help attract people away from traditional activities. And yearly before the holiday, people were made to study editorials on the virtue of passing a frugal Spring Festival.

In spite of these attempts to simplify the festival, it remains the most important and most elaborate holiday of the year. In the 1970s, worship of the kitchen god only rarely preceded the festival, which is one change from the past. But the days prior to the festival were still busy with preparation for the special family meal on New Year's Eve. This remained possible in part because the government continued to provide extra rations of sugar, meat, sesame oil, bean curd, eggs, glutinous rice, peanuts, and other goods appropriate to the season. If at all possible, family members in the other parts of the country continued to return home for this New

22. On traditional festival activities, see Tun Li-chen, *Annual Customs and Festivals in Peking,* 2d ed., Derk Bodde, trans. (Hong Kong: Hong Kong University Press, 1965); Wolfram Eberhard, *Chinese Festivals* (London: Abelard Schuman, 1958); V. R. Burkhardt, *Chinese Creeds and Customs* (Hong Kong: South China Morning Post, 1953).

Year's Eve meal. Formerly the meal was an important occasion for remembering the family's ancestors, and even today some families who worship at no other time may place the evening meal before the ancestor's picture or other memorabilia of the deceased in order to pay their respects.

The succeeding three days are filled with visiting close kin and friends, strolling through parks, going to the cinema, and other family get togethers. Children enjoy new clothes and shoes, as well as small red envelopes with a few cents from senior kinsmen—but not from just any visiting adult as might have happened in the past. The traditional fireworks continued through the 1950s, and parks gave free admission to enter and enjoy the numerous special performances of music and plays. Stadiums had sports events. But during the Cultural Revolution, parks had far fewer activities and fireworks were unavailable in major cities. The couplets posted outside doorways and greetings given on the street have changed. The emphasis on good luck and wealth have long disappeared, but the attempt to put political slogans into doorway couplets and personal greetings on the street had little staying power. Instead by the 1970s, most people either posted no couplets or only ones mentioning such general themes as good health. The same was true of greetings exchanged on the street. The attempt to infuse revolutionary character into the holiday continued to receive reinforcement through some work units' organizing visits to families of army martyrs and veterans as well as visits to some retired workers. Nevertheless the primary emphasis of the lunar new year continued to be reaffirming family ties and long-standing friendships through a series of family meals and visits back and forth between each other's homes.

The other traditional holidays fared much more poorly under the new regime. None of the other holidays warrant time off from state work units, and most provide no special food rations either. As a result they are only a pale image of their former selves. Through the 1970s, the traditional lantern festival on the fifteenth day of the lunar new year was generally no longer observed. And, as already noted, the spring Qingming festival for sweeping and worshipping before ancestral graves was only minimally observed in major cities, though it was not completely forgotten. Schools in some places tried to organize children to go pay their respects before the graves of revolutionary martyrs on this day. And it was on this day in 1976 that the Tiananmen incident occurred in Peking when supporters tried to present wreaths in memory of the deceased Zhou Enlai. But the significance and attention paid to the day is still much less than in the past.

Where it was observed, the Duanwu festival on the fifth of the fifth lunar month preserved only the special food of sticky rice cakes wrapped in lotus leaves. The dragon boat races that had given so much spirit to this day were disbanded virtually everywhere. The ghost festival on the fourteenth or fifteenth of the seventh lunar month as well as the Seven-Daughter Festival on the seventh day of this month were unobserved in cities. The mid-autumn festival on the fifteenth of the eighth lunar month remained important in some small towns where leaves from work were more lax. And in large cities the state provided special rations of the traditional mooncakes on this day, but otherwise there was little attention. The fall Chongyang festival for sweeping graves and the winter solstice were generally not observed. Thus, except for some sweeping and wor-shipping of graves on a Sunday near the spring Qingming date and except for some special foods at Duanwu and the mid-autumn festival, the tra-ditional festivals other than lunar new year's had passed by the way.

New Values

In the major cities, much of the old religion and festivals that had once given meaning and structure to people's lives had passed away or been suppressed by the 1970s. These practices and beliefs were supposed to have declined not only because of increasing security, knowledge, and selective coercion, but also because people embraced alternative values and symbols celebrating the new socialist order. In China, perhaps more than any other socialist regime, the spread of these new values was not left to chance. Rather, they were continually reinforced through political study among small groups of peers at work and in each neighborhood, through heavy doses of indoctrination in the public school curriculum, and in periodic political campaigns that focused attention on a single set of issues in the media, political study groups, and elsewhere throughout the nation. If new values were to be embraced, that embrace should have been particularly strong in China.

There is considerable evidence that many did adhere to new socialist values in the initial years of the new regime. The small group political study process, often with intense criticism and self-criticism among close friends, had a considerable impact on many urbanites when it was first introduced. In addition, many went along not just because of criticism and self-criticism, but because they identified with the regime's goals of building a strong China. With rapid economic growth accompanying the restoration of order in the early 1950s, many felt that the socialist regime did indeed provide the only answer to China's century of internal disorder and weakness in the face of foreign incursion. Also, many went along with the new values, feeling that they would be rewarded individually with meaningful roles in the new socialist order.

Under these conditions, idealism was quite widespread among many sectors of the population. Blue collar workers were often concerned as much about building a strong nation and a new way of life as about their individual economic welfare. For example, when comparing work in China to that in Hong Kong, a worker from a lock factory reported: "Hong Kong workers have no aspirations other than earning more money. Chinese workers pay less attention to money. Prior to the Cultural Revolution, being influenced by Communist thought, young workers in China were much more concerned about the collective good, the future of the nation, and so on. They were very idealistic."[23] Similarly, those emigrés who could have left legally because of foreign kin ties report that in the difficult Great Leap years of 1959–61 when they seldom had enough food to fill their stomachs, they nevertheless served contentedly and never thought of leaving because of a sense of participating in the common cause of building a new nation.

Idealism was also extremely intense among many students, and it was to students that Mao Zedong turned in order to attack the established bureaucrats at the start of the Cultural Revolution. Several of the young people we interviewed testified somewhat sheepishly to how committed to utopian ideals they had been during these years. This commitment helped support the late 1960s attempt to elevate Mao and his writings to sacred status. Students marched the streets waving the little red book of his quotations, statues of Mao sprouted everywhere, and a short prayerlike invocation to Mao's thought preceded many public ceremonies and even some family meals.

Yet, this attempt to sanctify Mao and the extreme idealism were short lived for many people. With the increasing shortage of jobs in cities, the absence of mobility opportunities in existing jobs, the increasing number and intensity of attacks for political errors, and the increasing disorder in the urban environment, people came to feel that they had no meaningful role in the socialist order. The increasing disillusionment is reflected both in our interviews and in many reports in the press today. A frequent theme in the interviews was how the emphasis on class struggle and random political attacks had destroyed a sense of participation in a grand national purpose. The same people who said they never felt like leaving during the economically difficult years of 1959–61 reported that they chose to leave in the 1970s because there was no longer any place for them in China. The Cultural Revolution shattered the formerly unifying goal of building a strong nation.

23. KSM25:6.

The disenchantment of many others who could not leave began to come out in other ways. Workers who had been highly committed to their work for the sake of a larger social good began to lose interest and to retreat to their home and hobbies. In a Peking factory, managers and other staff people would run home to tend their hobbies at every opportunity. The flower collection within the work unit compound became quite splendid.[24] In Canton, the mania for hobbies and card games became known among some as the "mass movement," welling up from below, as opposed to the numerous "political movements," which descended from above. Among others, it became known as the "army, air force, navy movement," with crickets being the army, birds the air force, and goldfish the navy. Making furniture from scrap wood also became popular, and even raising chickens could become a hobby.

> Raising chickens can be said to have been a hobby in those families who raised special large, foreign varieties. They would chop special foods for the birds, feed them vitamins, and compare how many eggs one's chicken laid relative to a neighbor's. It's like raising dogs in some other societies. Others went in for raising white geese, with both the geese and chickens being kept in special pens on roof patios.[25]

Untold hours that might have been spent on work were diverted to these kinds of activities.

Other adults would gather under the nearest street light in the evening in warm weather for a game of cards, with both men and women joining in. Chinese chess (qi) was popular among others, and even before the Cultural Revolution, poker was a favorite among cadre bureaucrats. Most of these games were played without money. But gambling, which was illegal, did exist, and it is said that groups of men would gather huddled on the sidewalk in certain districts to gamble in the open—their only precaution being to keep the money figures in their heads so that they would not be hassled by the police.

Perhaps the most disillusioned of all were the youth, now threatened with a possible lifetime in the countryside and with little hope of returning to the city or finding a meaningful job. This disillusionment appeared in both their recreational and quasi-religious activities. In Canton and surrounding towns that had much Western exposure, some youth gathered in each other's homes to play old records of traditional songs that were banned in the Cultural Revolution. Others took out their own instruments to play

24. PKD1. On hobby mania in the 1970s, see John Fraser, *The Chinese* (Toronto: Collins, 1980), pp. 354–56.
25. KSM30:9. This was in Canton. In Shanghai and Peking, such activities were illegal.

and sing these same songs together. Bolder ones would even listen to songs from foreign shortwave broadcasts or Hong Kong radio, if they could get it, and then sing them privately among themselves. Some novels also passed among youth. These varied from the salacious to more refined attempts at capturing the pathos of the Cultural Revolution to simply older books that had since been banned or become suspect. For example, one female student from Canton reports,

> Yes, there were underground books. The most famous was a hand copied book passing among students that was titled, *A Young Girl's Heart*. It was only about 5,000 words long and told about a girl who first had an affair with her cousin and then with another fellow. I never saw it, though a friend did and said it was nothing we would normally want to read. It was really hot stuff among students, though, and rented out for a certain fee for twenty-four hours. There were a few other short, hand-copied contraband books. More popular among my friends were novels, including Russian novels left over from before the Cultural Revolution.[26]

Besides seeking new diversions, some youth turned to older religious practices in an attempt to get some control over their uncertain future. Though they still avoided traditional gods and ancestors as an answer to their problems, quite a few flocked to divination devices. These were used to provide simple yes and no answers as to when and if they would be returned to the city, get a job, get married, escape to Hong Kong, and so on. One practice was for close friends to huddle about a table in a dark room with a plate in the center. When everyone placed their hands on the table and concentrated, the table would begin to vibrate and the plate move toward one participant or another, providing answers that had been put to the "spirit plate." Another was to balance a rice sifter on chopsticks, put a question, concentrate with the chopsticks in hand, and then determine the answer by how the sifter fell.

Others turned to fortune-telling, done both by facial and palm reading and from one's date of birth. Some did this by finding old books on fortune-telling so as to do it on their own. Others sought out underground fortune-tellers. Old fortune-tellers had been ready targets for political criticism in successive campaigns throughout the 1950s and 1960s, and by the 1970s they had been largely driven out of work in cities. But many still operated surreptitiously in small towns and villages. With proper personal introductions, youth would pay a yuan or so to have their fortunes told. Even the doubters might go before any particular dangerous moment, such as

26. STC1:9.

when they were about to try to escape to Hong Kong, to have the fortune-teller pick a propitious date.

Most fortune-tellers were blind or otherwise handicapped. Around the city of Liuzhou in Guangxi Province, one blind palm reader was said to be able to make ten to twenty yuan a day by charging fifty cents for a simple life line reading, one yuan for more complex readings, and several yuan for the whole family. A Swatow reader charged fifty cents for a simple fortune-telling, but one and a half yuan to tell one's fate for the year, and two yuan for one's lifetime fate.[27] This blind fortune-teller was simply ignored by the neighborhood officers since they had no other means of support to offer.

Other youth would make trips to the few temples that remained open to try their luck. For example, the Zu Temple in Foshan outside Canton has a square pond in which sits a stone turtle with a carved snake down the back. If one can land a coin on the back of the stone figure, it is thought one's luck will improve. If the coin falls into the water instead, one will not be so fortunate. In the 1970s when the temple had reopened, the pond had a large sign in front of it warning against superstition, but as any tourist can testify, the pond was full of coins throughout these years.

Certainty about life chances, then, does have some bearing on religious practice. For the youth of the population in the 1970s, that certainty was not being provided, and increasingly they turned from new values to selected versions of the old.

The lack of enthusiasm for the new values was also reflected in the reception of the new national holidays that were supposed to take the place of some of the old religious festivals. National Day, on 1 October, celebrating the revolutionary victory in 1949—our 4 July—attracted some attention. With two days off from work and extra food distributions as well as occasional public parades and firework displays, this holiday provided some relief from the grind of work

The other holidays provided less. Most workers in Chinese cities work eight hours a day, six days a week, fifty-two weeks a year. For most there is no annual vacation time, a two to three week paid leave period being limited to only that minority with a spouse elsewhere—or, if unmarried, with parents elsewhere. And among blue collar workers, family life has been disrupted by factories trying to save scarce electricity and reduce congestion by rotating each factory's day off.[28] Thus some families find

27. From interviews LCM2:20 and SWP1:12.

28. Bureaucrats, teachers, and other skilled white collar workers are more likely to get Saturday afternoon and Sunday off consistently, allowing more time to be with their families. But in the past, some of them have lost this advantage because of the necessity to attend

their children off from school on the weekend, the husband off on Tuesday, and the wife on Thursday, making it difficult to spend much time or eat special meals together.

One of the virtues of the remaining holidays of the year is that they give the family a rare chance to relax together and eat a better meal, and this is the quality of national holidays that the people we met most frequently mentioned. Through the 1970s, there were only two other national holidays, except for women who got an extra half day on 8 March, International Women's Day. The other days were solar new year on 1 January and May Day on 1 May. Providing only a few extra rations and few activities in parks or elsewhere, these two days were not counted as very special through the 1970s.

Altogether, for most state workers, national holidays—three days at the lunar new year, two days at National Day, and one day each for solar new year and May Day—provided a total of only seven full days off from work during the year. The lunar new year continued to have some of its former spirit of restoring ties with family and friends and the new National Day with its entertainment and special rations was often welcomed. But the old holidays had mostly lost their spirit while the new ones provided little more than a day off from work.

In general, then, one is struck by how the new socialist values and rituals failed to provide meaning and structure to urban life in the 1970s. To be sure, significant groups of ardent believers remained, trying through the first half of 1976 to force their beliefs on everyone else by concentrated political study and domination of the national media. But the average person was often repulsed by this strident dogmatism, and many youth and workers who had been firm believers in the cause of a strong socialist China found no place for themselves in the radicals' utopia. As we saw in our discussion of crime in chapter 8, the loss of legitimate channels of opportunity and access in the new socialist order caused many to lose faith in the central tenets of that order. For the lucky ones who continued to hold state jobs, the security may have helped them turn from old beliefs. But for the youth who remained without such security there was a scurrying about for other means to bring order and predictability to their lives. The frequent flipflop in official policy and ideological explanations for these policies made it even more difficult to know what to believe in. In

---

evening study and planning meetings, including a Friday night "Party life" meeting for Party members. In our 1970s sample of neighbors, almost 40 percent of the adult labor force had to attend evening meetings at least once a week. Another 4 percent went to evening meetings every other week or so. Political study for blue collar workers tended to be scheduled during, or just after, work.

the end, then, we are less impressed with the ability of the new socialist values to provide an alternative belief system than in the ability of the new order to mobilize coercive and administrative sanctions against old beliefs and practices. The result was that many in the population were left without any firm set of principles to believe in or structured rituals to bring order to their lives. Instead of eliminating alienation, the radical socialist order was helping produce alienation.

Neighborhood Variation

The degree to which people turned from the old and embraced the new varied somewhat from neighborhood to neighborhood, and this variation provides additional clues about whether the transition from old to new was based upon increasing knowledge and security or simply coercion. Our data is on deviation from ideals of the new socialist order. Two of the activities were typically engaged in by adults—covert worship, typically worship of ancestors by older women in the privacy of their home, and gambling, by men. Another three activities were typically engaged in by youth—divination to determine one's fortune, foreign radio listening, and the playing of underground music in private meetings in one another's homes. Each of these items is based on the reported frequency of such activities in a neighborhood.

Should these practices respond primarily to political control efforts, we would expect them to be least common in neighborhoods where deterrence efforts were most intense. We would also expect them to be less common in work unit compounds where there was more mutual surveillance by people who knew one another from work. In older and more stable neighborhoods in the old urban core or in smaller towns, we would expect that these surveillance efforts would be less successful and that neighbors might even turn a blind eye to violations of new cultural norms. To the extent that these practices responded not to direct control efforts but rather to the presence of meaningful social opportunities, we would expect them to be less common where there was less unemployment, where people had higher status jobs, and where the provision of supplies was more stable.

The data in table 36 give some support to the legitimate opportunity explanation but very little to the administrative control explanations for the kinds of cultural deviance being examined here. Covert worship was least common in neighborhoods where employment was high and most neighbors had white collar jobs. It was also less common in large cities, but more common in old, stable neighborhoods. Gambling, another adult activity, also tended to be less common where there were more legitimate opportunities, particularly more employment, and where residence was stable. In contrast to most other forms of cultural deviance in this table, gambling did appear to respond to active deterrence efforts in a neighborhood. The youthful deviations of divination, foreign radio listening, and underground music playing responded more simply to job opportunities. Where there were ample jobs, youth had less reason to turn to divination to predict their fate and less time or reason to turn to other kinds of deviant activities as well. Divination was more common in small towns with less bureaucratic control and where the youth could simply go to fortune-tellers in nearby villages. But the question here was less the control on youth but on adults who provided the fortunes. Household control efforts that included frequent inspections tended to reduce foreign radio listening. But for most youth, whether one turned to deviant cultural outlets depended primarily on the presence of legitimate job opportunities.

In sum, deterrence efforts had some effect particularly on adults, who tended to avoid gambling and fortune-telling in tightly controlled neighborhoods. And in the past, deterrence efforts effectively drove most priests and other religious professionals out of work while closing temples and emptying homes of their ancestral plaques. However, for youth, the major

Table 36   Cultural Deviation by Selected
                                            Characteristics (Partial
                                            Correlations)[a]

	Covert Worship	Gambling	Divination	Foreign Radio Listening	Underground Music
Neighborhood Structure					
Stability	.23*	.35*	-.20*	-.15	-.11
Homogeneity	.06	.10	.04	.14	.31*
Unit quarters	-.17	-.19*	.00	.06	.04
Deterrence Efforts					
Infrastructure	-.05	.20*	-.14	.02	.08
Household control	-.14	.31*	-.08	.32*	.21
Radical year	-.14	-.15	-.03	.12	.11
Opportunity and Access					
Ration-supply scale	-.02	-.16	.18	-.08	.11
Ration amounts	-.05	-.18	.06	.18	.07
Low unemployment	-.26*	-.31*	-.07	-.26*	-.50*
White collar neighbors	-.21*	-.18	-.07	.06	.13
Private housing rare	-.17*	-.09	-.07	.16	-.05
City Characteristics					
Administrative level	-.36*	-.16	-.49*	.12	.00
Median N	(58)	(49)	(44)	(35)	(24)

Source: Sample of neighborhoods, Lingnan Region only.

[a]Quality of interview controlled.

*p ≤ .05

question was one of legitimate opportunity. When they had a secure future, they were less likely to turn to foreign radio listening or other kinds of deviance. Again, this pattern replicates our findings on crime. In the Chinese context, most deviant activity has been more in response to inadequate legitimate opportunities than to an absence of control efforts. Control efforts (and the new political ideals) without opportunities failed to prevent deviant behavior.

Current Developments and Conclusion

In the 1980s, the restrictions on traditional religious activity have been relaxed somewhat. More churches and a few more temples and mosques are open, and freedom of established religion has been reaffirmed in the constitution. But as before, this is only a limited freedom. Superstition and all that supposedly goes with it is still forbidden.[29] The number of popular temples, as opposed to show-place temples for tourists, is still extremely restricted, and many of the inconveniences that inhibited family worship remain. Christianity is having a modest revival, both among old believers and among curious youth looking for something to hold on to. But religion generally remains extremely subdued in comparison to other Chinese settings such as Taiwan and Hong Kong.

Ritual activities and festivals of a traditional sort have made more of a comeback. There are better supplies of food, fireworks, and entertainment for the major festivals. Some places even have dragon boat races at the Duanwu festival in the fifth lunar month. Family rituals such as weddings and funerals have become more elaborate, and in some places the press has begun to complain about too much money being spent on these activities. However, with the continuation of cremation, and people still having only seven days off from work a year, the time available for activities such as these remains extremely limited.

It is harder to ascertain what has happened with levels of commitment to new socialist values. However, one impression is that for many older people, the levels of commitment are much higher now than a few years ago. Freed from some of the immediate threats of political attack and with a return to the goal of national growth, this time under the rubric of "modernization," many older people are solidly behind the new national

29. The 1 January 1980 criminal code stipulates that those who preach superstition to make money or spread rumors can get up to seven years imprisonment. See Xiao Wen, "Policy on Religion," p. 15. The limits on Christian activity appear to include no evangelization outside the church walls and no celebration on non-Sunday holidays such as Good Friday. See Charles Antoine de Nerciat, "Visit with Anglican Bishop," *AFP* (Paris), 4 April 1980, in *FBIS*, 9 April 1980, p. O2.

program. This is particularly true of intellectuals who have been given more of a role in national endeavors and more of their former pay and privileges.

Commitment to utopian socialism and to the personage of Mao is unlikely to become a secular religion, as some radicals would have had it during the Cultural Revolution. Despite the building of the large mausoleum in Tiananmen Square in Peking, Mao is now a flawed figure, and has been subject to too much cold analysis of his failures in official documents.[30] Unlike Lenin, Mao lived too long and became connected with too many distasteful policies. Nevertheless, the degree of diffuse idealism around building a strong and better China still remains quite high among many people that the visitor meets in China, and this idealism among older people may be called on for several years to come.

Among young people the issue may be somewhat more problematic. Today the press often complains that the young have little idealism or commitment to higher socialist values. To correct these sorts of problems, the press periodically calls for more political study among the youth. And it now appears that each spring will be devoted to a publicity campaign to instill better manners and civil courtesies, particularly among the young.[31]

Perhaps more problematic among the young is whether any new values can be found to reinstill the hard work ethic characteristic of Chinese of earlier generations. There are complaints about their lack of initiative both in China and abroad. In Hong Kong, employers complain that emigrés lack the motivation that they have come to expect from native-born workers. We suspect that one of the problems may be the destruction of the old beliefs about ancestors and obligation to the family line. Those beliefs still remain strong in much of the rest of East Asia which has become famed for its dedicated workers and rapid economic progress. If this source of motivation has been destroyed in China and nothing has been found to replace it—or if the dedication to the nation that was present

30. For a typical attempt to save Maoism (or Mao's thought) even while criticizing Mao the person, see Zhichao Lu, "China Upholds Principles of Mao Zedong Thought," *Beijing Review,* no. 24 (1981): 13–17.

31. The despair of a young factory worker, Ban Xiao, was recounted in a 1980 letter to the editor titled, "Why Has Life for Me Become Increasingly Meaningless?" After publication in *China Youth Magazine,* this letter elicited 40,000 additional letters, many from youth who identified with its content. For a summary of this exchange, see Richard Bernstein, *From the Center of the Earth* (Boston: Little, Brown, 1982), pp. 171–72. Another youth's loss of faith is recounted in Liang Heng and Judith Shapiro, *Son of the Revolution* (New York: Knopf, 1983). China's current attempt to instill new values among youth responds to many of the same pressures that caused Soviet rulers to restress socialist symbols and rituals for their youth in the 1960s and 1970s. See Christel Lane, *The Rites of Rulers* (Cambridge: Cambridge University Press, 1981), chap. 2.

before the Cultural Revolution has been permanently lost among the young—China may be forever impaired in its effort to modernize in a hurry, and it may long lag behind such rapidly growing Chinese settings as Singapore, Hong Kong, and Taiwan.

In conclusion, then, one is struck by both the difficulty of providing new sources of meaning in a socialist state and by the relative ease with which old systems of meaning were destroyed in China. The result was that instead of eliminating alienation, as is the frequent socialist promise, the new policies increased the sense of alienation and the lack of attachment to central values that would give meaning to life. In the early years of the regime, there was rather widespread commitment to the values of the new socialist order. This helped lead some people away from traditional values that honored the family across generations as well as a host of gods and ghosts. But the commitment to new values proved fragile, and with the excesses of radicals pursuing a new socialist utopia many people lost faith in the proposed new secular religion which tried to deify Mao Zedong and in the extremes of socialist virtue. Both the threat of political blacklisting for failing to hew to narrowly defined political dogma and the loss of opportunity for a meaningful role in this new order caused many to turn away.[32] The result has been a cooling of political commitment and China has come to approximate many other socialist states where Marxism is enthusiastically embraced by only a small percentage of the total population.[33] In China, that loss of faith in the central tenets of socialism may be even more severe because so much of what was central to the utopian version of Chinese socialism was associated with the now flawed figure of Mao.[34] The fear that the rejection of Mao may lead to a

32. The Chinese press in the early 1980s was discussing increasingly openly the crisis of confidence in the Party, socialism, and Marxism-Leninism. The media examined such manifestations as loss of faith in the official ideology or turning to "renegade" Marxists like Trotsky and Djilas (see Lin Honglin, "What Does the 'Confidence Crisis' Show?" *People's Daily,* 11 November 1980, in *FBIS,* 13 November 1980, pp. L8–13; "Strive to Further Improve the Party's Image," *People's Daily,* 31 December 1980, in *FBIS,* 5 January 1981, pp. L7–11); public scorn and ridicule for "activists" and "advanced individuals"; and sympathizing for those under criticism ("Give Play to the Good and Curb the Bad, Support the Progressives," *Shaanxi Daily,* 22 July 1981, in *FBIS,* 12 August 1981, pp. T4–6; "It Is Imperative to Correctly Deal with Press Criticism," *China Youth Daily,* 26 September 1981, in *FBIS,* 5 October 1981, pp. K13–14).

33. Paul Hollander discusses how, in spite of a massive ideological apparatus, Marxism in socialist states tends to be less fervently embraced than among some people in the capitalist West ("Research on Marxist Societies," *Annual Review of Sociology* 8 [1982]: 323–27).

34. Hollander notes that typically in socialist states, the legitimacy of the new regime has depended not just on belief in Marxism, but also on belief in a central founding leader, Stalin, Castro, Kim Il Sung, Enver Hoxha, Ho Chi Minh, and others. See "Research on Marxist Societies," p. 324.

much broader rejection of the socialist program is reflected in the criticism of Bai Hua and others, discussed in chapter 9.

Overall, the cooling of commitment to socialist values in China suggests that concerted childhood political education, adult political study, special political campaigns, and incessant media attention without the fulfillment of the promises of socialism eventually wear thin just as they have worn thin in other socialist states. Without economic security for youth and political security for adults, and without some gains in consumption, people grow weary of unrealized promises. Realizing these problems, the post-1976 leadership has tried to provide more opportunities, including more economic and political security as well as more consumption goods, but the experience of other socialist states suggests that this will at best go only part way in restoring the idealism of the past.

China's experience also illustrates deeper problems within Marxism that inhibit its becoming a secular religion illiciting deep commitment. Compared to the religions it is to replace, Marxism has little to say about the existential problems of life, and especially of death. In place of beliefs about one's condition after death, beliefs about one's place relative to departed ancestors, and elaborate funeral rituals that reinforce these beliefs, the Party has little to offer. The other-worldly focus of traditional religion provides a framework of meaning in comparison to which Party doctrine and ritual seems anemic. This may well help promote rather than ameliorate alienation.

In addition, Marxism has a certain schizophrenia concerning the ultimate values for which citizens should be striving. Whether the ultimate goal of life should be utopian socialism or national economic development has long troubled socialist states.[35] In China, as elsewhere, many people were attracted to the socialist cause because it promised to restore order and promote development. It was this goal of national unity and growth that attracted them more than the utopian ideals of equality and selflessness alone. And it was around this ideal of national growth that many people could unite. However, as in other socialist states, there was a small group of revolutionaries at the core more attracted to the utopian ideals, and in China this group may have been unusually large because of the protracted nature of the revolutionary war that began in the 1920s and was completed only in 1949. As Lowenthal suggests for other socialist states, the utopian ideals of extreme equality and selflessness that could

35. Richard Lowenthal, "Development versus Utopia in Communist Policy," in *Change in Communist Systems,* Chalmers Johnson, ed. (Stanford: Stanford University Press, 1970). Benjamin Schwartz traces this schizophrenia from its origins in seventeenth-century Western reformist thinking, "China and the West in the 'Thought of Mao Tse-tung,' " in *China in Crisis,* Ping-ti Ho and Tang Tsou, eds. (Chicago: University of Chicago Press, 1968).

elicit so much fervor finally are incompatible with the goals of development. The goals of development may not attract the same amount of fervor, but they are widely shared and provide a much safer way of trying to unify the country. China now appears to be settling into that safer path along with other socialist states.

Finally, China illustrates how some traditional belief systems may be particularly vulnerable to coercive pressures. In the early years of the new regime, some people turned from traditional religious beliefs because of commitment to new socialist values. And some people turned from traditional public and family religions simply because they found great security and predictability in the new economic order with its lifetime employment and ample fringe benefits. We see this in the greater turning from traditional practices both in large cities, where state-sector economic benefits are more widespread, and in those neighborhoods where economic opportunities have remained more secure. But we are also impressed with how Chinese religious practices have yielded steadily to coercive pressures: the closing of churches and temples, the closing of cemeteries, the arrest and reassignment of religious professionals, the attacks by radical Red Guards on family ancestral plaques, and the closing of factories making incense, paper money, and other religious paraphernalia. The success of these measures in China compared to some other socialist states with no less antipathy toward religion illustrates the weakness of a traditionally diffused as opposed to centrally organized religion. With only a minimal priestly hierarchy and few organized congregations to protest, and with such an eclectic set of beliefs, the population appears to have been more susceptible to religious change than in some other settings where socialists have come to power.

Family religion and the ancestral cult, around which there was more consensus and which was more central to people's self-understanding, has been somewhat slower to change—particularly in small towns and in some working class neighborhoods. But in major cities and among youth the changes in this area are profound as well, breaking three thousand years of tradition and raising major questions about the central direction of the lives of urban Chinese for generations to come.

11 Personal Relations

In the writing of many critics, modern urbanites have been said to suffer not only from powerlessness and meaninglessness, but also from social isolation. This isolation is thought to have many sources. For authors such as Durkheim, Simmel, and Wirth, the causes of social isolation include the increased residential mobility of modern cities, the mixing of people from differing backgrounds, and the segregation of work, residence, and other spheres of social life. For authors as diverse as Karl Marx and Ferdinand Toennies, isolation results from the increasing cash nexus in personal relations. As people become more concerned about getting ahead or simply surviving in their own careers, making money, and acquiring goods, traditional obligations to family, friends, and neighbors are left behind. People become more concerned about the utility of a relationship for their own personal good rather than social rewards. In the Marxian account, this problem would be solved by the security and equality of the new socialist order that would reduce the individual struggle for survival and replace it with more collective solidarity.[1]

Regardless of any debate about how accurately these ideas describe problems or solutions for modern Western cities, Chinese cities present a clear alternative. In contrast to the situation described in the West, Chinese residential and occupational mobility remains uncommon, with neighbors and workmates having ample chance to get to know one another. Work is often joined with residence, with one seeing the same set of people at work and at home. Through the mid-1970s, one's own planning and

1. Emile Durkheim, *The Division of Labor* (1893; 2d ed., New York: Free Press, 1933), Introduction; Georg Simmel, "The Metropolis and Mental Life," in *Classic Essays on the Culture of Cities,* Richard Sennett, ed. (1905; reprint ed., New York: Appleton-Century-Crofts, 1969); Louis Wirth, "Urbanism as a Way of Life," *American Journal of Sociology* 44 (1938): 1–24; Ferdinand Toennies, *Community and Society* (1887; reprint ed., New York: Harper and Row, 1957).

scheming for individual success was only weakly connected to income and other rewards, inhibiting some of the individual striving seen as hindering close personal relations in the West. The cash nexus was less important. And although Chinese neighborhoods had greater occupational heterogeneity than the average Western neighborhood, income and consumption remained so minimally differentiated by occupation that heterogeneity alone may not have hindered close ties among neighbors. On these dimensions, then, Chinese cities should have had closer personal relationships and less social isolation than modern Western cities.

These dimensions were countered, however, by the threat of political attack. Barrington Moore describes how during Stalin's time in the Soviet Union people drew into themselves so as to avoid revealing information to informers and other acquaintances who might be pressured into revealing information to be used in political attacks. Political pressure had an atomizing effect on society that could not compensate for the greater economic security which might have promoted solidarity.[2] Hedrick Smith discusses for later years in the Soviet Union how political pressure, though mild in comparison to Stalin's time, continued to limit the range of friends and acquaintances to whom one might be truly open.[3] Our problem in this chapter, then, is to examine the balance of forces in Chinese cities that either support or hinder close personal relationships and the improved quality of life that these relationships might bring.

Secular Trends

There have been some dramatic changes in relations with neighbors, friends, workmates, and kin since 1949. A doctor in her seventies provides a succinct summary of some of the major changes:

Neighbor relations are clearly closer now than before liberation [1949]. Everyone knows all about their neighbors—extremely close, you might say, from the many meetings. There was nothing like this before liberation. But knowing all about all does not mean that feelings toward all are close—some you have close feelings for, others not. Friend relations, in contrast, are not so close now, for one sees them less often and invites them for meals less . . . you might say that over time the immediate family has become more central in social relations—more inward-turning. With fewer kin and friend ties, people spend more time when off work simply with their immediate family . . .[4]

2. *Terror and Progress: USSR* (Cambridge: Harvard University Press, 1954), pp. 158–59.
3. *The Russians* (New York: Ballantine, 1976).
4. PEP3:35.

This pattern of drawing inwards to the immediate family and neighbors while losing contact with kin and friends is special compared not only to China's past but also to cities in other societies. In both the U.S. and India, for example, ties to neighbors remain very weak and inconsequential in comparison to ties to kin and friends.[5] The special character of interpersonal relations in Chinese cities has several sources. Some of the sources are based on secular trends having to do with time at work, neighborhood services, and the increasing stability of residence in Chinese urban neighborhoods. Others have to do with more transitory political pressures that may now fade as Chinese society attempts to reduce political fervor and the danger of political attack. Since our informants were very sensitive to both sources of change, it is best to let them speak for themselves.

First, on the secular sources of change, several informants note that with both husband and wife working eight hours a day, six days a week, and with shopping and other household tasks so time consuming, there is little time for activities outside one's immediate neighborhood. A high school teacher in her late thirties who had lived in her school's residential compound, reports that,

> People had little contact with friends in other places. On Sunday, by the time one got through buying food, cleaning house, cooking a little better, and occasionally visiting kin, there was no longer any time left for visiting anyone else. Sunday is the only day people have for doing all these things.[6]

For those blue collar workers in factories that give time off on days other than Sunday, friends and even family were not often off on the same day of the week. Thus one is thrown back on whatever neighbors happen to be nearby and off on the same day.

Visiting in the neighborhood is also encouraged by the paucity of communication and transport facilities, the scarcity of outside entertainment, and the physical setting of cities.

> In Canton, one visits kin only on big holidays. With no telephones, one has to go over by bicycle or public transport and then may not catch the other person at home. It is not like Hong Kong, where one can arrange a get together with kin on a moment's notice.[7]

5. See Claude Fischer, *To Dwell among Friends* (Chicago: University of Chicago Press, 1982), pp. 40–41; and Subash Chandra, *Social Participation in Urban Neighborhoods* (New Delhi: National Publishing House, 1977), chap. 5.

6. KSS4:5.

7. KSM30:9.

(There are neighborhood call boxes but virtually no private phones).[8]

The absence of TV and other diversions throughout the 1970s also helped promote visiting among neighbors. This was particularly true on the inner lanes in the old urban core and in work unit compounds where motorized vehicles could not go. "For anyone over thirty years of age, the major form of entertainment is sitting around with neighbors, soaking up the cool in summer, conversing, and playing [Chinese] chess," suggests a former Canton lane resident.[9] In a factory compound outside a small city, "everyone's door is open and people are always going back and forth. In the evening, people sit outside the door on the ground floor enjoying the cool breeze and conversing. People enter and leave each other's rooms as they please."[10] A large percentage of all residents live in these kinds of settings.

Comparisons to highly commercialized Hong Kong, where extended kin networks remain important even though neighborhood relations have dissolved, provide several other insights. Describing his immediate neighbors, a young man says,

> It is seldom that one sees kin visiting these neighbors, and this is true throughout Canton. It is not like Hong Kong where there are all sorts of occasions to meet kin throughout the year—at lunar new year, at old people's birthdays, marriages, funerals, full-month celebrations. All of these events have essentially disappeared in Canton.[11]

This situation is overstated by this person who had no immediate family left in Canton, but it describes a tendency to which others allude and one that was particularly true during the spartan 1970s.

Kin are not completely forgotten. There is less need to call on kin in emergencies these days because the state provides a subsistence floor for most. But when the rare emergency does occur and money or assistance with an ill person is needed, people do still call on kin. With the increase in unemployment, kin have been called on to help with job contacts. Kin working in shops or elsewhere in the commercial network are called on to help find scarce goods. And when kin live in the nearby countryside,

8. The call box is typically just a table with a phone on it attended by some old person appointed by the residents' committee. To call out, one pays a nominal one to two cent fee to the attendant. One can receive calls as well, with the attendant either simply writing down the message or running to get you while the other person waits on the other end of the line. The fee for this service is somewhat higher, generally three to five cents. Some people can also use a phone at their workplace or in a nearby store.

9. KSM2:4.

10. CMD:6.

11. KSP6:8.

there may be frequent visiting back and forth—the urbanite bringing gifts of consumer goods that cannot be found in the countryside and the villager bringing gifts of foods often absent in cities. Despite these kinds of assistance for people in special need or among those in special position to help each other, the generalization still holds that for the average person kin contact has declined relative to contact with neighbors and immediate family.

The shortage of free time, the paucity of communication and transport facilities, the reduction in festival occasions, and the absence of outside entertainment, as well as an increasing stability of residence, all helped create this turning away from distant kin and friends toward the immediate family and neighborhood. There is little here of the beneficial interpersonal relations that are supposed to result from increasing equality and security of living conditions in socialist societies.

Mutual Aid and Comradely Concern

There is another side to Chinese personal relations, however. To see the role of increased job security, equality, and collectively organized activities, one only needs to ask informants a bit more about relations with coworkers and neighbors—especially in comparison to these relations in Hong Kong.

Life in factories illustrates the pattern. With lifetime employment, there has been little fear of losing one's job to another worker who works faster. Jobs tend not to be finely divided, and there has been ample time for workers to get to know one another through years of contact. For skilled workers, this process begins with a two- or three-year assignment as an apprentice to an older "master" in the factory. In the past, this relationship has often been close, with master and apprentice sometimes continuing their relationship years after the initial apprenticeship period. Annual holidays provide opportunities for former apprentices to pay their respects to former masters, bringing a few gifts at times. And at the apprentice's wedding and birth of a child, the master may play an important role. Larger factories also tend to get involved when workers are sick and at funerals, sometimes delegating a member of the work group to call on a fellow worker or pay respects to the family. In these respects, Chinese factories are rather like large Japanese factories.

These simple courtesies, or acts of comradeship, so lacking in ultra-capitalist Hong Kong, often lead to favorable evaluation of factory life in China. A worker from a scrap steel factory notes,

> Things are more comfortable in China than in Hong Kong. There
> is no piece rate there to make one work hard and there is no
> threat of being laid off tomorrow or the week after as there is in
> Hong Kong. True, there is more political threat, but there is still
> less pressure than in Hong Kong and interpersonal relations are
> less tense.[12]

A lock factory worker, who evaluates Chinese factories negatively in several other respects, agrees: "There is more human feeling in China than in Hong Kong. If one's child is sick all one's coworkers will be concerned about it, asking what they can do to help and continuing to ask until the child is well."[13] Many informants concur in this assessment of considerable mutual aid in Chinese factories.

Mutual aid and comradely concern are also common among neighbors and friends, and the relatively small gaps in incomes and consumption of people in different occupations as well as in the noncompetitive nature of work life have had a role in this. This generalization is again particularly striking in comparison to Hong Kong, with its major gaps between rich and poor, an emphasis on piece rates at work, and high mobility among jobs and residences. When confronted with the situation in Hong Kong, some of the emigrants respond much like the residents of European cities at the start of the industrial revolution—it is the "cash nexus" that dominates their impressions.

> In Hong Kong friendship relationships, considerations of education
> and money are very important—not in China. In Hong Kong there
> are all sorts of fees for introductions and other services—not in
> China where these services would be performed by one's friends
> for free. In China, there was more loyalty and not so much nar-
> row-mindedness. In Hong Kong, if you have money many con-

12. FSP1:15. Hong Kong provides an extreme comparison to be sure. In a survey of urban residents in Hong Kong, Taipei, Singapore, Bangkok, and Malaysia, the Hong Kong residents almost invariably had the weakest ties to kin, coworkers, friends, and neighbors. Rapid economic change, huge influxes of migrants, forced high-rise living, the mixing of people from different backgrounds, and an uncertain political future have all taken their toll on interpersonal relations in Hong Kong. Nevertheless, in the comparative survey, the Chinese in Hong Kong were not completely deviant. Throughout Southeast Asia, the Chinese tended to have weaker interpersonal ties than the Malay, Thai, and Indian ethnic groups in these same cities. Thus, the quality of interpersonal relations in socialist China stems not just from these people being culturally Chinese, and the contrast with Hong Kong is not inappropriate in trying to determine how interpersonal relations have changed under socialism. See Robert E. Mitchell, *Levels of Emotional Strain in Southeast Asian Cities* (Taipei: Orient Cultural Service, 1972).

13. KSM25:6.

sider you a friend. In China even if poor you still had friends—it just depended on what kind of person you were. It's a big difference which I can't get used to. Hong Kong is much colder in human feelings, and there is much mutual suspicion.

You can see it in the way wages are handled. In China one knows the wages of all others, but in Hong Kong they won't tell you what their wages are. In Hong Kong, they are always calculating how they stand in wages relative to others, but not in China. In China, my best friends came from all groups—the second Party secretary of the factory, the Party secretary of the workshop, and also some hooligans—from all ends of society. I didn't even know the names of some of them, but I would wave to them and give out ball tickets to them and so forth.[14]

This overseas Chinese manual worker, originally from Indonesia, was far more extroverted than the average worker, but his frustration in Hong Kong illustrates issues perceived generally.

Another young woman from Canton comments,

In China we were pretty much all in the same situation, wearing the same clothes and having about the same amount of money. If I needed money, my friends would know it even before I told them and give it to me. But here [in Hong Kong] there are major gaps in society, and everyone is trying to put on airs at being successful, and I myself buy clothes that I cannot afford in order to appear successful. Now, I wouldn't ask my friends for money for fear of losing face, even if I was hungry, and some of these are the same friends I had back in Canton.[15]

Organized neighborhood activities such as sweeping streets, getting people together for a film while fumigating each house in the neighborhood, or meeting for public announcements has helped bring neighborhoods together. In a county seat with about 80,000 population, an informant told us,

Neighbors . . . come in contact through the cleaning of public places or their kids' activity, allowing each family to develop close livelihood contacts. Thus when a family has a problem, all others know about it. For example, when I married, all the neighbors on the whole street came to my home saying they wanted a look at the new bride, and mother invited each of them in for candy and tea.[16]

14. LCM1:42.
15. KSM4:8.
16. CHS4:15.

Long years of residence together, common activities, minimal gaps in income and consumption, as well as a lack of mutual competitiveness, then, often lead to close relations as expressed in visiting back and forth and multiple forms of mutual aid. Our informants describe best the many ways in which neighbors can help one another:

There was a lot of exchanging of mutual favors in Canton. Neighbors helped each other buy vegetables, grain, and the like. If one had a neighbor working in a pork store, he would help one get pork. Usually one would give meat coupons, but not always, and even when one gave a coupon, he would cut off a little more than you were supposed to get. The policeman (who lived next door) helped a lot of people get bicycles, which were hard to come by. He was often waving a bicycle purchase certificate around and asking who would like to buy one. It is said that he had a friend working in one of the department stores. When my brother came back from Hainan Island he would always bring lots of salted fish with him, for all the neighbors wanted to buy some from him and to those with whom we were closest he just gave some. (One simply cannot buy salted fish in Canton except around the time of the major holidays.)[17]

There is no lending of money among neighbors, but they help each other buy vegetables, or when they make special foods or sweets, they take a little to the neighbors to try.

When a child is born the neighbors give presents, but not in Hong Kong.

In a work unit compound, in North Central China, the neighbors

watched the fire in the stove for you, unlocked the door for your child, and even if you had to go to the countryside for two days on business, they would watch your child while you were gone.

There are no major kinds of assistances among neighbors, but there are lots of small assistances—giving small packets of food at lunar new year's, giving extra pork, fresh vegetables, or cloth that one has acquired through nonrationed channels.

Among the five households that I have described, our relations were best with the old couple [husband 90, wife 70 years old]. Whenever we had time, we helped them write letters to send to the younger sister in north Guangdong. The younger sister came every year and she brought special products from her area, and when she left we gave her cakes and noodles. The old wife also comes over in her spare time to converse and pass the time of

17. KSM13:7; HHH1:2; KSM9:45.

day—we discussed everyday life, not politics. In part, having no
children, and being old, we just felt we should show a little extra
concern for them so that they would not feel too lonely. But also
this old couple really knew how to talk, they were polite, and a
lot of fun to be with.

We were next most close with the teacher whose wife died. Before his wife died, we would help one another—for example, in
buying vegetables, my mother would also pick up some for them.
If it began to rain while their clothes were out, and no one was at
home, we would bring their clothes in, and then hang them back
out when the rain stopped.[18]

This example may illustrate a more general pattern in Chinese cities.
As a person from Jilin suggests, two families may be closest when one
of the families has old people and the other does not. Then, the family
without an old person home during the day will give their key to the old
person to let the children in when they return from school, and they will
provide all sorts of other mutual favors for one another.[19]

Overall, in our weighted sample of neighborhoods, less than ten percent
are reported to be without at least some form of assistance among immediate neighbors, and almost thirty percent were reported to have very
extensive patterns of aid among neighbors. This pattern of aid and mutual
concern leads four-fifths of our informants to describe neighborhood life
as closer in China than in Hong Kong. Only a fifth described neighborhood
life as about the same, and none described neighborhood life as being
better in Hong Kong than in China. Clearly, then, life in cities with minimal
mobility, minimal income or consumption gaps, minimal competiveness,
and many organized neighborhood activities has a distinct impact on the
nature of interpersonal relations, creating far more mutual concern and
assistance among neighbors and friends than occurs in other cities around
the world.

Conflict

In spite of the mutual aid and favorable evaluations, conflict among neighbors is not uncommon. Some of the same conditions that lead to mutual
knowledge and assistance can also create high levels of friction. The
sharing of facilities is a common source of friction.

In a Shanghai neighborhood, we were told,

18. CHDl:64; CCSM:5; KSM4:5.
19. CLD1:16, also KSP1:7.

Because these houses used to be single family dwellings, the toilets, kitchens, and baths are designed all wrong for sharing. . . . In kitchens, the placing of burners is very crowded and there are disputes first over who gets what space for one's burner and then disputes over storage and people spilling over into the other's space. Then others hook their stove to your natural gas. The cadre upstairs does this. She has the largest household of any in the building but she consistently has the smallest bill since she hooks to our outlet when we are not at home. She also uses our cooking oil. Some places (not us) have fights over these sorts of things.

Toilets are also a source of contention. We haven't had this problem, but others in the lane have a severe problem when all three floors use the same toilet and bathe on the second floor. In the evening, everyone wants to bathe about the same time. One family member will stretch out his time in the bath until another family member comes up and knocks and the member inside just lets in this late arriver. There are similar problems in the morning when some people take their time, holding up others and making them late for work. They use your soap. If there is severe conflict, it may go to the residents' committee, but there isn't a great deal they can do since they can't move people.[20]

These types of conflicts are most common in older neighborhoods with housing converted to multifamily use in the last three decades.

The problem of sharing facilities is mentioned in several other accounts as well. It is not surprising that demands for private baths and kitchens are very common. One of our research assistants still remembered vividly the time he had been taken to the police station and locked in a pitch-black room for two hours when he was still in primary school because of conflict with a neighbor over the use of the shower. Another person from Zhanjiang City in western Guangdong reports,

In my building and nearby, there were frequent small conflicts over sharing the kitchen. . . . The line between each family's side of the kitchen is not clearly marked, and one person spilling over into another family's area causes some small disagreement.[21]

Conflict may also extend to neighbors in other buildings, especially when they must share facilities outside the home and when children get

20. SSM1:8. In 1980, forty-two percent of Shanghai's residents had natural gas, but throughout the large and medium size cities of China, only fifteen percent had natural gas for cooking (*FBIS*, 2 June 1980, pp. L7–8). Most of the rest used some form of coal, typically "beehive" coal.

21. CCSM:5.

involved. In a Canton neighborhood with a public water tap, the maternal grandmother in one family,

> often argues with the neighbors over the use of the public tap. And the kitchen drains are often clogged with garbage she puts there, and the neighbors are upset. Also her grandchildren get into fights with other neighborhood children, and she argues with neighbors about this.[22]

In a prefectural city,

> Two kids were playing together in the street. For reasons unknown, they started swearing at each other and then fighting. One was beaten in the head, bleeding and swollen. The other got bruises in the face. Weeping sadly, they ran home to tell their mothers. With each mother believing her son's story, each decided to take the matter up with the other. They met in the street. First, pointing at each other's noses, they quarreled. They swore at each other's ancestors. While exchanging vulgar words, one's finger touched the other's nose. She, in turn accused the other of starting a fight and touched her opponents nose. Then they started fighting, tearing each other's clothes, pulling each other's hair, and scratching each other's face.
>
> The husbands heard the ruckus and came out to stop the fighting, but one of them got scratched in the hand and turned on the woman who scratched him. Then her husband gave him a slap, and the two began fighting each other. Seeing their parents fighting, the children did not want to lag behind . . . so the children had their own battlefield. Woman fought with woman, and husband with husband.
>
> The neighbors tried to stop the fighting but failed. So they just stood aside to watch. They had been fighting some time before the neighborhood picket corps, the neighborhood police, and ward committee people came to stop them. They were all taken to the office of the picket corps to be questioned, criticized, warned to not do it again, and then let go. The two families have remained hostile ever since, often quarrelling with each other.[23]

As a former resident of a county seat notes, after commenting favorably on cooperation, "There are also some conflicts with neighbors that can't be avoided by moving away such as in Hong Kong—so there is more of both cooperation and conflict among neighbors in the county towns as compared with Hong Kong. In Hong Kong one is simply more separate

22. KSP3:8.
23. CCM1:7.

from neighbors."[24] This generalization seems to be true for many of the neighborhoods that we studied. Long years of common residence breed both cooperation and conflict.[25]

The family fight described above also illustrates how the official neighborhood apparatus may have only minimal success in helping to prevent conflict. In another example from Zhanjiang City,

> the household with the worst relations with neighbors is a family living in a very small, dark room on a nearby lane. They keep leaving their excess goods outside in the narrow lane so that others have difficulty getting by. Their neighbors fuss at them and it has almost come to blows at times. The residents' committee has tried to mediate, though there is no special mediation committee.[26]

Were the 1950s regulations establishing neighborhood organizations followed, there would be a special mediation committee in each neighborhood to handle these kinds of disputes among families as well as within families. But as noted earlier, most of these committees were defunct in the 1970s, and most disputes were handled by the residents themselves or in a very ad hoc manner, with residents' committee leaders being called only as a last resort when violence was threatened.

Political Pressure

To this point, we have emphasized only those aspects of the socialist system that create greater mutual involvement and support among neighbors and workmates. (The presence of conflict among neighbors who have lived together too long and the failure of neighborhood leaders to resolve all conflicts are but minor subthemes in this larger picture of mutual involvement and support.) In this emphasis we have ignored some major problems created by the political pressure that has come along with increased equality, security, and residential stability. Political pressure has created significant problems among friends and among certain groups of workers—indeed part of the retreat from the wider world of kin, friends, and some workmates is explained as much by political pressure as by any of the other more benign factors that we have mentioned.

24. STH1:12.

25. Using Latin American data, William Whyte argues that cooperation and conflict are not opposite ends of a single dimension but two separate dimensions that may vary independently of one another. See William Whyte and Giorgio Alberti, *Power, Politics, and Progress* (New York: Elsevier, 1976), chap. 19.

26. CCSM:5.

Intellectuals and people of suspect class background were the ones most threatened by the possibility of political attack through friends and work units (see chapter 9). For them, the awareness of this danger came early. From the 1950s, in successive political campaigns, friends and workmates were quizzed for information that might be used against a person suspected of committing political errors. Work units were typically the center of this quizzing and subsequent criticism, for it was in work units that permanent dossiers detailing one's performance in past political campaigns were kept, and it was in work units that one was subject to criticism and self-criticism among a small group of peers. The result was that some people began to be very cautious about making friends, especially among workmates. A young woman worker from a neighborhood machine parts factory reports, "I was not so close to workmates. In general I felt that one could get into conflicts with fellow workers, and dared not talk too freely with them for fear of political problems in the future. If you are in trouble, the authorities will find your closest friends to interrogate. So I avoided workmates outside of work."[27] The son of a trade company official who lived in a work unit building, notes after observing that most of his family's friends came from outside their work unit, "It is common knowledge that one should not be too close to those in the same work unit lest they have to report on one in the next campaign."[28] And a worker in a leather and plastic products factory reports, "In Canton, workers . . . just maintain average ties to coworkers, especially to workers in the same group, for fear of exposure in the next campaign."[29]

This cautiousness about workmates sometimes extends to residence in work units compounds as well. The daughter of a financial cadre reports, "Some people don't like to live in their unit's quarters because there is no privacy—no freedom. One's workmates and superiors will immediately know who comes to visit you and every harsh word you say to your wife and kids."[30] Commenting on life in the 1970s, a former high school teacher who used to live in her school's quarters among workmates remarks,

All sort of opinions could be interpreted as political opinions—for example, one's expressed attitude toward study or how much effort should be spent on study as opposed to anything else, one's attitude toward the rural branch school, one's complaints about standing in line to buy things could all be taken as complaints

27. KSM17:42.
28. KSS1:4.
29. KSP11:3.
30. KSM1:17. For a vivid account of some of these themes see the stories "Chairman Mao Is a Rotten Egg" and "Residency Check," in Chen Jo-hsi's, *The Execution of Mayor Yin* (Bloomington: Indiana University Press, 1978).

against the socialist system. So one had to be careful about everything one said. . . . Yes, this was worse in unit quarters. Things
were freer in nonquarter areas, and freer among manual workers
regardless of where they lived.[31]

This variation in political pressure is also related to several other conditions. A person whose father lived in a factory dorm replies, "Yes, my
father had a lot of coworkers come by, but this was just because he worked
in a big factory, was in a nonthreatening staff position, and because he
made it clear right off to everyone that he wasn't going to assume any
direct responsibility."[32]

Relations in and outside of work could also be good in those work units
which remained out of the mainstream of political currents. In a county
light industry,

there are some who are like sworn brothers (*sidang*), spending all
their spare time together. There are two in particular who spend
every evening together playing chess, drinking tea, chatting. And
there are several groups of young workers who spend many days
off riding their bicycles to nearby villages to buy pork, seafood,
chicken, and ducks.[33]

This informant's factory was one of five in town that kept working throughout the Cultural Revolution. An informant in another county told us, "My
brother and sister-in-law's friends were all workmates. They sometimes
played cards together and sometimes went out to travel together [to a
nearby city]."[34] Both the brother and sister-in-law were manual workers
in light industry. As we have already noted, political pressure throughout
the 1970s remained less intense for manual workers and for those in
smaller and administratively lower level towns. Thus, the possibility of
more open, spontaneous relationships with fellow workers was easier in
these types of places.

In most places, however, the Cultural Revolution was a time of retreat
from friendship and fellow worker contacts. The daughter of a school
teacher reports, "Prior to the Cultural Revolution my parents had lots of
fellow teachers coming to visit them, but after the Cultural Revolution,
when teachers had such a hard time, few came."[35] Even before the Cultural
Revolution, it was common practice to back off from people who were
under political suspicion. The doctor in her seventies reports,

31. KSS4:6.
32. KSM24:7.
33. CSH4:8.
34. HHH1:2.
35. FSP3:6.

If a friend had a political problem, then one avoided them. We were all afraid of having these kinds of contacts for fear of being questioned about it and having the problem shift to our own heads. . . . Even if you viewed them as falsely accused, you wouldn't get too close—not just from fear for yourself but also from the feeling that it would be better for the targeted person as well. If the person is eventually exonerated, then one can repair the relationship later. Of course, it is pitiful for a while to be ostracized like that.[36]

This feeling of ostracism or social distance among people was originally concentrated among intellectuals who were common targets in early campaigns. But with the start of the Cultural Revolution, the feeling became more general, drifting on down among some blue collar workers as well. As a worker from the vinyl products factory reports, "There was more distance among workers following the Cultural Revolution, especially following the Clean the Class Ranks campaign. In this campaign, workers were forced to expose their friends."[37] Or describing what used to be very close relations between masters and apprentices in a factory, a worker from a transformer factory reports, "Taught by their experience in the Cultural Revolution, people didn't trust each other or tell what was really on their mind. They talked ritualistically. . . . They talked about technical questions, but never about political matters or things in the factory."[38] According to our informant from the lock factory:

Prior to the Cultural Revolution, there were no serious conflicts among workers. They not only were very cooperative and helpful to one another but also very open with one another. Today they are still helpful. . . . But since the Cultural Revolution there has been a lot of mental pressure. Workers have come to fear that in the next political campaign, old historical political problems will be dragged up and fear that errors that they themselves did not commit but were committed by their parents and siblings will be brought up and held against them. Because of this, people will not say what is in their hearts. The Cultural Revolution had a lasting effect, which was to make people very cautious of what they said to one another. Everyone began to think before they spoke and refused to say what they really felt. A distance grew between workers.[39]

36. PEP3:36. For a vivid account of this kind of ostracism during the Cultural Revolution, see Ruth Earnshaw Lo and Katherine S. Kinderman, *In the Eye of the Typhoon* (New York: Harcourt Brace, 1980).
37. KSP11:3.
38. KSP13:3.
39. KSM25:5.

The response by some people to this situation was to select their friends very carefully. A restaurant worker reports that, in contrast to Hong Kong where money is emphasized, "in China, people viewed one's character or virtue in picking friends. People worried about being betrayed or sold out by their friends. Thus, before they understood the character of a person well, they would not easily pour out what they really had on their mind."[40]

An intellectual from a cultural unit explains in greater detail,

It is only with reliable people that one talks freely. A reliable person is one who will not try to make something big out of your minor errors or to make something out of minor indiscretions in conversation. Most people are not afraid of criticism, but they are afraid of those who would take their words and distort them or tell lies about what they have done. Prior to the Cultural Revolution people talked openly in meetings and there was debate over differing opinions. But in the Cultural Revolution people soon learned not to be so open, to reserve their frank talk not for meetings but for discussions with trusted friends afterwards. Things were not so bad in our unit as in some other places, but still there was a chilling atmosphere.

Choosing reliable people with whom to talk freely depends on having known them over a period of ten years and knowing what they have done in each successive political movement. One avoids people who just try to please others—we call them [court] jesters (*xiao-qiu*), one who lives by toadying up to others and making them smile, opportunists who are likely to turn on you if there is suddenly someone else they want to please. If one is with friends and one of these jesters walks up, one changes the subject to discuss weather or some other innocuous topic. There were no jesters on our floor, but still one did not talk freely with everyone.[41]

People were not just cautious in selecting friends, however. Quite the contrary, some people engaged in an apparent effort, perhaps subconscious, to search out two, three, or four friends with whom one could spill out one's true feelings. These contacts became increasingly valuable as the political environment intensified. While mouthing what was required to survive in public settings, saying what was really on one's mind to select friends became one of the few ways one could maintain one's sanity and sense of integrity. Typically these friends could be trusted not to reveal your inner thoughts even when under severe criticism them-

40. CCM1:15.

41. PED1:2. In some places this cautiousness is generalized to anyone who is a known Party member.

selves. If forced to, they would talk only of "chicken feathers and garlic skins," of minor errors, such as dreaming of having a gold watch, rather than of what you might have really done wrong. The search for close friends of this sort was most typical of intellectuals who were under greater pressure, but it occurred among others as well. A county light industry worker explained that, "I had only two or three close friends—former middle school classmates whose families lived close and who also got factory jobs in town. I considered them sworn brothers, and among ourselves we could express gripes and talk of our dissatisfaction."[42]

That political pressure induces people to form a tight circle of friends even while inducing them to reduce the total range of friends is a phenomenon that has not always been correctly perceived. Barrington Moore notes this phenomenon in the Soviet Union, suggesting that Stalinist terror both destroyed and created personal relationships, friendship groupings, and protective cliques.[43] Also, in the early 1970s, after more than a decade or more of political relaxation, Hedrick Smith found that "precisely because their public lives are so supervised and because they cannot afford to be open and candid with most people, Russians invest their friendships with enormous importance. . . . Their social circles are usually narrower than those of Westerners . . . but relations between Russians are usually more intense, more demanding, more enduring and often more rewarding."[44]

In his account of friendship in China during the early 1960s, however, Ezra Vogel gave just one side of the picture, emphasizing how political pressures destroyed traditional friendship.[45] Later work on China in the 1960s and 1970s has tended to see close friendship of a traditional sort as also providing a potential "haven" from the world of politics.[46] These

42. CSH4:15. For a detailed account of selecting trusted friends, see Tung Chi-ping and Humphrey Evans, *The Thought Revolution* (London: Leslie Frewin, 1967).

43. *Terror and Progress*, pp. 160–61.

44. Smith, *The Russians*, pp. 143–44. There is a maudlin character to Russian friendship not shared by the Chinese, but otherwise the resemblances are quite striking. Smith also speaks of the schizophrenic separation of existence into public and private lives with accompanying "official" and personal relationships (pp. 138–40). Here too, the resemblance to Chinese practice is striking—though these days the schizophrenia does not seem quite so deep in China. Victor Zaslavsky uses the term "political diglossia" to describe the tendency in the USSR (and in China) for there to be two completely distinct styles of discourse, one the slogan-filled form used in meetings and other public settings and the other the informal, everyday type used in normal contexts. See his *The Neo-Stalinist State* (Armonk: M. E. Sharpe, 1982), p. 42.

45. Ezra F. Vogel, "From Friendship to Comradeship," *China Quarterly* 21 (1965): 46–60.

46. Susan Shirk, *Competitive Comrades* (Berkeley: University of California Press, 1981), chap. 5; and Gordon Bennett, "China's Mass Campaigns and Social Control," in *Deviance*

findings and our own work on the continuing importance of a small circle of friends provide insights that should not be lost. They help explain how people can endure threatening or difficult government policy, mouthing one thing in public and then another among close friends.

Ezra Vogel's original work on the shift from friendship to comradeship also provides valuable insights into Chinese society. Vogel argues that in the 1960s, even while traditional friendship was disappearing, a new ethic of mutual assistance and comradely concern was appearing. Although people might not be free and open with one another, they were concerned about one another's well-being in a comradely sort of way. Our work on the 1970s suggests that this pattern has continued. Despite some common Western assumptions to the contrary, both mutual aid and a certain cautiousness with workmates and other potential friends can exist at the same time. Or, as our informant from the county light industry factory who had sworn brothers outside but no friends at work reports,

> In the factory with workmates one is very cautious and correct, but in livelihood matters everyone can lend mutual help. For example, whoever at work has been able to buy some meat or a special dish in the countryside will pass it around to others. And whenever there is a household problem such as a child or parent ill, then all will show concern. And when someone is upset, then all will try to offer comfort.[47]

Thus, a comradely ethic can exist even while friendship networks are severely retracted. This is the third unity of opposites that we have noted in this chapter: close interpersonal knowledge and contact in neighborhoods and work units often coexists with conflict in these same units; the retraction of the range of friends with which one is open often coexists with the seeking out of one, two, or three friends with whom one can reveal and reaffirm one's true beliefs; and even among those with whom one feels a certain distance or cautiousness there can still be an ethic of comradely concern. All three unities must be kept in mind to appreciate the full range of interpersonal relations in China.

Sources of Variation

To this point we have discussed mostly general trends that apply to the average citizen in an average neighborhood and work unit. There are some

---

and Social Control in Chinese Society, Amy A. Wilson et. al., eds. (New York: Praeger, 1977), pp. 135–36.

47. CSH4:15.

sharp variations, however, by both individual and social setting. We have already alluded to one of the clearest. Intellectuals and those of negative class background have suffered more from political pressure and hence been more likely to restrict their friendship networks.

In addition, employees in large factories and especially those living in work unit compounds tend to violate the norm that friendship contacts with workmates should be avoided. Indeed, those in unit compounds would have a hard time avoiding them, for workmates are synonomous with neighbors, and it is difficult to maintain close relationships with people living in other parts of the city. According to our interviews, 65 percent of the work units with considerable housing for their employees also have considerable interaction among employees after work. In those without housing, only 40 percent have frequent interaction among workers after work.[48]

The pattern of interaction with kin, friends, and neighbors also varies by age. Two emigrés suggest the possible permutations:

> Old families get together mostly with kin and close neighbors. But in young families with no old kin present, most of the contact is with colleagues and friends. With the death of old traditions there is less emphasis on kin contact. In Canton, one hops on one's bicycle after dinner to go visit friends. Since there is not much else to do outside and since one can't sit at home and be entertained by the TV like in Hong Kong, the major form of entertainment for youth in Canton is to go meet with friends and just talk. . . . Yes, that is right, kin are more important than friends in Hong Kong while the reverse is true in Canton. . . . Yes, it is slightly different for older people in Canton, for them neighborhood contacts substitute for friend contacts.

> Most youth have contact mostly with friends. Older people just visit with their neighbors. They don't go out to look up friends like young people do. And some youth have friends mostly among coworkers as they live in dorms surrounded by coworkers.[49]

Assuming these emigrés are correct, then older people meet more with neighbors and possibly some kin as well. Young people visit more with friends and to some extent other young coworkers.

Variations by type of neighborhood suggest some additional complexities. We have data on three kinds of neighborhood relations—mutual

---

48. With complete data on only 35 work units, none of the relationships can be statistically significant, but frequent after-work ties among coworkers correlates positively with both work unit compounds (gamma = .47) and large work units (gamma = .51).

49. KSP6:8; KSM28:3.

involvement, mutual aid, and neighborhood harmony. "Mutual involvement" is a summary scale including whether neighbors play a role in mediating local disputes, whether they play a role in detecting and reporting crime, and whether they speak to other neighbors about how each should raise their children. "Mutual aid" includes reports on the extent of mutual aid among neighbors and favorable comments on neighborhood life in China as compared to Hong Kong. "Neighborhood harmony" is simply the absence of reports of conflict between families in the same neighborhood. These are all difficult things to measure, especially when they rely on flexible yardsticks and are examined from a distance, but the observed patterns make some sense nevertheless.

Following Louis Wirth, one would expect closer neighborhood relations where there was greater stability of residence, greater homogeneity of residents, and where work combined with residence, such as in work unit compounds. From our earlier discussion of evidence from both China and the Soviet Union, we would expect neighborhoods with intense political pressure to have weaker relationships—even though on the average we expect neighborhoods to be less affected by political pressure than are work units or wider-ranging friendships. And then one would expect a number of ad hoc relationships, such as weaker neighborhood ties, in large cities and high-rise buildings. All of these suppositions are examined in table 37.[50]

The most striking finding in this table is the negative impact of political pressure on neighborhood ties (rows 4–6). Not only in neighborhoods with control efforts such as frequent household residency checks and neighborhood patrols but also in radical years when these and other political pressures are intensified, mutual involvement, aid, and harmony tended to decline. This finding replicates the anecdotal evidence discussed earlier. Political pressure hinders close personal relations.

Contrary to our earlier impressions, this table shows very little relationship between stability, homogeneity, work unit compounds, and neighborhood ties (rows 1–3). Except for the moderate relationship between work unit compounds and mutual aid, there are no relationships between these variables and neighborhood ties. A closer inspection of the characteristics of neighborhoods suggests why this is so. The stable neighborhoods tend to be old, inner-core neighborhoods where control efforts are particularly well developed and where services are provided through bureaucratic rather than informal channels (see appendix 2). Also, as we have already suggested, homogeneity of residents by occupation is not

50. Table 37 is restricted to just the Lingnan Region to avoid nonlinear problems with some variables. The opportunity and access items that are unrelated to neighborhood relations are omitted from this table.

Table 37   **Neighborhood Relations by Selected Characteristics** (Correlations)

	Mutual Involvement	Mutual Aid	Harmony
Neighborhood Structure			
Stability of residents	-.10	-.12	-.05
Homogeneity of residents	.09	-.09	-.05
Work unit compound	.13	.22*	.05
Deterrence Efforts			
Service infrastructure	-.21*	-.20*	.20*
Household control	-.32*	-.40*	-.26*
Radical Year	-.28*	-.22*	-.07
Other Characteristics			
Administrative level	-.26*	.06	-.18*
Outskirts location	.47*	.19*	.31*
Low-rise housing	.22*	.05	.03
White collar neighborhood	.05	.07	.25*
Median N	(44)	(48)	(64)

Source: Sample of neighborhoods, Lingnan Region only

*p ≤ .05

all that great in any Chinese neighborhood. They tend to be mixed occupationally but involve minimal differentiation in income, consumption, and style of life. Thus relative homogeneity is not a major determinant of neighborhood relations in this context.[51] And, finally, work unit compounds are also places with considerable political pressure that can help offset the potential closeness of neighborhood ties. Thus, we conclude that on the whole stability, homogeneity, and shared work promote closer ties in Chinese cities, even if their effects are muted by political pressure and difficult to detect in comparisons among neighborhoods.

There are a number of other characteristics that shape neighborhood life. There is somewhat less mutual involvement and harmony in larger cities, in part because these cities have more bureaucratic services and control. Neighborhood ties are closer on the outskirts of the city, where

51. There is also the following complexity: "As for frequency of conflict, generally if the people in the same building are of different class origins or if one is a cadre and one is not, on the surface things will be very polite and there will be little outward conflict. If, instead, they are all of the same class—all workers or all of capitalist origins—there will be lots of fighting" (SSM1:8). This former Shanghai resident goes on to elaborate that those from the wrong class background or of nonofficial status would fear offending someone of better background because of the political difficulties that this might cause. In the 1970s, it was differentials in political activism rather than differentials in occupational status that caused conflict. Thus, it is not too surprising that homogeneity of status was unrelated to neighborhood harmony.

informal services substitute for the bureaucratic services and where political control is weaker. Mutual involvement is greater in low-rise housing.
And there is more harmony in white collar neighborhoods—not so much
because white collar residents are more civilized, we suspect, but because
they are less likely to be forced into the conflict-generating sharing of the
toilet, bath, kitchen, and other facilities.

Again, the major theme that arises from this study of variation is the
negative impact of political pressure. Intellectuals have had narrower
social circles because of the threat of political attack, and social circles
have narrowed for virtually everyone in the most extreme periods of
political dogmatism. Neighborhoods under tight control have fewer ties
among neighbors, and where bureaucratic controls are greatest the effects
of residential stability, homogeneity, and common work may not be felt.
The other themes that arise from the study of variations across groups
and neighborhoods are only minor ones, but ones consistent with our
earlier observations. A major restriction on social networks is the shortage
of time as well as weak transportation and communication facilities. The
young, being able to bicycle about on their own and having fewer family
responsibilities, are able to overcome some of these obstacles and have
somewhat wider social networks. The old, being tied closer to home, are
more likely to take just the neighborhood and immediate family as their
most significant social world.

Future Trends and Conclusions

All these patterns may change somewhat in the 1980s and beyond. There
will be tendencies for personal networks to both expand and contract.
The relaxation of political pressure should allow people to establish closer
relationships with a wider network of friends and workmates. The construction of many new apartments with private toilets and kitchens should
also help reduce conflict among neighbors even as there is less necessity
for daily interaction. Contraction of social networks will come from several other sources. With increased construction of new residences, residential mobility will increase so that neighbors will not have such long
histories of contact. With more televisions, people will stay at home more
for entertainment rather than go next door or down the street to meet
and talk with neighbors. And with the introduction of piece rates and
more competition among workers in some work units, comradely relations
of mutual help and concern may be muted.

Nevertheless, we see these as only minor trends within a dominant
pattern of Chinese urban relations that has already become firmly established. These patterns started in the 1950s and were already firmly in place

by the early 1960s when Vogel did his work on the change from friendship to comradeship. The characteristic pattern of low residential mobility, great equality, lifetime job security in most jobs, and shared housing facilities is not going to change that quickly. And even the danger of possible political criticism will not completely disappear, for work units still keep dossiers on workers and political study groups still meet, and to an extent political campaigns still continue, even if in reduced form. Crowded work schedules will persist for both husband and wife, allowing little time for activities beyond one's immediate family and neighborhood.

The dominant tendencies will be much as in the past. Chinese personal relationships will be characterized by intense relationships to the immediate family and a close circle of friends. This will be accompanied by continuing "comradely" relations among workers and neighbors—relations characterized by an absence of great openness but a high degree of mutual aid and concern mixed with occasional conflict and ill feeling from too many years together in difficult situations and the inability to change jobs or move to another location.

Besides giving us some clue as to trends in Chinese personal relations in the future, our work also suggests some conclusions about common Western beliefs concerning interpersonal relations. In recent years there has been much scoffing at the suggestion of authors such as Durkheim, Simmel, and Wirth that modern urban life causes social isolation. The critics note that most people make new friends rapidly after a residential move and that with new transportation and communication facilities, kin and friendship ties can be maintained over great distances. The closed solidary community may be gone, but a widespread social network ranging throughout the city and beyond has taken its place. The critics also delight in pointing out how friendship and kin ties are not just utilitarian or dominanted by the "cash nexus" but include many aspects of obligation and alternative social rewards.[52] In the light of these findings, the ideas passed down by Durkheim, Simmel, Marx, Toennies, and Wirth seem a bit outmoded.

The data from China suggest that we should not be so quick to toss out these older ideas. In Chinese cities with minimal residential mobility, minimal differentiation by income or consumption, little opportunity for reward for individual striving, and the frequent joining of work and residence, personal relations include much more mutual knowledge, involvement, and concern than reported for cities in most other societies. Since residential mobility, income differentials, status striving, and the sepa-

52. Claude Fischer summarizes much of the available evidence in his *To Dwell among Friends.*

ration of work and residence were taken as critical features in shaping the nature of modern cities, earlier authors would not be too surprised that rather traditional relations—gemeinschaft—have reappeared in Chinese cities. The reaction of Chinese residents to life in their own cities and Hong Kong also suggests that earlier authors may have been right about the very sharp contrast between traditional rural community life and that in newly emerging industrial cities. We tend to have lost sight of these old distinctions because our urban and rural areas have been almost equally affected by modern communication and transportation. But those Chinese who have been yanked out of their old environment and plopped down in Hong Kong have not lost sight of the difference, and they use language with a very nineteenth-century flavor to describe what they often see as the overriding "cash nexus" of social relations outside their own society. All this gives further support to earlier authors who suggested that modern capitalist cities had individuating tendencies that could often be experienced as isolating and utilitarian to the exclusion of more human concerns—at least in the early stages of industrial development.

At the same time, one should also note with Durkheim, Simmel, and others that an environment with minimal separation of work, residence, and other spheres of life can often be stressful. The mutual knowledge and involvement in Chinese neighborhoods and work units is often not one of great closeness and openness. Knowledge and involvement come from being placed in the same situation for many years, and from the ethic that everyone should help everyone else. But these are not contacts that are chosen because of mutual attractions. Contacts of mutual attraction and agreement are reserved for a much smaller circle of friends. Indeed, the interaction in neighborhoods and work units can lead to conflict when people have been together too long sharing scarce facilities and suffering through political campaigns in which one person has criticized another. With little option of picking and choosing a work unit or neighborhood, one has the experience, much as would a traditional villager, of simply being stuck with immediate associates and having to make do as best as possible.

One is struck, then, not so much with the great benefits of an urban environment in which mobility, inequalities, personal striving, and work-residence separations are reduced as with the mixed blessing that it brings. On the one hand, these conditions bring greater mutual involvement, concern, and a sense of place in society. On the other, there is the danger of conflict and political attack from those who know too much about one. With political reform, some of the danger of political attack will decrease, causing social networks to expand and become more open. But the conditions of low mobility, equality, job security, and so forth depend to a major extent on a highly centralized economy run by a large bureaucracy bent on protecting the present order. Thus the two sets of conditions— the promise of relations of mutual concern and involvement and the threat of political criticism—may continue to go together.

Overall, in reviewing the quality of life in Chinese cities, one is impressed by how many things have to go together, and how, like Humpty-Dumpty, they are very fragile and difficult to put back together once broken apart. The socialist promise has been that with increased economic security and the end of economic exploitation, alienation, social isolation, and many of the other problems of modern capitalist cities would be solved. We have seen how some of these promises have been realized. In the initial years of the new regime, the increase in opportunities for education and work helped reduce the crime rate. But with an emphasis on heavy as opposed to light industry, the promise of meaningful jobs for the young proved difficult to fulfill. Without these opportunities, youth turned increasingly to crime, divination, and other activities indicating their sense of having no meaningful role in the new society. The patterns of modern capitalist societies were replicated rather than avoided.

Similarly, in the early years of the new regime, many people felt that the new socialist cause gave them a meaningful set of beliefs for guiding their life and directing their energies as a strong new national and social order was constructed. But this sense of purpose within developmental socialism was lost as utopian socialists came to the fore. In the aftermath, the sense of new economic security was overridden by the sense of political insecurity (and for the youth, increasing economic insecurity as well). As a result, powerlessness and meaninglessness, both important components of alienation, grew, and people increasingly became socially isolated or restricted to a very narrow circle of close friends. Again, the patterns of alienation and partial isolation of the capitalist West were being repeated rather than avoided.

12   Conclusions

It will come as no surprise to the reader to learn that we argue that the Chinese model of urbanism, especially as it was developed in its "purest" form during the Cultural Revolution decade, possessed a number of very distinctive features. In conclusion, we want to review the nature of this distinctiveness, examine the lessons it provides about the forces that shape urban forms, and speculate about the kinds of policy options that remain open to Chinese urban policy makers.

As suggested in the Introduction, Western scholars have had a profound ambivalence toward the rise of the modern city. They have both celebrated its liberating elements and condemned its social problems. They have debated, often without resolution, the sources of the benefits and liabilities of the modern city. Marxist scholars have tended to find the source of the cities' liabilities in their capitalist origins, while non-Marxist scholars have often seen them as universals.

The debates have centered on a number of key elements identified as shaping the character of modern cities. Some authors, such as Toennies, Durkheim, Simmel, and Wirth, identify the dissolution of tight, solidary communities as one of the principal defining characteristics of the modern city. This dissolution provides the ambiguous heritage of increased individual freedom, initiative, and creativity combined with moral confusion, loneliness, crime, and other forms of social deviance. Other authors, following Marx, put more emphasis on the increasing inequality and insecurity that accompany capitalist development and the host of social problems that these tendencies produce. One of the resulting problems is alienation: Loss of control over work induces a sense of meaninglessness and powerlessness. Then there are authors like Weber who emphasize the growth of bureaucracy in all modern societies, and like Hayek and Friedman who suggest that the increased bureaucratization of modern urban life is only exacerbated under socialism. In short, modern urban life is seen as being shaped by a loss of community solidarity, decreasing equality and security, increased alienation, and spreading bureaucratic control. Whether these are characteristics that could be changed in a socialist, as opposed to capitalist, setting has remained unresolved.

China's experience of the 1970s helps resolve some of the issues in this debate. In each of the areas enumerated above, Chinese cities have experienced very different conditions from what has been known in the capitalist West, currently developing market societies, and most other socialist states as well. In each area, China tried in the 1970s to implement extreme socialist ideals more thoroughly than in preceding societies, thereby providing a test of the limits of urban reform.

Distinctive Features

We will not attempt to recapitulate all aspects of the "pure" form of the Chinese model of urbanism, but among the basic structural elements of this model were strict migration controls and minimal urbanization in spite of considerable economic development; a penetrating residential work unit organizational system; a highly developed bureaucratic allocation system; an emphasis on production rather than consumption; a relatively egalitarian distribution system; a rejection of schools as the basic mechanism for sorting talent; much stress on citizen involvement in public health, social control, and other realms; and rigid taboos on all forms of dress, expression, ritual life, and communication that did not conform to the official ideology. These elements were supposed to make possible cities that were spartan, productive, egalitarian, stable, solidary, and economically secure, with an atmosphere that would make urbanites feel well provided for and involved, so that they would express their positive commitment through vigorous work efforts and active participation in social life. The structural changes in urban institutions contributed to a number of social consequences that also seem quite distinctive—high stability in jobs and residences, involvement and familiarity with neighbors and workmates, minimal differentiation of consumption patterns and life styles, low divorce, high female work participation, and rapid changes in fertility, religious customs, and other realms of behavior.

It should be clear by now that most of these features arose not from a special Chinese historical and cultural tradition, but from changes introduced after 1949. We have seen this in comparisons both to China's own pre-1949 urban tradition and to Hong Kong, Singapore, and urban Taiwan. Some features, such as low divorce rates and preference for extended household living, are shared with these other Chinese cities. Some contemporary practices also have common historical precedents—for example, the efforts to register the urban population and to exile criminals from urban areas. A good many visual images are held in common as well—older residents practicing the graceful *taijiquan* exercises in parks in the early morning and junks moving up and down the rivers. But still much about contemporary Chinese cities is very different. Some relatively large firms in pre-1949 China provided housing and other amenities for their employees, but the extensiveness of the resources provided to, and of the controls exercised over, employees by modern work units in China has no real parallel. Residential stability and great involvement with neighbors is more the creation of modern conditions than a carryover from the past. Other features, such as nearly universal female labor force participation and minimal religious activity, also have no comparison in other Chinese environments. We have previously noted that many other sights and sounds of Chinese cities today are dramatically changed, as anyone who has taken the train between socialist Canton and capitalist Hong Kong can testify. Overall, the face of Chinese urbanism has been transformed in a revolutionary way.

Many of the changes implemented and many of the features we have listed are shared to one degree or another with other socialist societies—an emphasis on production rather than consumption, controls on expression and religion, high female labor force participation, and so forth. Of all our comparative frameworks, the similarities with urbanism in Eastern Europe and the Soviet Union are most apparent. This is not too surprising, for the ideas that animated the Chinese urban reforms have their roots in Marxist-Leninist ideology, and the basic institutional framework was borrowed from the Soviet Union in the 1950s. Still, there are features of the Chinese model of urbanism, particularly as it developed in the Cultural Revolution decade, that are distinctive even in comparison with European socialist societies. For example, in Eastern Europe restrictions on urban migration have not been as strict or as effectively applied, people have been more free to change jobs and residences, the market plays a somewhat greater role in distribution (and direct bureaucratic allocation and rationing less), schools have a highly emphasized role in sorting talent, more inequalities in consumption patterns have been allowed or even encouraged, divorce is much more prevalent, and restrictions on unorthodox thinking and behavior generally have not been as strict.[1] The features of the contemporary Chinese political economy that we have stressed as primary—relative equality, bureaucratic allocation, persistent

1. There have, of course, been variations over time and by country in European socialist societies that these generalizations ignore. In certain respects, conditions in the late Stalinist Soviet Union are more similar to those in 1970s China, and places like Yugoslavia much less so, than these statements recognize.

political campaigns, and a tight-knit and penetrating organizational system—are all more developed in China than in Eastern Europe. Thus, more clearly than most socialist states, China allows us to test how extreme forms of socialist organization might reshape urban life.

Chinese cities are distinctive not only with respect to Chinese cities elsewhere and with respect to other socialist cities, but also with respect to the contemporary Chinese countryside, thereby increasing our appreciation of how China's urban form leads to special social consequences.[2] In comparison to cities, Chinese villages have remained much freer of a bureaucratic presence, more able to follow the dictates of local public opinion, and more able to ignore external political commands. This degree of autonomy is based on several characteristics that diverge sharply from the characteristics of urban neighborhoods—including the small population of each unit, the kinship basis of these units, their leadership by locals rather than outsiders, and their considerable distance from police stations and other modes of external control. Thus, villages can serve as a partial buffer between the individual and the bureaucracy above and allow peasants to act in ways that they see fitting their own needs.

The needs of peasants are quite different from those of urbanites because of the structure of their political economy. Even before the post-1978 reforms that restored quasi-family farming, peasants had to depend heavily on their families. Family members were paid, not according to need, but according to how much they worked, males earned significantly more than females, and incomes averaged only about a third of that of urbanites and went up and down sharply with each year's harvest. Housing remained in private hands, as did pigs and other domestic animals, and a private plot usually brought in about a fourth of the peasant family's income. Virtually all old-age support was the responsibility of sons, and much of a family's schooling and medical expenses were private, not public, responsibilities. It is of little surprise, then, that when combined with the internal solidarity and relative autonomy of the village community, familism remained dominant in many spheres. In comparison to cities, birth control made slower progress, there was more favoritism to males, bride prices continued to be paid, weddings remained lavish, and domestic ancestor worship persisted in significant ways.

In spite of a proclaimed policy to narrow the gap between city and countryside, that gap has become increasingly sharply defined. In traditional times the line between urban and rural was only vaguely drawn, mobility into and out of cities was high, and many kin groups had links

2. See William L. Parish and Martin K. Whyte, *Village and Family in Contemporary China* (Chicago: University of Chicago Press, 1978).

in both town and countryside. Today, with the emphasis on household registrations labeling one as agricultural or nonagricultural from birth and confining most peasants to the countryside, the line is sharply drawn. Through the 1970s, most Chinese urban residents grew up expecting to rely on the state for housing, income, pension, education, and medical care while rural residents grew up expecting to look to their families and close neighbors for these same services. The two spheres became increasingly distinct from one another, with very different political and economic structures leading to very different social consequences. Ironically, then, one consequence of socialism in China has been to increase, rather than reduce, the rural-urban gap.[3]

Lessons from the Chinese Experience

As outlined in the introduction to this chapter, Western scholars have identified a limited number of characteristics as shaping the nature and problems of modern cities. This list of characteristics, with differing emphases by Marxist and other scholars, typically includes the growth of bureaucracy, growing inequality and insecurity, alienation and a loss of sense of purpose, and a dissolution of community ties. Chinese cities provide examples of very special attempts to introduce reform in each of these areas and an important test of whether common urban ills can be avoided and a new, more perfect form of urban life created.

One of the attempted reforms was to make the bureaucracy responsive to popular needs, thereby avoiding the problems associated with the growth of bureaucracy elsewhere and especially in socialist states. This proved difficult to implement. From the 1950s on, recurrent political campaigns and purges were used to force reform, and these mechanisms probably did reduce bureaucratic corruption to very low levels compared to many other developing societies—at least for a time. But in other respects, the campaigns only heightened responsiveness to higher authority, or encouraged bureaucrats to play it safe and avoid making decisions in order to protect themselves. By the 1970s, with bureaucratic allocation almost completely replacing markets in the distribution of goods and replacing exams in the allocation of students to schools and workers to jobs, the role of the bureaucracy became ever more pervasive. The radical leaders' attempt to simplify administration by eliminating most rules and procedures had the unanticipated effect of allowing some bureaucrats to use

3. See Martin King Whyte, "Town and Country in Contemporary China," *Comparative Urban Research*, Summer 1983. These basic policies have been retained since Mao's death. One leading official, Wan Li, states bluntly, "There is no need for peasants to work as workers in the cities." (Peking Radio, 24 February 1983, in *FBIS*, 28 February 1983, p. K13.)

their power for personal advantage. The result was that urbanites increasingly felt themselves under the control of inefficient and often capricious authorities. In terms of fostering bureaucratic efficiency and responsiveness, the Cultural Revolution reforms must be judged a failure, and this is ironic because they were motivated to a considerable extent by the antibureaucratic feelings of Mao Zedong and other radical leaders.[4]

Another attempted reform was to create greater equality and security. This was in some respects a major success and in others a major disaster. It did provide widespread basic education, health care, pensions, job security, and income equality. And during the 1966–76 radical decade the emphasis on equality in dress and consumption helped further blur the distinctions among people in different occupations.

However, urbanites did not lose all sense of the relative worth of different jobs. Preferences for different jobs and marriage mates revealed a clear sense of a status hierarchy based upon power, education, income, job prestige, political labels, and other factors. With a few exceptions, jobs continued to be evaluated much the same way as in other countries, whether socialist or capitalist. Professional and administrative jobs were placed on top. Jobs that use only the hands and brute strength rather than the mind were placed near the bottom. Thus, even within a regime of relative income equality, the prestige hierarchy of occupations remained relatively undisturbed, and as elsewhere, that hierarchy placed mental labor on top and manual labor at the bottom. Relative income equality and socialist propaganda about the worth of manual labor have been unable to break this universal tendency.[5]

Also, in spite of the relative income equality, high level administrative cadres have often been perceived as living exceptionally well. High level officials do indeed have special perquisites, and the use of these perquisites may have become somewhat more free wheeling over the last decade.

4. On the actual consequences, see Andrew G. Walder, "Work and Authority in Chinese Industry" (Ph.D. dissertation, University of Michigan, 1981). On the nature of Mao's feelings on the matter, see Martin K. Whyte, "Bureaucracy and Modernization in China: The Maoist Critique," *American Sociological Review* 38 (1973): 149–69.

5. Ruth Lo notes that by punishing people with manual labor the authorities implicitly recognized the lower status of manual labor. Ruth Earnshaw Lo and Katherine S. Kinderman, *In the Eye of the Typhoon* (New York: Harcourt Brace, 1980). The evidence on the similarity of prestige rankings in both socialist and capitalist societies is reviewed in Walter Connor, *Socialism, Politics, and Equality* (New York: Columbia University Press, 1979). As in other socialist states, one of the apparent ironies is that service jobs such as being a waiter in a restaurant rank particularly low in prestige despite the emphasis on "serving the people." One study of ranking is in Lan Chengdong and Zhang Zhongru, "The Aspirations and Inclinations of This Year's Upper Middle School Graduates," *Shehui* 2 (1982): 22–25.

But other factors also shape the perception of elite privilege. One of these factors is that there is but a single status hierarchy. Instead of elite businessmen, elite government officials, elite lawyers, doctors, artists, and writers as we know them in market societies, there is a single elite with its privileges closely tied to a uniform, graded bureaucratic hierarchy. Along this hierarchy, income, consumption, status, and power all cohere to a remarkable degree. Therefore, there is less confusion about elite status than in other societies and perhaps a heightened sense of "them," the elite, against "us," the masses. Also, in a society with few differences in income and consumption, and with most people having little of their own, small differences in income and consumption may well take on an exaggerated significance. And, as in other socialist states, the public morality of equality learned in school and elsewhere may cause people to be more critical of small differences and of the violation of norms about equality in consumption than would be the case in other settings. Thus, *actual* inequality need not necessarily correspond with *perceived* inequality, especially when it comes to elite positions in society.[6]

The more serious problems with equality, however, had to do with the failure to provide employment and the attempt to invert the old class order. Many of the social problems of the 1966–76 decade can be traced to these two features of the radical program. Under this program, people were no longer free to compete for the best education or job that their abilities allowed or to rise in their jobs on the basis of work performance. Opportunities in these spheres came to rely heavily on class background and political commitment—and, in this highly bureaucratized environment, often on personal connections as well. The transmission of parental status to children was disrupted, a highly unusual experience in any society, and so was any sense of predictability and fairness in society. There was no longer any link between effort and reward. When combined with the emphasis on heavy industry and the failure to provide jobs for urban youth, these policies undermined the sense of justice and security that had been present in earlier years.

The problems, then, came not so much from the emphasis on equality of distribution as from the effort to equalize mobility opportunities and an absence of predictable opportunities. The Chinese experience shows clearly how these two sets of issues need to be separated. Some Chinese officials and professionals complained about the limits on incomes, housing, and other amenities, but the more frequent complaints from all sectors of society were about the interference with normal opportunities for them

6. For a similar set of points based on Eastern European and Soviet data, see Frank Parkin, *Class Inequality and Political Order* (New York: Holt, Rinehart, and Winston, 1977), pp. 156, 162.

and their children and about the use of class labels, political criteria, and personal connections in place of predictable, objective performance. It was this absence of predictable mobility opportunities that led to the social disasters of the 1970s, including poor school performance, low work productivity, alienation, and juvenile delinquency. The Chinese experience, then, demonstrates the extreme importance of legitimate opportunities and the dangers of utopian experiments that fail to recognize this fact.

Another goal of urban reforms was to reshape people's sense of moral purpose. For a time it seemed that Chinese cities had moved toward eliminating the alienation described for other urban dwellers around the world. By joining in the grand national effort to make China strong, people began to feel that they had a meaningful role in a noble, patriotic cause. The dramatic changes in China's national unity and stature in world affairs might make people feel their contributions were effective, even if as individuals they had little power. Small study groups with criticism and self-criticism caused people to internalize or at least adjust to the values of the new society, setting China apart from other socialist states where efforts at producing the new socialist man have been less thoroughgoing. Many people turned from old beliefs and practices and began to accept significant parts of the new socialist order and the leadership of the Communist Party and Mao Zedong.

In the end, however, this sense of national purpose and commonly shared values proved somewhat tenuous. When the values of developmental socialism were replaced by those of utopian socialism, when people began to be attacked for beliefs that lay outside the bounds of this narrow utopianism, and when legitimate opportunities in schools and work declined, alienation spread. People felt increasingly powerless and unable to control their own or their nation's destiny, and many lost the sense of having a meaningful role in building a new society and a strong China. This experience demonstrates how difficult it is to find unifying values in modern society, and how the most commonly accepted unifying value is still that of simple nationalism—one shared by both market and socialist states. The experience also demonstrates how shared values are closely linked to the availability of legitimate opportunities and a sense of fairness in allocating these opportunities. Without access to jobs and education allocated on the basis of commonly agreed principles, a sense of fairness and trust in the society can be lost. And without a modicum of political as well as economic security, people will withdraw into a narrow circle of family and friends and fail to give commitment or energy to their work or society.

Chinese leaders not only tried to create a new sense of moral purpose but also a new sense of community. As with the other reforms, the results were not always as anticipated. True to what one would have expected from the low rates of residential and occupational mobility, relative equality, and the occasional joining of work and residence, over the course of years people got to know a considerable amount about the lives and personalities of other members of their work groups and neighborhoods. In these units individuals came to be seen not just as holders of roles as Party secretary, foreman, janitor, and so forth, but as whole people with individual quirks and with particular family problems and concerns. The impersonality and anonymity experienced in many other cities were avoided—this is particularly apparent in comparisons to life in Hong Kong. Relations with colleagues, superiors, and neighbors may not have always been pleasant and might even have been filled with conflict, but there was little likelihood of feeling isolated and of no concern to others. These consequences were not always the result of conscious policy choices on the part of the leadership. The reduction in inequality and status differences as well as the ethic of comradely concern was consciously supported as a means to increase solidarity among different groups in society, but other factors such as the reduction in residential mobility were artifacts of policies designed for other purposes, such as keeping peasants out of cities and reducing urban costs. The results, nevertheless, support much of the earlier scholarly thinking on the factors that shape patterns of urban anonymity versus community.

Unfortunately, these unusual communal, or gemeinschaft-like, relationships in settings where we would normally expect less intimate gesellschaft-like relationships depend to a considerable degree on an all-pervasive bureaucracy, which in turn has unusual consequences for personal relationships. Without the bureaucratic control of jobs, incomes, consumer goods, housing, and urban residence permits, the equality, infrequent migration, and the joining of work and residence that help support communal relationships would not exist. But in turn, pervasive bureaucracy increases the possibility of political threat, and this gives personal relationships a very special flavor. Personal relationships, particularly during the Cultural Revolution years, have been of a type that discourages the spontaneous expression of thoughts and feelings. Instead, elaborate role playing developed in which what was said and how others were treated were carefully considered and regulated in order to create the proper impression. The roles were things like Party member, activist, backward element, and relationships came to be characterized by "comradeship"—

a curious blend of amiability, helpfulness, and potential hostility.[7] So in these urban cells relationships were not segmental and impersonal, but at the same time they were still highly formalized rather than spontaneous. Given this atmosphere, it is understandable that urbanites cultivated a few very close ties with family members, former schoolmates, and others and were completely open only with this limited set of people. The Chinese experience, then, provides new understanding of how interpersonal relationships can involve seemingly contradictory aspects of knowledge and conflict, cautiousness and concern, as well as emotional distance with many and intense relationships with only a few. The experience also leads to a new appreciation of older ideas about how mobility, inequality, and work-residence separation shape these relationships as well as a sense of how the conditions needed to recreate communal relationships in the modern age create unanticipated problems.

The Chinese experience also leads to a new appreciation of the difficulty of reshaping loyalties to the larger social world. We noted in chapter 2 that a number of features of the social structure of traditional Chinese cities inhibited the development of any sense of urban community and citizenship, and instead kept concern focused on one's own family, native place association, or other narrow grouping. In the enthusiastic atmosphere of the 1950s, many urbanites felt that the narrow compartmentalization of urban life was breaking down. The disappearance of many of the previous organizational forms, the building of new, more all-encompassing organizations, and the frantic participation of people of different statuses and backgrounds in the reforms and campaigns of the period all created a sense of people being drawn out of their shells into the affairs and concerns of the broader community.[8] But, again, this sentiment seems to have been eroded in more recent years. As work units and neighborhoods gained increasing control over resources and over the lives of their members, new, highly inclusive compartments arose to replace the old forms of association and to monopolize people's energies and concerns.

7. Of course, it can be argued that in all societies people are continuously involved in various forms of role playing, even with intimate friends and family members. For a classic statement of this theme, see Erving Goffman, *The Presentation of Self in Everyday Life* (Garden City: Doubleday, 1959). However, it can still be argued that in the tense political atmosphere of Chinese urban organizations even before the Cultural Revolution decade the nature of role playing became unusually elaborate and contrived, with a much clearer recognition that individuals were presenting a manufactured image of themselves. For vivid personal accounts of the manufacturing of such images, see Robert Loh, *Escape from Red China* (New York: Coward-McCann, 1962), and Tung Chi-ping and Humphrey Evans, *The Thought Revolution* (London: Leslie Frewin, 1967).

8. This sense is vividly conveyed in William Sewell, *I Stayed in China* (New York: A. S. Barnes, 1966), especially pp. 107–8.

There do not appear to be mechanisms to promote communication and a shared sense of community between, say, an urban hospital and a large factory located right next door to it.[9] The growing sense of disorderliness and danger of the urban environment in the Cultural Revolution years also encouraged this retreat into the private concerns.

In this setting one might expect strong loyalties and a sense of community to develop around individual work units and neighborhoods, but there is precious little evidence of such sentiments in our interviews, except in a few especially large and prosperous units such as the army and the railroad. Feelings of patriotism and national pride are often intense, as are sentiments of family loyalty and obligation, but pride or attachment in intermediate levels of urban organization are curiously weak. The overarching stress on national symbols of loyalty—the motherland, the Party, and Mao Zedong—may help prevent the sort of "company spirit" or "town pride" that exists, say, in Japanese factories or American towns.

Also contributing to the weakness of work unit and neighborhood identification may be the inability of urbanites to choose where they will live or work, the absence of any direct connection between the success of one's work unit and level of pay, and the inability to express one's interests through local elections and other forms of local political participation. In contrast to Chinese villages and local communities in some other societies, Chinese urban communities do not serve as a buffer between the central government and the local population. Instead the central government has been able to capture leadership of each local neighborhood and work group for its own purposes. In a few areas such as gambling and covert family worship, having a highly solidary neighborhood with residents who have known one another for many years does provide some leeway for behavior that is officially frowned on. But by and large Chinese neighborhoods and work units have represented the interests of the central government and whichever political group was in charge rather than the interests of the local population.

This effective control of local communities has meant that the government did not have to rely primarily on harsh, secret police rule for control of the population. But in political attacks and the stifling of individual expression the results were much the same. Thus, the lack of identification with local neighborhoods and work units is not too surprising. The Chinese experience suggests that older theories about community identification need to be amended. It is not just residential and occupational mobility,

9. This particular example comes from observations of just such a side-by-side unit situation in the city of Wuhan in 1980. See Gail Henderson, "Danwei: The Chinese Work Unit" (Ph.D. dissertation, University of Michigan, 1982).

separation of work and residence, and differentiation and heterogeneity of occupations that can cause a decline in community solidarity. The absence of free choice of one's neighborhood or work group and the inability of that group to express local interests appear to be equally important in weakening community identification.[10]

In sum, the Chinese urban experience of recent years does have a number of lessons to teach us. First, it shows the great difficulty of changing some urban characteristics, such as bureaucratism or the urban prestige hierarchy. Second, it shows that while some aspects of urban organization can be changed, the results are not always as expected. The pursuit of equality through class struggle and an emphasis on class labels alienated many and failed to eliminate awareness of occupational rank and privilege. The pursuit of comradely relations produced more interpersonal knowledge and concern but also a certain interpersonal wariness and weak attachment to middle level community and work organizations. Several reforms proved to be contradictory—the pursuit of equality through class struggle, for example, destroyed much of the former unity of purpose of the goal of national strength and growth. The characteristics of cities that some Western theorists saw as immutable are not, but the Chinese experience shows that reforming the nature of modern cities is a complex business.

There are other, more specific lessons as well. In Chinese cities in the 1950s, through a combination of increased bureaucratic control, more secure job opportunities, and mutual surveillance, many social problems were handled successfully. Starvation, begging, drug addiction, prostitution, and organized crime were eliminated or drastically reduced in scope. Individual crime was also significantly reduced. But in the 1970s, with a reduction in economic security for youth, the mechanisms of bureaucratic control and mutual surveillance alone proved unable to prevent juvenile delinquency and other forms of petty crime. This experience helps delineate more clearly than before the independent role of legitimate opportunities in controlling crime and related social problems.

Family life has also not proved to be as amenable to change as anticipated. In a few areas, it is true, dramatic changes have occurred. The move of urban women from the home and into the work force has been impressive, as has been the speed with which urban fertility has declined. The decline in ancestor worship and related family ritual life, which were once seen as giving Chinese families much of their meaning in life, has also been startling.

10. On the role of political participation and competition in shaping identification with communities in Chicago, see William Kornblum, *Blue Collar Community* (Chicago: University of Chicago Press, 1974).

But in other important respects urban family life in China has changed only modestly, and the changes that have occurred reflect distinctive socialist patterns less than trends toward more "conjugal" family forms that are occurring in many parts of the globe. Less autocratic relations between the generations, more freedom of mate choice for the young, and rising marriage ages all fit these worldwide patterns, although the specifics vary somewhat from country to country. Extended kinship relations seem to be giving way somewhat to reliance on neighbors, friends, and workmates, a pattern also commented upon in other societies. And in spite of the tumult of change in the society outside, economic considerations still have a pervasive impact on family relationships and women continue to manage the bulk of family chores, thus producing the "double burden" of work at home and on the job that employed women in other societies are familiar with.

In some ways what may seem most remarkable is that basic elements of Chinese family life have changed so little. There are few signs of the kinds of family disorganization that sometimes accompany urbanism. Families have retained much solidarity, and marriages stability, in spite of the major changes that urbanites have been subjected to. What socialism may have to do with this enduring strength of urban Chinese families is debatable, since we have noted that solidary families and stable marriages are also characteristic of capitalistic Hong Kong and Singapore. But we speculate that to some extent the bureaucratic nature of Chinese socialist urbanism and its political turbulence may have helped to maintain strong family ties, as individuals have pooled their efforts in family units in order to survive in the contentious world around them. So the peculiar nature of the urban reforms in China has had mixed consequences for family life—certain features have been changed dramatically, but many others only modestly, and in certain respects contemporary urban forms reinforce traditional family strengths and orientations.

Then there are additional lessons about the costs and benefits of modern cities. Even while bemoaning the loss of community, Western theorists have often praised modern cities for the sense of self, individuality, creativity, and freedom that they provide. Cities have been seen as places where individuals can escape the conventionality and traditionalism of village life and where freedom and diversity promote innovation and reward eccentricity; as places where, according to urban sociologist Robert Park, "Everyone is more or less on his own."[11] Not much recapitulation of the material covered in this study is needed to see that contemporary Chinese cities do not fit this conception. Of course, in Chinese cities,

11. Robert Park, *Human Communities* (Glencoe: Free Press, 1952), p. 74.

there is more diversity in types of people, occupations, and so forth than is found in Chinese villages. But the bureaucratic structures and rigid controls of the contemporary urban system work to ensure that this diversity is molded into acceptable and standardized forms of behavior. Village superstition may be escaped, but a new set of constraints on thought and action has prevented the sort of freedom and experimentation that Park and others describe. In fact, it could be argued that the controls on behavior and expression are more restrictive in the cities than in Chinese villages, where bureaucratic controls are less directly and pervasively felt. And while it is true that in China most academic learning and research are concentrated in urban places, it is also apparent that very little that could be called an urban "high culture" has been allowed to survive and develop. Again the bureaucratic control system, in this instance that presiding over culture and the arts, has effectively prevented the emergence of cultural products aimed at a specialized and refined audience.

The rigidity of the urban controls raises an issue about a related trait that is supposed to be a universal and positive trait of cities. Whatever their faults, cities are generally seen as centers of innovation and catalysts for social change, partly as a result of the freedom for innovation and cultural experimentation occurring there. We noted earlier the claim that imperial Chinese cities served this innovative function less than did cities in the West because of the ways in which the imperial bureaucracy controlled urban places and institutions. After the fall of the Manchu dynasty in 1911, cities became much more visible as centers for new ideas and reform efforts, with new magazines, a vernacular literature movement, political protests, the Chinese Communist Party, and other new phenomena all growing from urban roots. After 1949 the Chinese Communists did not see the issue as one of an innovative city versus the conservative countryside, but as a bourgeois and consumption-oriented city versus the productive and proletarian village. They set about to transform urban places to productive and spartan places, as we have seen. But in the process, by the nature of the institutions and controls instituted to eliminate the "bourgeois" aspects of urban life, did they also snuff out much of the creative potential and innovativeness of urban areas? Did the effort to keep cities from being "cancers" result in their having less of a role as "catalysts" as well? Recent Chinese press articles extolling the virtues of large cities and of their specialized intellectual activity suggest that China's post-Mao leaders may be coming around to this view.[12]

12. In the wake of a national conference on urban planning in October 1980 there was a shift in official favor back in the direction of large cities and a revival of the 1950s slogan, "Learn from Shanghai," although the further expansion of Peking was supposed to be halted. See Editorial, *People's Daily*, 31 May 1981, in *FBIS*, 1 April 1981, pp. K3–5. Similar

Overall, one is reminded of the ambivalent feelings many early Western theorists such as Durkheim and Simmel had over the emergence of the modern city. On the one hand they wrung their hands over the loss of supportive social relationships and clear social values inherent in traditional communities. On the other they celebrated the new freedom, individuality, and creativity that looser community structures encouraged. When faced with this same conflict, Chinese leaders over the last three decades chose to come down hard on the side of tight social communities directed by a centralized bureaucracy with clear prescriptive values that allowed little room for deviation. The more radical leaders thought that this program would be liberating, but instead it introduced even tighter regimentation than had been true of Chinese communities in earlier centuries. In this, as in several other respects, Western theories turn out to contain considerable truth after all.

Future Trends

We have concentrated on the radical decade ending in 1976 not only because this is the period on which we happen to have the richest data but also because this is the period which provides the clearest alternative in urban form and which puts many ideas about urban dynamics to a test. We are also interested in this period because it helps set the stage for contemporary urban policy, frequently providing a negative example for the post-Mao leaders of things to be avoided. Understanding what they are trying to avoid, and the potential dilemmas they face, helps one better appreciate current policy trends and evolving urban social forms. Also, by looking as far back as the 1950s, we have been able to see the formation of many institutions—the household registration system, the neighborhood control system, all inclusive work units, and the rationing of vital supplies such as grain, oil, and cotton cloth—that remain unchanged even under the present reform regime.

As indicated in previous chapters, reform policies instituted since the end of the 1970s have led to some very distinctive changes in urban social life. Some of these changes take advantage of choices within the larger socialist model which can make for quite different types of cities even while many of the larger goals of socialism remain intact. One is the choice between utopian and developmental socialism. The present leaders have

---

sentiments seem to underlie efforts to get intellectuals and specialists transferred back to work appropriate to their skills in large cities and provide them with the necessary comforts and privileges to encourage their creativity.

shifted clearly toward the latter, making Chinese cities much less threatening places than they were before 1976. Chinese cities may remain clearly under the control of an extensive bureaucracy anxious to set limits on public criticism of its rule, but this is still very different from the reign of virtue and terror under the utopian socialist model.

The reform rulers have moved not just away from the utopian to a developmental socialist model, but away from the extremes of both models. The extreme utopian model forces a limited set of standards on everyone, while the extreme (Stalinist) developmental model depresses current consumption to very low levels in favor of investment for long-run growth—particularly in favor of investment in steel and other heavy industries. In the 1966–76 decade, radical leaders pursued extreme utopian and developmental models at once—promoting a narrow ideology that everyone had to embrace while reducing consumption, increasing investment, and favoring heavy industry over light industry and agriculture. By following the extreme Stalinist model of development, employment opportunities failed to grow, housing standards declined, and consumer supplies failed to keep pace with growing demand. All these trends helped create the feeling that the socialist promise of a better society was not being met and in turn helped produce the many social problems that we have enumerated.

By moving away from the extreme Stalinist model of development, many new opportunities have been created and people can begin to feel that more of the socialist promise is being realized. This, then, provides a clear break with the past and will improve the quality of life in Chinese cities in the 1980s. Another clear break with the immediate past is the decision to assign educational and career opportunities primarily on the basis of performance on objective tests and job related standards rather than on the basis of political commitment and class origin, providing perhaps more of a sense of equity or fairness in the way that social rewards are distributed.

Despite these clear changes, some quandaries remain, and they are likely to cause some wavering in the 1980s and a partial return to some of the tendencies of the past. This wavering will come from a number of trade-offs that are endemic to modern societies. We have alluded to these trade-offs in earlier chapters as those between market distribution and bureaucratic allocation and between equality and efficiency, and they are fundamental factors distinguishing capitalist from socialist societies.[13] Market distribution systems have a number of positive features, but they

13. Consult Charles Lindblom, *Politics and Markets* (New York: Basic Books, 1977); Arthur Okun, *Equality and Efficiency: The Big Trade-off* (Washington: Brookings Institution, 1975).

also have undeniable drawbacks, particularly in developing societies—
sharp income differences and class differentiation, inflation and unemployment, slum creation, and simply the inability of the authorities to
predict and control the behavior of urbanites in a situation of "consumer
sovereignty." Many of these problems can be reduced or overcome if a
switch is made to state socialism, direct allocation, and an egalitarian
distribution policy. This was the choice made in China and other socialist
societies, and for very much these reasons. But in making such a switch,
the advantages associated with a decentralized market system were lost,
while problems that are by-products of direct allocation were spawned.

Fundamentally, the switch involves concentrating vast amounts of authority and control in the hands of a centralized bureaucracy in order to
enable that bureaucracy to combat the previous set of evils. When the
matter is put in these terms, the costs should be obvious. The many ways
in which market forces, even if imperfectly developed, contribute to high
motivation, productivity, innovation, and efficiency are lost. People are
not able to arrange their lives in ways they would choose, and this fact
may weaken motivation and creativity. Decisions that should be made
quickly have to pass through multiple layers of the bureaucracy and await
the necessary "chop" at each layer. Irrational actions by bureaucratic
authorities cannot be criticized or checked before they lead to waste or
human suffering. Individuals who are victimized and persecuted have no
protection or recourse and must simply try to survive until later policy
changes may result in their "rehabilitation." The nature of the bureaucratic system that develops helps to overcome previous problems and
mobilize resources, but as new problems proliferate the disadvantages of
this form of social organization, at least in its extreme form (as in China
after 1966), become increasingly obvious.

State authorities have been only too eager to persuade urbanites that
they should be given credit for the improvements that have taken place
in their lives, but in doing so they have played a dangerous game. If large
numbers of urbanites begin to feel that their lives are unsatisfying, unpredictable, or oppressive, then they are not likely to blame themselves,
the gods, or fate. In view of the bureaucratic system that dominates their
lives, they are likely to hold the state responsible. Thus this new set of
problems can undermine public support for the state and produce a growing sense of alienation and anger, even if these sentiments cannot be
openly expressed.

This, then, appears to us to be the nature of the urban crisis of post-
Mao China. Pursuit of one alternative way of organizing urban life in a
relatively pure form led to problems that eventually threatened the political order and jolted the post-Mao leadership into taking action to change

the situation. This has not meant simply eliminating utopianism or undoing irrational policies and returning to the "correct" way of organizing urban life. Nor is it a matter of Deng Xiaoping and other post-Mao leaders claiming a nonexistent crisis in order to justify their repudiation of Mao's legacy. Instead, it has been a question of how to come to a new balance in the trade-offs between equality and efficiency, between control and initiative. Since the 1950s, East European socialist societies have grappled with this central dilemma—with the need to counteract the inefficiencies and rigidities their bureaucratic systems produced, without reviving all of the problems associated with the previous market regime—and they have arrived at a range of compromise solutions. Some, such as Yugoslavia and Hungary, have made a major shift away from the direct allocation mode, with some enhancement of efficiency and productivity but also renewed problems with things like inflation and unemployment. Others, such as Czechoslovakia and the Soviet Union, have had reform efforts watered down or reversed, and as a result have remained much closer to their bureaucratic mold.

China's post-Mao leadership has since the late 1970s been wrestling with the dilemma outlined here. A large number of reforms are either being implemented or at least discussed. As noted earlier in this study, a wide variety of incentives and sanctions have been reinstituted to stimulate work efforts and creativity, collective and private enterprises have been released from some of the restrictions placed upon them, consumer goods production is being emphasized, enterprise profit-retention and other reforms are being experimented with, regular raises based upon contributions are being promised, and efforts are being made to concentrate day-to-day authority in the hands of managers and experts and move Party committees back into more of a supervisory role. Efforts to restore career opportunities for young people and to link present behavior to future rewards and opportunities are underway. Individual needs and preferences, not just the needs of the state, are supposed to be given more attention now, and this entails things like allowing career preferences to be expressed and considered, permitting rusticated youths to return to the city, trying to find out what products consumers would like to buy, taking opinion polls to see what young people want in life, encouraging discussion of romance problems, and reuniting some separated couples while allowing other couples to divorce somewhat more easily. The dangers of persecution and abuses of authority are supposed to be countered in a number of ways—by enhancing the role of the legal system and formalized court procedures, by encouraging newspapers to print letters of complaint, by allowing people's congress representatives and workers' congress delegates to criticize bureaucratic problems, by establishing a Communist Party disciplinary commission, and by publicizing cases of past persecution in the media.

These reforms seem like a near total repudiation of the legacy of Mao Zedong, and to the extent that political campaigns and the reign of virtue that so threatened people have really been called off for good, this is a clear break with the past. Social change via political ideals is being emphasized less than in the past. Nevertheless, many of the early 1980s' changes in urban bureaucratic institutions must be judged as modest—much less far-reaching, for example, than the reforms implemented in Hungary or Yugoslavia. The system of migration controls and direct job allocation has still not been fundamentally changed, nor is the state backing off much from direct efforts to control most prices, production targets, fertility levels, and many other areas of urban life. In essence, the egalitarian policies of the Cultural Revolution decade have been denounced, but efforts to modify the basic urban political economy established in the 1950s are mostly only in the "trial balloon" stage. While there has been a significant reduction in the dangers of political attack from political purists and some reduction in egalitarian programs, the fundamental features of most urban institutions we have described have only been changed marginally.

Even these modest changes have given rise to negative reactions within at least segments of the Chinese leadership and population, and a number of reform efforts have been stalled or reversed even as others continued. In our view, the negative reactions stem not simply from "die-hard Maoists" or Gang of Four supporters or bureaucrats whose accustomed ways of doing things and posts and privileges the reform efforts threaten. Rather, even the modest reforms made in the five years after Mao's death show signs of contributing to the return of an older set of urban problems. Urban inflation, long kept under effective control, has spurted ahead at a rate variously estimated between 6 and 15 percent. Urban youths, now given more say in the matter, are increasingly selective about job assignments and unwilling to go to the countryside for even a limited stint, and as a result, reports have begun to circulate that the population in China's largest cities is once again growing out of control. Consumerism stimulated by the economic liberalizations has fostered enthusiasm for foreign goods and styles and has led to new concern about "decadence" and the loss of spartan "fear neither hardship nor death" spirit fostered in earlier years. Lavish spending on wedding feasts is also seen as representing contamination by "bourgeois" influences. Reports have even appeared of the revival of urban drug and prostitution problems.[14] Signs of public resentment by ordinary workers and peasants against the new housing advantages, keypoint school access, and foreign travel privileges enjoyed by urban elites and their children have surfaced as well. In general, signs of what might be called a "socialist neoconservatism" indicate that at least some portion of the population feel that things were better back when Mao Zedong was in charge.[15] Similar sentiments have arisen in reaction to reform efforts in various East European countries, and in some cases they have won out and in others they have not. What the outcome will be in the Chinese case remains to be seen.

This discussion allows us to throw light on our earlier question about whether the Chinese model of urbanism provides a model for other societies to copy. The issue is really one of trade-offs, rather than of finding the "correct" way to organize urban life. Particular approaches have their advantages but also their associated problems. Whether the Chinese model is seen as desirable depends upon both the particular set of urban problems faced in a society and the set of values believed in. Given the complexity of urban institutions and the nature of the liberal political values in America and other Western societies, the Chinese model of bureaucratic control and direct allocation does not look very attractive upon close inspection. To put it in other terms, for Western cities the costs seem much larger than the benefits that might be gained. For other developing societies, for socialist societies, and for China itself, the matter is not quite so clear. What sorts of urban problems are Chinese authorities (and urbanites) willing to tolerate or ignore in order to avoid others? Which is the more important problem, conspicuous consumption or shoddy quality goods? Which is a more important goal, rough equality of rewards or encouragement of experts? These are the kinds of difficult decisions China's leaders will have to make as they try to grapple with universal urban dilemmas.

14. On the problems of refusing job assignments and population growth in Peking, see Peking Radio, 6 May 1979, in *FBIS*, 30 January 1980, pp. R1–2; Peking Radio, 11 January 1981, in *FBIS*, 4 February 1981, pp. R2–3. On reaction against signs of "decadence," see Shanghai Radio, 9 February 1979, in *FBIS*, 12 February 1979; "Resist Corrosion, Establish a New Style," *Wenhui Bao*, 12 June 1980, in *FBIS*, 8 July 1980, pp. L9–14; "An Important Measure for Preserving Socialist Morality," *Southern Daily*, 18 August 1981, in *FBIS*, 25 August 1981, pp. P1–2; Chen Bo, "Films Should Contribute toward Developing a Socialist Spiritual Civilization," *Red Flag* 19 (1981): 22–33, in *FBIS*, 28 October 1981, pp. K6–12.

15. A Hong Kong newspaper published a purported conversation with a Chinese army officer that reflects this sort of dismay at current "liberal" trends to a considerable extent. The conversation, which occurred during the course of a long train ride, was serialized in *Zhengming Daily*, 14–24 July 1981, and translated in *FBIS*, 16–22 July 1981, sec. W.

Appendix 1   **Methodological Notes**

This is a study based primarily upon the material gathered from intensive, semi-structured interviews conducted in Hong Kong with 133 former residents of cities in various parts of China. In most respects this research was conceived as a companion and parallel investigation to our earlier research on rural China, although the issues focused on are somewhat different. The methods used in the current research are very much those used in our previous research and described in the methodological appendix to our rural study.[1] For readers unfamiliar with our earlier work we describe here how we deal with the methodological problems presented by "emigré interviewing."

The Interviews

Grants from the National Science Foundation and from the National Endowment for the Humanities supported our year of interviewing in Hong Kong and two subsequent years of data analysis back at our home institutions. The interviewing and associated library research were conducted during a year we both spent in Hong Kong, in 1977–78. As in our earlier work, we conducted our research at the Universities Service Centre, the primary base for scholarly research on contemporary China for the last two decades. We were assisted by five Chinese research assistants, all of whom were themselves former residents of cities in China. A fairly detailed interviewing topic outline had been worked out at the time of our research grant application. This was modified and supplemented by a number of specialized forms during our initial weeks in Hong Kong, and our assistants were trained in interviewing procedures using these instruments. The final instruments included a revised interview topic outline and standardized forms for recording the characteristics of individuals in our census of neighboring households (on which more later), a family income and possessions form and a family chore division and daily schedule form for those households, and a form for recording rationed items and the amounts and procedures used in rationing in

1. See William L. Parish and Martin King Whyte, *Village and Family in Contemporary China* (Chicago: University of Chicago Press, 1978), appendix 1.

each city. Copies of either the interview outline or any of these supplementary forms can be obtained by writing to either of us.

The time period during which we conducted our interviews was relatively favorable in terms of there being a large number of people with urban experience who had left China for Hong Kong either legally or illegally during the previous years.[2] Thus there were many suitable potential interviewees available. As in most Hong Kong interviewing projects, we relied upon a variety of informal networks to locate people to interview, having research assistants, other researchers, previous interviewees, and acquaintances and friends to help us. No systematic sampling procedure is possible in Hong Kong conditions, but informal procedures were used to maximize the diversity among those actually interviewed. It was assumed that it would be easiest to locate people from cities in Southeastern China near Hong Kong, and particularly from Guangdong Province and from its capital city, Canton. Thus after initial interviews, we screened potential interviewees from this region to see if they came from smaller cities or cities not yet described by other informants, or if they came from Canton whether they had lived in neighborhoods, or worked in organizations, that were different from those described by earlier informants. Such interviewees were eagerly sought, while people similar to those we had already talked to we often declined to interview. For areas outside of Guangdong we generally accepted such referrals as we could find, hoping to obtain a fair spread of cities on which we could collect information.

The final spread of interviews was as follows (also see map 1 for the location of many of these cities).[3]

Guangdong Province:

Canton City	54	Other county seats and	
Swatow City	4	small towns	10
Foshan City	3	subtotal	94
Zhaoqing City	3		
Haikou City	2	Guangxi Province:	
Zhanjiang City	2	Liuzhou City	3
Jiangmen City	1	Nanning City	2
Shaoguan City	1	A county seat	1
Zhongshan County	7	subtotal	6
Shunde County	4		
Dongguan County	3		

2. Those leaving illegally were the main type of emigrés up until about 1972, and they mostly escaped to Hong Kong by swimming or in small boats or flotation devices. Since that time, the Chinese have allowed substantial numbers of people to apply for exit permits and come to Hong Kong legally. As we have seen, generally only those with overseas relatives, or individuals who grew up overseas and then went to China in the 1950s or 1960s, are eligible for such exit permits. Just preceding and during our Hong Kong stint, over twenty thousand legal emigrants and several thousand illegal refugees were entering Hong Kong each year (Far Eastern Economic Review, *Asia Yearbook, 1981* [Hong Kong], p. 138).

3. The number of interviews reported for counties includes those for small towns in addition to the county seat. Counties with more than one interview are shown separately.

Other South China:		Small towns in Anhui and	
Kunming City, Yunnan	3	Sichuan provinces	2
Nanchang City, Jiangxi	1	subtotal	9
Changsha City, Hunan	1		
Other towns in Hunan,		North China:	
Fujian, and Yunnan		Peking Municipality	9
provinces	3	Tientsin Municipality	2
subtotal	8	Jilin City, Jilin	1
		Zhengzhou City, Henan	1
Central China:		Small towns in Shanxi,	
Shanghai Municipality	6	Ningxia, and Qinghai	
Wuhan City, Hupei	1	provinces	3
		subtotal	16
		Total	133

The 81 percent of all interviews from Guangdong, Guangxi, and the other parts of South China provides a firm basis for discussing conditions in a range of cities of all sizes in this region. The smaller percentage of interviews from North and Central China includes some particularly long and detailed interviews on large city conditions that provide some basis for generalizing findings from the South to much of the rest of China.

The actual interviews were conducted by one of us or by one of our Chinese assistants who had been trained for this task. This was not a questionnaire study focusing on the attitudes of the people interviewed. Instead we used intensive, semistructured interviews that were designed to get as full a picture as possible, in an ethnographic sense, of the specific urban environment in which each informant had worked and lived. The topic outline was not followed in a rigid order; rather, new topics introduced by informants were followed up immediately, and loose ends from other topics were attended to later on. Generally informants were interviewed several times in sessions of three hours each until the outline had been fully covered. Occasionally an informant would show a lack of detailed knowledge or a fuzzy memory, and then we would decide to terminate the process after only one interviewing session. In all, our interviews totaled 1,382 hours, or 10.4 hours per informant on the average.

The interviews were all conducted in Chinese. Interviews were not recorded on tape but in the form of detailed notes, which were typed into full transcripts immediately after the interviews. In appropriate places during each interview, our standardized forms were filled out with the aid of our informants to supplement the transcribed notes. One of our Chinese assistants was bilingual, but the others wrote out their interview notes by hand in Chinese, and these were then translated and typed up in English by one of us or by our bilingual assistant. In all, we accumulated 2,369 single-spaced, legal-sized pages of interview transcripts (or an average of almost 18 pages per informant), plus the additional pages represented by our standardized forms.

Informants were generally paid standard fees for participating in these interviews. At the time of our research, the customary fee was HK $45 (about US $9) for a three-hour interview. Although payment is less desirable in a Chinese context than developing a close personal relationship as the basis for an interview, it is unavoidable when large numbers of individuals are being interviewed, as in our project. These payments have become a fairly well-established practice in Hong Kong, and for newly arrived emigrés in particular, the funds come in very handy. However, in a few instances reservations expressed by an informant about accepting this form of payment led us to substitute meal invitations or less precisely calculated "Chinese lesson fees" from the hourly interviewing fees. In order to discourage elaboration and invention motivated by the desire for cash, informants were told in advance that the interviewer had a set number of topics to cover, dealing with common experiences from daily life, and that as soon as this was done the interviews would terminate.

Methods of Analysis

The transcribed material from our interviews forms the raw material for most of the analysis presented in this volume. At many points the reader will note that we have simply extracted the general pattern or major variants from the interview transcripts in a qualitative fashion to illustrate general points about urban life. But we have also dissected these materials in order to subject some of our impressions to quantitative tests. To do this we have constructed a number of "samples" from our interview information and have coded certain kinds of standard information for all the units in these "samples." (We use quotation marks because these are not random samples of Chinese urban areas, and we cannot be certain just how representative they are. See below, however, for more discussion on the issue of representativeness.)

One sample is simply of the fifty cities represented in our interviews. For each city we have coded information on its location, the size of its population, and its administrative level (see appendix 2 for details). Another sample is of the 133 individual neighborhoods described by our informants. Using our informant accounts, we have been able to code a wide variety of characteristics of the organization of each neighborhood (e.g., the occupational composition of residents, the number of ward-run factories) and of the social life of the people who live there (e.g., crime prevalence, extent of mutual aid among neighbors). We also have been able to construct a parallel sample of 91 urban work organizations experienced by our informants, pertaining to the organization of those work units and the patterns of social life within them.[4] The reader will be aware that this sort of coded information has been used throughout our study to check whether patterns of social life vary by city or by neighborhoods and work organizations within cities.

4. There are only 91 work units described, compared with 133 neighborhoods, because a fair proportion of our informants were students, former students, or temporary workers who had not accumulated sufficient experience in a particular work unit to be of value in our analysis.

Another very important kind of sample we constructed from our interview materials was what we call our neighbor household census sample. As already noted, our focus in this research is not on our informants and their traits, but on the social worlds in which they lived. In our effort to try to obtain a population sample for urban China that is more representative than our sample of informants, we asked each person we interviewed to describe the family characteristics of individuals in up to five or so neighboring households whose circumstances they were quite familiar with. The fact that most informants could easily comply with this request is testimony to the level of interpersonal familiarity and lack of privacy that is characteristic of contemporary Chinese cities. We used standardized forms to record the features of each family member—relationship to the family head, age, marital status, work history, and so forth—as well as in many cases information about the chore division and daily schedule of each family listed and economic information about each family as a unit. The result was a sample of 581 urban households consisting of 2,865 individuals (termed "sample of neighboring households" and "sample of neighbors" respectively in tables).

Since cities in the Lingnan Region (roughly Guangdong and neighboring Guangxi provinces) were heavily overrepresented in our interviews, and since within this region cities of various sizes are not evenly represented, any efforts to compute average population parameters from the neighborhood household census sample are likely to be off base. To deal with this, we constructed a "weighted" Lingnan neighbor census sample from the broader sample. To do this we first eliminated all households from cities outside the Lingnan Region and then employed a weighting procedure to compensate for the fact that cities of certain sizes were underrepresented, and of other sizes overrepresented, even within our cases from this region.[5] The weighted Lingnan neighbor census sample is our effort to approximate what we think a sample of the urban population in China would look like (at best, in the Lingnan Region), and when we try to give information on the characteristics of the average for Chinese urbanites, we use only this weighted sample.

In all cases we can use our coded data on cities, neighborhoods, and work units in which particular families in our neighbor census samples lived so that we can examine how characteristics of families or individuals vary by city, neighborhood, or work unit characteristics. For example, are families smaller in large cities (chapter 6), or are weddings more frugally celebrated in work unit-dominated neighborhoods (chapter 5)? These neighbor census samples contain information on topics besides member characteristics that permit further quantitative analysis—for example, on family chore participation and whether kitchen or toilet facilities were shared with other households. The neighbor census samples are also the basis for specialized subsamples we have used in examining particular

5. To be specific, we used a code based on the listed population of each city in the 1974 atlas, *Zhonghua Renmin Gongheguo Fensheng Ditu Ji* (Peking: Map Press, 1974). Then we weighted cases from cities under 50,000 and from 300,000 to one million by 3, from 50,000 to 300,000 by 1, and cities over one million by .333. Cities in Guangdong and Guangxi not falling in Skinner's Lingnan Region (specifically, Swatow in eastern Guangdong) were also eliminated from this weighted sample.

topics. For example, women of childbearing ages in the included households were used to construct a fertility sample to examine changes over time in childbearing in chapter 6, and father-son dyads in the sampled families were used to construct a social mobility sample to investigate status transmission in chapter 3.

Several other samples were constructed for more limited analysis. We constructed a sample of 831 marriage cases described in our interviews for the analyses reported in chapter 5. Of this total, 515 came from married couples described in our neighbor census households, 181 came from descriptions of weddings observed or recently attended by our informants (from a separate part of the interview schedule), and the remainder were cases of marriages or couples described by informants in miscellaneous other parts of the interviews. We also collected a modest amount of information on 66 divorce cases and on the personal characteristics and roles of 181 local neighborhood leaders. Data from these samples are also analyzed in appropriate places in our study.

All of these samples permit us to carry out rudimentary quantitative analysis to test a number of ideas about Chinese urban life. For example, we have used these data to show that the "break" in status transmission from father to son brought about by the Cultural Revolution was surprisingly effective, but that no clear trend is visible for newly marrying couples to move in with the bride's parents rather than the groom's. In our research we utilize a variety of statistical procedures familiar to social scientists. Often we simply examine how marriage behavior, perceived crime problems, the quality of relations among neighbors, or some other phenomenon varies by city, neighborhood, or family characteristics, using correlation statistics or an ordinal measure of association, gamma.[6] As in our earlier research on rural China, some of the independent or explanatory variables we are using are themselves statistically related, so that it is often hard to sort out the "true" effects of any single one. To deal with this problem we have used partial correlations and regression techniques, statistical procedures designed to filter out the effects of these other confounding variables so that the residual effects of the variable we are interested in will be visible. Although significance tests are not strictly appropriate to our data, which do not come from a random sample, we have also included information on significance levels in many tables as a way of helping the reader to see how likely or not a particular result could occur by chance alone. We have tried to use quantitative analysis to support and illuminate our arguments rather than to impress or confuse, and much preliminary and background statistical analysis has not been presented in the text to avoid overburdening our readers. Still, our methods should be recognized for what they are: efforts to use imperfect techniques to scrutinize imperfect data in

6. Strictly speaking, ordinal association statistics, such as gamma, are most appropriate for much of our analysis, since they do not assume that our variables are based upon an interval scale. However, available computer procedures using ordinal statistics are fewer and generally costlier than those using interval measures, such as the product moment correlation. We carried out much of our preliminary statistical analysis using both types of measures, but for the ease of our readers, we often present only the more familiar interval statistics in tables here, where we do not feel the conclusions reached would differ much either way.

an effort to move beyond impressionistic statements and polemical arguments on the nature of Chinese society.

Problems of Selectivity and Bias

The general criticisms of emigré interviewing as a research technique are well known. Briefly, it is claimed that emigrés are not representative of individuals who remain in China and often come from places and organizations that are also not representative (the selectivity issue), and that most are alienated individuals who have rejected Chinese society and cannot be expected to give an accurate account of that society (the bias issue). There is substantial truth to both these charges, but in our view the advantages of emigré interviewing still outweigh the disadvantages. If used carefully to study certain kinds of topics, these interviews provide more useful and accurate information than other methods.

To begin with, we should state that all sources of information on China today are subject to serious problems of bias and selectivity. Three sources can be considered—the official media, trip observations, and fieldwork in China. The places and institutions reported on in the Chinese media are predominantly model institutions, most of them located in well-endowed and modernized parts of the country. The messages in the media are also often normative and exhortative—tending to say more about how authorities would like things to be than how they actually are—a trait of official communications in China that has persisted down through the centuries. Moreover, on many topics of interest to us the official media do not provide the detailed information about local life and customs that emigrés can provide. In recent years, the Chinese press has become more informative and less slogan-dominated, and as a consequence it has become increasingly useful as a supplementary source of information, as we have used it in this study. But still media reports have too many drawbacks to form the main basis for an analysis of patterns of urban social life.

When we conducted our Hong Kong interviewing there was no possibility of conducting a field study of urban social life within China. Since that time, however (since 1979, to be exact), a few American researchers have been able to go to China to carry out field investigations, and this exciting possibility represents the obvious real alternative to the sort of Hong Kong interviewing research we have relied upon primarily. Even in this case, though, it is not clear which approach is preferable. There are obvious advantages to being able to conduct field research within China—for example, one can examine people's lives in their natural setting rather than relying on verbal recollections, and one has some prospect of developing collaborative relations with Chinese researchers. But there are also major limitations on research within China that are avoided through Hong Kong research. One does not need to gain Chinese approval for visas, research topics, and even specific interview questions, one can achieve a degree of anonymity and protection for informants that is impossible in China, and one can deal with a broad range of issues and research sites that would not be feasible within China. At the time we are writing a "backlash" is visible, with authorities in China trying to block further field research by foreign social scientists, at least temporarily. Only time will tell what opportunities for field research will develop in China in the future, but for the present it is clear that this option is highly constrained, and that even before the recent "backlash," the sort of broad-ranging investigation described in these pages would not have been possible within China.[7]

The value of Hong Kong interviewing research becomes more apparent once one eliminates several misconceptions about this approach. To begin with, most emigrés are not bitter anti-Communists. Several stints of such interviewing over the years have convinced us that the main reasons most emigrés have for coming to Hong Kong are to be found not in political ideology but in the quest for opportunity—opportunity to get more education, to find a rewarding job, to rejoin relatives there or overseas, to find a spouse. Most do not reject the entire society built in China since 1949. They can give a picture that includes positive features as well as negative, as should be apparent to readers of our study. The rumored "professional informant" who makes up tales of life in China to please the ears (and tap the wallets) of foreign researchers is also, in our experience, not a serious problem. The large number of emigrés streaming into Hong Kong in recent years means that one cannot really make a career of being interviewed unless one were to have some sort of specialized and high-level knowledge, and a study such as ours that deals with mundane facts of everyday life, and which has an announced brief duration, is not likely to attract such individuals. In a study like ours, it is also not that important to find "virginal" informants who have never been interviewed before, since the topics of interest to each researcher are different and thus previous experience cannot prepare one in how to say what a new researcher "wants to hear." Of course, it is still important to check into the background and reliability of those interviewed and to compare each account with many others, rather than relying on one individual informant to supply "the truth" about life in China.

Still, one cannot assume that problems of bias and selectivity are unimportant. Instead, one must utilize a variety of cautions and checks to avoid problems from these sources and to take fullest advantage of the rich potential of this sort of research. Procedures to control for informant bias have been introduced in both the interviewing and analysis stages of our research. In interviewing, we picked topics for investigation that were sufficiently mundane and open to casual daily observation that fabrication and anxiety would not be major problems. Any former resident of a city in China can describe such things as the roles of the local residents' committee and how a recent wedding was celebrated without feeling that this information is of much concern, one way or the other, to foreign governments and intelligence services. Assurances about our academic credentials

7. The merits of Hong Kong interviewing versus field research in China are discussed in more detail in Martin King Whyte, "On Studying China at a Distance" (Paper for the annual meetings of the American Association for the Advancement of Science, Toronto, January 1981). Of course, for many topics the ideal approach is to combine Hong Kong interviewing with a stint of China field research, as a number of scholars now have done.

and of our scholarly intent helped to set the stage for the interviews. Guarantees of anonymity served to protect the informant and relatives in China.

In the interview, we repeatedly pressed informants to give concrete examples and personally observed details rather than hearsay and subjective impressions. We of course also utilized standard interviewing precautions of avoiding leading questions and refraining from stating our personal views. In analyzing our coded data, we utilized other checks for informant bias. There is sufficient variation in the backgrounds of our 133 informants so that we can perform "quality control" checks to see if informants who might be expected to have more bias than others may be distorting the picture we get of Chinese urban life.[8] The following figures summarize informant background characteristics:

Sex: 101 males; 32 females.

Age: 20–29—71; 30–39—51; 40–49—5; 50–59—2; 60–69—1; 70+—3.

Marital status: 81 single, 47 married; 5 no information.

Class origin labels: "Good" labels (worker, poor or lower middle peasant, revolutionary cadre, etc.)—33; "Middling" labels (middle peasant, employee, professional, etc.)—47; Overseas Chinese—27; "Bad" labels (rich peasant, capitalist, merchant, landlord, etc.)—20; no information—6.

Educational background: Some or completed primary schooling—6; some or completed lower middle schooling—36; some or completed upper middle schooling—59; some or completed university education—27; some postgraduate education—2; no information—3.

Political affiliation: "Masses"(not a member of either Youth League or Party)—114; present or past Youth League member—13; present or past Party member—1.

Native locale: In the city described—46; elsewhere in the same province—41; outside the province—36; no information—10.

Occupation: Professional, managerial, technical—30; clerical, other white collar—7; sales and service—9; industrial or construction worker—36; agricultural worker—5; temporary worker—4; no job—41; no information—1.

History of trouble with authorities: None—86; minor trouble (e.g., caught on an attempt to escape Hong Kong)—36; major trouble—8; no information—3.

How left China: Legal exit visa—59; illegally—74.

Time since last in the city described: 1 year or less—12; 1–2 years—27; 2–3 years—61; 3+ years—32; no information—1.

The basic idea in these quality control checks is to see if informants of one type supply information about urban life that is systematically different from informants of another type. In a quantitative analysis one can partial out the effects of such informant biases and observe how other statistical results are affected. In general we have not found the "data quality" problems to be very

8. These techniques have their origins in those developed to screen biases out of cross-cultural anthropological surveys. See Raoul Naroll, *Data Quality Control* (Glencoe: Free Press, 1962).

severe in this investigation. Even in cases where informants differed on important points, as in regard to crime problems in chapter 8, when we controlled for informant differences the remaining results were not much affected. This finding gives us some confidence that our conclusions on various topics are not simply the product of our having interviewed a politically biased group of informants.

Even if precautions are taken to deal with the issues of bias, they do not resolve the selectivity issue. Of concern here is whether, even if our informants are fairly accurate and unbiased, they come from such an unusual selection of urban settings that piecing together their accounts will give an unrepresentative picture of urban realities in China. We adopted several procedures to deal with selectivity. First, we used emigrés as informants rather than as respondents. Not the attitudes of the individual interviewed but his or her account of a particular corner of urban social life is the focus. The technique is basically that used by ethnographers who do research on other cultures by talking to knowledgeable informants, although in our case this talking occurred "at a distance" from the actual cities described.[9] Since our unit of analysis is not the individual interviewee but rather the neighborhood, work unit, neighbors, and so forth, the essential question is no longer whether informants are representative (they surely are not) but rather whether the reported neighborhoods, work units, and neighbors are representative (they may be). We have already noted that we used other sources of information on the distribution of cities of different sizes in the Lingnan Region to construct an improved weighted household sample which we feel is likely to be more accurately representative of the urban population than our unweighted sample is.

Second, throughout our analysis we have been as much concerned with internal variations in urban life as with the average level of urban incomes, frequency of political study meetings, or number of tables at wedding banquets. We wanted to know, for example, whether weddings were simpler in larger cities or in work unit-dominated neighborhoods than they were in other urban settings. So long as we are concerned with the relationship between two urban characteristics, then having a precisely representative sample of urban places is less important than having a sample with sufficient variability to cover the extremes of urban conditions that are found within China. We believe our samples are satisfactory on this latter count. They include information from Peking as well as from rural commune towns, from the interior of China as well as the coast, from industrial, academic, bureaucratic, and other settings, and about people who are unemployed as well as those who hold prestigious positions.[10] We are therefore fairly confident that we have been able to investigate variations in urban social life relatively well even without a representative sample of all urban places in China.

9. See Margaret Mead and Rhoda Metraux, *The Study of Culture at a Distance* (Chicago: University of Chicago Press, 1953).

10. We have noted earlier, however, that there are some gaps in our coverage. For example, we have much better coverage of cities in the developed coastal areas than in interior and minority regions. And, as noted in chapter 4, because of the small sample of only a little over 1,600 workers, our neighbor census includes only one of China's high-ranking cadres—those with an official rank exceeding 13.

Finally, in places we can compare the results we obtain from our admittedly imperfect procedures with data released by the official media in China to see how representative or unrepresentative our samples are. We cannot do this in every instance, but when we can we have found that the correspondence between our figures and the official figures is quite close. Unfortunately there is still not an exact match in these comparisons, since we generally rely on our weighted Lingnan neighbor census sample, while official figures are generally for the whole urban population or some subset of larger Chinese cities. But nonetheless the similarities in eight sets of data are remarkable:

1. Data on the age structure of the city of Canton alone show a quite close match with our sample calculations from that city, which are circa 1975 for the most part. In our Canton figures 26 percent of the individuals were under 16 years of age, 67 percent between 17 and 60, and 7 percent 61 or older. In a 1975 report the corresponding figures were 30 percent, 62 percent, and 8 percent, and in a 1978 report 26 percent, 65 percent, and 9 percent.[11]

2. Our estimate of the average urban family size in the Lingnan region was 4.4 persons. This figure fits neatly between the figures of 4.3 and 4.5 persons given in two different surveys of Chinese cities in 1980.[12]

3. Our weighted sample estimate of 76 percent of the urban labor force in socialist enterprises employed in state firms and 24 percent in collective firms is not far different from the 79 and 21 percent figures given for 1977 in an official source.[13]

4. A detailed occupational distribution comparison yields the following picture:[14]

	Sample (ca. 1975)	Report (1978)
Industry (mining & manufacturing)	44.6%	47.9%
Construction	3.0	7.9
Health	5.7	4.0
Education, culture, & science	8.3	12.0
Urban public utilities	0.7	0.3
Govt. admin. & mass organizations	6.5	6.1
Transport, post & telecommunications	10.4	8.4
Trade, restaurants & hotels	18.0	12.4
Finance, banking	0.5	0.7
Other services	1.9	0.4
Total	99.6%	100.1%

11. Our figures are computed from the sample of neighbors in Canton alone. The comparison figures come from Zhu Yuncheng, "On the Question of Controlling the Size of Canton City's Population," *Zhongshan University Journal*, no. 1 (1980): 45.

12. The 4.3 figure comes from a survey of 7,962 families of workers and employees in China's forty-four largest cities in 1980 (*Xinhua* [Peking], 22 April 1981, in *FBIS*, 24 April 1981, p. K13) and the 4.5 figure from a survey of 86,955 families of wage and salary earners in forty-four cities in 1980 (in *Xinhua* [Peking], 30 December 1980, in *FBIS*, 5 January 1981, p. L20).

13. State Statistical Bureau, "Communique on Fulfillment of China's 1978 National Economic Plan," *Beijing Review*, no. 27 (1979): 40.

14. *State Statistical Bureau, Statistical Work in New China* (Peking, 1979), adapted by

5. From our weighted sample we estimate that 53 percent of the urban population is employed. In official surveys about 49 percent of the urban population was employed in 1978.[15]

6. From our weighted sample we calculate that the average monthly wage of state employees circa 1975 was 46 yuan; of collective firm employees, 39 yuan; and that the monthly per capita income of the urban population was 24 yuan. Official figures for 1977 yield corresponding figures of 50, 39, and 23 yuan.[16]

7. From our weighted urban sample we can rank individuals on the basis of their household per capita income (which is slightly different from the ranking in chapter 3 on the basis of total household income). In this ranking, the richest 10 percent of all individuals get 18 percent of all income while the poorest 40 percent get 29 percent. This is similar to the percentages implicit in a State Statistical Bureau survey of 86,555 households in China's forty-four largest cities that were 15 and 30 percent, respectively.[17]

8. In both our weighted sample of neighboring households and implicit in official reports, households spend 55 percent of their income on food.[18]

Not all of the figures correspond exactly, and without knowing more about how urban social life in the Lingnan Region corresponds with that in other regions it is difficult to be conclusive. And we should note that there is at least one instance in which an officially released figure differs sharply from our own. We have calculated from our urban weighted sample that 47 percent of the urban labor force is female. However, a 1980 press report from a national trade union conference stated that women make up about one-third of all workers in China. We are unable at this point to account for such a large discrepancy. Perhaps this latter figure refers to a different base population from ours or perhaps either our calculation or the official report is simply in error.[19] Even taking into account this one discrepancy and other smaller differences in the figures cited above, on balance we are struck by the rather close correspondence between figures calculated from our interview samples and official figures that were not available at the time we made our calculations. These comparisons give us added confidence that, even

---

John Phillip Emerson, "The Labor Force in China, 1957–1980," in *China under the Four Modernizations*, U.S. Congress, Joint Economic Committee (Washington, D.C.: U.S. Printing Office, 1982), p. 247.

15. This figure comes from the statement that each employee in the state sector supported 2.06 persons (including him or herself). This same statistic implies that urban employment rose to 56 percent by 1981. See Li Chengrui and Zhang Zhongji, "Remarkable Improvement in Living Standards," *Beijing Review*, no. 17 (1982): 16.

16. The collective income figure is estimated by the formula (reported collective enterprise wage bill)/(mid-year number of employees in such enterprises)/12. The monthly per capita income figure is based on (reported total wage bill)/(total mid-year Chinese population × .20)/12. See *Xinhua* (Peking), November, 1979 in *FBIS*, 9 November 1979, p. L12; State Statistical Bureau, "Communique."

17. Adapted from *People's Daily*, 31 December 1980, p. 1. Similar official figures, apparently from the same survey, are also circulating in World Bank circles.

18. See chapter 4.

19. *Xinhua* (Peking), 5 January 1980, in *FBIS* 10 January 1980, p. L5.

if our samples are not exactly representative, they still come close enough to the mark so that computations based upon them will give us a fairly accurate reading of urban social patterns in China.

We have tried to make the fullest and best use of the data provided by our informants. Though emigré interviews present a number of problems to the researcher, we believe that through the procedures outlined above we have been able to control or eliminate many different sources of bias, selectivity, spuriousness. The personal details and vivid anecdotes that only informants speaking in complete confidence can provide have done much to enrich our understanding of what social life is like in contemporary Chinese cities, and we hope some of this flavor has come through to the reader. Although no amount of caution and scrutiny can remove all the problems in our data, we hope that the scope and detail of the picture of Chinese cities presented here will serve as testimony to the continued importance of the research methodology we have employed.

Appendix 2   Neighborhood and Work Unit Characteristics

At various points throughout this study we have utilized quantitative analysis of variables and scales derived from our interview data to test ideas about urban social relationships. The variables and scales used for this purpose were derived by coding information supplied by informants into categorical form. For example, in our interviews we asked our informants a systematic set of questions about the neighborhoods they had lived in, such as whether most of the neighbors had lived there since before 1949 or whether some or many of them had moved in there recently. Then we coded their responses into three categories to represent our measure of the relative stability of residence in the neighborhood (see variable number 1 below). In some cases, as noted in appendix 1, we used specialized forms to record information from our interviews, and in these cases we could often base our variables directly on the data supplied on these forms, rather than on coding of verbal material in our transcripts. In a number of places, we have also combined single, interrelated variables into scales designed to measure certain general urban phenomena. In doing this we followed the same general procedures in each case. We computed a mean of all the separate variables used in the scale.[1] The resulting continuous scales were then used in a number of analyses, and were subdivided into categories (generally three) when an ordinal version was desired for use in tabular analysis. In this appendix we supply details on the major neighborhood and work unit independent variables that have been used throughout the study and how they are interrelated. As noted in appendix 1, this information on intercorrelations has been used in our quantitative analysis to allow partialling out or control for some independent variables in order to observe whether others have a residual effect on each dependent variable, or whether an original bivariate association was spurious, attributable to the confounding produced by the controlled variable. Though not every variable below is reported in every table, each

1. Before adding, the separate items in each scale were recoded to all fall in the same range—for example, one to two—and missing values assigned a score of zero. Then, the sum of the constituent items was divided by the number of items with known values to give a mean or average score. Scales with more than half the constituent items being of unknown value were typically deleted.

was examined for possible confounding effects in our reported findings. This is particularly important for the variables concerning the Lingnan Region and Canton as well as the variables for informant optimism and quality of interview. When these variables were significantly related to the variable to be explained, they were introduced as controls and reported in the tables in the text.

For the composite scales including several different items summed together, we provide the average interitem correlation (AIC) of these constituent items as an index of whether the items really cohere in a single scale.

Neighborhood and City Characteristics

1. Stability of residents. Ranges from 1 = many residents new since 1960s, to 3 = most people there from before 1949.

2. Homogeneity of residents. 1 = residents of a mixed variety of occupations, 2 = residents mainly of one occupational type.

3. Low-rise buildings. Ranges from 1 = three to five story buildings predominant locally, to 4 = mainly one to two story detached houses.

4. Unit compound scale. Based on five items: extent of residents under residents' committee supervision (from 1 = most households, to 3 = few households); type of neighborhood (1 = residential or mixed, 2 = work unit quarters); general distance to work unit (from 1 = elsewhere in city, to 3 = same locale); type of residents (from 1 = varied work units, to 3 = single work unit); and degree of work unit/neighborhood overlap (from 1 = none, to 3 = extensive). AIC = .80.

5. Infrastructure scale. Composed of nine items: extent of ward-run enterprises (from 1 = none, to 4 = six or more); extent of ward or residents' committee-run service facilities (from 1 = none to speak of, to 3 = extensive); ward-run health stations (1 = none, 2 = some); ward-run nurseries and kindergartens (1 = none, 2 = some); local reading room or culture station (from 1 = none, to 3 = yes, actively used); ward welfare activities for the poor (from 1 = none, to 3 = major); role of neighborhood authorities in birth control work (from 1 = none, to 3 = major); role of neighborhood authorities in sending youth to countryside (from 1 = none, to 3 = major); and ward or residents' committee role in street sweeping (from 1 = none, to 3 = active). AIC = .25.

6. Household control scale. Composed of five items: involvement of residents in security patrolling (from 1 = none, to 3 = frequent and active); level of police or militia patrols (from 1 = absent, to 3 = frequent); frequency of household registration inspections (from 1 = never or rare, to 3 = frequent); strictness of household registration reporting enforcement (from 1 = lax, can ignore for short stays, to 3 = quite strict, can't ignore even briefly); and local sentencing meetings among residents (1 = none, 2 = some). AIC = .21.

7. Political study. Frequency of political study meetings for residents (from 1 = not held, to 4 = meetings every day).

8. Controls over sent-down youths. Strictness of controls over illegally returned sent-down youths or other unregistered individuals in neighborhood (from 1 =

Table A

	ST 1	HO 2	LR 3	UC 4	IN 5	HC 6	PS 7	CY 8
1. Stability	--							
2. Homogeneity	-34	--						
3. Low-rise building	26	-02	--					
4. Unit compound	-53	41	-31	--				
5. Infrastructure	37	-22	03	-48	--			
6. Household control	03	-01	-11	-23	33	--		
7. Political study	-02	10	02	-00	22	30	--	
8. Control SD youth	-02	00	-19	-03	-12	15	-10	--
9. Radical year	07	-22	-02	-23	32	15	-06	01
10. Ration-supply scale	-42	-07	-06	41	-35	-19	-01	10
11. Ration amounts	-10	-10	-16	22	-07	03	16	-23
12. Public housing	-49	33	-49	57	-15	05	21	01
13. State employment	-34	22	-23	31	05	26	-01	11
14. Low unemployment	-27	13	09	15	-01	-07	01	-01
15. White collar nbhd.	-20	-18	-07	03	11	07	12	-15
16. Lingnan Region	39	-19	17	-36	17	05	-28	06
17. Admin. level of city	-23	28	-17	04	22	32	22	-01
18. City population	-03	22	-15	-07	33	41	28	-05
19. Canton	30	-02	-02	-36	35	30	-04	-02
20. Interview quality	-50	15	-12	52	-29	01	18	-06
21. Informant optimism	-22	05	-04	32	-28	-25	09	24
Median N	115	120	111	121	97	85	68	90

Source: Sample of neighborhoods.

[a]Decimal points omitted.

Correlations among Neighborhood and City Characteristics[a]

RY 9	R 10	RA 11	PH 12	SE 13	LU 14	WC 15	LR 16	AL 17	CP 18	Ca 19	IQ 20	IN 21
--												
07	--											
02	42	--										
-05	21	11	--									
-05	31	32	42	--								
-05	36	23	17	26	--							
03	23	22	05	02	06	--						
02	-40	-27	-43	-23	-14	-26	--					
05	13	24	39	64	19	12	-32	--				
09	-11	15	27	55	04	03	-08	89	--			
02	-46	-22	-15	17	-14	-12	51	41	64	--		
59	60	35	28	20	20	24	-47	20	02	-35	--	
-21	28	05	16	17	20	-04	-17	01	-06	-08	27	--
132	84	72	124	108	91	120	133	133	132	133	119	66

can stay long periods if no trouble, to 3 = strict controls, risky to try to stay even briefly).

9. Radical year. Based on years to which the interview information refers and political campaign pressures experienced in those years: 1962–65, 1972, 1973, 1977, and 1978 coded as 1 = moderate; and 1966–71 and 1974–76 coded as 2 = radical.

10. Ration-supply scale. Based upon eight items: grain ration sufficient for needs (from 1 = no, to 3 = yes); pork ration sufficient (from 1 = no, to 3 = yes and usually no lines); controls over pork and fish (from 1 = both rationed, to 3 = neither rationed); tobacco rationed (from 1 = yes, to 3 = no); coal rationed (from 1 = yes and not sufficient, to 3 = unrationed); general prevalence of lines to buy goods (from 1 = common, many items, to 3 = rare, special items); general sufficiency of supplies recently (from 1 = very insufficient, to 4 = enough or more than enough); and the number of items listed as rationed on the special ration form used in interviews (from 1 = seven to eleven items, to 5 = seventeen or more items).

11. Ration amounts scale. The average monthly supply of five items: cooking oil, sugar, fish, pork, and soap. Prior to adding, we standardized the actual amounts of each item in kilograms or pieces by subtracting the mean supply of each item and then dividing by the standard deviation for that item. The items thus all have a common mean and similar range before they are added into the composite measure.

12. Public housing. Type of housing in neighborhood (from 1 = private housing predominant, to 3 = no private housing, all public).

13. State employment. Pattern of local employment (from 1 = most in collective enterprises, to 3 = most in state enterprises).

14. Low unemployment. Extent of local unemployment or underemployment (from 1 = serious problem, to 3 = none to note, or very little).

15. White collar neighborhood. Occupations of most neighbors (1 = manufacturing or service, 2 = mixed, 3 = white collar, intellectuals, cadres).

16. Lingnan Region. Whether or not city is in the Lingnan Region, as described in G. William Skinner, *The City in Late Imperial China* (Stanford: Stanford University Press, 1977), p. 213 (1 = outside Lingnan, 2 = inside Lingnan).

17. Administrative level of city. 1 = market town that is not a commune seat, 2 = commune seat, 3 = county seat, 4 = district or prefectural city, 5 = provincial capital, 6 = national level city (Peking, Tientsin, or Shanghai).

18. City population according to Chinese atlas (1 = under 10,000; 2 = 10–49,000; 3 = 50–99,000; 4 = 100,000–299,000; 5 = 300,000–999,000; 6 = 1 million +).

19. Canton. 1 = other city; 2 = Canton.

20. Interview quality scale. Composed of six items: informants' socioeconomic status (a measure itself composed of an equally weighted average of informant education, monthly income, industry, and occupation); informant maturity (composed of an equally weighted average of informant age and marital status); informant political membership (from 1 = masses, to 3 = in Party); informant class background (from 1 = bad, to 3 = good); informant familiarity with city (a

measure composed of whether the informant was a native of that place and the degree of continuity of residence there over time); and the depth of the interview (a measure of the number of hours of the interview, the number of pages of transcript resulting, and whether one of us—as opposed to assistants—did the interview). AIC = .26.

21. Informant optimism. This is a continuous scale based upon the gap between rationed items supplied locally and the actual amounts of the monthly rations supplied as described that taps one sort of informant bias—whether he or she reports that material supplies are better or worse than the amounts listed would warrant concluding. It is computed to the following steps: (1) ADEQUACY = sum of informant judgments about the adequacy (from 0 = insufficient, to 3 = more than enough) of grain, oil, cotton cloth, pork, and coal supplied locally. (2) QUANTITY = (9 × catties of oil) + (meters of cotton) + (3 × catties of port) / 3,000. The multiplications used here are designed to put the items in roughly the same metric as cotton cloth, thus giving them equal weights in the final variable. Grain is omitted here as it does not appear to vary much from city to city. (3) OPTIMISM = Ln (ADEQUACY + 1) − (−1.4842 + .5173 × QUANTITY). In the resulting variable, then, those who see supplies as more abundant than they really are in relative terms (the "optimists") receive a positive score, and those who underestimate their adequacy receive a negative score.

Work Unit Characteristics

1. Unit size. From 1 = 2,000+ employees, to 9 = 10 or fewer employees.

2. No shift work. Work on shifts? (1 = yes, 2 = no).

3. Unit inclusiveness scale. Composed of five items: existence of dependents' committee or organization (1 = no, 2 = yes); role of work unit in memorial meetings or funerals (from 1 = none, to 3 = for all staff); unit leaders send representatives to visit sick and hospitalized employees (1 = no, 2 = yes); cases of offspring succeeding their parents in their jobs (1 = none, 2 = some cases mentioned); unit arrangements for cultural, sports, and recreational activities for employees and dependents (from 1 = none, to 3 = regular and active). AIC = .37.

4. Employee contacts off the job. From 1 = little contact, to 3 = much contact.

5. Mass organizations in unit scale. Composed of four items: unit women's federation (from 1 = does not exist, to 3 = exists and has some concrete role in unit); campaign pressures since the Cultural Revolution (from 1 = minor, to 3 = many, hectic); trade union activities (from 1 = no union, to 3 = exists and has some concrete role in unit); and unit militia organization (from 1 = none, to 3 = exists and has regular activity). AIC = .45.

6. Management and labor. Nature of management participation in manual labor (from 1 = little or none, to 3 = regular and institutionalized).

7. Unit sanctions scale. Composed of nine items: role of work unit in approving marriages (from 1 = none, to 3 = active); unit role in mediating marital disputes and approving divorces (from 1 = none, to 3 = active); unit role in sending

Table B

	SUS 1	NSW 2	UI 3	COJ 4	MO 5	ML 6	US 7
1. Small unit size	--						
2. No shift work	36	--					
3. Unit inclusiveness	-50	-16	--				
4. Contacts off job	-17	-15	-04	--			
5. Mass organizations in unit	-51	-54	53	11	--		
6. Management do labor	12	-30	-19	-14	09	--	
7. Unit sanctions	-56	-55	63	19	69	06	--
8. Criticism/self-criticism	-04	-26	37	19	17	18	32
9. Political study	-13	-22	08	02	14	03	09
10. Birth control activities	-44	-46	37	-02	29	-02	43
11. Model workers	-37	-52	06	51	57	21	45
12. State enterprise	-47	03	54	-04	43	-02	47
13. Resources	-63	-33	44	20	55	-20	67
14. Heft	-67	-51	73	25	82	-01	88
15. Level of administration	-41	19	64	04	29	-08	20
16. Wage raises	10	-11	-28	-28	13	-03	-30
17. Low wage span	12	51	-35	-07	-57	-20	-59
18. Material incentives	07	-39	06	-26	15	-01	14
Median N	(74)	(53)	(49)	(39)	(69)	(41)	(62)

Source: Sample of 91 work units.

[a]Decimal points omitted.

Correlations among Work Unit Characteristics[a]

CSC 8	DS 9	RCA 10	MWS 11	SE 12	R 13	H 14	LA 15	WR 16	LWS 17	MI 18
--										
16	--									
-08	07	--								
39	06	20	--							
07	21	25	10	--						
-17	09	52	12	66	--					
16	11	40	48	52	80	--				
-11	13	29	-02	61	59	40	--			
-05	-29	-12	-01	-22	-12	-23	-19	--		
-20	-01	-37	-47	-13	-20	-53	09	03	--	
13	-41	-03	-06	-13	-21	09	-22	28	-11	--
(48)	(67)	(63)	(40)	(89)	(69)	(73)	(89)	(42)	(49)	(45)

offspring of employees to the countryside (from 1 = none or nominal, to 3 = major responsibility); unit role in enforcing birth control (from 1 = minimal or none, to 3 = very active); "controlled elements" supervised in the unit (1 = none, 2 = some mentioned); sentencing meetings held in the unit (1 = no, 2 = yes); cases of firing staff members (1 = none, 2 = some); study group criticism of staff members (1 = none, 2 = some); and number of wage supplements received by employees (from 1 = one, to 3 = five or more). AIC = .21.

8. Criticism and self-criticism. Occurrence at meetings (from 1 = rarely or never, to 3 = regularly).

9. Political study. Frequency of employees' political study meetings (from 1 = never or infrequent, to 3 = three times a week or more often).

10. Birth control activity. Level of activity to enforce birth control campaign (from 1 = little or no activity, to 6 = regular filling out of birth control forms, setting of birth control plans and designation of those eligible to become pregnant each year, threatened sanctions for unauthorized pregnancy, and the designation of a lower level staff member to monitor compliance).

11. Model worker selection. Regularity of selections (from 1 = none, 3 = regular and stressed practice).

12. State enterprise. Type of enterprise (1 = collective, 2 = state).

13. Resources scale. Composed of eleven items: unit canteen for staff (1 = no, 2 = yes); unit procures scarce food items or other goods for staff (1 = no, 2 = yes); quality of health care received by employees (from 1 = poor, some problems, to 3 = high quality, ample medical personnel and equipment); medical insurance coverage for employees (1 = none, 2 = partial or full); nature of medical insurance coverage (from 1 = none, to 3 = employee fully covered, dependents at least partly covered); unit supply of housing (1 = none, 2 = partial or full); unit provision of hardship allowance for employees (from 1 = none, to 3 = regular practice); unit help to employees in finding housing (1 = none, 2 = some); nature of unit medical facilities (from 1 = none, to 3 = full clinic run by unit); unit education and training programs (1 = none, 2 = some or access to); and unit child care facilities (from 1 = none, to 3 = has nursing station, nursery school, and kindergarten). AIC = .46.

14. Heft scale. A composite scale made by taking the mean of the unit inclusiveness scale (no. 3 above), mass organizations scale (no. 5), unit sanctions scale (no. 7), resources scale (no. 13), and what might be called a unit inequity scale, the reversal of our low wage span scale below (no. 17). This scale thus taps all aspects of work unit size, resources, and inclusiveness. AIC = .55.

15. Level of administration. Level of administration under which the work unit falls (from 1 = urban district or lower level, to 3 = provincially or centrally run unit).

16. Wage raises. Recent wage increases in the unit (from 1 = none since the Cultural Revolution, to 3 = more than one in this period).

17. Low wage span scale. Composed of three items: extent of elite privilege and influence in the distribution of housing and goods within the unit (from 1 = extensive, to 3 = minimal); maximum/minimum monthly wage ratio (from 1 =

5:1 or greater, to 3 = 2.5:1 or less); wage ratio for blue collar workers only (same code as previous item). AIC = .45.

18. Material incentives. Use of bonuses or piece rate in unit currently (1 = not used, 2 = currently used).

Other Scales

1. Neighborhood crime scale. Composed of seven items: examples of post-Cultural Revolution crime to own family (1 = no, 2 = yes); examples of post-Cultural Revolution crimes to neighbors nearby (1 = no, 2 = yes); examples of crimes committed by nearby neighbors since the Cultural Revolution (1 = no, 2 = yes); safe walking alone at night locally (from 1 = yes, to 3 = no); residents lock doors when they go out (from 1 = no, to 3 = always); gang fights and similar disturbances nearby (from 1 = none, to 3 = serious problems); and general extent of crime locally (from 1 = very little, to 3 = major problems). AIC = .37. The scale was reversed so that a high score = low crime.

2. Neighborhood economic deviance scale. Composed of eleven items: extent of private peddling and illegal marketing nearby (from 1 = none or isolated, to 3 = widespread); examples of moonlighting or underground factories (1 = none, 2 = some); local individuals refusing to take jobs (1 = none, 2 = some); people staying locally without proper registration (from 1 = none or minimal, to 3 = many or common); cleanliness of local neighborhood (from 1 = generally neat and clean, to 3 = serious problems); extent of grain coupon sales locally (from 1 = negligible, to 3 = common); extent of black market in food and other items locally (from 1 = negligible, to 3 = common); extent of going "by the back door" to get needed items not readily available (from 1 = negligible, to 3 = common); extent of violation of housing regulations, squatting, illegal building, etc. (1 = none, 2 = some); ability of local youths to evade the campaign to send them to the countryside (from 1 = practically impossible, to 3 = many escape); and youths who refuse to go to the countryside get jobs locally (1 = none, 2 = some cases). Average item-to-item intercorrelation = .31. Again, this scale was reversed so that a high score = low economic deviance.

3. Work unit crime scale. Composed of four items: theft of unit materials (1 = none, 2 = some); unit corruption and graft (1 = no instances, 2 = some cases); crimes within work unit or unit dormitory (1 = none, 2 = some); and crimes committed by unit personnel (1 = none, 2 = some). Again, this scale was reversed, so that a high score = low unit crime problems.

4. Occupational status scale. Composed of three items from marriage sample, computed separately for males and females: industry (1 = primary, e.g., agriculture, forestry, 2 = manufacturing or construction, 3 = services, 4 = education, culture, health care, 5 = administration, 6 = military, 7 = other); occupation (1 = no work, agricultural work, temporary work, 2 = industrial or construction worker, 3 = sale or service, 4 = clerical and other white collar, 5 = professional or managerial), and the monthly wage. AIC = .29 or .37, depending on sex.

5. Male leadership scale. Composed of three variables from marriage sample: political membership of the male (from 1 = none, to 3 = in Party); military service of male (1 = none, 2 = veteran, current service); and special leadership posts held by the male (1 = no, 2 = yes). Note: too few females in the marriage sample have served in the military or held leadership posts to allow us to create the comparable scale for females. Instead the female political membership item was used alone. AIC = .53.

6. Socioeconomic status of parent scale. Composed of seven items from marriage sample: industry of mother (as in no. 4 above); industry of father (the same); occupation of mother (as in no. 4); occupation of father (the same); level of ownership of mother's work unit (1 = self-employed, commune, or town, 2 = ward, collective, 3 = state enterprise); level of ownership of father's work unit (the same); and estimated monthly income of parents at the time of the couple's marriage. AIC = .51 or .56, depending on sex.

7. Freedom of mate choice scale. Composed of four variables from the marriage sample: how the couple first met (1 = by introduction, 2 = directly); type of introduction utilized (1 = family or marriage arranger, 2 = neighbors, workmates, or friends, 3 = no introduction); how long the couple knew each other before marriage (from 1 = under six months, to 5 = five or more years) and intensity of proto-dating activities (from 1 = little or none, to 3 = frequent joint activities). AIC = .44.

8. Wedding simplicity scale. Composed of seven items from the marriage sample: gift demands from bride or bride's family (1 = yes, 2 = none); value of gifts supplied to bride's side (from 1 = 300 yuan or more, to 3 = under 100 yuan); unit wedding celebration (1 = absent, 2 = present); nature of wedding banquet (from 1 = elaborate, more than five tables, to 4 = none held); traditional rituals observed at wedding (1 = some, 2 = none); total cost of wedding to the male side (from 1 = 1000 yuan or more, to 3 = under 300 yuan); and total cost of wedding to both sides (from 1 = 1000 yuan or more, to 4 = under 200 yuan). AIC = .35.

9. Occupational level. A categorical measure used in the neighbor household census sample (1 = unskilled and marginal workers, 2 = ordinary and semiskilled workers, 3 = service worker, 4 = skilled manual worker, 5 = clerical and sales worker, 6 = lower professionals, 7 = managerial cadres, 8 = administrative cadres, 9 = high professionals). Note: in some places in our analysis of the household census data, we use instead an occupational measure that is closer to a continuous measure and is based upon the average wage of people in the sample who fall into thirty-two different occupational categories (see table 24 in the text).

10. Consumption index. The total number of the following four items in a household: bicycles, radio, wristwatches, and sewing machine.

11. Household amenities. The number of the following four amenities that are present in a home: running water, bath, kitchen, and toilet.

12. Mean chore performance scale. Composed of the mean of the scores on the chore subsample of five items: buying vegetables, cooking, washing dishes, sweep-

ing the floor, and washing clothes (each score from 0 = no role, to 4 = sole performer in household; see figure 5). AIC = .59.

13. Mutual involvement scale. Based on three items: neighbors report crime (1 = no, 2 = yes, some examples noted); neighbors play a role in mediating local disputes (from 1 = no, avoid it, to 3 = active involvement); and neighbors voice their views on how one should raise one's child (1 = no, rarely, 2 = sometimes).

14. Mutual aid scale. Based on two items: extent of aid and concern among neighbors (from 1 = minimal, to 3 = extensive); comparison of the quality of relations among neighbors in the city in China and in Hong Kong (2 = about the same, 3 = China much better).

15. Harmony scale. Composed of two items: concrete cases of severe interpersonal disputes in the neighborhood (from 1 = many, to 3 = none); extent of conflict among neighbors generally (from 1 = much, some severe, to 4 = very little).

Index